Revolutionary Morality

REVOLUTIONARY MORALITY

A Psychosexual Analysis of Twelve Revolutionists

William H. Blanchard

ABC-Clio Information Services
Santa Barbara, California
Oxford, England

Library of Congress Cataloging in Publication Data

Blanchard, William H.
    Revolutionary morality.

    Bibliography: p.
    Includes index.
    1. Revolutionists—Case studies. 2. Revolutions—
Psychological aspects—Case studies. 3. Revolutions—
Moral and ethical aspects—Case studies. 4. Motivation
(Psychology)—Case studies 5. Equality Case studies.
6. Masochism—Case Studies. I. Title.
HM281.B563 1983   303.6'4   82-22679

ISBN 0-87436-032-3

10 9 8 7 6 5 4 3 2 1

ABC-Clio Information Services
2040 Alameda Padre Serra, Box 4397
Santa Barbara, California 93103

Clio Press Ltd.
55 St. Thomas Street
Oxford OX1 1JG, England

Manufactured in the United States of America

To Marichen

Contents

Preface ix

Acknowledgments xiii

Introduction xv

Part I: The Social Rebel, 3

Introduction 5

1 T. E. Lawrence: The Role of Guilt 7

2 Jean Jacques Rousseau: The Spirit of Revolt 15

3 Count Leo Tolstoy: Return to God and Nature 31

Part II: Revolutionary Conviction without Combat, 45

Introduction 47

4 Prince Peter Kropotkin: The Gentle Revolutionary 51

5 Mohandas K. Gandhi: The Power of Suffering 61

6 Karl Marx: Romantic Origins 87

7 Karl Marx: The Antagonism to Capitalism 103

8 Karl Marx: Revolution in Theory 115

Part III: Victory without Power, 135

Introduction 137

9 Sun Yat-sen: The Eclectic 139

10 Leon Trotsky: The Internationalist 153

11 Ché Guevara: The Romantic Revolutionary 181

Part IV: The Successful Revolutionary, 197

Introduction 199

12 Fidel Castro: Maximum Leader 205

13 V. I. Lenin: The Stoic 219

14 Mao Tse-tung: The Return to Romanticism 225

15 Beyond Masochism 231

Selected Bibliography 245

Index 275

Preface

This book represents the culmination of over fifteen years of research and writing on the subject of revolution and the psychology of politics. It began with an earlier work, *Rousseau and the Spirit of Revolt* (University of Michigan Press, 1967), a psychological study of the origin of Rousseau's political ideas. This study extends the work to a broad examination of the chief psychological factors behind revolt or rebellion against the state, provided the rebellion is based on some moral principles or a theory which seeks to create a better life for humanity. I have excluded the palace coup or military junta when it involves merely a change in the ruling clique or the substitution of one leader for another with no basic change in the society.

The outstanding feature of this book is that it brings together revolutionary ideologies and tactics from a number of diverse sources, some of which seem directly opposed to each other (such as violence and nonviolence) and demonstrates a common psychological dynamic behind the urge toward revolt against established state authority. I regard *moral* rebellion as the principal subject of study—a characteristic shared by the theorist and the activist, the violent and the nonviolent, and even the rebel and the revolutionary.

A rebel always mounts some form of protest against the state in word or deed. Whether or not the rebel becomes a revolutionary may depend on the situation in which he finds himself. Such factors as the degree of acceptance given his ideas or proposals by the population; the degree of violence used against him by the state; the challenges and competition from others within his own group; and the degree to which he develops a need for action to prove his sincerity to himself and others (to demonstrate that he is not a mere tool of the state, and show that he is willing to risk safety and security for the noble cause) can all impact the formation of a revolutionary.

I have long felt that a common psychological characteristic underlays revolutionary behavior, but I have never believed this trait would be simple or easily described. The behavior of some revolutionaries differs so markedly from that of others that they seem to have no connection. Karl Marx, the fierce advocate of violence, the avowed atheist who took a special delight in his demonic image, seems, at first, to have little in common with the gentle and saintly Mohandas Gandhi. Rousseau, the reclusive thinker who sought a retreat from the world and who was easily intimidated in social situations, was clearly different in personality and temperament from Ché Guevara, the activist, guerrilla fighter, and leader of men. Even Marx and Guevara form quite a contrast. While both were apostles of violence, Marx seemed content to advocate violence in elaborate theoretical models that encompassed highly ambitious and intellectual ideas. He worked on paper and never fired a gun in combat. Guevara, on the other hand, was primarily an activist. He left behind extensive writings on guerilla warfare and revolutionary consciousness, but he is best known for what he did and not for what he wrote.

There is, I believe, a common idea of the self, a common moral attitude underlying the behavior of these men and others that we will examine in this study. Victor Wolfenstein in his *The Revolutionary Personality*, suggests that his three subjects (Gandhi, Trotsky, and Lenin) each carried a burden of guilt that he was unable to relieve in the context of the family, and each had difficulty in coming to grips with paternal authority. Wolfenstein views these conditions as necessary but not sufficient for revolutionary involvement. Bruce Mazlish in *The Revolutionary Ascetic* writes of a "prototypic revolutionary personality," an ideal type approximated to a great extent by Lenin and Mao. Important characteristics of the revolutionary ascetic were few close libidinal ties, a sadomasochistic orientation, and the capacity to gain ascendency over others through suffering and self-denial.

My early study of Rousseau outlined similar characteristics. However, I have stressed the role of masochism in its classical psychoanalytic significance, i.e., the sensuality and the virtuous thrill derived from suffering rather than the stoic satisfaction of asceticism. I have also emphasized the importance of attention-getting behavior as a child and the need for some demonstration of love for and love from the masses as an adult. Perhaps a more important difference from the work of Mazlish is my effort to place twelve individuals on a four-stage continuum of revolutionary development, from the primitive moral masochist to the successful revolutionary.

If we accept a common pleasure in suffering for both the sexual masochist and the martyr for a cause, we have taken an important step in understanding the pehnomenon of rebellion. The ferocity of Marx and the timidity of Rousseau are brought closer together when we learn that Rousseau's childhood hero was Scaevola, who held his hand in a flaming brazier to demonstrate his ability to undergo suffering, and the childhool hero of Marx was the defiant Prometheus, who brought fire to humanity, but who suffered for his heroism by being chained to a rock while an eagle devoured bits of his liver. Tolstoy had an aunt who also admired Scaevola and who became an important influence in his life. The childhood hero of Ché Guevara was Don Quixote who set himself against the same impossible odds that faced Ché himself in his final battle. In a last letter to his family, Ché remarked, "Once again I feel between my heels the ribs of Rosinante" (the horse of Don Quixote).

Still, a difference exists between the blatant sexual masochist who seeks a private, secret, highly personal pleasure, and the political savior who suffers for humanity. Rousseau was sexually stimulated by a spanking at the age of eleven and T. E. Lawrence hired a sergeant to whip him to orgasm, but both men managed at various times in their lives to transcend these private sexual desires and suffer in a larger, more political sense for the freedom of others. The search for a moral truth and the desire for personal goodness, as well as the conviction that this goodness could be found only in suffering for others, was a prime characteristic of the rebels we will study.

Mazlish has also stressed the moral aspect of revolutionary motivation and its strong affinity to religious idealism. It is the moral aspect that I highlight in this study. I have examined the motivation of individuals who perceive and protest a lack of equity in society. Not all of us are sensitive to this lack of equity or aroused by it to the same level of moral indignation. What are the personal sources of this moral indignation? What induces an individual to become so identified with an oppressed group that he feels he must do something about the problem? These are the questions I attempt to answer.

Acknowledgments

The idea for this book emerged in 1968 from a conversation with Dick Doctor who was then chairman of the Psychology Department at California State University, Northridge, and from the encouragement he gave me to offer a course on the psychology of revolution. I have since prepared somewhat different versions of this same course for the Psychology Department at the University of California at Los Angeles and the California School of Professional Psychology, as well as a number of seminars on this subject during four years on the staff of the Urban Semester at the University of Southern California. During this period I have profited from the discussion of some of these ideas with Gerald Shure, Meryl Ruoss, and Terry Cooper. I am particularly grateful to the staff and Directors of the Planning Analysis and Research Institute where I have been a Senior Research Fellow for the past five years.

I owe a special note of thanks to Elizabeth Parry Catenaccio who has taken time to go over the manuscript in detail and who has been particularly influential in strengthening the preface and introduction. Lloyd Moote has been of immense help as an idea man, particularly in overall organization and structure. The principal source of support for this book has come from my wife, Hitchie, whose enthusiasm for the project and whose willingness to read and critique the several versions of the manuscript have made it a much more readable book than it would have been without her help.

Introduction

The Psychological Basis of Political Action

I have a fundamental quarrel with the belief that the liberal democrat is the most effective opponent of the tyrant. Certainly most of us would prefer to live in a democratic society managed by reasonable and humane people who believe in political freedom. But this does not mean such people will be the first to detect abuses of freedom or the first to react against such abuse. In their study *The Authoritarian Personality*, Adorno et al. present the liberal democrat and the tyrant as polar opposites.[1] There have been too many criticisms of this study to present here, but I do not question the primary finding of the study—that an association exists between extreme authoritarianism and sadomasochism. I *do* question the conclusion that the most effective opponent of the "sick" tyrant is the "healthy-minded" liberal. More vocal and active than the liberal is the chronic protestor who serves at all times as gadfly in the hide of the state. He is always fulminating against privilege and injustice, even in a democratic state where the majority of citizens are quite satisfied. If police orders prohibit parading down the main street, but offer a back street as a compromise, he refuses the compromise and courts arrest. He is seldom reasonable in the way society defines reason. Regardless of his primary profession of attorney, actor, businessman, or student, he appears also to be a professional social activist who is never really content without a cause. The sense of anger and righteousness he derives from defending the weak satisfies a deep psychological need within him.

It is my contention that this type of person will be first into the field in the battle against injustice. He will be there long before the injustice is evident to others. He will stay and fight longer, not just because he is courageous (for courage is also necessary in such struggles), but because he has a personal need to be there. He can endure more punishment than others because he is rewarded by struggle and punishment in ways that others do not understand. He thrives on unjust treatment because he knows how to use his own wounds to convince others to join his cause. Every defeat represents another step toward final victory. Even loss of life is a pleasure if death comes in such a way as to stimulate others to a heroic anger and thus help to ensure the final victory.

xv

I do not intend to imply that in politics one must be sick to join the struggle in the first place. Rather I will try to show that impulses, which may adversely affect the individual if confined to private life, can play a productive role in the sphere of politics. In "normal" times most "normal" people are content to direct their attention to earning a living and caring for their families. This is true in both socialist and capitalist societies. Most of us do not thrive on crisis. We are not trying to establish a new system of political and/or religious beliefs. Politics is not our life, although we may become more involved in politics during an election.

The professional protestor, be he reformer or revolutionary, is different. He lives to remake the world, to build a better society, to create a new image of humanity. Any job or profession is secondary to this goal. He is always on guard against injustice and prepared to defend its victims. He is, in fact, deeply identified with the victim, the underdog, and one of his greatest joys comes from the thrill of righteousness he derives from his actions.

While protesting government injustice, the revolutionary is not content with a mere overthrow of the government or the assumption of power for its own sake. He is seeking something more vague and indefinable than political or military power. In this introduction I describe briefly the "something," but in the process it will be necessary to outline some of the differences between the rebel and the tryant, to make clear what I mean by revolution, and to define the limits of this study.

The Moral Aspects of Revolution

The term "revolution," as used in this study, involves the kind of mass movement that aims at major political and social change. Various other forms of palace revolution or military coup represent a change of individuals in power, but they do not require the period of preparation and incubation necessary for mass revolution. Such mass revolutions are of a fundamentally moral character, although I would not suggest that this is the only factor involved. It is my contention that the revolutionary moralist is that individual who initiates mass revolutionary movements and (while tactics and behavior may change as the revolution progresses) whose primary goal is a mass moral awakening, similar in some respects to a religious awakening.

Crane Brinton has described several stages of revolutionary development: the alienation of the intellectuals, the overthrow of the government, the rule of the moderates, the rise of the radicals, and the final return to order (termed Thermidor). Sometimes this final stage involves the same repression which characterized the old regime. [2] In this study we deal with men who participated in the stage of alienation and held some responsibility for the development of theory, whether or not they engaged in armed conflict. They were all revolutionary moralists. There are no Thermidorians in this study, no individuals who followed behind in the theoretical stages and who took control of the movement only after revolutionary victory (such as Stalin and Napoleon).

Despite the fundamentally moral quality of his leadership, the revolutionary may press hard for action, believing true commitment impossible without action. Action, then, for some revolutionary leaders, brings about moral change. It is the mark of sincerity, the final test of belief that awakens the thinking process and causes the person to reflect on what he is doing. In others, thought must come before action. In certain circumstances, thought in the form of speeches, books, and pamphlets *is* a form of action. Sun Yat-sen argued at great length on this subject of what ought to come first, but it does not seem to me that he resolved the problem, for a fundamental difference in the temperaments of individual leaders remains.

In this study I examine the lives of revolutionary ideologists because they are the instigators of mass revolutionary movements. I try to tie their lives together with the single dynamic of sacrifice and suffering and the meaning it held for these men.

Because the revolution itself moves from a period of selfless sacrifice to one of authority and control, we would expect those individuals who are more idealistic and self-sacrificing to be successful in the initial stages of a revolution and those more comfortable with a position of command to rise to power in the later stages. However, it is difficult to take a categorical classification of a person's role or profession as an indication of his inner concern for morality. T. E. Lawrence was a military leader assigned to use the Arab revolt to aid the British cause in World War I, but Lawrence soon became a moral leader and found success dependent on fostering within the Arab people a belief in their rights and a search for freedom and self-determination. In the end he became so thoroughly committed to what he construed as the moral basis of the Arab cause that he was unable to accept the British and French partition of the Arab territories. He had adopted the Arab people as his own and had deeply identified himself with them. Thus, while he was quite capable of deeds of terrorism and became a skilled guerrilla fighter, his leadership was of a moral quality and he could not continue to represent the British position to the Arabs after he felt they had been betrayed. He became so repelled by the notion of command that he resigned his rank of colonel and later joined the RAF as a private, refusing any rank above corporal.

Numerous studies of political leadership have been directed toward revolutionary leaders or revolutionary "elites." For this reason it is important to emphasize that this work is a study of the qualities that make for rebellion and revolt *against* power—a revolt which may or may not result in the actual achievement of power for the individual. While many of the men in this study will be leaders, it is not a study of leadership or the qualities that make leaders. Instead I concentrate on the impulse toward *moral* rebellion, disagreement with power, and the revulsion from power. This revulsion may often conceal an attraction toward power, a secret urge to dominate others in an autocratic manner. This urge is something that we will sometimes observe in the further study of the individual.

The fact that this secret urge to dominate often emerges in the personality of the rebel (coupled with the frequent accusation that some rebels have become tyrants once they have gained power) means that we should look at the personality of both the tyrant and the rebel before we begin our study of individuals.

The Emergence of Independent Moral Belief

Sigmund Freud has suggested that the basic moral support for a culture comes from the development of a superego in its citizens. The superego is the restraint against murder, rape, cannibalism, and other forms of aggression. This restraint is instilled in us by our parents and cemented first by a fear of punishment and finally by the development within ourselves of an internal representative of parental standards. This superego is partly conscious in the sense that we are aware we should not do certain things, but it is also partly unconscious in the sense that we experience guilt or shame before or after some action without understanding why we feel the way we do. The standards that form our superego come in part from our parents and in part from the culture in which we are raised. Speaking of the superego as a source of support and cultural stability, Freud remarked:

> The strengthening of the superego is a highly valuable psychological possession for culture. Those people in whom it has taken place, from being the foes of culture, become its supporters. The greater their number in a cultural community, the more secure it is and the more easily can it dispense with external coercion.[3]

Everyone does not have this superego to the same degree and some are restrained from murder, robbery, and other aggressive acts only by fear of punishment. The problem is aggravated if the satisfaction of one group within the culture necessarily involves the suppression of another, such as a master–slave culture. Freud clearly disapproves of such a culture and says, in effect, that it tends to stimulate rebelliousness in its citizens and that, if it leaves unsatisfied the drives to rebelliousness of a large number of its citizens, it does not deserve to exist.

As already noted, the mere existence of injustice—even poverty and starvation—is not sufficient to produce rebellion. Many slaves have defended the lives of their masters out of a sense of loyalty and duty. They have incorporated the moral values of a master–slave culure and regard themselves as good virtuous slaves if they obey and serve their master well, particularly if he feeds them and punishes them only when indolent or lazy. Even in a popular revolution such as the French Revolution of 1789, peasants in certain districts may fight beside their lords against a republican army seeking to liberate them from serfdom. In such cases, an important moral force behind the peasant armies was the local clergy, who claimed that God was on the side of the monarchy and the local aristocracy.

For years colonial governments of white Caucasians have ruled Africa and India, with soldiers from the native population loyal to their colonial officers. The native soldiers felt they had a special position somewhere above their fellow nationals. When they smashed in the skull of a local dissident with the butt of a rifle, they were proud that their officer had placed such trust in them.

In the dutiful slave we see a special sadomasochistic psychology that perpetuates the dominant culture, but represents merely a distortion or exaggeration of the obedience and conformity that characterizes a stable culture as a whole. Against this stable society are two types of rebellion: the individual deficient in superego control who will commit minor fraud and theft or even robbery and murder for private gain; and the individual who puts forth a different set of moral standards, who will suffer personal privation and discomfort to uphold these standards against those of the dominant culture. Sometimes this rebellion is supported by religious principles, sometimes by a deviant set of ethics. But it always takes place in the name of some larger group, an oppressed minority or even a majority, which the rebel feels is being misled and dominated.

In this book we will be seeking a common source for this moral rebellion; that is, a rebellion that claims to be an effort to create a new and "better" set of moral standards for the culture. The people who fall into this category include both reformers and revolutionaries. Their chief characteristic is that they both look toward a new morality, rather than personal gain, as the basis for their revolt.

In the end one is forced to raise the question of whether obedience (conscious or unconscious) really constitutes morality at all. When we speak of ethical standards of personal conduct, do we not really mean standards that represent some conscious thinking about right and wrong, some personal principles of justice based on some belief about the nature of humanity and supported by some evidence? Is not all genuine morality a refusal or revolt of some kind? The decision to live by one's own standards, the very existence of personal standards of conduct which may or may not differ from those of society, represents a form of moral independence on which all personal integrity is based.

The Intimate Relationship between Pain and Morality

The real test of personal standards occurs when they come into conflict with generally accepted social values or the force of some established authority. Without this sense of physical opposition there is no way to be sure that such standards are more than an idea—a thought which may change its direction when opposed by force. Our first childhood lessons in morality were enforced by a real or implied threat, by someone considerably larger and more powerful than ourselves. We have all felt that power in some way, if not by a sound rap on the ear, then by the sheer physical strength involved in restraint. Pain and discomfort are a way of helping us understand what we really believe, or whether we have any beliefs at all that cannot be changed by another sound rap on the ear.

In the final analysis there is no moral belief or moral courage without physical courage. All power is held by force. Even the force of public opinion represents an implied physical force and even nonviolent rebellion against this force involves the risk of violence.

But, just as a sharp blow from the policeman may help us discover we do not hold certain beliefs as strongly as we thought, so the arousal of our anger by the opposition of others may cause us to discover a reservoir of imperiousness in ourselves that we have never before experienced. Thus action, in one form or another, has a way of clarifying moral issues, particularly if we believe that moral issues are a mental phenomenon only and not related to the body at all.

The "Right" to be Cruel

In the modern Western world it is no longer fashionable to be a tyrant or to wish to be a tyrant. Former kings boasted of their power and considered the conquest of new territory as an indication of their increased worthiness. They dragged conquered chieftains in chains behind their chariots in a victory parade and demanded payment of a "tribute" from subject peoples. Today we can accept a difference in intelligence, physical strength, and other characteristics among individuals, but it is no longer acceptable to speak of a weak people, a cowardly nation, or an inferior race. Such things, if they are said at all, are spoken of quietly among friends who will answer with a knowing smile. They are never uttered in the presence of reporters with the television cameras rolling.

But there remain cultures in which torture and hanging are forms of entertainment and cruelty is considered a form of manliness. For a while we believed such ideas were part of our precivilized past, but the rise of the Nazi party in civilized Germany exposed many of our modern ideas about equality and justice to be only a thin veneer covering more primitive beliefs capable of rising to the surface on slight provocation. When such feelings are manifested in action they are seen to be more than mere abstract philosophical beliefs; they are connected with deep sources of emotion and erotic pleasure.

Friedrich Neitzsche was perhaps the last philosopher to attempt an open justification for tyranny. He proposed the existence of one morality for the strong and superior and another for the weak.

> Every elevation of the type "man" has hitherto been the work of an aristo-cratic society and so it will always be—a society believing in a long scale of gradations of rank and differences of worth among human beings, and requiring slavery in some form or another. To be sure one must not resign oneself to any humanitariam illusions about the history of the origin of an aristocratic society. . . . Men with a still natural nature, barbarians in every terrible sense of the word, men of prey, still in possession of unbroken strength of will and desire for power, threw themselves upon weaker, more moral, more peaceful races. [4]

Nietzsche saw all morality in terms of dominance and submission, master and slave.

> In a tour through the many finer and coarser moralities which have hitherto prevailed . . . two primary types reveal themselves to me. There is a *master-morality* and *slave-morality*. [5]

The master-morality upholds virtues such as bravery, hardness of heart, pride, disdain for the weak. In slave-morality

> those qualities which serve to alleviate the existence of suffering are brought into prominence and flooded with light; it is here that sympathy, the kind, helping hand, the warm heart, patience, diligence, humility and friendliness attain to honour; for here these are the most useful qualities. . . . According to slave-morality, therefore, the "evil" man arouses fear; according to master-morality, it is precisely the "good" man who arouses fear and seeks to arouse it, while the bad man is regarded as the despicable being.[6]

It is characteristic of the extreme polarity of Nietzsche's moralities that they should have a sexual basis. Slave-morality is feminine; it is the morality of weakness and submission. Master-morality is masculine; it is the morality of dominance.

> It is thus conceivable that it is just from woman . . . that *they* have learnt so readily those outbreaks of boundless devoted *sympathy*. . . . This sympathizing invariably deceives itself as to its power; woman would like to believe that love can do everything—it is the *superstition* peculiar to her.[7]

Sympathy for the suffering is thus a disgusting, feminine trait. Sympathy should be reserved for the strong.

> There is nowadays, throughout almost the whole of Europe, a sickly irritability and sensitiveness towards pain, and also a repulsive irrestrainableness in complaining, an effeminising which, with the aid of religion and philosophical nonsense, seeks to deck itself out as something superior—there is a regular cult of suffering. The *unmanliness* of that which is called "sympathy" by such groups of visionaries, is always I believe, the first thing that strikes the eye. . . .[8]

The Sexual Aspect of Dominance and Submission

Aggression in all animals is related to survival. Much of what Nietzsche wrote has a certain element of truth for animals and primitive humans. The brute who seizes the fruit from a tree and keeps his fellows at bay until he is full, then goes to sleep in the sun not minding if others eat. The remarks of Nietzsche reveal a certain anger toward the weak, a contemptuous description of the femininity of submission that goes beyond the aggression needed for survival. There is a certain sensual glory in being strong that contains a definite erotic component. The joy of beating or dominating another is greater if that other is a woman, or a man who is being emasculated or "made into a woman." According to Reza Baraheni, this attitude is more striking in those cultures which have recently emerged from matriarchy. In his book, *Crowned Cannibals*, and particularly in his chapter on "Masculine History," he emphasizes the extent to which masculinity in Iran is associated with power and femininity with shame and weakness.[9]

But if this were the substance of the psychology of tyranny, we could say merely that all tyrants were sadists. Freud, who examined this phenomenon in some detail, stressed not only the sadistic, but also the masochistic side of the tyrant. He showed that the two impulses generally occur together in the same individual.

The Work of Freud

Freud gave the name sadism to pleasure derived from inflicting pain on others. Closely related to this was the act of dominating or humiliating another, which inflicted a certain psychological pain. The counterpart to sadism was masochism, the pleasure in receiving pain and being dominated or humiliated. He called these "partial instincts" because he believed (in his early theory) that sadism was derived from the normal aggression of the male in his efforts to overcome the resistance of the female by means other than courting.[10] However, these normal partial instincts could become distorted into a "perversion" when hurting the sexual partner became the primary means of stimulation and the source of orgasm. In like manner, normal "feminine" masochism, the desire to submit to the male, to be dominated by him, to receive his penis, could also become distorted into perverse behavior in which the woman desired to be hurt and/or could not achieve orgasm except through a beating. Freud also recognized that masochism could occur in men and sadism in women. In fact, the two impulses, in their extreme form, were usually interchangeable, hence the term "sadomasochistic personality." If the masochist does not receive the beating he wants, he may become provocative, striking his partner in order to stimulate anger and aggressive behavior. If he still does not receive a beating, he may become the sadist, torturing his victim, challenging him to dare to strike, humiliating him and laughing at his impotence.

Freud regarded men as normally the active partners in sexual relationships. While our modern society is beginning to take a different view of the "normal" passivity of the female and the "normal" activity of the male in both sexual and social encounters, it should be recognized that the roots of this stereotype of masculine and feminine behavior go far back in our history and still have an important influence on our attitudes and beliefs. There is a fear of femininity in men which may not be directly related to genital sexuality, but may have a more diffuse connection with dependency and power.

Freud saw another important derivative of the masochistic impulse. This was the association between suffering and virtue. He believed that some people punish themselves for aggressive and competitive feelings toward a parent by (unconsciously) arranging for their own failure. In this way they express their guilt about aggression, but also gain a sense of virtue from their own suffering. He called this "moral masochism" to indicate that the direct motive of physical pain has been transformed and partially sublimated by a more generalized desire to suffer morally. Theodor Reik carried this subject a step further in its political implications by a discussion of what he called "social masochism."[11] He described the rebellious element in masochism and how masochism is directly related to political revolt as sadism is related to political domination or tyranny.

Sadomasochism and Political Power

While both sadistic and masochistic impulses exist in the political tyrant, he cannot display both of them openly. Like Nietzsche, he is proud of his will to power, but he is ashamed of his secret desire for submission and humiliation. Therefore, masochistic impulses, if they are discovered at all, are usually a part of his private relationships with women or men.

Some evidence exists for believing Adolf Hitler, who gloried in his own urge for power and who spoke of a "master race," was a secret sexual masochist. The sources of this evidence are numerous and fairly consistent.

During his rise to power, Hitler took his niece, Geli Raubal, as a mistress, but their relationship soon developed tensions due to Hitler's extreme jealousy and his refusal to allow her to be seen in public with any man but himself. He was also fearful that she might talk with others about their private life. Konrad Heiden maintained that Hitler wrote a letter to his niece Geli in which he was quite explicit in the expression of his masochistic desires.[12] The letter fell into the hands of his landlady's son and had to be purchased by party members at great expense. Ernst Hanfstaengl, a former friend of Hitler, described him as "an impotent man with a tremendous nervous energy. Hitler had to release this tension somehow. He was in turn sadist and masochist. . . ."[13] Otto Strasser once tried to date Geli Raubal, but Hitler objected. Strasser claims that Geli described in detail for him some of Hitler's perversions, but his own account is lacking in specific facts.

> She did not need much questioning. With anger, horror and disgust she told me of the strange proposition with which her uncle pestered her.
> I knew all about Hitler's abnormality. Like all others in the know, I had heard all about the eccentric practices to which Fraulein Hoffman was alleged to have lent herself, but I had genuinely believed that the photographer's daughter was a little hysteric who told lies for the sheer fun of it. But Geli, who was completely ignorant of the other affair of her uncle's, confirmed, point by point, a story scarcely credible to a healthy minded man.[14]

We have another secondhand account of Geli's experiences with Hitler from Walter Langer. "It was of utmost importance to him [Hitler] that she squat over him in such a way that he could see everything." Here the source is not mentioned. Langer took this as evidence of Hitler's voyeurism, but the position is also one which suggests a submissive, humiliating role.[15]

In another interview Langer obtained more specific information about Hitler's masochism.

> Rene Mueller . . . confided to her director, Zeissler (who had asked her what was troubling her after spending the evening at the Chancellory) that the evening before she had been with Hitler and that she had been sure that he

was going to have intercourse with her; that they had both undressed and were apparently getting ready for bed when Hitler fell on the floor and begged her to kick him. She demurred, but he pleaded with her and condemned himself as unworthy, heaped all kinds of accusations on his own head, and just groveled in an agonizing manner. The scene became intolerable to her and she finally acceded to his wishes and kicked him. This excited him greatly and he begged for more and more, always saying that it was even better than he deserved and that he was not worthy to be in the same room with her. As she continued to kick him he became more and more excited. Rene Mueller committed suicide shortly after this experience.

Hanfstaengl, Strasser and Rauschning, as well as several other informants, have reported that even in company when Hitler is smitten with a girl he tends to grovel at her feet in a most disgusting manner. Here too he insists on telling the girl he is unworthy to kiss her hand or to sit near her. . . .[16]

It is important to note that, in his period as chancellor and dictator, this desire for submission could be expressed only in relation to women. Even in such cases it was a shameful thing to be kept secret. In his public behavior, Hitler was a man who believed in dominating others, not being dominated. He first hired a group of ex-convicts and war veterans to silence hecklers at his meetings, a group which later became the SA (*Sturmabteilung*), but he soon took his brownshirted troopers into other public meetings to break them up. In 1921 he personally led his storm troopers in an attack on a meeting to be addressed by a Bavarian federalist. He was sentenced to three months in jail but regularly continued breaking up the meetings of others by force. Still, the really sadistic element in this urge to dominate appeared only when Hitler was thwarted. He arranged for the slaughter of the SA (officers and men) when he suspected the group of a growing disloyalty. According to William Shirer, when army conspirators were arrested (for attempting to kill Hitler by bombing an underground bunker), a particularly painful method of execution was selected for them. They were strangled slowly by piano wire while hanging from meathooks. To make sure he would not miss the event and could view it in privacy, Hitler ordered films made of the strangling. "The developed film, as ordered, was rushed to Hitler so that he could view it. . . . Goebbels is said to have kept himself from fainting by holding both hands over his eyes."[17] On the surface, Hitler was clearly both authoritarian and sadistic, but he may also have had secret masochistic needs which he was unable to express openly.

This sadomasochistic character of the "authoritarian personality" was also expressed in the literature of liberals and left-wing writers. Jean-Paul Sartre's "Childhood of a Leader" and Alberto Moravia's *The Conformist* were essentially examples of the consequences of the "sick" sadomasochistic character who turned to politics.

Rebel and Tyrant

Psychological research such as the studies in Adorno et al., *The Authoritarian Personality*, as well as the many psychoanalytically based studies of power and submission do bring out an important point. There are differences in attitude and identification between the rebel and the tyrant. Hitler outwardly exhibited the personality of the tyrant, even during the period when he was an outcast and rebel against the German society of his time. He never made a secret of his belief in elitism. In fact, his strong emphasis of it may have covered his secret desire for submission and humiliation. While the term sadomasochistic personality has been applied to the tyrant, I believe it applies to the rebel as well. The rebel may make such a strong point of his weakness and his willingness to suffer, in order to conceal from himself and others his underlying urge to dominate. With this understanding of an underlying similarity in motive forces, a mutual concern for power and its use, I will try to highlight some of the outward and *conscious* differences between the rebel and the tyrant, again keeping in mind that these are ideal types or polar tendencies to which no one individual will conform perfectly.

We have two very different types of sadomasochistic personalities of the political Right and Left. On the surface, right wing authoritarianism is sadistic, stressing the "natural" rights of the strong over the weak, of the inherently superior over the inherently inferior. The rebel challenges traditional meanings of superiority. On the surface he stresses the rights of the disenfranchised, the poor, and the weak against the strong. But as his power increases (in terms of number of followers, force of arms, and media support), this sense of strength may release latent sadistic forces in his personality. As a result he may become as morally inflexible as his opponent. The rebel may begin by demanding justice. He may end by imposing a dictatorship.

From the political standpoint, the primary distinction between the sadist and the masochist lies not in the degree of violence versus nonviolence or dominance versus submission, but between what Nietzsche has called master-morality and slave-morality, identification with those in power (by strength or tradition) versus identification with those who suffer. The rebel, while capable of fighting and killing in a moment of passion, finds cold cruelty extremely difficult. He may punish a subordinate with great cruelty, but it always grieves and sometimes incapacitates him. He takes no *conscious* pleasure from punishing others, but may experience conscious pleasure from his own suffering. The tyrant, on the other hand, takes an open delight in cruelty. He feels his personal superiority to those he punishes, a superiority that derives, in part, from the power he has over them.

The rebel dreams of adulation from multitudes praising his virtue, or of future generations weeping over his tomb. The tyrant dreams of a mountain of skulls celebrating his triumph and victims trembling in fear before his power. The ideal of the rebel is complete equality among all people, men and women, an ideal seldom achieved in any social system. The ideal of the tyrant is a complete system of aristocracy with upper and lower ranks based on a system of slavery for the lowest orders of humanity.

But again, remember that we are talking of sadomasochism. History reveals many examples of benevolent monarchs and tyranical rebels in whom these two tendencies were always at war. The actual possession of unlimited power can release a bloodlust in individuals who seemed at first to be gentle, mild, and self-effacing. This is what is meant by Lord John Acton's famous remark about the tendency of power to corrupt.[18] Many of us have latent sadistic tendencies which can be aroused if the situation is sufficiently encouraging to them. It may also explain why certain of our rebels refuse power, even when it is thrust at them (as did Trotsky and Guevara). Perhaps they sense their corruptibility and do not want to expose themselves to temptation. But this very refusal of power merely emphasizes, once again, that there *is* a difference between the masochist and the sadist, the rebel and the tyrant. The rebel feels comfortable only as an underdog. He is concerned with virtue, in the traditional Judeo-Christian sense, and feels virtuous only in revolt against a more powerful adversary. The tyrant takes a delight in domination for its own sake and feels his own strength when his adversary is weak.

Revolutionary Suffering

If the tyrant shows an overt pleasure in domination, the rebel often begins his life with an excessive interest in suffering and submission. But the suffering of the revolutionary, unlike that of the sexual masochist, often has a moral basis. Like the early Christian martyr, the rebel seems to seek out punishment. He might court arrest for many practical and strategic reasons, but the emotional involvement in suffering and sacrifice seems to go beyond these matters. In early childhood he is often found testing himself to see how much pain he can bear or deliberately prolonging some painful experience because of a belief that it will make him strong and virtuous. Such was the case with Lawrence, Rousseau, Tolstoy, and Gandhi.

It was Theodor Reik who stressed the rebellious element in moral masochism and emphasized the degree to which not only success but moral superiority and moral victory (i.e., the complete moral subjugation of others) are important elements in moral masochism. The masochist feels blocked and thwarted in the direct expression of his aggressive impulses. He is inhibited by a fear of punishment or (often in later development) a fear of hurting his parent, but his reaction to this frustration is defiance. He never really gives up this feeling of anger or his desire for the assertion of his will to dominate. Reik contrasted his view with that of Karen Horney and Freud.

> The masochist is a revolutionist of self-surrender. The lambskin he wears hides a wolf. His yielding includes defiance, his submissiveness opposition. Beneath his softness there is hardness; beneath his obsequiousness, rebellion is concealed. ... No mythological figure can better impersonate this masochistic defiance than the Titan Prometheus who is chained to the rock by the highest of the gods. The wrath of the fettered hero equals the character of the hidden defiance in masochism.[19]

Prometheus was, in fact, the favorite saint and martyr of Karl Marx.

Reik investigated moral masochism in more detail than Freud. He pointed to the frequent social success of certain masochistic individuals. While he doubted that these could be genuine cases of sublimation, he nevertheless noted certain traits which moral masochism had in common with sublimation. He felt the entire phenomenon could best be designated by the expression "social masochism," a more general term which clearly points out the sphere of life in which this instinctual inclination is manifested.[20]

Social Masochism

Another more deeply buried motive lies beyond virtue in the social masochist. Reik saw victorious revenge as the primary aim of masochism, particularly in those cases where direct sexual pleasure is completely repressed. *"Despite the outward appearance of guilt and suffering, pleasure is the aim in masochism.* And when the directly sensual and sexual elements are denied, the notion of a final victory over one's enemies becomes more prominent."[21] This dynamic is particularly appropriate for the revolutionary, whose needs are transposed onto society as a whole. He is socially humiliated and condemned in the present, but his fantasies turn toward the future. His very persecution proves his own importance to himself. Despite his immediate humiliation and provocation of social abuse, the fantasy of the final triumph of his own will keeps him going.[22]

Reik is clear about the masochistic nature of these drives, but seems to place a higher social value on masochism than generally found in the psychoanalytic school.

> I do not share the view of most analysts, who look down on such phantasies. I see in these phantasies one of the previous means of preservation of individuals and groups. Perhaps it is mostly due to them that people like the Jews and Armenians can survive national catastrophes, because they permit those groups to adapt, and yet to remain the same. The supremacy of the will is not only expressed in open flight. It can be demonstrated in the determination to yield only exteriorly and yet to cling to life, nourishing such phantasies, anticipating final victory.[23]

According to Reik, Jesus was a good example of social masochism "in its noblest and most spiritualized forms."[24] Reik saw the paradoxes of Jesus turning upside down the traditional opinions of his times. Paradoxical sayings like "many that are first shall be last and the last first" (Mark 10.31) and "whosoever will save his life shall lose it and whosoever will lose his life for my sake shall find it" (Matt. 17.25) fit the psychic basis of social masochism, in their glorification of the humiliated one, the despised one who finally surpasses even the greatness of kings.[25] The paradox and all forms of inversion and reversal are ways of upsetting conventional meaning in a peculiar manner that assumes the character of an *intentional absurdity*. We will examine this same tendency to invert ideas in Karl Marx.

Some Caveats

In the initial phases of this study I have assumed that many social rebels (those who rebel against their government *for moral reasons*) share a common dynamic. However, the manner of expression varies greatly from one individual to another. First of all, we have stepped outside the realm of the psychoanalyst's case history. The people in this study are not neurotics, dissatisfied with their lives and regarding themselves as failures, who have come to seek help. The revolutionaries we are studying are motivated by sources other than the promptings of their own instinctual needs. This may also be true of the neurotic patient, but it is a matter of degree. The neurotic feels a certain helplessness, an inability to run his own life. He feels chained to his instinctual needs. Such is not the case with the revolutionary who is motivated primarily by a sense of justice and reasoning about the nature of society and government.

Reason plays a significant role in the behavior of the revolutionary, as does the interpretation of the moral principles of others. While all human behavior is overdetermined (in the sense that it is the product of more than one source), the degree of this rational determination is greater in the revolutionary than in the neurotic. Therefore, when we speak of the role of social masochism in the life of the revolutionary, it should be regarded as a tendency to behave in a certain manner. At a crucial moment of opportunity the revolutionary may well cast aside his inhibitions and move to seize power. How then can we say that this impulse of masochism is operative at all if it does not prevent the revolutionary from achieving the success he desires? I will outline some of the characteristics of social masochism as we would expect it to manifest itself in the behavior of the revolutionary. Reik described some of the general characteristics of the masochist as follows:

> *Inhibition of aim*—a holding back of the aggressive drive for success in life. This may manifest itself as overt submissiveness or an indirect and "inadvertent" arrangement to be dominated by others, against which the individual rebels.

> *Provocative behavior*—the social masochist may be on the way to success but at this point he becomes insulting or provocative to those in power and thus undermines the very opportunities he had created for himself. He needs to show that he is not unduly cowardly or submissive and his repressed rebellious impulses burst forth and destroy his success.

> *Delay of gratification*—the masochist gains a special pleasure from prolonging the suspense. Masochism vacillates between the pleasurable and the anxious and it tends to delay the moment when tension is discharged. Apparently this putting off, or rather shunning of the end pleasure, conforms with the nature of the suspense feeling. . . . In the suspense factor the stamp can be recognized that masochism places on sexuality. It repre-

sents an alloy composed of the contradictory striving both for pleasure and for self torment.[26]

Revolutionary Psychodynamics

We have moved a long way from the dynamics of masochism (even the moral masochism of Freud) when we address the masochism of the revolutionary. Is this still masochism? If so, how will we recognize it in the lives of the men we will study? When I speak of the psychology of the rebel, I will be describing someone who has a psychological need to be in revolt. Unlike the masochist, who must arrange for his own defeat and humiliation, the rebel is motivated by the desire for heroic opposition. In one sense the rebel strives for success rather than failure, but success to him means being in the right—maintaining a sense of personal virtue and not the achievement of power. In fact, the revolutionary seeks to avoid power, and to prolong the position of opposition, by one of the following means:

Nonviolence—the refusal to use force against the government. By refusing to take up arms the revolutionary increases the sense of personal virtue and prolongs the period of opposition, avoiding an immediate overthrow of the government and his own assumption of power.

Rationalization of delay—if the revolutionary accepts the necessity for armed revolution, he discovers a reason for prolonging that period in which he must struggle for power and avoid the moment in which he must take responsibility for the government. This does not mean he is inactive during the period of delay. He uses his time productively, developing revolutionary theory, organizing the opposition, and propagandizing against the government. But he always finds a reason for discouraging an immediate armed assault or, if a revolution actually occurs, he sees it as a preliminary step to the final revolution, i.e., his revolution. The social masochist has a fantasy of eventual success or a final revenge and domination of his enemy. But the realization of this fantasy is constantly postponed by one device after the other until we realize that it is the anticipation of victory that is so sweet and not the victory itself. The aim of the masochist is actually to continue the struggle and the position of underdog during his lifetime.

Resignation in victory—if the social masochist leads a successful revolution, he may resign or refuse a position of leadership so he can stay "close to the common people." Or he may act as a perpetual gadfly to the ruling revolutionary council, always reminding them they are not doing enough, not living up to the highest principles of the revolution. In this way, he continues as the underdog and the outsider.

Even after victory and the assumption of power, he may deliberately seek moral reform *against his own administration.* He may seek to divorce himself from administrative authority and create a movement of moral reform against the very administrators he has placed in power. In this way he demonstrates his deep discomfort with power and his strong attraction toward moral righteousness.

The Role of Theory

In this goal of being a revolutionary but forestalling the actual revolution, the individual who produces revolutionary theory and/or propaganda is in a much better position. He can continue to perceive himself as bold and intrepid. He can consciously strive for action and keep busy during periods of delay. The development of theory serves several purposes. First, it justifies his own position and enhances his feeling of personal virtue by explaining to himself why it is necessary to take a position of outright rebellion. He must not rebel to obtain power for himself, but out of a desire for what is right. Second, theory explains the reasons for delay to others and so forms a rationale for keeping his followers in check. Third, if properly conceived and rationalized, the very activity of theory development can be regarded as a form of revolutionary action, in the sense that "the pen is mightier than the sword." Every stroke of the pen can become a blow against oppression.

The revolutionary who accepts the need for violence generally wants to emphasize the outwardly aggressive and active aspects of his personality and to deny his need for a more passive and submissive role. Still, his need for a sense of personal virtue is as strong as that of the nonviolent revolutionary. Therefore, the two criticisms he most fears and the two extreme images he most tries to avoid are: (1) that he is self-seeking and there really are no principles behind his position. He only wants to fight, kill the enemy, and take the power for himself. He really seeks the same things that the old regime enjoys, i.e., personal self-aggrandizement and a life of luxury. He does not really care about the oppressed people; or (2) he is afraid of action or is deliberately prolonging the moment of action. He does not want to face the discomfort and suffering of a real revolution and will falter and compromise with the opposition if given the opportunity. Again, he would rather talk about noble motives and pretend to moral aspirations than risk injury in a real fight for the oppressed.

In many respects these are opposite images, but the more the revolutionary struggles to avoid one of these images, the more he begins to take on the lineaments of the other. The more he develops theory and explains his principles, the more he can be accused of talk instead of action. The more he is inclined to rush into action without fully developing and explaining his principles, the more he can be accused of a mere selfish and egotistical struggle for power.

A Step toward Revolutionary Typology

This study does not attempt to cover the entire spectrum of revolutionaries.

Rather, the subjects of this study share one important characteristic—all were deeply involved in the effort to convert others to their way of thinking, to create not only a revolutionary protest, but a revolutionary ideology, a change in the mass consciousness to a new way of perceiving reality. To some degree, they were all theoreticians who believed their theories could be realized in the form of a major social change, either in their lifetime or in some future generation.

The more advanced, more successful examples of this kind of revolutionary were Lenin, Mao, and Castro. If we wish to see the working of revolutionary motivation in its more primitive and undisguised form, we must examine some of the precursors of the revolutionary ascetic. For this reason, I have examined other leaders who rebelled against the authority of the state and who moralized about their reasons for revolt, but who fell short of the level of control and success exemplified by the masters of revolution.

For this study, I have selected those people who left behind them enough material, in the form of letters, personal memoirs, and autobiographical writings, to provide some evidence of their personal motives for revolt. With some, the material is much more ample and intimate than with others. This fact accounts for the difference in the level to which we can penetrate each personality. The tendency to leave such material is in itself an indication of certain personality characteristics. In this respect, the study is self-limiting. We must deal with those people who have a sufficient need for self-justification to tell us something personal about themselves, even if they tell it inadvertently.

All psychoanalytical research is essentially anecdotal. This is because one expression of aggression or masochism is never exactly like another. Rather than present these cases in the order of their occurrence, I have arranged them in an order that best demonstrates an increasing consciousness of the revolutionary intent of the individual as it emerges into action. Movement is primarily from a sensual pleasure in self-sacrifice toward a more directed, cause-oriented action in which the sacrifice of the self becomes incidental. This approach has certain drawbacks. It is impossible to make a perfect fit of the individual to his level of social consciousness and his distance from the more private, self-centered pleasure in suffering. Each one vacillates back and forth in both intention and in the consciousness of sensual pleasure. T. E. Lawrence was ahead of his time in some respects. A man of action, he was the first to perfect the art of guerrilla warfare. His reasoning about revolution and his identification with the oppressed developed after his action was well under way. He conceived theories of guerrilla warfare and methods for ensuring the revolutionary motivation of local tribal chiefs as a result of his experience. His moral outrage at the British and French followed his full realization of what they were doing to the Arab territory won by his revolt. Furthermore, his intent did not remain fixed on revolution throughout his life, but slipped back into the realm of private suffering. Mired in guilt much of the time, his effectiveness as a social rebel was blunted. For this reason I have placed his story at the beginning of revolutionary development rather than toward the end.

In all, these revolutionaries were deeply concerned with the notion of sacrifice for others and suffering as the path of virtue. In the first rebels we encounter, the suffering seems to be deliberately sought, almost as though it was more important than the reasons for suffering. As we progress, suffering is seen more often as a consequence of revolutionary action, an unfortunate but necessary side effect of a noble goal. It is revolutionary morality and revolutionary consciousness rather than revolutionary suffering that gains ascendency in the later subjects of our study.

To clarify this point I have divided the subjects of this study into four types. Part I consists of those men who were never conscious revolutionaries. These are the social rebels without a world mission. Part II contains those who consciously viewed themselves as bringing about revolutionary change and had a clear vision that their work could apply beyond the boundaries of their own country. Part III contains men who were both theoreticians and activists, but who found difficulty accepting victorious leadership and who, even after revolutionary victory, constantly worried about the moral development of their people rather than the problems of administering an empire. In Part IV we see the victorious revolutionaries who have thrown aside their scruples about exercising power. But here, too, we will find some doubts and hesitation, some longing for former days of rebellion, and some attempt to retain the outward trappings of the rugged unkempt revolutionary, sometimes accompanied by growing wariness about the permanence of mere administrative power and a sudden outbreak of the old urge to bring about some moral awakening in the masses. Thus, it is clear that we are not describing discrete types, but a continuum of revolutionary development in which there is much shifting and regression to earlier levels. Nevertheless, while there is a pull backward toward private primitive masochism, there is also a push forward toward some other goal that leads far beyond the self.

This leads us to a search for other sources of revolutionary motivation. When one experiences only the sensual aspects of suffering, we are dealing with simple masochism. Suffering for a cause involves something more than displaced eroticism. Revolutionary morality may have other roots than those we have uncovered in the childhood experiences of the individual, roots which carry us beyond suffering and even beyond revolution itself. This is the subject of the final chapter of this study.

The revolutions and revolutionaries I describe are a special type. This introduction outlines some of their characteristics and some of the research which demonstrates how sexual impulses can be related to political ideology. This field is rich in research and I have described only a part of it. A bibliography is provided to give the interested reader access to more background information.

NOTES

1. T. W. Adorno et al., *The Authoritarian Personality* (New York: John Wiley and Sons, 1964).

2. Crane Brinton, *The Anatomy of Revolution* (New York: Vintage, 1958).

3. Sigmund Freud, *The Future of an Illusion* (Garden City: Doubleday Anchor), 14.

4. Friedrich Neitzsche, *Beyond Good and Evil* (Chicago: Great Books, 1949), 191.

5. Ibid., 194.

6. Ibid., 197.

7. Ibid., 210–11.

8. Ibid., 222.

9. Reza Baraheni, *The Crowned Cannibals: Writings on Repression in Iran* (New York: Random House, 1977). Baraheni is widely traveled and has taught at the University of Tehran, but he was born and raised in Azerbaijan, a fiercely independent, Turkish-speaking province. His frequent use of examples from Tabriz, one of the major cities in this province, suggests that this sadistic concept of sex (and particularly the homosexual aspects of domination and power) may be an important aspect of the Turkish as well as the Iranian culture.

10. Sigmund Freud, *The Basic Writings of Sigmund Freud*, translated and edited with an Introduction by A. A. Brill (New York: Modern Library, 1938), 569. In his later writings, Freud associated sadism with a more basic, primary drive which he called the death instinct. It was the task of the libido to defuse and neutralize this instinct by directing it toward objects of the outer world where it is described as an urge to destroy or a will to power. The death instinct is generally not given much credence by modern psycho-analysts, but its assumption is by no means necessary to believe in a will to power.

11. Theodor Reik, *Masochism in Modern Man* (New York: Grove, 1941).

12. Konrad Heiden, *Der Fuehaer* (New York: Houghton Mifflin, 1944), 383–88.

13. Ernst Hanfstaengle, *Unheard Witness* (New York: J. B. Lippincott, 1957), 130.

14. Otto Strasser, from the Introduction to Kurt Kruger, *I Was Hitler's Doctor* (New York: Biltmore, 1941), xv–xxi.

15. William C. Langer, *The Mind of Adolph Hitler: The Secret Wartime Report* (New York: Basic Books, 1972), 168.

16. Ibid., 171–73.

17. William L. Shirer, *The Rise and Fall of the Third Reich: A History of Nazi Germany* (Greenwich: Fawcett, 1960), 1391.

18. John E. Acton, *Essays on Freedom and Power* (Boston: Beacon, 1948), 365.

19. Reik, *Masochism in Modern Man*, 156–57.

20. Ibid., 292–93.

21. Ibid., 319.

22. Ibid., 310.

23. Ibid., 322.

24. Ibid., 346.

25. Ibid., 344–45.

26. Ibid., 61.

Revolutionary Morality

Part 1

THE SOCIAL REBEL

Introduction

I have described the social rebel as one who was not a conscious revolutionary. Yet the term "conscious" is clearly a matter of degree. T. E. Lawrence was a revolutionary activist almost from the beginning of a military career which started shortly after the university. He viewed himself as a soldier charged with a mission to stimulate revolt in others; he did not see himself as a professional revolutionary nor did he have, in the initial stages, the moral fervor of a revolutionary. His strong moral convictions about the Arab revolt seemingly emerged from some deep sense of justice and equity that was stimulated by his experiences, an aspect of himself that might have received only partial expression had he not received this specific assignment.

Lawrence stumbled into revolution almost by accident, although much of his early life appears to have been an unconscious preparation for such an ordeal. Jean Jacques Rousseau wandered into revolutionary ideology through an essay on the arts and sciences and their relation to modern morals. But here too, in the extreme emotion he experienced at seeing a prize offered for such an essay, we can see that it triggered something laying dormant within him, something waiting to be aroused. It is significant that both Lawrence and Rousseau, who were stimulated to revolutionary enthusiasm by seemingly accidental circumstances, were both deeply attached to the physical and sensuous aspects of masochism. Both experienced a period of guilt following the height of their enthusiasm, a kind of fall from grace in which they could no longer participate in political activity. Both experienced a sense of revulsion toward their greatest periods of success.

While guilt plays an important role in the lives of many other revolutionaries, in their later years we do not find the same paralysis in regard to political action that characterized Lawrence and Rousseau. These two men were not really conscious of themselves as revolutionaries or of revolution as a political ideology, although Rousseau clearly saw himself as part of a line of thought, the beginning of a new way of looking at humanity and society.

Tolstoy, a great admirer of Rousseau, was raised by the prescriptions in *Émile* and had an aunt who admired Scaevola. He should have been a revolutionary, or at least a social philosopher, from birth. Instead, he became a famous writer whose novels carried no great revolutionary message, but whose life was troubled by a sense of guilt, a feeling that something terribly important was missing from his life. His role of social rebel evolved slowly in midlife from a fruitless attempt to find God. While Tolstoy exhibits the same deliberate self-torture evident in Lawrence and Rousseau, there is no suggestion of sexual arousal. Whatever sexual masochism he may have experienced as a child was clearly redirected into moral channels before his social rebellion began. Tolstoy wrote much about social injustice and actually developed an organization of followers, but he continued to see himself (like Lawrence and Rousseau) as a moral critic of the way society operated and not as one who would overthrow the whole order of society and replace it with something new.

Perhaps the most striking feature to appear in these prerevolutionary activists and ideologists is the emergence, particularly in Rousseau, of the masochistic life-style, the mark of "sincerity" in the social protestor. Many who have been sympathetic to the poor were embarrassed by their own riches. Rousseau was the first to make a virtue of neglect and shabby dress. But to *dress* for a part, to *display* one's sincerity, places one in a position of conflict. Clothing is a covering of the naked self. "Sincere" covering is, to some extent, a contradiction. The real self is underneath the clothing, even under the skin. One can never really display "sincerity," but only what one hopes to be taken for sincerity. Rousseau was sincere in the sense that he felt he should act and live according to his beliefs, but he was also an actor. He was caught in the paradox of the moral masochist who, though he is often shy, loves attention if he can convince himself that he is not seeking it. He must not want attention for selfish or egotistical reasons, but it is quite acceptable if his life-style inadvertently draws attention to himself.

We will find a persistent tendency in revolutionaries and rebels of the Left toward a Rousseau-like neglect of the physical person and dress. In most cases, as with Rousseau, it is a studied neglect designed to attract notice and impart a message—here is one who suffers with the poor. Kropotkin, Sun Yat-sen, Trotsky, and Lenin stressed simplicity rather than shabbiness. Tolstoy and Gandhi exhibited an increasing tendency to simplify, beginning with the discarding of formal attire and leading, in the case of Gandhi, to the wearing of almost no clothes at all. By contrast, Lawrence maintained a strict cleanliness and adopted a very specific and even elegant costume, provided it was the costume of the oppressed. Guevara and Castro placed special emphasis on dirt as an indication of poverty and self-abnegation. The important point in all of these examples is that the costume or the life-style is meant as a message of protest, not that it is always the same or that it is always conscious and deliberate. In both the scrupulously clean and elegantly attired Lawrence and the deliberately and ostentatiously dirty Guevara, we witness a means of drawing attention to one's life-style and deep identification with the oppressed as well as an insistence on the depth and sincerity of one's moral convictions.

It is the same message expressed by Thoreau in his life at Walden Pond and the modern hippie who scorns the convenience and dress of the middle-class liberal, wearing jeans and long dresses from the thrift shop. It may end in the incongruity of the rock guitarist singing songs of protest while wearing designer jeans, Gucci moccasins, and a gold head band. The costume remains a device for attracting attention, but the original meaning of its message has been lost.

Chapter 1

T. E. LAWRENCE:
The Role of Guilt

His Uniqueness

Lawrence has been selected to begin this series of studies because he illustrates in a more primitive, undisguised form much of the moral conflict and guilt that is usually masked in the character of the masochistic rebel. Unlike many revolutionary leaders, he did not develop a philosophy in opposition to his own culture. While he was certainly influential in the Arab revolt, he accepted his position, initially, as an act of obedience which was part of his effort toward success in his own culture, although he was disgusted by the hypocrisy of much of British social life and sought the desert life as a refuge. He was also unique among rebels in that he desired virtue and a virtuous image for himself while being convinced of his own unworthiness and even evil. No amount of punishment or persecution ever changed this self-image. Thus Lawrence was a moral (and sexual) masochist as well as a masochistic *character.* He was genuinely chained by his own guilt and, particularly in the years following the Arab revolt, forbade himself the rewards of victory.

John E. Mack provides a detailed account of the psychology of Lawrence in his book, *The Prince of Our Disorder.*[1] Only a brief and highly selective description of some of the principal features of this psychology is included in this chapter. I do not intend to explain the full motivation for Lawrence's behavior, but to highlight those aspects of his personality that tie him so closely to other social rebels. The origin of the Arab revolt and Lawrence's role in it is best described by Mack.

> The revolt of the sharif of Mecca, Husayn Ibn Ali, and his sons against the Ottoman [Turkish] authority in June 1916 provided Lawrence with a unique opportunity to exercise his diverse talents. These abilities, the most important of which was his capacity to enable the fragmented Arab tribesmen of the Hijaz and portions of Syria to translate their passion to be free of Turkish rule into an effective military operation, had to be exercised in the context of British war policy in the Middle Eastern theatre. This dual purpose—of motivating and guiding the Arab Revolt, while at the same time, as a British officer, serving his country's military and political policies—was inescapable having been built into his situation from the outset.[2]

At first this appears to be a simple assignment of a military officer to a special duty, but Lawrence was already deeply involved in the Arab world. He had traveled extensively through the Middle East, prior to his military service, on a study of medieval castles. He had learned the Arab language and schooled himself to tolerate desert heat, mosquitoes, and long treks on foot. There are numerous instances of his overstudy and overwork in apparent attempts to harden himself for some as yet unknown task.[3] During his travels he often stayed with families in the area, eating the food of the people. He traveled extensively in Syria and Palestine and came to love the simplicity of the Arab people and to despise the hypocrisy of civilization.

Once he had the assignment, Lawrence began a deep identification with the Arab cause. He dressed, lived, ate, and slept as an Arab; he helped plan their campaigns and took an active part in the fighting. A few quotations from his own work will suffice.

> In my case, the effort for these years to live in the dress of Arabs, and to imitate their mental foundation, quitted me of my English self, and let me look at the West and its conventions with new eyes: they destroyed it all for me. At the same time I could not sincerely take on the Arab skin: it was an affectation only.[4]

Nevertheless, any casual use by the British of Arab lives wounded him and insulted his sensibilities as an Arab. He began to feel guilty about his participation as a British soldier.

> Vickery, who had directed the battle was satisfied, but I could not share his satisfaction. To me, an unnecessary action or shot, or casualty, was not only a waste but a sin. I was unable to take the professional view that all successful actions were gains. Our rebels were not materials, like soldiers, but friends of ours, trusting our leadership. We were not in command nationally, but by invitation; and our men were volunteers, individuals, local men, relatives, so that a death was a personal sorrow to many in the army.[5]

An even deeper reason for Lawrence's guilt was the Anglo-French Sykes-Picot agreement which called for a postwar partition of the Middle East according to a typical colonialist plan of spheres of influence. Lawrence felt he had disclosed this plan to Feisul (Husayn's third son), but Feisul did not fully understand its implications. He continued to trust in Lawrence's grand generalizations about Arab freedom and believe the Arabs would really control their territory.

Lawrence, a colonel who hoped to be a general before he was thirty, was becoming increasingly conscious of the role of his own egotism in fostering the Arab revolt and in the consequent loss of Arab lives. After the capture of Jerusalem and the final British victory, he tried to inject himself into the bargaining process on the side of the Arabs, but he was mostly unsuccessful. He retired, joined the RAF as a private, and refused any promotion above the rank of corporal. He constantly berated himself for his personal ambition.

There are many testimonials to Lawrence's incredible charm, but he blamed himself for exploiting others through this charm and failed to credit himself when he had a positive influence. He knew that he was widely loved and admired, but he despised the admiration thinking it undeserved, and he hated himself for wanting it anyway.

> There was a craving to be famous: and a horror of being known to like being known. Contempt for my passion for distinction made me refuse every offered honour. I cherished my independence almost as did a Beduin, but my impotence of vision showed me my shape best in painted pictures, and the oblique overhead remarks of others best taught me my created impression. The eagerness to overhear and oversee myself was my assault upon my own inviolate citadel. [6]

Sexual Masochism

Lawrence's guilt about his role in the Arab revolt was clearly reinforced or perhaps initiated by *sexual* guilt. He longed for punishment that Mack associates with the beatings given him by his mother in childhood. [7] This desire for physical pain was closely associated with the thought of humiliation and degradation of his own ego, the restraint of his hated ambition. It is clear that he had already found some satisfaction for this desire in the Arab world. In his own notes on the Bedouin life and the campaign, "the cruel rather than the beautiful found place." [8] In many places his description of the self-abnegation of the desert Arab sounds like a self-description: ". . . he hurt himself, not merely to be free, but to please himself. There followed a delight in pain, a cruelty which was more to him than goods. The desert Arab found no joy like the joy of voluntarily holding back. He found luxury in abnegation, renunciation, self restraint. He made nakedness of the mind as sensuous as nakedness of the body." [9]

It is in the directly sensual quality of his masochism that Lawrence differs from other revolutionaries. Most revolutionaries identify with others who suffer, are willing to endure pain, or even seek pain as a test of strength. But the pain is almost always perceived as unpleasant. It is a sign of virtue, a sacrifice of one's pleasure for the good of others. It is only in Lawrence (and possibly in Rousseau in his early years) that one finds this direct sensual enjoyment of pain. Perhaps for this reason Lawrence never gained a sense of personal virtue from suffering. For him, suffering was a perversion, not a sacrifice. He was directly conscious of the sensuality it aroused in him and it could not, therefore, make him feel "good" in the moral sense.

This may not always have been the case. In the early days of the campaign against the Turks, Lawrence seems to have gained a sense of moral worth from his identification with the Arab cause and the friendship he inspired in others. An incident in Deraa, in which he was captured, severely beaten, and raped by a Turkish Bey, evidently intensified his sensual connections with pain and perhaps also his own awareness of the homosexual content of the fantasies associated with being beaten. Beyond doubt, this experience left Lawrence with a desire for repeated beatings. We do not know what steps he may have taken to inflict pain upon himself directly after the beating at the hands of the Turk; but later, in the

Tank Corps, he hired a sergeant to whip him. This whipping had a clear sexual significance, for it was continued to the point of orgasm.[10] Possibly, the sensual aspects associated with suffering were largely unconscious prior to the incident in Deraa. In Lawrence's account, the beating by the Turkish Bey and his corporal aroused sexual feelings but the incident was not clearly a homosexual rape. After a part of the beating in which they "play unspeakably with me," he was kicked with a nailed boot. "I remembered smiling idly at him, for a delicious warmth, probably sexual, was swelling through me." After this he was beaten further and rejected by the Bey as "a thing too torn and bloody for his bed."[11] However, other letters concerning this event uncovered by Mack seem to suggest that Lawrence finally yielded to the homosexual advances of the Bey out of fear of further pain and that this may have been a factor in the intense guilt he felt about the incident.[12]

This episode alone was not the source of Lawrence's conflict over fame, ambition, and self-regard. However, by its intensification of his awareness of the sensual element in his suffering, it may well have deprived him of a sense of virtue, often an important aspect of the masochistic character. From this point on he could no longer see himself as a suffering hero, and it may have impaired his zeal to be a leader in social reform. His refusal of promotions in the RAF and the Tank Corps is strongly associated with this need to be degraded to a lower level, to be put in his place from a moral standpoint.

> ... my way will lie with these fellows here (in the Army) degrading myself ... in the hope that some day I will feel really degraded, be degraded, to their level. I long for people to look down upon me and despise me, and I'm too shy to take the filthy steps which would publicly shame me, and put me in their contempt. I want to dirty myself outwardly, so that my person may properly reflect the dirtiness which it conceals. . . .[13]

This extreme guilt and the desire for punishment, if it was indeed reactivated by the homosexual advances of the Bey, may have been related to a homosexual desire which Lawrence could not acknowledge, or which he both acknowledged and despised in himself. On this point the evidence is rather curious. Lawrence seems to have been repelled by the thought of *himself* in sexual intimacy with a man or a woman, but Mack points out that he was less uncomfortable with homosexual than with heterosexual concepts and behavior. He spoke openly of "man and man loves" which he had observed and felt to be "very lovely," and he understood women could be the same way, "and if our minds so go why not our bodies."[14] In his *Seven Pillars of Wisdom,* Lawrence suggested a certain sensual delight in the *thought* of male homosexuality.

> The Arab was by nature continent; and the use of universal marriage had nearly abolished irregular courses in his tribes. The public women of the rare settlements we encountered in our months of wandering would have been nothing to our numbers, even had their raddled meat been palatable to a man of healthy parts. In horror of such sordid commerce our youths began indifferently to slake one another's few needs in their own clean bodies—a cold convenience that, by comparison, seemed sexless and even pure. Later,

> some began to justify this sterile process and swore that friends quivering together in the yielding sand with intimate hot limbs in supreme embrace found there hidden in the darkness a sensual co-efficient of the mental passion which was welding our souls and spirits in one flaming effort. Several, thirsting to punish appetites they could not wholly prevent, took a savage pride in degrading the body, and offered themselves fiercely in any habit which promised physical pain or filth.[15]

Here, too, we see that combination of homosexual encounter with physical pain, filth, and degradation. Thus, while the *fantasy* of homosexuality was not difficult to accept (in fact, it seems to have pleased him to dwell upon it) the actuality of such an experience was evidently not acceptable to him—at least it was fraught with guilt and with thoughts of physical pain and defilement. The notion, in his literary work, that such encounters were "pure" and even "sexless" probably represents his own attempt to reduce the guilt he felt about his homosexual feelings.

Self-Sacrifice, Suffering, Pain, and Morality

It is clear that Lawrence's attraction to the Bedouin life existed much earlier than his direct involvement in the Arab revolt. Most likely his superiors encouraged his efforts because of his long experience with the people and the region—tramping about on his own, eating with Arab families, learning the language, absorbing the culture. Mack notes the numerous tests of endurance and suffering that Lawrence prepared for himself in these early years as well as the basis for his attraction to the Bedouin.[16] This attraction also contained a strong moral element. Lawrence found a candor and naturalness in desert life that he had long sought in society.

This moral element is seen in all of Lawrence's relationships. He seemed to make others feel better about themselves just by being with them. Although overly severe, even cruel, with himself, he was tolerant and open with others. Mack, who has talked with a number of Lawrence's former companions in the RAF, gives this account of his influence.

> Lawrence's generosity with money could only be described as saintlike, and he gave away any savings he might accumulate from his wages, royalties or other sources of income so readily that he was in fact constantly quite poor. . . . Lawrence's influence on these men was considerable. Several of his former companions have told me of the difference he made in their lives. Some spoke of being shown aspects of the world they had been ignorant of, while others stressed a kind of moral lift or turn their lives took following the association with Lawrence. Some he introduced to literature, which then became a life-long interest for them. All experienced an increased confidence and an ability to think things out for themselves as a result of knowing him.[17]

This combination of the search for personal virtue with severe personal restraint, self-denial, and even self-cruelty, is a common characteristic of saints, martyrs, social reformers, and revolutionaries, i.e., people in whom the dynamic of social masochism is evident to one degree or another. An important source of the self-punishment is the very height to which the saint aspires. Lawrence wanted his motives in the revolt to be absolutely pure, and when he found in himself an element of egotism about his role, he was mortified and self-condemning. In his deep identification with the Arabs he came to despise his role as the Englishman who manipulated the Arab revolt for British military ends.[18] This growing doubt about his personal virtue was intensified or perhaps even initiated by the incident in Deraa. A similar combination of personal guilt and direct sexual excitation from flagellation was characteristic of some of the great religious saints. Reik has described in detail the self-tortures of Theresa of Avila and Catherine de Siena, particularly the close relationship between sexual orgasm and the height of religious ecstasy.[19] The close relationship between guilt, self-torture, and sexuality is evidenced by the frequent warnings to monks against too much self-torture or the sinful pleasures of punishment.

The Final Act of Self-Abnegation

While Lawrence became deeply involved in the moral aspects of revolt, he never lost his strong need for some physical expression of his sacrifice. In the early years this need was filled by his constant exposure to the danger of combat. Later, the whipping he received at the hands of his sergeant does not seem to have satisfied this need for risk. His letters reveal a sense of having "crashed my life,"[20] his longing for the old days, the old sense of justification in danger, as well as his inability to come back. His problem was further complicated because no one in the military would accept his desire to remain in the ranks for what it was. When the story of his heroic feats were disclosed in the press he was discharged from the RAF because the enlisted men believed he was a spy for the officers, and the officers resented commanding him because they believed he was secretly laughing at their directions.[21] In fairness it should be noted that Lawrence was an ardent defender of the rights of enlisted men, and had a way of embarrassing junior officers by exaggerated compliance with an overly strict or severe order. Indeed, his way of mocking officers could not be punished because he was only following orders. In 1923 he entered the Tank Corps as a private, but he continued to seek readmission to the RAF. In 1925, in a letter to Edward Garnett, he threatened suicide.[22] He had made up his mind to "come to a natural end" around Christmas and might have done so had it not been for the intervention of George Bernard Shaw who wrote the prime minister on the possibility of "an appalling scandal." Lawrence was readmitted to the RAF in August 1925 and posted at the Cadets College at Cranwell. Unfortunately, in early December, near the time he had planned to "come to a natural end," he suffered a serious motorcycle crash which left him limping for over a year.

With the impending publication of *Revolt in the Desert,* Lawrence sought transfer to India to avoid publicity, leaving Cranwell in November 1926. In 1929 rumors claimed that he was being used by the British to foment revolution in Afghanistan, and he was hustled back to England and assigned to Cattewater, a station near Plymouth which was later renamed Mountbatten. Here he taught himself to work on boats and became an expert mechanic, repairing boats until his retirement in 1935. Throughout this period he was an ardent motorcyclist and seemed to take delight in the risks he encountered. In a conversation in June 1934 with Liddell Hart, he spoke of the way he would avoid running over a hen and the risk that one took in swerving, for "only on a motorcycle was the driver compelled to take a fair proportion of risk."[23] In 1935 he wrote to a friend, "Early in March I 'get my ticket,' [out of the RAF]. It's like a blank wall beyond which I cannot even imagine . . . I can only say that I wish it had not to be."[24] After retirement, he settled at his place at Cloud Hill, but frequently explored the territory on his motorcycle. After the death of his friend Frederic Manning, he wrote to Peter Davies, "I find myself wishing all the time that my own curtain would fall."[25] On May 13 he rode his cycle to Bovington to wire a friend to come for lunch. His final ride was on the return trip.

> Lawrence was traveling 50 to 60 miles an hour—an unsafe speed, but one he could ordinarily have managed—when he came suddenly upon two boys at a rise in the road just before the cottage. They were on bicycles, going one behind the other. . . . Lawrence swerved suddenly to avoid the boys, flew over the handlebars and fell in the road, suffering fatal head injuries. He lingered for nearly six days in a coma at the Bovington camp hospital and died on the morning of May 19, 1935.[26]

Lawrence was forty-six at the time of his death. While there is no evidence of a deliberate act of suicide, it is clear that he was toying with his own life, deliberately exposing himself to physical danger and that, once he had left the RAF, he wished his life would end. In Lawrence we find a heightened emphasis on the importance of physical danger; the thrill of risking death was an element in his own satisfaction, even his peace of mind. The chance that he might die at any minute consoled his doubts about his own moral worth. We will find a similar self-destructive tendency in other revolutionaries, but in the cases that follow, the element of death is further removed. Lawrence died cut off from his own rebellious impulses, unable to find a satisfactory vehicle for their expression. His was an intensely physical suffering.

While there is a suicidal element in the deaths of other revolutionaries (Tolstoy, Trotsky, Gandhi, and Guevara), in each case it was not necessary for them to court death as openly or to bring it on by their own hand. Tolstoy was eighty-one when he died, and his death was caused, in part, by his insistence upon escape from the luxury of his surroundings and a need to keep moving when he was in poor health. Gandhi and Trotsky were both assassinated, but only in the case of Trotsky is there evidence that he knew his killer and may have deliberately walked into his trap. With Gandhi it was more a matter of refusing protection when he knew he was in danger. Guevara's last mission had a similar suicidal element, but here also he made sure the enemy struck the final blow.

NOTES

1. John E. Mack, *A Prince of Our Disorder: The Life of T. E. Lawrence* (Boston: Little Brown, 1976).

2. Ibid., 113.

3. Ibid., 58.

4. T. E. Lawrence, *Seven Pillars of Wisdom* (Garden City: Doubleday, 1935), 31.

5. Ibid., 163.

6. Ibid., 563.

7. Mack, *A Prince of Our Disorder*, 417–20, 455,

8. Lawrence, *Seven Pillars of Wisdom*, 31.

9. Ibid., 41.

10. Mack, *A Prince of Our Disorder*, 428–41, but especially 433: "He required that the beatings be severe enough to produce a seminal emission."

11. Lawrence, *Seven Pillars of Wisdom*, 444–45.

12. Mack, *A Prince of Our Disorder*, 438–40, 457.

13. Ibid., 357.

14. Ibid., 424. Quoted from a letter to Charlotte Shaw.

15. Lawrence, *Seven Pillars of Wisdom*, 30.

16. Mack, *A Prince of Our Disorder*, 294.

17. Ibid., 323–24.

18. Ibid., 213.

19. Theodor Reik, *Masochism in Modern Man* (New York: Grove, 1941), 414.

20. Mack, *A Prince of Our Disorder*, 421.

21. Ibid., 339–40.

22. Ibid., 253.

23. Ibid., 400.

24. Ibid., 403.

25. Ibid., 407.

26. Ibid., 409.

Chapter 2

JEAN JACQUES ROUSSEAU: The Spirit of Revolt

Psychological Aspects of Revolt

Irving Babbitt tells us that "if we wish to see the psychology of Rousseau writ large we should turn to the French Revolution."[1] John Morley[2] and E. P. Oberholtzer[3] would probably agree, as they see his hand in the American Revolution as well. Others, such as Joan McDonald[4] and Paul Spurlin[5] find little evidence in books and newspapers of Rousseau's influence. Yet, a real cult of Rousseau worship grew up during the height of the French Revolution. His bust was carried in parades and celebrations; his works were presented several times to the National Assembly; a section of Paris was named *Contrat Social;* and his remains were transferred to the Pantheon in 1794.[6] Why did the revolution pay so many honors to a man who apparently had so little influence? Rousseau, as I have shown, was influential not through his specific ideas for change, but through the intensity of his infectious rage against injustice, his romantic view of man as naturally good, his ringing phrases, and his "spirit of revolt."[7] I think it significant that Babbitt refers to the "psychology" of Rousseau, not his philosophy or politics, in regard to his influence on the French Revolution.[8]

Rousseau was one of the first political reformers to stress the importance of life-style in cultural change. He was aware of the subtle psychological influences in society which direct and dominate the individual consciousness. He felt that he must start with himself to escape the social, political, and psychological constraints upon his behavior. He sought to strip himself of all artificial forms of dress and manner, to be open and direct with people, to discover his own identity and real needs that he might understand more clearly the needs of social and political man.

In Rousseau's concept of a "natural man" we see the first effort to reach for something beyond the mere form of government. It was an attempt (although not a conscious and deliberate one) to alter people's perceptions of their society and their relationships with each other. It was an example of the "Social Myth" described by Lyford Edwards.[9] Rousseau created a fiction of an earlier state of man, the way he felt life must have been before man was civilized by society. He painted this image with charm and conviction and compared this "natural" way of behaving with the artificial manners and the formality of the French court and

15

salons. The result was a general and broad influence on the French people through the wide popularity of his work. The American colonists had already developed a society without rank, but Rousseau's vision went beyond that. He challenged the very basis of any government's power over its people.

A shy and even diffident fellow, Rousseau was capable of lordly indignation in his writing. He could make people feel the absurdity of their lives and the injustice of poverty like no other writer of his times. He was particularly clever in describing the psychology of power—how the mind of man was enslaved by his immediate environment and his daily behavior—and he was adept in the use of powerful analogies.

> An unbroken horse erects his mane, paws the ground and starts back impetuously at the sight of the bridle; while one which is properly trained suffers patiently even whip and spur: so savage man will not bend his neck to the yoke to which civilized man submits without a murmur, but prefers the most turbulent state of liberty to the most peaceful slavery. We cannot therefore, from the servility of nations already enslaved, judge of the natural disposition of mankind for or against slavery; we should go by the prodigious efforts of every free people to save itself from oppression. [10]

Rousseau pointed to the fact that sometimes an intellectual argument about a way of life is rather meaningless if the individual lacks the capacity for such an experience himself. He urged the people of his time to look beyond the wit and repartee of the salon and recognize a different way of "feeling" about authority. In a similar manner he illustrated the process by which people are seduced into abandoning their liberty through co-optation by the powerful.

> ... individuals only allow themselves to be oppressed so far as they are hurried on by blind ambition, and looking rather below than above them, come to love authority more than independence, and submit to slavery, that they may in turn enslave others. It is no easy matter to reduce to obedience a man who has no ambition to command; nor could the most adroit politician find it possible to enslave a people whose only desire was to be independent. [11]

As to the argument that the strong would dominate the weak in a state of nature, Rousseau claimed that it was only in society that this was possible. [12]

The Life-Style as Revolt

While there is a certain logic in this argument, if one considers the situation among savages, it is more than logic and more than an argument. It is designed to open the eyes of the subservient courtier to his own capacity for freedom, to make him aware that most domination in society is a psychological domination and, once he no longer conceives of himself as an inferior or one destined to serve another, the largest step toward freedom has already been taken. Rousseau's natural man had no basis in anthropology or natural history. It was a device for altering the perception of the individual.

To carry this process further, Rousseau determined to live the part of a natural man, as much as it was possible for him in eighteenth-century France. He resigned his position as the cashier for M. de Francueil, the receiver-general of finances for France, and determined to make his living copying music. He no longer wore gold lace or white stockings, gave up his sword, replaced his elaborate wig with a simple round one, and sold his watch saying he no longer needed to know the time. When the brother of his mistress stole his fine linen shirts, he replaced them with a common variety. Somehow he felt that this reform in his dress was an essential step in altering his perception of himself and changing his character. But this was only the beginning.

> Having thus completed my reforms, my only thought was to make them solid and lasting by striving to uproot from my heart all tendencies to be affected by the judgement of men, and everything that might deflect me, out of fear of reproach, from conduct that was good and reasonable in itself.[13]

This was the ostensible motive for reform. Rousseau was a Swiss country boy charmed by French society and the brilliant conversations about elevating one's character, but lacking the refinement and experience to adapt to the elaborate manners of the salon. Furthermore, he was shy and awkward in conversation. Since it was hopeless for him to be like the French, he determined to set a new style and make them want to be like him.[14]

Rousseau, then, did not view himself as a revolutionary nor did he regard his change of dress and occupation as a "revolutionary life style." But just as some Americans had discovered that slaveholding, as a part of their domestic living arrangements, made them uncomfortable when they spoke of freedom and self-determination, Rousseau found that he could not truly understand "natural man" while wearing an elaborate wig, white stockings and gold lace, nor speak of personal independence while serving as cashier to the receiver-general of Finances. It is significant that Rousseau was almost alone in this attitude. Voltaire continued to live in the style of a wealthy bourgeois and take gifts from the nobility, as did Diderot, d' Holbach, d' Alembert, and many other literary rebels of the period. Rousseau's reputation is not spotless in this regard. He accepted a number of small gifts, the use of a cottage, occasional food and clothing, and came very close to accepting a pension from the king of England. But in the end he had an attack of panic for his own independence of mind and turned down the pension, continuing to live primarily from his music copying for the remainder of his literary and political career.

In Rousseau we see the growing awareness of a connection between life-style and belief in a very tentative form. His friends did not understand this attitude. They regarded him as a poseur and, to a large extent, they were right. Rousseau had taken hold of something of great importance, but his own ego was involved in a very sticky way. He was a natural actor who loved to play himself, but who was uncertain of his position. He was always stepping forth boldly and disdainfully in his new style, only to have doubts about the new reality he was trying to create in the face of the overwhelming presence and certainty of the old reality.

A classic example of this uncertainty is his appearance on the occasion of his own opera, *The Village Soothsayer,* at a special performance for the king and queen of France. He expected jeers for his outlandish behavior and dress and steeled himself for social disapproval, but when people were nice to him in spite of his conduct, he was completely disarmed.

> On that day I was dressed in my usual careless manner; with a growth of beard and a poorly combed wig. Regarding this lack of propriety as an act of courage, I entered, in this fashion, the very hall where the King and Queen, the royal family and the whole court were soon to arrive. I went from there to take the seat to which M. de Cury conducted me, which was his own. It was a large box seat opposite a smaller and higher one where the King sat with Mme de Pompadour. Surrounded by ladies and the only man in the front of the box I could not doubt that I had been placed there for the very purpose of being seen. When the house lights came on and I saw myself, dressed as I was, in the midst of people very elegantly attired, I began to be ill at ease. I asked myself whether I was in my proper place, if I was suitably dressed and after some minutes of uneasiness I answered, 'yes,' with a firmness which perhaps came more from the impossibility of undoing what I had done than from the strength of my conviction . . . But whether it was the effect of the presence of the King or the natural disposition of those around me, I saw nothing but civility and kindness in the curiosity of which I was the object. I was so touched by this that I commenced to be disquieted all over again about myself and the fate of my play. . . . I was armed against their raillery, but their benevolent attitude, which I had not expected, overcame me so completely that I trembled like a child when the play began.[15]

Despite his discomfort, Rousseau regarded his impropriety as an act of courage and personal honesty. One can make a number of psychological interpretations of this kind of behavior, but in his adoption of the style of simplicity and poverty and in his selection of the royal performance as the time and place to make his stand, Rousseau was clearly performing a political act.

It was an act not understood by the other liberals of his time. Voltaire, Grimm, Diderot and others chided him for his affectation and his refusal to accept a pension (although the kings of France, Prussia, and England made offers). It was fashionable for liberals in Rousseau's time to live well while they wrote and spoke eloquently about the struggle for equality and the battle against poverty. They saw no inconsistency in such a position and no lack of authenticity. They prided themselves on their boldness and originality and insisted that the gifts from the nobility had not affected their freedom to criticize the *ancien régime.* Rousseau's reply was to mock them with a question. How did they know what they might have written were they not in the pay of the nobility? Could they really be sure there was no restraint on their behavior? Was not the need to live well, to be comfortable, in itself a form of insincerity and a source of corruption?

In Rousseau's time the notion that one's life-style could have an influence on one's political beliefs or political consciousness was relatively unknown and certainly unappreciated. Rosseau had an inner conviction that he could not maintain his own independence once he had accepted the living standards of the "gentleman," but he was one man alone in a society that seemed to contain only two opposing forces: the nobility and the liberal bourgeoisie. For both sides his manner of dress and frugal way of living were regarded, at best, as a charming eccentricity and, more often, as a sign of rudeness and bad manners. Why did Rousseau pursue this life-style in the face of such opposition and what was the source of his "inner conviction" that he must live simply and suffer like the oppressed if he were to formulate an effective attack on the rich? In the course of this narrative we will discover that Rousseau had a need to suffer and even to display his suffering and his humiliation in public, a need that would probably have persisted throughout his life whether or not he ever became involved in politics. His unique skill was that he shaped his personal need into a virtue and, instead of being ashamed of his secret desire for humiliation, he practiced it in public and developed a following of people who regarded him as a hero in the cause of justice and truth.

The Childhood Pleasure in Suffering

Jean Jacques Rousseau was born in Geneva, Switzerland, June 28, 1712. His mother died eight days after his birth and this fact proved to be a central aspect in his image of her as a virtuous woman, and also in his guilt about having "killed" her. The death of one's mother so soon after one's birth might easily raise such guilty fantasies in any child, but in Jean Jacques' case the connection was made quite explicit by his father, who described his mother as a woman of almost saintlike goodness. He reminded the young man, in his grief, that Jean Jacques had taken his wife from him and he would cry out "Give her back to me! Console me for her."[16] However, this was more than a mere accusation. The young Rousseau was reminded that he too had lost a great woman and his father was struck by the resemblance between Rousseau and his mother. Thus when he cried out "Give her back to me!" he was also demanding that Jean Jacques repay him for the loss of his wife by assuming her identity, particularly her great virtue.

Rousseau and his father would often weep together remembering his mother. It was a sadness tinged with pleasure, for the older man would hug the younger close to him because of his resemblance to the dead wife. Thus Rousseau became a kind of substitute wife for his father through their mutual suffering. The father, Isaac, read many tales of virtue and heroism to the son in the hope that he would grow into a noble person like his mother. The young Rousseau was deeply impressed by these stories, particularly the one in which Scaevola, the Roman warrior, held his hand in the flame of a burning brazier to show his indifference to pain when Porsena threatened to have him burned alive. One evening when Rousseau was reading the story of Scaevola to his family he suddenly grasped a hot chafing dish in imitation of his hero, startling everyone.

Isaac Rousseau was an excitable and emotional man who left town impulsively one day after a dispute with a French captain, and Jean Jacques was then placed in the care of his uncle Bernard who sent him to board with the Pastor Lambercier. It was with the pastor's sister Mlle. Lambercier, who permitted Rousseau and his cousin Abraham to sleep with her, that he first became aware of the masochistic nature of his sexual feelings. In his *Confessions* he describes the experience as follows:

> As Mlle. Lambercier had a mother's affection for us, she also exercised a mother's authority, which she sometimes carried to the point of inflicting some children's punishment on us when we deserved it. For a long time she was content to threaten, and the threat of a punishment which I had never experienced appeared very frightening. But when it came I found the reality less terrible than the anticipation; and the strange thing is that this punishment increased my affection for the one who inflicted it. It required all the strength of my affection and all my natural gentleness to prevent me from seeking the return of this same treatment by further disobedience, for I had found in the suffering, in the very shame of the beating, an element of sensuality which left me with more desire than fear of receiving another punishment by the same hand . . . Who would have believed that this childish punishment . . . should decide my tastes, my desires, my passions, my very self for the rest of my life, and in a direction quite opposite from the one in which they should have developed naturally.[17]

It was not the spanking, as such, that *caused* Rousseau's sexual masochism. He was eleven at the time, but was thoroughly prepared for this reaction by his earlier childhood experiences which I have covered in more detail elsewhere.[18] Further, this was not the end of the development of his attitude toward suffering. Mlle. Lambercier evidently suspected that her charge was enjoying his punishment and, on the next infraction, the breaking of some teeth in her comb, Rousseau's uncle Bernard was sent for. He administered a severe spanking to both boys (Rousseau and his cousin Abraham) and both believed they were innocent at the time. Now the element of injured innocence entered the picture.

> The bodily pain, although severe, I hardly sensed; I felt only indignation, rage, despair. My cousin, in a case very much like my own, had been punished for an involuntary fault as though it were a premeditated action. He became infuriated after my example and, so to speak, raised himself to a level of excitement in keeping with my own. . . . I feel, in writing this, my pulse beating faster; these moments will always be with me even if I should live a hundred thousand years. That first sense of violence and injustice has remained so deeply engraved in my soul that every idea related to it brings back my first emotion, and this feeling, related only to myself in its origin, has developed such a consistency in itself and has become so detached from personal interest, that my heart is inflamed at the spectacle or the tale of every act of injustice whoever may be the object and wherever it is committed, as though the effect of it were to fall upon myself.[19]

Identification with the Oppressed

While there was a sense of righteousness connected with this second spanking, it was not without its sensual element as well. The two boys, Rousseau and his cousin Abraham, embraced each other with "convulsive transports" while they cried out against the man who had inflicted this punishment upon them. Throughout his childhood Rousseau longed for a domineering woman who would beat him on the buttocks. On one occasion, he exposed his buttocks to a group of girls in a perhaps unconscious desire to stimulate such a response, but the severe reprimand he received for this behavior was enough to inhibit further expressions of this kind. Thus the two feelings in relation to punishment—sexual arousal and righteous anger—existed side by side in Rousseau throughout most of his youth and early manhood. But the feelings of righteous anger were more easily generalized to other phenomena. He could feel this sense of indignation not only for himself but for others as well. He could feel a companionship with all whom he felt were unjustly treated by society. There emerged in the young Rousseau a strange combination of tenderness toward the oppressed and ruthlessness toward those he regarded as oppressors. It is a quality that we have already noted in T. E. Lawrence and one which will appear in all the revolutionaries in this study. Mohandas Gandhi possessed this quality in reverse; his ruthless and demanding side was reserved for his most devoted followers and his gentleness was directed toward his enemies.

In Rousseau's case the feelings of tenderness and pity came first. It was only then that he began to look around for the cause of the misfortune which aroused his compassion. When he found the "enemy" the full fury of his resentment would rise once more. Even reading or the casual conflicts among animals could arouse this fury in him. He tells us:

> When I read of the cruelties of a fierce tyrant, or the subtle atrocities of a rascally priest, I would willingly go and stab these wretches, even if I should perish a hundred-thousand times in the act. I have often worked up a sweat chasing or throwing stones at a cock, a cow, a dog, any animal that I saw tormenting another merely because it felt itself stronger. [20]

Freud has remarked on the close relationship between masochism and sadism. In Rousseau we can see the one feeling emerge from the other. It is his deep identification with the oppressed, his need to suffer with the victim, which arouses his anger and even his cruelty toward anyone whom he can describe as an oppressor.

This deep identification with the oppressed was demonstrated in his later travels over the French countryside. Rousseau stopped at the house of a farmer to ask for food and drink, but the fellow was familiar with the devices of the tax inspectors who tried any ruse to discover how well a farmer could live. At first he gave his guest only coarse barley bread and skimmed milk. Rousseau consumed the food so eagerly that the watchful peasant became convinced he was not a spy and delved into his secret hoard, bringing forth fine bread, a ham, and a bottle of wine, while refusing Rousseau's offer of payment. This incident reawakened the anger against injustice that always boiled just beneath the surface of his personality. He left the farmer's house filled with indignation "against the vexations which these unhappy people must suffer. That man, although in easy circumstances did not dare to eat the bread he had earned by the sweat of his brow and could only avoid ruin by displaying the same misery which prevailed all around him."[21]

In a brief summary of this kind there is much of Rousseau's life that must be ignored because it is not directly related to his masochistic orientation. However, his long affair with Mme. de Warens deserves some comment. She was much older than Rousseau and adopted him as a kind of runaway child when he left Geneva. She instructed him through much of his early youth and finally took him to her bed. He lived with her in a childlike paradise for a long period in which she took care of all his needs. For this reason, his shock was intense when she ultimately abandoned him for another lover. Rousseau's account of this moment in his *Confessions* is marked by a kind of righteous indignation at the injustice of his abandonment in view of his innocence.

This emotional component was a central feature of Rousseau's work. He had a gift for contrasting the innocence and essential goodness of the poor and oppressed against the calculating wickedness of the rich and powerful. We do not find, in his adult life, the same blatant sexual masochism that characterized his early association with punishment. Instead, the pleasure related to the suffering in his adult years seems more directly associated with a sense of virtue, the need to "suffer for truth." It is to this dynamic that we owe the evocative quality of his writing.

Much of Rousseau's suffering was self-inflicted. Some rather direct examples of this are evident in his childhood. In his adult years he was never aware that he was the author of his own suffering. He seemed to put himself in circumstances in which he was threatened with arrest, persecuted or socially humiliated because of his noble ideals. His letters and his *Confessions* show that he often "inadvertently" provoked persecution, although the punishment always seemed to come from the outside and against his will.

The Ascetic Life-Style

I have described Rousseau as the philosopher refusing the support of kings, living frugally, and cherishing his independence. Rousseau's intense need for independence was based on his awareness of his vulnerability, his strong need to be cared for and nurtured; in short, his tendency to become dependent on others and grateful to them in a childlike manner. Voltaire could accept an invitation from a king, enjoy his hospitality, and then write about the injustices of kings. If he felt slighted or ill-treated he could express his anger in a barbed remark. Rousseau was overwhelmed with love for those who treated him well and he could not express the slightest conscious anger toward them. As a result, he knew that he must be independent precisely because he had such a dependent and sensual nature. He loved the luxuries of life and therefore denied himself even a taste of them. He was fearful of becoming a loving slave of the rich and he therefore bristled at every kindness. This characteristic extended to his sexual relationships as well, for he was never attracted to shop girls, only to fine aristocratic ladies. Still, he was fearful of becoming too dependent and obedient to such women and so chose Thérèse Le Vasseur, a sewing maid who aroused his pity more than his passion, for a mistress. He met her at a small hotel in Paris where he was working on an opera. From his description of their meeting, she clearly offered him one more opportunity to defend the underdog.

> The first time I saw this girl appear at table I was struck by her modest bearing and still more by her lively and gentle glances, of which I had never seen the like before. The company at table . . . teased the little one; I defended her. Immediately the gibes were turned against me. Even if I had not felt a natural liking for that poor girl, compassion and defiance would have given me one. I have always admired decency in words and demeanor, particularly in the opposite sex. I became her avowed champion. I saw that she was touched by my protection and her looks, animated by a gratitude she dared not express in words, became all the more eloquent. . . .[22]

But Thérèse satisfied only his sexual desires, and Rousseau had a strong unfulfilled need for a romantic, emotional attachment to a fine lady. This need resulted in many temporary liaisons with ladies of society who prepared some small retreat for him where he could work undisturbed and be near them. Evidently he could accept help from a woman, but not from a man.

Even such small favors as a cottage made him uneasy and fearful of the slightest sign of luxury. His approach to the Hermitage offered by Mme. d' Epinay was characteristic of his general attitude toward such arrangements. When he first saw the Hermitage it was an old rundown cottage on Mme. d' Epinay's estate. Rousseau exclaimed with delight that it was a perfect refuge for him. But Mme. d' Epinay felt she could not offer it to him in such condition and had it remodeled to suit her image of a philosopher's retreat. Rousseau covered her hand with tears of gratitude when she finally proposed that he stay there, but he became somewhat uneasy when he saw the newly painted and remodeled quarters. To make matters worse, Mme. d' Epinay mentioned that she had certain "projects" with which she wanted help and that she could offer him some "compensation" for his assistance. Rousseau indignantly replied that he would be no one's valet and that he was not for sale. Mme. d' Epinay apologized, suggesting that he did not understand. Then Rousseau apologized, explaining that she must learn to read his heart and pay little attention to the words he used. She assured him he could have complete freedom and she would make no demands upon him. With this he became so enthusiastic that he moved into his new retreat before the snow was off the ground.

In reality, the two had not really reached an understanding, for Mme. d' Epinay was a lady of fashionable French society, the society of the salon and the philosopher. Regardless of her assurances, she reserved the right to trot him out for company on special occasions. She also expected a certain amount of attention from him; this proved the deadly element in their relationship. Rousseau, who would do anything for love, would do nothing out of social obligation. He finally presented Mme d' Epinay with the ultimate insult by falling in love with her sister-in-law the Countess d' Houdetot, after Mme. d' Epinay had introduced them. This romance became a long protracted affair, devoid of consummation and leading to a break not only with Mme d' Epinay but with many of Rousseau's other friends as well. I have described this debacle in more detail elsewhere. [23]

The incident with Mme. d' Epinay is only one of Rousseau's many encounters with the "lady of quality," all repetitions of his early relationship with Mme. de Warens in which he sought the kind of childlike trust and dependency never experienced with his own mother.

The Role of Trust

Rousseau has often been described as extremely suspicious, even "paranoid." He was also very trusting of others. He was a man who made a great distinction between friends and enemies and had no tolerance for ambivalence. Once he decided a person was his friend, he trusted that person completely, telling his friend everything about himself, good and bad, and following his friend's advice in a childlike manner. His decisions to accept someone as a friend were often based on very flimsy evidence. Before he had even met David Hume (the two men had exchanged a few letters), Rousseau was rushing across Europe toward England to "throw myself into your arms."[24] This complete abandonment, this total trust, made him vulnerable and always on his guard against betrayal. He trusted others like a child, expecting the unquestioning love a mother gives her infant. Any ambivalence on their part, any criticism of him, any suggestion that he had obligations to them because of what they had done for him wounded him deeply. If they helped him because of love, he owed them nothing but love. If they expected more, then their friendship was merely a trap, a means of manipulating him, a clever trick in which his so-called friends were really in league with his enemies. Total trust, doubt, and suspicion were all related elements in Rousseau's personality.

When Rousseau discovered that David Hume had friends among the d'Holback circle (particularly Diderot, Grimm, and d' Alembert whom Rousseau regarded as enemies), he became increasingly suspicious. But by this time he had already abandoned himself. He was living in England in the house of a friend of Hume in a country whose language he did not understand. He had placed himself in a position of complete dependence on Hume and was therefore wary of anything less than Hume's complete and undivided loyalty. By his very suspicions he aroused Hume's anger and the two men began a famous quarrel that became the talk of all the salons of Europe.

Throughout his lifetime Rousseau was the victim of the situations he provoked. His friends often found him guilty of such provocation, but all the time he was preparing his defense. In his *Confessions* he put forth the details of his quarrels so future generations might find him innocent. In writing his *Confessions* he treated future readers very much the way he did a newfound friend. He determined to tell everything about himself, good and bad, in the belief that future society would find him blameless. In the sense that innocence is naivté, Rousseau was certainly innocent, yet he was able to prepare not only his own personal defense but an indictment of the French regime which undermined the very basis for authoritarian rule. Thus Rousseau combined this peculiar naivté with a deep understanding of the psychology of power and submission. Much of what he did not understand in himself he projected onto society and described in minute and graphic detail with an eloquence that has seldom been equaled.

Rousseau saw in his *Confessions* the vindication of his life and victory over his enemies. In all probability it was to be a victory that would occur after his death, thus heightening the sense of contrast with the persecution and humiliation of much of his life. But there is little doubt that while he sought eventual victory he also desired humiliation. One of his final letters to Hume illustrates his fantasy of an idealized conclusion to their quarrel.

> I am the unhappiest of men if you are guilty, I am the most unworthy if you are innocent. You make me desire to be this despicable object. Yes, the state in which you would see me, prostrate, trampled under your feet, crying for mercy and doing everything to obtain it, loudly proclaiming my indignity and rendering the most glittering homage to your virtue, would be for my heart a state of full-blown joy, after the breathless and deathlike state in which you have put me. [25]

The Inhibition of Aim

Rousseau clearly separated the humiliation he expected and even desired in his life, from the vindication he expected after his death. While this is true to some extent of all revolutionaries who devote their lives to theory rather than action, many revolutionary theorists and agitators at least describe a goal of revolution in their lifetime. In this respect Rousseau can be regarded as a prerevolutionary writer. The vindication which he visualized after his death was highly personal— a restoration of his reputation for virtue. The revolutionary consequences of his political writings and the final destruction of the French society he criticized was an unconscious product of his work. Rousseau forecast revolution and suggested the fall of kings, but he nowhere called upon the people to take up arms and overthrow the French monarchy. He despised the rich and noble but his approach was essentially nonviolent, although his style and way of thinking often inspired violence in others. One might even conclude from his writings that he desired violence as long as he did not have to raise his own hand in the final act. If this is true, the French Revolution was certainly a fitting encore for his work. Rousseau recognized most of his aspirations, particularly his desire for vindication after his death, for a virtual revolutionary cult of Rousseau sprang up after 1789. [26]

Ironically, Rousseau understood the dangers of submission because he felt such a strong urge to submit. He hated the idleness, luxury, and sensuality of the rich because of his own deeply sensual nature and secret longing for luxurious idleness. But it was characteristic of Rousseau that, for most of his life, he fought against these desires in himself and yielded to them only periodically.

Rousseau was unsure of himself and confused about his political purpose. We will find less of this doubt and uncertainty in other revolutionaries. But in none of our revolutionaries, including Rousseau, do we find the kind of need for failure that has so often been associated with the social masochist. Rousseau, Gandhi, Tolstoy, Kropotkin, Marx, and Guevara were all successful individuals within their own lifetime, although they often looked to posterity for an even greater victory. Freud, Otto Fenichel and even Reik (in the majority of his work) were dealing with the pathological manifestations of the masochistic impulse. With the revolutionary, we are looking at the accentuation or exaggeration of certain aspects of the personality which seem congruent with the political climate of the times. Our subjects represent more flexible personalities, less directly tied to their personal needs, as is the case with the neurotic. They are more capable of redirecting their needs in such a way as to realize them through a social goal shared with others.

The Final Years

There are many contradictions in the life of Rousseau. He loved children and completed a kind of novel on child care, but he reared no children of his own. In his *Confessions* he tells us that his five children by Thérèse were all sent to the foundling hospital. Despite the denials by many of his partisans, I see no reason to doubt this statement. In fact, his feelings of guilt and longing for children in later years may have been a factor in his writing of *Émile*.

His character was one of sharp contradiction. He could be friendly one moment and suspicious the next. The climax to his fear and doubt about others was reached in the relationship with Hume. This relationship is often used to support the belief that he was mentally ill, but no evidence of delusional ideas exists prior to his meeting with Hume in his early fifties. While it is possible, paranoid schizophrenia rarely develops that late in life and senility comes much later. His illness did not get progressively worse; many of his famous works were written after this period. Clearly, there were moments in his relationship with Hume when he was delusional. He believed Hume was plotting to destroy him by enlisting the aid of liberal intellectuals throughout the world as well as the king of England. He had become so paranoid that even an offer of prunes from a friend became part of some vast secret plan. Still, his behavior differed in many ways from the psychotic individual. When the elder Marquis de Mirabeau, a stranger to Rousseau at the time, told him in a frank letter that his accusations against Hume sprang from an overheated imagination, Rousseau could respond with warmth and friendship. Further, he had many real enemies and there was still a warrant for his arrest in France because of his political writings. When he left

England to arrive at Amiens, the Prince de Contí warned him that the news of his arrival was everywhere in Paris. Many friends believed a plot against him existed, and even if they did not accept every piece of evidence he found, some were inclined to forgive his excesses.

The Fall of Jean Jacques Rousseau

In a more detailed study I have presented evidence that Rousseau's personality had a strong sadistic-authoritarian side, an aspect of himself which had a negative influence and which marred some of his greatest works.[27] It is probably because of the emergence of this tendency in his own works that Rousseau reached a point in his life when he began to have doubts about the virtue of his political motives. His attack on French culture as "effeminate" and his disdain for ribbons and decorations on a uniform as "feminine adornment" suggest a growing note of protest in defense of his own masculinity.

He became aware that something was not quite right about his political writing. It was a slow, developing awareness and he never reached a sudden and awful confrontation with his own desire for domination. It was merely that the pleasure of his work became infused with a certain disgust and self-contempt. In his later years Rousseau began to have moments of lucidity in which he felt the great international plot to destroy his reputation might be imaginary. These moments were infrequent and distinctly uncomfortable for they undermined his belief in his own motive of noble self-sacrifice.

While other writers implied that Rousseau was making such an issue of his persecution in order to draw attention to himself, Rousseau had never believed this himself. Now the suspicion of his motives began to lead him on a long trail of introspection and self-justification. Much of his energy was spent defending himself against this unpleasant awareness through a search of his childhood and a complete confession of all his thoughts and deeds. He was determined to justify himself, but in the process of introspection he turned toward the kind of aimless reverie that characterized his childhood. He spent hours lying at the bottom of a rowboat, looking at the sky and watching the clouds drift along. He engaged in imaginary conversations with himself, outlining his defense.

Still, he could never escape a sense of discomfort with regard to his political works. This feeling gradually increased until he determined to write nothing more about politics. He was frequently both tempted to return to the field of political combat and determined not to be drawn in. Perhaps the books and personal correspondence of the Marquis de Mirabeau represented his strongest source of conflict. There is something almost sexual about this temptation. After refusing Mirabeau's request for some political commentary, Rousseau told him he had decided to remove, once and for all, every temptation to write on politics by confining his reading to botany and even avoiding those parts of Mirabeau's letters that referred to politics. But alas, one day in Mirabeau's home he casually opened a book that the Marquis had left on his desk. Rousseau came upon some arousing political ideas and sensed he was "about to become hooked." Hastily he shut the book before being completely taken.[28]

While Rousseau gave as his reason for refusal to write on politics the persecution he experienced in the past and the personal conflicts with his friends over his political works, this does not seem valid. Rousseau was proud of his courage to speak out and he delighted in the experience of "suffering for truth." If his friends had not understood him, there was an even greater need for a final work that would summarize and clarify his ideas. The frantic, repressive aspect of his refusal and the seductive quality in his frequent temptation leads me to believe he felt something a bit unclean, perhaps even corrupting, about political writing—at least his own political writing.

After his return to France, Rousseau accepted the hospitality of Mirabeau and the Prince de Contí. From 1767 to 1770 he changed his residence several times in response to various signs that his persecutors had found him out. But in the spring of 1770 the weather improved and so did his disposition. In June he made a triumphant entry into Paris where he was hosted and dined by prominent people throughout the city. No attempt was made to arrest him and he settled at the Hotel du Saint-Espirit to write and to continue his work of music copying and composing. He made sporadic attempts to get a hearing of the case against his enemies. In 1770 he began a public reading of his *Confessions* which was finally stopped by the police. But he continued to be capable of quiet thought and musical composition with his friend Corancez. In 1778 he was offered a small home at Ermenonville by M. de Girardin. Here he spent the last few months of his life, dying of apoplexy on July 2, 1778, at the age of sixty-six.

The Limits of Psychological Analysis

We must use a certain caution in our attempt at a psychological understanding of Rousseau. An exclusive concentration on his psychodynamics implies that all his ideas are a product of his personal conflicts. Rousseau read extensively. He wrote to Voltaire and argued with Diderot, Grimm, d' Holbach, and others. His ideas were certainly his own, but they were also the product of his reading and discussion. He was in revolt against a real world situation and a French society that he both loved and despised. To treat all rebellion as merely a product of the internal psychodynamics of the individual is to deny that moral claims have any reality. To say that a man rebels against an unjust government because he has not resolved his own conflicts with authority is to dismiss all revolution as merely a private sickness of the revolutionary. Surely, great social movements such as the French Revolution spring from sources deeper than individual masochism, although the psychological characteristics of the leaders may be important in shaping the direction, intensity, and violence of the movement.

Most behavior is overdetermined. There are personal motives, but there are also real injustices in the world. Fortunate is the individual who can link his personal problems with the suffering of a nation or a people and find a host of allies for his cause. In doing this he may change the ethical nature of his own acts, redirect his aim, and even find a new source for his motivation. Thus an idea or a movement that begins as a private vendetta may expand to encompass the general cause of justice for all humanity.

NOTES

1. Irving Babbitt, *Rousseau and Romanticism* (New York: Meridian, 1957), 114.

2. John Morley, *Rousseau and His Era*, vol. 1 (London: Macmillan, 1923), 3.

3. E. P. Oberholtzer, *Philadelphia: A History of the City and Its People*, vol. 1 (Philadelphia: S. J. Clarke, 1912), 250.

4. Joan McDonald, *Rousseau and the French Revolution: 1762–1791* (London: Athlone, 1965).

5. Paul M. Spurlin, *Rousseau in America: 1760–1809* (University, Ala.: University of Alabama Press, 1969), xiii

6. McDonald, *Rousseau and the French Revolution*, 156–58.

7. William H. Blanchard, *Rousseau and the Spirit of Revolt: A Psychological Study* (Ann Arbor: University of Michigan Press, 1967).

8. Babbitt, *Rousseau and Romanticism*.

9. Lyford P. Edwards, *The Natural History of Revolution* (Chicago: University of Chicago Press, 1973), 92–96.

10. Jean Jacques Rousseau, *The Social Contract and Discourses*, translated by G. D. H. Cole (New York: Dutton, 1950), 256. From "Discourse on the Origin of Inequality."

11. Ibid., 264.

12. Ibid., 232–33.

13. Jean Jacques Rousseau, *The Confessions of Jean Jacques Rousseau*, translated by J. M. Cohen (London: Penguin, 1954), 340.

14. Rousseau, *The Confessions*, 343–44.

15. Jean Jacques Rousseau, *Les Oeuvres Complètes de Jean Jacques Rousseau*, vol. 1 (Paris: Galimard, Bibliothèque de la Pléiade, 1959–64), 377–78.

16. Ibid., 7.

17. Ibid., 15–16.

18. Blanchard, *Rousseau and the Spirit of Revolt*, 1–6.

19. Rousseau, *Oeuvres Completes*, vol. 1, 20.

20. Ibid.

21. Ibid., 164.

22. Ibid., 330.

23. Blanchard, *Rousseau and the Spirit of Revolt*, 23–41.

24. Jean Jacques Rousseau, *Correspondance Generale de Jean Jacques Rousseau*, edited and annotated by Theophile Dufour, vol. 24 (Paris: Colin, 1924–34.), 315.

25. Rousseau, *Correspondance,* vol. 15, 324.
26. McDonald, *Rousseau and the French Revolution,* 156–61.
27. Blanchard, *Rousseau and the Spirit of Revolt,* 245–46.
28. Ibid.

Chapter 3

COUNT LEO TOLSTOY:
Return to God and Nature

Learning to Endure

Three aspects are closely related in the social masochism of Rousseau: (1) the desire for personal virtue, (2) the association of this virtue with social humiliation and punishment, (3) the belief in some kind of vindication for one's self, indefinitely postponed, with the suggestion that one's true vindication will appear only after death.

In Leo Tolstoy we have an interesting variation on this theme, for Tolstoy spent much of his life as a successful writer, apparently unconcerned with his reputation for virtue. His emergence as leader of a group of dissidents occurred slowly and accompanied his concern about death which arose toward the height of his literary career. However, an examination of Tolstoy's childhood reveals circumstances similar to those surrounding Rousseau's early years.

Leo Tolstoy was born August 28, 1828 on the family estate of Yasnaya Polyana in the Russian province of Tula. A member of the nobility, he was Count Tolstoy until he renounced his title and his property late in his career. His similarity to Rousseau lies in some of the more personal aspects of his life. His mother died (like Rousseau's) when he was very young, before the age of two, and she was remembered for her unusual moral and spiritual qualities. When provoked to anger she would grow red in the face and even begin to weep. She admired the works of Rousseau and tried to raise Tolstoy according to the precepts of Rousseau's *Émile*.[1] From an early period in his life Tolstoy took a certain pleasure in deprivation and suffering. He remembers being pleased, following the death of his grandmother, to hear female relatives describe him and his siblings as "complete orphans."[2] The person with the "greatest influence" in his childhood was a woman he called Auntie Tatyana, who was actually his father's cousin. It is interesting that Tatyana, like Rousseau, was also inspired by the example of Mucius Scaevola. As a child, she startled her playmates by placing a red-hot metal ruler on her arm to show her endurance to pain when her courage was challenged.[3]

Tolstoy himself remembered something apparently from an even earlier period of his childhood. In it we see the connection with suffering and the strong sense of being in the right which he came to associate with suffering. Suffering, injustice, and the desire for freedom are all part of one feeling in this early memory. Tolstoy recalled being bound in some way as an infant. He did not know who tied him or who bent over him when he cried, but he imagined their attitude toward him.

> It seems to them that that should be (that is, that I should be tied), whereas I know that it need not be, and I want to prove it to them, and I burst into an irrepressible cry which disgusts me with myself. I feel the injustice and cruelty, not of men, because they take pity upon me, but of fate, and I feel pity for myself. I do not know and shall never know what it was: whether they swaddled me when I was a sucking babe, and I tried to get my arms free, or whether they swaddled me when I was more than a year old, to keep me from scratching off a scab; it may be that I have brought together a number of impressions, as is the case in a dream, but this much is sure—it was my first and most powerful impression of my life. . . . I want freedom—it does not hurt anybody, and I, who need strength, am weak, and they are strong.[4]

The impression was written during his declining years and may not be strictly accurate. He may have been tied up as an older child, perhaps by his playmates. Certainly his memory of anger and sense of injustice seem to be feelings associated with childhood rather than infancy. It should also be noted that Rousseau's *Émile*, which his mother evidently used as a guide, contains specific prohibitions against the swaddling of infants.

> Is not such a cruel bondage certain to affect both health and temper? Their first feeling is one of pain and suffering; they find every necessary movement hampered; more miserable than a galley slave, in vain they struggle, they become angry, they cry. . . . They cry because you are hurting them; if you were swaddled you would cry louder still.[5]

Knowing that Tolstoy regarded Rousseau as one of the two great influences on his life and that he had read and admired *Émile*, I am inclined to wonder if this memory of being bound may not be influenced, in part, by his deep personal attachment to Rousseau. It is possible, though rather unusual, that he was swaddled by his grandmother after the death of his mother. If this were the case, it would account for his clear memory of the experience. For a child, raised for a year and a half without swaddling, to be suddenly placed in swaddling bands would have been traumatic indeed. It could well have become a significant memory from his childhood.

The Suffering of Others

From an early age the suffering of others also filled Tolstoy with horror. He was shocked when he first discovered a servant on his way to the stables to be flogged, and he was outraged when his tutor had his own dog hanged because the animal had a broken leg.[6] But the incident that struck him most deeply was one involving his sense of personal injustice. When he was about nine years old, a new tutor, a Frenchman named Prosper Saint-Thomas, was introduced into the

Tolstoy household. Tolstoy detected a subtle contempt for these barbaric Russians in the new tutor and it was not long before his disobedience brought about confinement in a closet and threats of whipping. In his old age he still recalled this experience with intensity and anger.

> I experienced a terrible feeling of indignation, revolt, and aversion, not only to Saint-Thomas, but towards that violence which he wished to exercise on me. This occasion was perhaps one reason for that horror and aversion for every kind of violence which I have felt throughout my whole life. [7]

While he was outraged by suffering imposed on him against his will, he frequently engaged in self-inflicted suffering. He was convinced that he must learn to endure suffering if he was to achieve happiness, for only then would he be truly independent of the pressures of the world and of fate. Thus he would hold a heavy dictionary at arm's length for five minutes or lash his bare back until tears came to his eyes. [8] These feelings followed Tolstoy all through his life and gave him a horror of suffering and cruelty imposed on anyone and a conviction that self-imposed suffering was good for the soul.

In addition to the simple desire to suffer there was also a tendency to humiliate himself or call attention to himself in some public manner. He believed himself terribly ugly, but he would often do things to exaggerate his ugliness or to cause others astonishment at his behavior. He would sometimes bow backwards when introduced, just to startle people. Once he shaved his eyebrows and, on a trip with his aunt, he shaved half his head. He leaped eighteen feet from an upstairs window in an attempt to fly, receiving a slight concussion. On one occasion, when the family carriage stopped, he leaped out and ran to keep ahead of the horses until exhausted. He sometimes tried to impress people by an impolite frankness and he was called "the bear" because of his clumsy and awkward behavior.

The Early Years

The interesting thing about Tolstoy is the degree to which he concealed his urge for self-torture through much of his adult life. We can see this search for suffering in his childhood and later years, but in his youth and early manhood he became habituated to violence and often engaged in long bouts of debauchery. He suffered periods of guilt about these experiences, but evidently no repentance was serious enough to slow him down until after his marriage. However, it would be a mistake to view this period as one of thoughtless indulgence. Of his behavior he says in his *Confession*:

> With all my soul I wished to be good; but I was young, passionate and alone when I sought goodness. Every time I tried to express my most sincere desire, which was to be morally good, I met with contempt and ridicule; but as soon as I yielded to nasty passions, I was praised and encouraged. [9]

It was in the midst of this moral conflict that Tolstoy discovered Rousseau's work at the University of Kazan. He wore a picture of Rousseau suspended from a chain around his neck, as one might wear a cross, and during summers at Yasnaya Polyana, he wore a loose, shapeless canvas garment in imitation of his hero's simplicity. He was shy with women and in his university years was sometimes strongly attracted to men, particularly his friend Dyakov. While these relationships held a certain intense and emotional sensuality, he was repelled by the notion of sexual contact with another male.

Tolstoy soon lost interest in the university, it failed to arouse his curiosity and it did not stimulate him intellectually. He was interested in many of the subjects, but he thought the presentations, the formality of study, and the discipline a terrible bore. He was presented with facts when he wanted to understand the meaning of life. He felt the professors interfered with his quest for knowledge instead of fostering and stimulating his independent study. He resigned from the university and began a round of travels and pleasure with frequent visits to Moscow for bouts of gambling. When his brother arrived on furlough from the army, Tolstoy accompanied him to his assignment in the Caucasus and joined the army cadets. He became a good soldier and was cited several times for bravery under fire.

Throughout his army career, Tolstoy struggled with his own character, sensuality, and impulsivity. He sought self-reform and some lasting contribution to society. As his self-discipline improved, he spent his early mornings and evenings working on his first novel, *Childhood*. In July 1852 he contacted the editor of *Contemporary*, who agreed to publish *Childhood* in his magazine. The work was an immediate success and launched his literary career.

After the fall of Sevastopol, a new resolve for personal moral reform soon gave way to the usual drinking, gambling, and womanizing. At last he resigned his commission and left the army for the attractions of the literary circles of St. Petersburg. Ivan Turgenev presented him to the prominent writers and critics in the city. From St. Petersburg he moved to Moscow where he was again introduced to the literary figures of his time and honored with numerous dinners. He was at first flattered by all the attention, but soon developed increasing doubts about the significance of much of the literary work of his time. He felt few were willing to live their lives according to their own high moral pronouncements. When he expressed these views at public gatherings and in print, he angered many of his new friends and frequently became the center of violent arguments at social gatherings.

A regular pattern in Tolstoy's behavior becomes apparent with each new career. A mighty struggle for approval and acceptance was followed by short-lived pleasure with the admiration of his professional colleagues. At the university he did well at first, but soon felt the teachers an impediment to real, serious study. Among his young friends he excelled at drinking, gambling, and womanizing, but soon tired of these amusements and sought something beyond them. In the army he first distinguished himself for bravery and courage under fire, but his success led to an urge to tell everyone of the futility of mere physical courage.

Courage for what? Where did it lead? He wanted to demonstrate that he was more than a mere army officer; he was a writer and thinker as well. At first he was delighted to see his words in print, and he loved the admiration of the literary crowd. But here too, he sensed a certain conformity and similarity in all writers and literary critics and came to feel himself capable of more than mere writing. Of what value were mere words? It was easy to make fine pronouncements, but were these elegant literary liberals really capable of changing the world? Had they really helped one poor family or changed the habits of a single criminal? The question that characterized his later years, "yes, but then what?", was already haunting him in his youth, but, for the moment, it was a pleasant haunting. He loved being the dissatisfied dreamer who looked beyond other mere mortals. He loved the role of outcast and rebel because it made him feel above the crowd. His arguments with others contained a certain self-satisfied egotism. Always he dreamed of making his own work deeper, more penetrating than anything written before. For a long time he remained satisfied with this literary goal and it inspired his greatest works.

Marriage and Career Development

Tolstoy was thirty-two when he resigned from the army. His opposition to violence kept him outside most of the revolutionary movements in Russia during his time, but with the freeing of the serfs he was appointed arbiter of disputed land purchases between peasants and landowners, a position vigorously opposed by landowners who well knew his sympathies. He was a friend of Pierre Proudhon and Aleksandr Herzen and, even in his early years, the police suspected him of aiding revolutionaries and antireligious movements. Police ransacked and searched his house while he was in Moscow meeting his future wife, Sonia Bers. He was thirty-three and Sonia was eighteen, but she had long admired his works and looked up to him as Russia's great literary genius. They were married in 1862 and shared many years of domestic contentment, although not without moments of turmoil and stress. Much of Sonia's time in these years was involved with their growing family. Tolstoy loved the children and they idolized him. He invented games for them and they inspired him to new educational experiments in his school at Yasnaya Polyana. His early married years were also filled with his efforts to advance his literary career. Sonia loved to entertain friends and Tolstoy was a charming and lively host. Sonia managed many of the household activities and expenses not only for Yasnaya Polyana, but also for their home in Moscow. In his late thirties and early forties Tolstoy published his greatest literary work, *War and Peace*. It was not until 1872, when he was writing *Anna Karenina*, that he became disgusted with doing "merely creative work." In 1880, in his early fifties, he began a long examination of theology. Although shocked by the Tsar's murder in 1881, he wrote a letter to Alexander III asking pardon for the terrorists.

The Period of Reflection

In the 1880's Tolstoy became increasingly depressed by the self-indulgence that had characterized his life. Even his greatest literary work seemed to him a form of vanity. He began to express disgust toward his own work, similar to that of Rousseau, but with some differences. Rousseau's disgust with his writing drove him away from political works; Tolstoy's disgust increased his motivation toward political writing and action. Both men were repelled by the notion of self-aggrandizement which seemed to be associated with their earlier work, but Tolstoy seemed to have somewhere to go. He could reject everything he had written before as "mere vanity." Rousseau could not; his early work was the very substance of his life. Thus, while Rousseau lapsed into self-justification, Tolstoy moved from literature to politics.

However, it would be a mistake to regard this as a smooth and easy transition. Tolstoy had made a good deal of money from his literary work. He was a count, a member of the nobility. He had a wife, eight children, and a position to uphold in society. Simmons has given us an idea of the complexity of his situation and the regular expenses that were required to maintain it in 1884.

> Despite his wife's careful management, the family expenses in Moscow mounted. Social caste, tradition, and custom dictated a certain standard of living. No less than five tutors and governesses lived with the family, and as many more teachers were employed from outside to give lessons to the children. Eleven servants worked in the house, took care of the grounds and operated a carriage, calash, drosky, and two sledges. Food alone for the twenty-six members of this household was a considerable item of the budget. Sonia reckoned her monthly expenses at 910 rubles, a large but not extravagant amount for so numerous a family.[10]

As already noted, Tolstoy had really been a moralist all his life. He always believed he possessed a certain inner virtue and, like Rousseau, this belief in his own virtue was associated with both humility and extreme self-aggrandizement. He believed that true virtue was expressed in humility, but the very conviction that one is destined for a higher more exalted and virtuous path than that of ordinary men is a form of egoism. Thus, by a strange twist, his early self-indulgence and debauchery was a form of humility, an expression of his own worthlessness and a denial of his own inner conviction that he was destined for sainthood. As early as March 29, 1852 he was writing in his diary:

> There is something in me that obliges me to believe that I was not born to be what other men are. But whence does this proceed? From a lack of agreement, an absence of harmony among my faculties, or from the fact that I really stand on a higher level than ordinary people? I'm older, and the time of development is passed or is passing; and I'm tortured with a thirst, not for fame—I have no desire for fame and despise it—but for acquiring great influence for the happiness and benefit of society. Shall I die with this wish a hopeless one?[11]

Tolstoy was twenty-four when he wrote these lines, a young cadet about to write his first novel. He obviously did not understand his own need for fame and recognition, but he did understand, even in these early years, something more important about himself. He saw that he would never be content with fame, that he had a great need for a sense of moral worth, for self-approval, that could be only temporarily and partially satisfied by the approval of the crowd. But even a reputation as a great moralist and a profound thinker was not enough. It was a reputation in the eyes of the world alone. Tolstoy felt inside that he was a mere fraud, a faker who had done nothing but make a name for himself. It was a name and a recognition that he devoutly desired, while hating himself for wanting it.

Nothingness

As Tolstoy began to think seriously about changing his life, he began to have increasing difficulties in his marriage. Sonia was outraged by his letter to Alexander III and began to fear his growing resentment of his own wealth. She sensed an increasing tendency on his part to do something about his situation instead of merely complaining about the self-indulgent life they lived. She was afraid he would give away everything he owned and leave her penniless. Tolstoy was torn by guilt during this period. He was irritated by luxury, elegance, and social affairs, yet he felt responsible for making his family accustomed to this life. More and more he was depressed, brooding, and miserable, constantly thinking of religion and a more humble way of life.

There are revolutionary atheists and revolutionaries such as Gandhi who use orthodox religion as a basis for their teachings. Tolstoy could accept neither of these positions. He could not accept the Russian Orthodox faith nor could he found a new religion. In his own account, the basic doubt about the very significance of his life returned to haunt him again and again.

> I was overcome by minutes at first of perplexity and then of an arrest of life, as though I did not know how to live or what to do, and I lost myself and was dejected. But that passed and I continued to live as before. Then those minutes of perplexity were repeated oftener and oftener, and always in one and the same form. These arrests of life found their expression in ever the same questions: "Why? Well, and then?"[12]

A sense of nothingness and the thought that life was meaningless overwhelmed him. Every desire was followed by the thought that, whether he gratified it or not, nothing would come of it. We are reminded of Sören Kierkegaard's *Sickness unto Death*. Here was truly an existential despair, but also an element of terror.

> If I had simply comprehended that life had no meaning, I might have known that calmly . . . but I was like a man who had lost his way in the forest, who was overcome by terror because he had lost his way, who kept tossing about in his desire to come out on the road, knowing that every step got him only more entangled, and who could not help tossing. That was terrible. And in order to free myself from that terror, I wanted to kill myself.[13]

Tolstoy attempted to reason his way out of this problem. He read many books and talked with learned men, but nothing helped. He recognized that some had found escape in religious faith, but he no longer had the childlike naiveté that would have made religious faith possible for him. Further, he regarded the suspension of his critical judgment as worse than death. He could not let go, could not abandon himself long enough to experience the nonrational.[14] Nevertheless, he recognized that this nonrational acceptance of religion made it possible for others to go on living. He abandoned the priests and others who attempted to explain religion to him and began to cultivate the poor. He listened to them and found their expression of faith inspiring. He felt that his error lay not in the way he had reasoned, but in the way he had lived and he turned to manual labor for solace from his doubts. Instead of striving to find peace in religion, he sought peace in a continual search for God. This search did not lead him to the Russian Orthodox faith, but he determined instead to practice some of the principles of Jesus in his daily life. He could not accept the narrow belief that some people were saved and others condemned because of their particular religious faith. The attitude of Jesus toward the poor impressed him, and he was convinced that all men should be treated as brothers. The literal application of some of these ideas got him in trouble with the authorities.

Family Conflicts

Tolstoy's family, once the source of great enjoyment, now became a burden to him. He was annoyed by the social life of Moscow that Sonia so enjoyed. Sonia became increasingly miserable because of his frequent absences from Moscow and his various projects for social reform. He was often at his estate working in the fields beside the peasants. She frequently accused him of using this love of humanity as an excuse to avoid responsibility to his own family.

Tolstoy continued with his work. He learned shoemaking and made shoes for his friends. He worked with the peasants, building huts, and hauling manure. He emptied his own chamber pot in the morning, something that caused him great shame at first. He made other members of the family feel somewhat uncomfortable and guilty about their luxurious style of living and their style of entertainment. Finally his young son Ilya asked for work and was given a job in the fields. Sergei, Leo, and the girls followed and asked their father for work, and even Sonia participated to a limited extent.

Tolstoy began writing many works forbidden by the censor. His *Short Account of the Gospels* could not be found anywhere and hand-copied versions were passed from one person to another. The same was true of many of his other moral and semireligious publications. His works aroused the interest of a young captain of the guards, V. G. Chertkov, who also despised the debauchery of a military career and retired to his estate to help the peasants. Chertkov read the forbidden works of Tolstoy and wanted to meet him. Tolstoy heard of Chertkov through mutual friends and when they finally met they formed a close master-disciple relationship which further disturbed Sonia.

In 1884 Tolstoy abandoned his title and instructed everyone to call him plain "Leo Nikolayevich." In this same year he completed *What I Believe.* He not only worked on his estate and received a growing number of followers, but moved out into the world and tried to relieve the suffering of others. At first his awareness of this suffering was enough to immobilize him. His son Ilya gives a moving account of an experience in which he and Tolstoy were conducting the Moscow census. Ilya also experienced "horror and disgust" when they entered the quarters of the poorest people, but for him it was an experience of the moment.

> I looked at my father's face and saw written on it all that I felt myself, but in addition it was a look of suffering and repressed inward struggle; this look made a deep impression on me which I have never forgotten. I felt that he wanted to run away as fast as he could, just as I did, but I also felt that the reason he could not do so was because there was nowhere to run to; wherever he went the impression of what he had seen would remain with him and continue to torment him just the same, or even more. And this was indeed the fact.[15]

Tolstoy was not merely playing a game in which he hoped to become a new messiah. Sonia's critical remarks about his own self-aggrandizement and the neglect of his family were certainly true, but he was also genuinely touched by the suffering of others and the injustice of poverty when he had so much. As for his neglect of his family, he would have been pleased if they had ignored their own social life to follow him into a full-time devotion to the poor and moral reform. But as his work continued, few around him were willing to persist in this life and devote their entire energies to it. Chertkov, who rapidly became Tolstoy's chief disciple and Sonia's major rival, was the one possible exception. Sonia's letters to Tolstoy were bitter and critical, filled with her own desire for death and her resentment at the growing influence of Chertkov. Chertkov, unlike Tolstoy, had a distaste for physical work and sought to help others with "advice," which only added to Sonia's belief that he was a mere fraud. But Chertkov believed intensely in his own moral superiority. He became Tolstoy's chief confidante; the master discussed all his problems with the disciple, including his private problems with Sonia.

Sonia increasingly suspected their relationship was homosexual, but Tolstoy, despite his deep attachment to the sensual life, was moving away from sex and all sensual pleasure. He became a vegetarian, gave up smoking and wine, and no longer hunted. Young disciples surrounded him, copying and distributing his work. In 1885 he finished *What Then Must We Do?* In 1886 *The Death of Ivan Ilyich* and a play, *The Power of Darkness.* In 1887 he completed *On Life* and in 1889, the *Kreutzer Sonata.*

The government became increasingly fearful of his influence, but avoided any direct persecution of such a national saint and worldwide literary figure. In 1888 the governor general of Moscow sent a confidential letter to the Ministry of the Interior warning that any direct interference with Tolstoy would only bring him more publicity and aid the spread of his ideas. Finally, in 1889, Tolstoy announced to the outrage of Sonia that he would become a celibate. He had frequent relapses in his search for purity and Sonia felt a natural responsibility for distracting him from this noble aim while, at the same time, despising him for withdrawing from her and making her feel the source of all that was vile and impure in his life.

In the famine of 1891 he organized free food kitchens, thereby embarrassing the Russian government in its attempts to deny the famine. He renounced all his copyrights, giving anyone free permission to publish his works, and divided his estate into ten equal parts for his wife and children. The emperor had been desperately trying to suppress news of the famine both inside and outside the country but Tolstoy was openly soliciting help and donations throughout the world. The emperor was advised to arrest him but thought better of it and decided to offer government assistance to Tolstoy's effort. News of the great famine in Russia had spread throughout the world and there was no longer any hope of avoiding the embarrassment by insisting that people die quietly.

Tolstoy, at least in word, was now a full-fledged revolutionary, but still the government refused to act against him. The government jailed his disciples while the church sent the children of his followers to religious relatives. Chertkov was arrested and exiled. In 1901 the church excommunicated Tolstoy but only succeeded in increasing his influence and stimulating protest all over Russia.

The Need to Suffer

Success only increased his agony over the persecution of those who followed him. In one respect at least, the government had succeeded. His torture was all the greater since he could not suffer with those who followed him. He demanded the authorities arrest him as the author of those pamphlets for which they were arresting others. They refused. In 1908 plans were being made for the celebration of his eightieth birthday. Followers, family, and friends were all preparing for the great event. Once more, Tolstoy challenged the authorities to arrest him. His son Ilya described his misery at his failure to gain the punishment he desired.

> ...as everyone knows, neither this challenge nor the others that followed it led to any result, and the arrests and deportations of those associated with him still went on. My father felt himself morally responsible toward all those who suffered on his account, and every year new burdens were laid on his conscience.
>
> In 1908, just before his Jubilee, my father wrote to A. M. Bodyanski: "To tell you the truth, nothing would satisfy me so much, nothing could give me so much pleasure, as actually to be put into prison, into a real good prison—stinking, cold and 'hungry'. . . . It would cause me real joy and satisfaction, in my old age, so soon before my death; and at the same time it would save me from all the horrors of the intended Jubilee that I foresee."[16]

The physical suffering of others is even more unendurable if we cannot share it and have never experienced it ourselves. In the end it led Tolstoy toward an open desire for physical suffering as a form of relief for his sense of guilt—his feeling that he had been responsible for the suffering of others.

Much of his behavior in his final years is reminiscent of T. E. Lawrence. Admired by everyone as a saint, Tolstoy despised himself and sought self-humiliation. He even gained a certain pleasure from this self-contempt. "I feel well in my soul," he said, "but I am repellent to myself and am glad of it."[17] During his final year of 1910, he was impelled again and again by the need to experience the suffering of his followers and repelled by the luxurious surroundings of his estate. Giving away everything to his family changed nothing; he still lived with them and enjoyed the same luxuries as before. This concrete sense of guilt about his life-style was increased by a frequent sense of shame about something nameless. On June 24, 1910, he wrote in his diary, "I do not feel well in my soul somehow. Ashamed of something. Am going to bed, it is after eleven."[18] Some of this shame had a decided sexual aspect, a sense that he was somehow unclean, but one is also struck by the fact that it is disguised. He finds obvious and conventional reasons for his guilt. On July 16: "I must only be thankful to God for the mildness of His punishment, which I am bearing for all the sins of my youth, and the main sin, my sexual depravity when I married a pure girl. It serves you right you dirty debauchee."[19]

The pleasure he finds in unpleasure, the satisfaction he takes in ruminating on his guilt and castigating himself is striking. On August 10: "Everything is still depressing, and I am not well. It is good to feel that you are guilty, and that is how I feel."[20] Gradually every pleasure annoyed him, the slightest diversion, unless it was productive work or writing to his exiled friends, made him feel guilty. He felt ashamed of playing cards and made several resolutions against it. But there was also much joy. He rejoiced in his loss of memory as it made him live only in the present. Toward the latter part of October his feeling of shame increased as did the need to "take some step."[21] He felt compelled to do something about his dispicable condition of luxury and idleness.

Sonia also became increasingly upset in her later years over her growing estrangement from Tolstoy. She was clearly mentally ill during much of this period and under psychiatric care. One of her most prominent symptoms was an inordinate suspicion that he was about to do something to disgrace her or leave her penniless. She frequently rummaged through his desk and papers, reading his diary and watching his movements for some sign of betrayal, a frantic state that was clearly the product of a disordered mind. On the night of October 28–29, 1910, Tolstoy slept until 2 A.M. when he was awakened by Sonia who had a bright light burning as she rummaged about in his study. She became frantic if he closed any of his doors at night, terrified of being shut off from him. After she went to bed he could not sleep. He lit a candle which brought Sonia again, wondering why he was unable to sleep. As he talked to her, he gradually formed the resolution to leave his estate. After she went to bed, he packed with the help of his daughter and left by train to Optina accompanied by his friend and follower, Dr. Dushan Petrovich Makovitski, who also served as his personal physician. Sonia attempted suicide when informed by the family, but was easily restrained.

On the afternoon of October 31 he felt a severe chill. Dr. Makovitski examined him and asked that he be allowed to rest in the station master's shack when the train stopped at Astaporo. Chertkov, who had been allowed to return from exile, visited him there. He became feverish, convulsions followed and another physician was called for consultation. Soon there were five doctors in attendance, but his condition did not improve. Sonia was informed that he was gravely ill at Astaporo and hurried to be with him, but she was met by an army of physicians and family members (mostly her own children) who insisted she would upset him if he knew she was there. She was allowed in to see him only briefly after he had been given a morphine injection and was sleeping. He died on Sunday, November 7, 1910, at the age of eighty-one.

The newspapers were filled with the details of his last illness and people gathered daily to hear the latest word on his condition. At the news of his death, there was mourning all over Russia and the trains were filled with those traveling to his funeral.

Sources of the Final Agony

Tolstoy's decision to leave his estate and travel on his own was certainly stimulated by his conflict with Sonia. But his growing estrangement from the life of the country noble and his need to "take some step," which he expressed the day before his departure, show clearly that the incident in the night with Sonia was only the precipitating cause. Sergei and Sasha were his devout partisans, but some of his other children were less sympathetic. Ilya and Andrei firmly condemned him for deserting Sonia. It was only among his disciples and followers that he could feel complete support for his work and when he returned to Yasnaya Polyana he often felt a stranger. Ironically, it was he who set the style of laughter and thoughtless childish gaiety that he now despised, and this new self that he had created found the struggle that much more difficult because he was still living in the same body which inspired the same expectations from others.

Thus he drove his wife and children from him. The need to live simply and to suffer with the poor, which intensified in his middle and later years, actually produced the most acute mental suffering when he was not physically suffering. Again it is Ilya Tolstoy who describes this psychological suffering in such graphic detail.

> When we were setting up theatricals at Yasnaya . . . and we were all enjoying ourselves with games and croquet and talking about falling in love, suddenly my father would come in and with a single word or, even worse, with a single look, would spoil the whole thing. And we would feel bored and, as it were, rather ashamed at times: "It would have been better if he hadn't come." And the worst of it was that he felt this himself. He did not want to spoil our fun— for after all he was very fond of us—but nevertheless he did spoil it. He said nothing but he thought something. We all knew what he thought, and that was what made us so uncomfortable. . . .
>
> When I recall this period, I am filled with horror at the thought of what he must have been suffering mentally. . . . And when, to relieve the intolerable

oppression of the thoughts that tormented him, he tried to pour them out before us, we drew timidly away from him, in order not to have our childish, selfish happiness spoilt.[22]

The social masochism of Tolstoy was distinctly different from that of Rousseau. One finds here the same longing to suffer, but the suffering Tolstoy experiences is more the result of his guilt, his feeling he has not done enough. Rousseau's need for suffering was gratified by the state. He actually sought a place of rest (although he usually managed to arrange things so he was driven out) and thus his guilt and his self-torment were not so severe. Rousseau generally felt virtuous and justified in his behavior. Because he was punished by external forces, he had less need to punish himself with these inner feelings of guilt.

NOTES

1. Ernest J. Simmons, *Leo Tolstoy* (Boston: Little Brown, 1946), 11.

2. Ibid., 79.

3. Ibid., 15.

4. Leo N. Tolstoy, *Collected Works of Leo Tolstoy*, translated by Leo Weiner, vol. 12 (Boston: L. C. Page, 1904), 3–4.

5. Jean Jacques Rousseau, *Émile* (New York: Dutton, 1955), 11.

6. Simmons, *Leo Tolstoy*, 26.

7. Ibid., 31–32.

8. Ibid., 34.

9. Ibid., 59. From *Confession*, Maude edition, vol. 11, 8.

10. Simmons, *Leo Tolstoy*, 379.

11. Ibid., 86.

12. Tolstoy, *Collected Works*, vol. 7, 16.

13. Ibid., 24.

14. Ibid., 49.

15. Ilya Tolstoy, *Reminiscences of Tolstoy*, translated by George Calderon (New York: Century, 1914), 277.

16. Ibid., 369.

17. Leo N. Tolstoy, *Last Diaries*, edited with an Introduction by Leon Stilman, translated by Lydia Weston-Kesich (New York: Putnam Capricorn, 1960), 47.

18. Ibid., 122.

19. Ibid., 134.

20. Ibid., 156.

21. Ibid., 215.

22. Ilya Tolstoy, *Reminiscences*, 260–67.

Part 2

REVOLUTIONARY CONVICTION WITHOUT COMBAT

Introduction

The men in this section were all profound revolutionary theoreticians, but there is a gradual progression in the degree to which they made trouble for the government without coming into armed conflict. Kropotkin was gentle and nonviolent, but the Russian government considered him a serious threat and he was perhaps the most severely persecuted while giving the least offense. Marx, in sharp contrast to Kropotkin, was an open advocate of violence, but confined his own work to theory. He never fired a shot in battle and never found a revolution he could call his own—whereas even the good-natured and affable Engels participated, for a while, in the revolution of 1848.

Between the mild Kropotkin and the aggressive Marx, was Gandhi, a paradoxical figure. Although Gandhi was the most convinced believer in nonviolence, he brought about (in my own opinion) more violence than either Kropotkin or Marx, although he declined all responsibility for it. Gandhi expected too much of his followers if he expected them to remain nonviolent while he continued to arouse their hatred of the British. In fact, I believe there is evidence to conclude that Gandhi wanted violence (if it was the only way he could drive out the British) and that he wished to train the Indian people to use guns and ammunition in the expectation that they would someday use them in battle against British soldiers. The Gandhi I have described in this study is a figure much more aggressive and authoritarian than the saint so often presented by his biographers.

The life-style of the revolutionary continues in this section, but with some striking differences. Kropotkin shows little effort to create a revolutionary life-style. He began his life as a soldier, selecting the regiment with the most difficult and hazardous living conditions and the most drab and unpretentious uniform. For much of his life the Russian government created his life-style by jailing him for long periods of time. After his release, he lived frugally, but not in poverty. He had earned his reputation for suffering and had no need to seek any further privations.

Gandhi and Marx took to suffering and self-abnegation in a very different manner. Gandhi gradually moved from the attire of an English barrister to a loin cloth, but the transition (like Rousseau) was a voluntary and deliberate outward expression of his belief. He taught his family to fast and to eat a simple diet of fruits and nuts. If they complained of poverty, he explained sweetly that the world was his family and they must learn to share the poverty of his other "children." When his wife was close to death and the doctor advised her to take meat broth to survive, Gandhi, who forbade the use of meat in his family, left the decision to his wife but said, in his own case, he would rather die than break a vow. His wife refused the broth and lived anyway. Gandhi felt a religious and righteous vindication in her brave act.

Marx (who was not a Marxist but a bourgeois at heart) married the beautiful daughter of a German baron, who loved to wear the fine clothes Marx loved to

47

buy for her. He wanted a good education for his children, French and piano lessons for his daughters. He was horrified that they might become shop girls. Although his income was sufficient for a modest middle-class life-style, he mismanaged his way into poverty. He cursed bourgeois society for his financial disaster and he was bitter about the misfortunes of his family, which he did not consciously desire.

Thus one man had his life-style thrust upon him by the government, one carefully designed and sought a life of poverty, and one stumbled into poverty protesting loudly all the way, but did the very things that made it impossible for him to live any other kind of life. Gandhi sacrificed material comforts but seldom suffered emotionally. For Marx, the loss of material comforts for himself and especially for his family was the *cause* of his emotional suffering.

We must not neglect Friedrich Engels, the revolutionary dandy, who seems at first the exception to the rule of suffering and self-abnegation. As a youth he polished the buttons on his military uniform and sat near the front of a poetry session so the girls could see and admire his clothes. He always dressed well, as though he were a general in mufti. Indeed he was nicknamed "General," as much for his clothes as for his detailed critique of military strategy in every war he followed. While he was a devout revolutionary and party member, he was also a successful businessman in Manchester and a notorious womanizer. But the profits from his business and much of his salary were sent to the perpetually impoverished Marx and (after the death of Marx) to Marx's son-in-law, who touched him regularly for frequent never-to-be-repaid loans. Engels, while he did not live the outward life of a revolutionary, remained self-effacing in a more profound way. While he made an important contribution to his work with Marx, he regarded himself as a mere helper and financial provider for Marx, the real genius of revolution. He carried on this role of helper and assistant all his life and characterized himself in this role publicly in a speech at Marx's graveside. A man who had considerable talent and conviction in his own right, and certainly a gift for financial survival, he chose a subordinate position, and, even after the death of Marx, devoted himself to revising the works and editing the correspondence of the master.

The Cure of Body and Soul

In the introduction I noted a similarity in psychodynamics between the revolutionary and the religious leader. In the developmental stages of the revolutionary vocation this trait can be described more adequately as a "nurturing tendency." It is not always clear what formal vocation the individual will adopt, but it is obvious that he wants to help, to lift up and nurture others. Whether this takes a religious, medical, legal, or educational form will depend on many circumstances—the goals of parents or the strong childhood impressions of heroic figures. But in the end it is the nurturing personality that shapes the profession. Church doctrine, legal or medical ethics, and educational methods are easily cast aside if they interfere with revolutionary goals.

All of our nonviolent revolutionaries give the feeling that religion was never really rejected, although all scorn the narrowness of a single faith. They seemed to seek some universal moral principle applicable to life as well as religion. Rousseau began as a Protestant, became Catholic, returned again to the Genevan Calvinism and finally rejected all orthodox faiths for a "supreme being." Tolstoy accepted the message of Jesus but his literal interpretation resulted in excommunication by the church. Kropotkin showed little interest in religion but much concern with morality and ethics. He sought a morality liberated from religion, more universal and standing on a higher plane—a natural morality.

Gandhi experienced a return to his own religion; but instead of a revival of fundamental teachings, he gave his own unique interpretation to the Hindu religion, enlarging its scope. His religion was Jainism (a heterodox Hindu faith in which respect for all life plays a prominent role), but he generally avoided references to specific articles of faith or religious rituals. While he considered himself a religious person, he did not wish to exclude Moslems, Parsis, Jews, or Christians from his followers. Thus he applied religious principles in a way acceptable to all men of good conscience from whatever religion.

Gandhi combined his religious beliefs with a severity of diet that went far beyond the requirements of the Hindu religion. His diet had a religious significance and was part of what he called his "quackery," his practice of medicine for himself and others. He loved to nurse those in physical suffering back to health. The more severe and repulsive the illness, the more others turned away from the sick one, the more Gandhi was attracted to the act of helping, advising, and nursing. Like Ché Guevara, he spent a period of his early years working in a hospital for lepers. One finds a similar concern with the sick and suffering in other revolutionaries. Guevara, Sun Yat-Sen, and Franz Fanon all began their careers as physicians (Fanon was a psychiatrist) and all, like Gandhi, were involved in anticolonial revolutions. The unsanitary conditions and lack of doctors in many colonial countries make it easy to see how an individual seeking to help his countrymen escape from debilitating disease might be attracted to medicine. However, most doctors learn to live within the limits of their profession. If they discover that disease is a product of poverty and poverty is the result of political oppression, they are inclined to continue with the modest goal for which they were trained. Only the rare individual is prepared to do whatever he must to help a "sick" society—even if this means attacking a problem for which he has had no previous training or experience.

Gandhi's principal field was law, not medicine. Politics and law are more closely associated and it is a common practice to move from law to politics. However, Gandhi was never content to confine himself to the orthodox aspects of his own field. His concern with the whole person frequently involved him in education, law, and the treatment of illness. Although he began with a concern for the sick that was similar to that of the doctor–revolutionaries, he was always more unorthodox in his approach. He was rather pleased and amused to refer to his medical treatment as "quackery," not only because he had no orthodox medical training, but because his work was always a combination of religion and medicine. It suited the humble position he desired to refer to himself as a quack. Yet when the time came to apply his treatment to himself or his family he was much more strict with his prescriptions than the average doctor and more confident of his absolute capacity for cure—or rather of God's capacity, in whose name he acted.

Thus the "prescripitions" of Gandhi always had more of religion than medicine, but here too he was unorthodox. According to Shri Pyarelal, Gandhi had no faith in the orthodox religious practices of his mother, but he had a deep faith in her sincerity as a person. Speaking to audiences later, Gandhi remarked that his mother fasted not for religious convictions, but out of her love "for us," her children.

While there are no professional educators among our revolutionaries, Marx would have sought a university post after his Ph.D. had he not been discouraged by the conviction that he could never be accepted by conventional academicians. Sun Yat-Sen saw education as the only effective long-term means of bringing about a lasting revolution in China. He would awaken the consciousness of the masses through education. Tolstoy, who was not a professional revolutionary, nevertheless had the same notion of awakening the masses through education. He started his own school and prepared his own textbooks. Trotsky, too, saw himself as an educator. As a speaker, he felt the "hunger to know" of his listeners and regarded them as starving children clinging "with dry lips to the nipples of the revolution." Here we see the nurturing and educational impulses graphically combined in a metaphor. But it is always nurturing, not education per se, that drives the educational efforts of the revolutionary. He becomes an educator because he feels no "proper" educators are available.

Chapter 4

PRINCE PETER KROPOTKIN:
The Gentle Revolutionary

Childhood

Peter Kropotkin was born December 9, 1842 in Moscow. He was born Prince Kropotkin in a family whose ancestors had once ruled the principality of Kiev. Like Tolstoy and Rousseau, he was a revolutionary whose influence came primarily from his words and ideas. He is said to have resembled his mother who died before he was three years old. Like the mothers of Rousseau and Tolstoy, she had a great reputation for virtue, not only among the immediate family, but also among the peasants on the family estate. The serfs, who had loved his mother, lavished attention on Peter and his brother Alexander. Peter remembered a striking incident in which the memory of his mother was called forth by an old peasant woman.

> . . . a peasant woman on greeting us in the fields would ask, "Will you be as good as your mother was? She took compassion on us. You will, surely." "Us" meant, of course, the serfs. I do not know what would have become of us if we had not found in our house, among the serf servants, that atmosphere of love which children must have around them. We were her children, we bore likeness to her, and they lavished their care upon us. . . .
> Men passionately desire to live after death, but they often pass away without noticing the fact that the memory of a really good person always lives. It is impressed upon the next generation, and is transmitted again to the children. Is not that an immortality worth striving for?[1]

Here, once again, we find the striving for immortality through goodness of character, a quality evident in both Rousseau and Tolstoy.

Kropotkin's father, a military man given to outbursts of rage, does not seem to have spared much attention for his young sons and daughter after his remarriage. The stepmother made an effusive effort to charm her new children, but Peter and his brother Sasha turned from her in suspicion. She lost interest in them when her own child was born. Peter and his brother Alexander found themselves virtual orphans. They spent much time with the servants or playing with each other, and a strong bond developed between them. Kropotkin's description of his childhood gives the feeling that his brother and the servants formed a separate community of the oppressed, ruled by the memory of his late mother. They kept their own secrets from the master of the house and they were bound together by a strong sense of personal loyalty.

> We never would have betrayed any of the servants, nor would they have betrayed us. One Sunday, my brother and I, playing alone in the wide hall, ran against a bracket which supported a costly lamp. The lamp was broken to pieces. Immediately a council was held by the servants. No one scolded us; but it was decided that early next morning Tikhon should at his risk and peril slip out of the house, and run to the Smiths' Bridge in order to buy another lamp of the same pattern. It cost fifteen rubles—an enormous sum for the servants; but it was bought, and we never heard a word of reproach about it. . . . I remember we never heard coarse language in any of the games. . . .
> In the servants' house, among themselves, they assuredly used coarse expressions; but we were children—her children—and that protected us from anything of the sort.[2]

What a terrible experience, then, to be reminded that one was not really a member of that select community, that one's birth and background placed one in the class of cruel oppressors.

One day Peter's father flew into a fit of rage over some broken plates. He called in the servants to see if anything else was missing or broken. He shouted at them and struck them, accusing them of theft and deceit. Finally, he settled on Makar, the piano tuner and sub-butler, accusing him of being drunk and breaking the plates. He sent the unfortunate man with a note to the police station to be given twenty lashes with a birch rod. Kropotkin gives this account of Makar's return to the family:

> Terror and absolute muteness reign in the house. The clock strikes four, and we all go down to dinner; but no one has any appetite, and the soup remains in the plates untouched. We are ten at table, and behind each of us a violinist or a trombone player stands, with a clean plate in his left hand, but Makar is not among them.
> Where is Makar? our stepmother asks. "Call him in."
> Makar does not appear, and the order is repeated. He enters at last, pale, with a distorted face, ashamed, his eyes cast down. Father looks into his plate, while our stepmother, seeing that no one has touched the soup, tries to encourage us.
> "Don't you find, children," she says, "that the soup is delicious?"
> Tears suffocate me, and immediately after dinner is over I run out, catch Makar in a dark passage, and try to kiss his hand; but he tears it away, and says, either as a reproach or as a question, "Let me alone; you, too, when you are grown up, will you not be just the same?"
> "No, no, never!"[3]

Even in the extreme anguish of this moment, we do not hear of any anger of Kropotkin toward his father. In fact, in a rather indirect way, he offers excuses. He tells us that, despite the above scene, his father was not among the worst of the landowners. On the contrary, cruelty was so common and so barbarous in those days that his father was one of the best.[4] Like Rousseau who pitied his younger brother when the latter was beaten by his father, and like Trotsky who was touched by the plight of the peasant when his father demanded the cow, there is pity for the oppressed but no sign of anger toward the parent. The anger and the fighting back come out years later and are directed toward the state, not toward the one who first brought forth this sense of injustice. Kropotkin's feeling for the oppressed, particularly the peasant, was a central aspect of his character and, like Trotsky, he was later attracted to the verses of Nikolai Nekrassov because they appealed to his heart by their sympathy for "the downtrodden and ill-treated."[5]

The Exile

Kropotkin was sent as a page to the court of Alexander II, a post of great honor for a young man. But his experience only taught him to despise the elegance and gossip of court life. He began with admiration for Alexander, his hero for freeing the serfs, but he ended his service by despising this frightened tyrant. When it came time for his graduation from the school for the corps of pages, each student was allowed to select his own regiment. Kropotkin determined not to enter a regiment of the Guard and give his life to fancy parades and court balls. He selected, instead, the severe black uniform of a Cossack regiment in Siberia with a plain red collar without braid. His comrades were horrified and the captain at first thought he was joking. When he realized the young man was serious, he looked at him with "astonishment and pity." This was the beginning of several years of hardship in the bitter cold where Kropotkin began his work as an explorer, geographhher, and naturalist. He was appointed aide-de-camp to General Kukel who was already well known for his radical opinions and who introduced Kropotkin to the work of Michael Bakunin and Alexander Hertzen. He also met a number of exiles in Siberia who convinced him that reform was hopeless for Russia and that revolution was the only course.

Kropotkin, in his selection of the Siberian regiment, seems to have had a natural attraction toward suffering and hardship. But this attitude differed markedly from that of Rousseau and Tolstoy. Like them, he was inspired by the virtue of his mother, while his father emerged as the family oppressor. But we do not find in Kropotkin the kind of deliberate self-torture that was evident in the childhood of Rousseau and Tolstoy. It is true that he selected the plain uniform of the Siberian Cossacks and chose a life which he knew would be cruel and difficult, but instead of inflicting physical punishment upon himself, he chose the *circumstances,* the *life* which would punish him for ostensibly *moral* reasons. This will be the case, to a great extent, with the revolutionaries we will study in the following chapters.

He welcomed an assignment in the Amur region in 1863 and spent much time exploring the area. Ordered to report to Moscow on the destruction of a fleet of barges, he was astounded by the ignorance of Moscow officials concerning this region. He returned to the Amur and spent much time exploring, mapping, and surveying the area. These years confirmed his initial impression of the futility of helping people in remote regions by working through the administrative machinery in Moscow. He observed the communistic communities of the Dukhobors and admired their successful colonization of the region, achieved through their own brotherly organization without reference to the plans and directions from Moscow. The harshness of this remote region forced people to rely on each other instead of government and proved an ideal training ground for a future anarchist, convincing him of the futility of all governments and administrative machinery.

It is unclear that the "idea" of decentralization of authority first occurred to Kropotkin in Siberia. Certainly he had become aware of the separate governance of the community of serfs and servants on his father's estate. In the academy of pages he made a point of the sharp distinction between students and administration and how the students could prevent harrassment if they would stand together. He was opposed to centralized authority before he sought out the Siberian assignment and, in addition to his attraction toward a life of hardship, he may also have been seeking in Siberia some concrete evidence of the value of small independent community effort, knowing that the very hardship of life in Siberia would make it necessary for people to rely more directly on each other. It is uncertain to what extent he was conscious of his own motives in the selection of such a remote outpost. He had a feeling there was something he could learn in Siberia and that he might look on the experience in a different way from his comrades, but his own ideas on government were still unformed.

The Revolutionary

By his return from Siberia in 1871, Kropotkin regarded himself as an anarchist in thought if not in action. He resigned from the army, angering a father who "hated the very sight of civilian dress," and entered the university to study physics, mathematics, and geography. He remained at the university for five years, spending much of his time correcting Russian maps of Asia. He became obsessed with the outrageous errors in some of these maps. Great mountain regions drawn on the maps in the eastern part of Stanovoi had no existence in nature. [6]

As a result of his research and "many months of intense thought," the whole geographic structure of Asia became clear to him. "The main structural lines are not north and south, or west and east; they are from the southwest to the northeast—just as in the Rocky Mountains and the plateaus of America." [7] This realization filled him with a great "joy" of discovery that what had seemed for years so chaotic and contradictory could finally "take its proper position among the harmonious whole." [8]

This belief in the "harmony" of nature and in the essential harmony of man, if left to his own devices, was a part of his revolutionary philosophy. It seems strange to find the principles of anarchism arising from the study of physical geography, but Kropotkin was a revolutionary at heart long before he became a geographer. It might be even more accurate to say that the value of decentralization (getting away from the seat of power) was a central idea behind the development of both his revolutionary idealism and his interest in geography.[9]

During his travels he also crossed into Western Europe where he learned much of the political ferment and the rising belief in socialism. He tended to seek out political as well as geographic hinterlands and was soon in Neuchatel, Switzerland, spending time among the watchmakers in the Jura Mountains. In 1872 when he arrived, the Jura Federation was already rebelling against the centralized authority of the International Workingmen's Association dominated by Marx. He was deeply impressed by James Guillaume, one of the most important leaders in the Federation, who was so busy working he had no time for a friendly chat. Kropotkin helped him wrap the local paper he was sending out and thus made some time for a talk. He was astonished by tales of the terrible suppression of the communal insurrection in Paris in 1871, but his informants focused on efforts to control the Paris Commune made by the London headquarters of Marx and Engels—or perhaps Kropotkin's own bias resulted in that interpretation.[10] Apparently, centralization of power, soon led to reaction and a return of bureaucratic control even in revolutionary movements.

Kropotkin's work was not confined to thought alone. From the moment of his return from Siberia he was active in revolutionary circles. He refused to toast the Tsar at public gatherings and he soon attracted the attention of the police. He and his brother Alexander were both distressed by the lack of revolutionary fervor among the intellectual and literary circles of St. Petersburg.

Kropotkin opposed violence but felt a revolution would be necessary to bring about change in the great monolithic apparatus of the Russian state. He hoped to minimize violence by first converting the middle class to anarchism, thereby making them conscious of the injustice of their privileges and more willing to accept the new order of things. He organized a system for smuggling forbidden literature into Russia, gave talks at private meetings on socialism and anarchism, and joined the Tchaykovsky circle for self-improvement. Self-improvement was certainly a mild objective, but the circle also included women, and university education was forbidden to women in Russia. This in itself made the circle suspect, for Alexander II had an open hatred for educated women. However, the Tchaykovsky circle rapidly advanced from self-improvement to socialist propaganda among the masses. The brothers Kropotkin were in the forefront of this activity.

In 1873, while preparing a large volume on his geographical work, Kropotkin realized that his arrest was imminent. He prepared a hurried paper and map describing his views and transmitted both to his brother. They were published by the Geographic Society while Kropotkin was in prison. He was able to return to his apartment, look through his papers, and destroy compromising material on the evening before his arrest. Charged with belonging to a secret society planning to overthrow the government, he was sent to the notorious Peter and Paul Fortress.

In his later years Tolstoy, yearned for ". . . a real good prison—stinking cold and 'hungry.'" Kropotkin suffered no such frustration; he was punished more than once by both imprisonment and exile. In prison he earned his right to join the ranks of the oppressed. Makar, his old servant, would have been proud of him and would have welcomed him with open arms. However, it becomes (and it will become) increasingly difficult to find evidence of a conscious desire for punishment as the revolutionary leader becomes more openly defiant and successful. As the moral element becomes more prominent, the masochistic element recedes into the background. Kropotkin clearly felt guilty about his "unjustified" position as a member of the nobility, but we do not find him begging for the whip. He knew he would be caught and imprisoned, but no clear evidence exists that he set himself up, or that he wanted to be caught. In Kropotkin it becomes more difficult to distinguish between masochism and courage. He fought against what he regarded as injustice until the last moment of his freedom. He continued to work for his cause from prison and, when the opportunity came, he pulled off a fantastic escape that soon reached the world press and further enhanced his fame as a revolutionary.

The World-Wide Anarchist Movement

Kropotkin remained in the Peter and Paul Fortress, a supposedly impregnable bastion, for two years. During this time some of his comrades died in prison and others became insane, but he received no notice that his case would ever be brought to trial. In early 1876 he arranged a spectacular escape with the aid of friends, after which he traveled to England with the intention of staying a few months before returning to Russia. At the time he did not fully appreciate his own notoriety or the extent to which the Tsar had been embarrassed and insulted by the escape of an infamous revolutionary from his capital in broad daylight. At first he merely extended his stay in England, but as he became more aware of the international character of the anarchist movement and his own position in it, he decided to settle in England for an indefinite period.

At the time, an intense and open antagonism existed between anarchists and communists. The International had been founded in London in 1864 and Karl Marx was already a central figure in this movement; carrying on an extensive correspondence; being interviewed by reporters; and writing pamphlets, books, and speeches on communism. Marx's principal adversary was another Russian anarchist, Michael Bakunin, who in 1868 in Geneva founded the Alliance of Socialist Democracy as a device for taking over the International. In 1872 at the Hague Congress, the Bakuninists were expelled from an International already destroyed by four years of factional strife. The seat of the General Council was transferred from London to New York, but it dissolved in Philadelphia four years later.[11]

The Marxist theory of revolution designated Great Britain, the most advanced capitalist nation, as ripe for revolution, while Russia was still a barbarian state yet to evolve capitalism (a necessary stage prior to communism). Marx's conflict with Bakunin was not merely one of communism versus anarchism, it was also Marx's notion of the complicated and slow development of revolutionary conditions versus Bakunin's call for immediate revolution. The result was Marx's general antagonism toward not only Bakunin, but all "Muscovite optimists" who "attack Western civilization in order to minimize their own barbarism."[12]

Marx and Kropotkin were natural antagonists. Kropotkin opposed the very idea of a *leadership* or *governing body* for any international revolutionary organization and had no desire to associate with the communists in either London or Russia. He felt that Marx had hampered the revolution of the Paris Commune of 1871 by a clumsy effort to impose his leadership from London. Marx chose to ignore Kropotkin altogether and devote his attention to Bakunin, his only active threat at the time. Kropotkin admired Bakunin, although he never met him. It is perhaps just as well they did not meet, for Kropotkin's opposition to violence would have been unacceptable to Bakunin.

Kropotkin, while he described himself as a "revolutionist," actually believed that the ideas of anarchism, if they permeated all classes of society, would result in the conversion of much of the middle class as well as the working class. He saw the possibility of a "peaceful revolution" or one in which violence was at least minimized. "The question is, then, not so much how to avoid revolutions, as how to attain the greatest results with the most limited amount of civil war, the smallest number of victims and a minimum of mutual embitterment."[13] In any event, a revolution "whether peaceful or violent" would not occur until the new ideals had "deeply penetrated into the very class whose economical and political privileges were to be assailed."[14]

In 1878 Kropotkin married Sophie Ananiev, a Russian woman of Jewish and Slavic descent. By 1882 the French anarchist movement was very strong and he and his wife left for the excitement of France. Kropotkin was certain he would be arrested in France, but he was bored with the quiet life in England and joined the active and violent anarchists in the Lyons region.[15] As a figure of international reknown, he was the first to attract the attention of the French police and was warned several times to leave. But many of his friends had already been arrested and this made him determined to stay.[16] He was arrested on December 22 and visited in jail by an English friend whose offer of bail he refused. He was sentenced to Clairvaux Prison, a terrible dungeon. Friends sought his transfer to a more comfortable place, but he refused their help and insisted on remaining with his fellow revolutionaries until he was finally released three years later due to ill health and pressure on the authorities.[17]

For the remainder of his life Kropotkin continued to write on revolution and anarchism. His gentle quality, his tolerance for dissenting opinion, and his generosity made him a patron saint among revolutionaries. He travelled throughout the world on speaking engagements, making several visits to the United States and frequently introducing himself as "an old jail bird." Kropotkin had estranged himself from much of the anarchist movement by his support of World

War I and his intense opposition to the Germans, but he was enthusiastic about the Russian revolt and was welcomed in Russia by Alexander Kerensky, M. T. Skobelev, and a cheering crowd of admirers. However, he opposed the ideas of Marx and particularly distrusted the Bolsheviks. Anarchists were among the first victims of the Bolshevik terror of 1918. Kropotkin was not harmed as he was a world famous revolutionary figure, for by attacking him the Bolsheviks would only have harmed their cause.

Throughout his life Kropotkin, like Rousseau, was extremely particular about gifts. He always wanted to know the source and would accept nothing from any government agency. He even refused membership in the Royal Geographic Society because of its sponsorship by the British government and the monarchist implications of its title. He maintained this position after the Bolsheviks came to power and would accept no aid, pension, or relief from them, even though he was living in difficult circumstances. In April Lenin contacted Kropotkin and asked him to draw his attention to any injustices he discovered within the new communist state. Kropotkin wrote vigorous letters of criticism and visited Lenin two more times with his complaints before his death in 1921, at the age of seventy-nine.

I have already suggested that Kropotkin did not display the same obvious need for persecution as Rousseau or Tolstoy. We must always be wary of interpreting any form of opposition to custom, convention, or law as a form of "social masochism." However, even with these caveats, I believe there is some evidence of deliberate provocation in Kropotkin's second arrest. Was he "brave" and "loyal to his friends" when he refused bail and special treatment in a more comfortable prison, or was this evidence of his need to suffer for truth? There is, of course, no categorical answer. Probably, Kropotkin refused all aid which might have prevented his second incarceration for many reasons. He was clearly acting in accord with his own principles of moral behavior, and it may be that all such behavior has in it some element of moral masochism. If so, we may be saying that masochism is a productive force in the advancement of civilization. Revolutionaries must be prepared to suffer if they are to advance their causes. They must show the government they cannot be broken, even by imprisonment. Perhaps the only people suited for such long ordeals of suffering are those who derive some satisfaction from the experience of suffering itself. Others, who gain nothing from suffering, may be too easily discouraged. They may finally ask if it was really worthwhile, and they may conclude that the pain and hardship, along with the small chance of success, is not worth the risk.

Kropotkin is difficult to understand without the assumption of some motive of moral masochism, a feeling of guilt that requires some compensatory behavior. If this is the case, we must also acknowledge that Kropotkin differs markedly from the other moral masochists we have encountered. We do not find evidence of self-torture as a child or a provocative need for beating. There are no signs of the sexual gratification in suffering present in T. E. Lawrence and Rousseau or the severe sexual shame that was evident in Tolstoy. From his early years, Kropotkin was characterized by a lack of any obvious interest in sex. He was a bit embarrassed when other people referred to it, although he always took an interest in the rights of women, particularly their right to education. But talk of sexual freedom as an aspect of political freedom seemed out of place to him. When Emma Goldman confronted him directly with this relationship, he told her that a woman will be free when she is man's equal intellectually and shares his social ideals.[18]

There is even a suggestion of sexual prudery in his avoidance of the subject in his many books on sociology, politics, and freedom and his contrast of the Italian opera with the "French stage, which even then was showing in germ the putrid Offenbachian current that a few years later infected all Europe."[19] In all probability, the absence of sexual references in his books is more than an oversight. There is some clue as to the feeling behind this inhibition in a remark made to Will Durant when Durant told him he was spending the afternoon with Havelock Ellis. Kropotkin smiled, "So you are interested in sex?" "Of course," replied Durant. "Yes, naturally," said Kropotkin, "but I find that those who make a special study of sex are abnormal either at the start or at the finish."[20] This remark suggests deliberate inhibition of sexual ideation and fantasies.

All we can say, then, is that Kropotkin was far less frank about his sexual feelings than Lawrence, Rousseau, or Tolstoy. Whether this was the reult of a lower sex drive or an intense guilt and embarrassment about secret sexual desires, we do not know. Perhaps his wife Sophie could tell us more, but she, like Kropotkin, is no longer available for questioning.

NOTES

1. Peter Kropotkin, *Memoirs of a Revolutionist* (New York: Dover, 1971), 13.

2. Ibid., 19–20.

3. Ibid., 51.

4. Ibid.

5. Ibid., 95.

6. Ibid., 226.

7. Ibid., 227.

8. Ibid.

9. Ibid., 240.

10. Ibid., 284–87.

11. Karl Marx, *The Karl Marx Library*, edited by Saul K. Padover, vol. 3 (New York: McGraw-Hill, 1973), 155–56.

12. Ibid., 166.

13. Kropotkin, *Memoirs of a Revolutionist*, 291.

14. Ibid., 290.

15. Ibid., 442.

16. Ibid., 450.

17. George Woodcock and Ivan Avakumovic, *The Anarchist Prince: A Biographical Study of Peter Kropotkin* (New York: Schocken, 1971), 188–97.

18. Ibid., 119–20.

19. Kropotkin, *Memoirs of a Revolutionist,* 119–20.

20. Will Durant and Ariel Durant, *Will and Ariel Durant: A Dual Autobiography* (New York: Simon and Schuster, 1977), 43.

Chapter 5

MOHANDAS K. GANDHI:
The Power of Suffering

Childhood

Mohandas K. Gandhi was born October 2, 1869, in Porbandar, a principality of Kathiawad, India. His father was the prime minister of the principality.

With Gandhi, we see for the first time the power that personal suffering can have as a political weapon. Gandhi learned from his parents, particularly his mother, how to use suffering to control others. Wolfenstein[1] believes Gandhi identified with his mother, as was certainly true for Rousseau, Tolstoy, and Kropotkin. However, these three revolutionaries all lost their mothers before the age of three. They identified with an idealized image of virtue, an identification reinforced in each case by a significant female relative. The result was a general inhibition of aggressive impulses and a nonviolent approach to political change, even though their writings (particularly those of Rousseau) often stimulated violence in others. In the case of Gandhi nonviolence became an integral element of his political tactics and philosophy. With our early revolutionaries suffering was a consequence of their attitude and their way of life. With Gandhi it was deliberately and consciously sought as the very method of revolution. Wolfenstein has suggested the aggressive aspect of the self-suffering of Gandhi's mother.

> . . . if she was for some reason dissatisfied with the behavior of another member of the family she would impose some penalty on herself so that, out of love for her, they would cease the activity. . . . We do not know how often Putlibai used this technique in controlling Mohandas, but to the extent that she did he would grow up feeling that his actions and drives were potentially dangerous, that any, even covertly aggressive action on his part was likely to result in injury to another. . . .[2]

Throughout his youth, Gandhi was haunted by a feeling of unmanliness. He was shy, afraid of the dark, unathletic, and easily humiliated. Nevertheless, he very early believed that he would take part in driving the English from India. When a friend told him the English ruled over the Indians because they ate meat, he determined to try meat-eating to see if it would make him strong and cure what he regarded as his cowardice. He tried meat-eating several times and finally overcame his dislike for it, but the experience of lying to his mother and father on a regular basis was more than he could bear. He finally decided to give up meat-eating as long as he was in their home. The same friend also brought him to a brothel, but Gandhi was too shy to speak or take the initiative with the prostitute and she soon told him to get out. This made him feel even more unmanly than before and for years this feeling was the central problem of his youth. In his adult life he conquered the problem by yielding to it. In fact, he seemed to go out of his way to emphasize his weakness and womanliness to others.[3]

Suffering and Control

Weakness and womanliness are by no means synonymous. Gandhi was small and lacking in muscular development, but he had a powerful personality and incredible endurance. He spoke of his own shyness and reluctance to assert himself, yet his secretary Pyarelal described him in his adult years as a man with determination who enforced discipline.

> His energy was phenomenal. His iron will made every faculty of his body and mind obey its least command as an expert horseman does the animal under him. He could go on working day after day and week after week with only three or four hours of sleep—sometimes without any sleep at all. He enforced military discipline and clock-work regularity in his own case and expected the same from those around him. . . .
>
> He insisted on his desk being kept always clear and woe to anyone of his staff who referred to him a letter more than forty-eight hours old. Finesse or the dialectician's tricks in replies were severely deprecated. The answers had to be straight, clear and to the point.[4]

Gandhi achieved discipline among his followers simply by generating among them the fear that they might make him suffer. If they failed to work hard and to be sufficiently exacting, they might witness him working all night to correct their mistakes or he might fast because they had failed him in some way—an approach similar to that used by his mother.

While great emphasis is often placed on Gandhi's "feminine" identification, many writers overlook or minimize the role of his father, Kaba Gandhi, in his self-image of one who suffers for the sins of others. Gandhi's father had a temper which could explode when the children disobeyed. But he evidently also used self-suffering to control the children. Gandhi clearly feared his father and sought to appease him, but he claimed his father never beat any of the children.[5] On the one memorable incident in which he confronted his father it was fear of disapproval that was paramount in his own mind. He confessed a theft by sending a note to his father. Kaba did not grow angry or strike his own forehead as he often did when aroused, but the suffering of his father was still the primary element of his discipline. When Gandhi handed him the note:

> He read it through, and pearl-drops trickled down his cheeks, wetting the paper. For a moment he closed his eyes in thought and then tore up the note. He had sat up to read it. He again lay down. I also cried. I could see my father's agony. If I were a painter I could draw a picture of the whole scene today. It is still so vivid in my mind.[6]

Gandhi's father was the prime minister of Parbandar. As such, he was also a political leader. Like Gandhi, he had a reputation for incorruptability and he frequently invited guests, secretaries, and officials to his home. Pyarelal reminds us that Kaba Gandhi seldom sat down to eat with less than twenty guests. "This became a hereditary trait in the case of his son—the Mahatma."[7] Kaba also helped his wife Putaliba with the housework.

> It was a familiar sight, which the people of Parbandar still remember, of him sitting in the Shrinathji temple day after day, peeling and paring the vegetables for his wife's kitchen, while he discussed with his visitors and officials affairs of the State. Visitors to Gandiji's (M. K. Gandhi's) Ashram who had the privilege of being invited by him to join him in peeling and cutting vegetables for the Ashram kitchen, when they went to have a talk with him, will here immediately be reminded of their own experience.[8]

Thus Gandhi identified with both his parents, and the final resolution of his concern about manliness was not as difficult as might appear. Much of his initial conflict sprang from his belief that he must achieve the British ideal of masculinity if he were ever to become stronger than the British and drive them out of his country. The suffering he experienced in his early years in England, the efforts to wear English clothes and make public speeches, were all products of this effort to become something other than himself. His final adoption of the technique of nonviolent resistance and his abandonment of western dress was a return to what he regarded as his true identity (i.e., part of his search for truth).

Celibacy was another important element in Gandhi's adult morality. In some respects it can be seen as a continuation of his total effort to control all sensuality, although an incident in his youth may have had a special influence in this direction. He was married when very young to a girl, Kasturbai, chosen by his parents. His marriage began with an intense and possessive sexual desire. His desire to instruct his wife in writing and literature was impaired by his urgent desire for her body. Even his wife's pregnancy did not prevent him from sexual contact with her, although he regarded it as shameful at the time. His father became very ill during this period and Gandhi loved to nurse him, but when his uncle relieved him, Gandhi, pleased at the opportunity, rushed to his wife's room, woke her up, and began to have sex with her. When a servant knocked at the door to tell him his father was very ill, Gandhi knew at once what this meant and, when he insisted, the servant told him his father was dead.

> It is a blot I have never been able to efface or forget and I have always thought that, although my devotion to my parents knew no bounds and I would have given up anything for it, yet it was weighed and found unpardonably wanting because my mind was at the same moment in the grip of lust. . . . It took me long to get free from the shackles of lust, and I had to pass through many ordeals before I could overcome it.
>
> Before I close this chapter of my double shame, I may mention that the poor mite that was born to my wife scarcely breathed for more than three or four days. Nothing else could be expected. Let all those who are married be warned by this example.[9]

Gandhi felt himself responsible for the death of his first child and for his father dying without the comforting presence of his son. This was the result of his sexual lust but, in a general sense, one could call it the result of his desire for sensory pleasure.

While some individuals with a masochistic orientation punish themselves by inflicting physical pain or placing themselves in painful or uncomfortable circumstances, Gandhi'd approach to suffering was through self-denial. Gandhi's life-long attachment to the control and denial of sensual pleasure did not result solely from the circumstances surrounding the death of his father. His mother had already provided him with a perfect model of self-denial. This traumatic experience at the death scene of his father only reinforced his existing belief that sensuality was sinful.

A further aspect may also have intensified these feelings. The son in the Oedipal fantasy desires the death of his father and feels that his developing sexuality will be the instrument of that desire. Thus the aggressive feelings toward the father, which are associated with this developing sexuality, arouse feelings of guilt.[10] Surely this guilt would be intensified for Gandhi whose sexual desire actually prevented him from nursing his father, and perhaps in his own fantasy, from saving his life. His later desire to restrain all sensual appetites and to nurse the sick may well have been stimulated by this experience.

Education and Vocation

Through the help and advice of a family friend, Gandhi's family sent him to England to study law. He was eager for the journey, although his parents and relatives feared he would be corrupted by the experience. In England he discovered vegetarian restaurants and soon had a leading role in English vegetarian society. His shyness sometimes prevented him from speaking, but he became a highly regarded member of the organization.

We have examined the development of Gandhi's beliefs. While these beliefs were to shape his later development, the iron willed, charismatic leader of later years was not yet in evidence. The Gandhi who passed his bar examinations in London on June 10, 1891, appeared a timid, nervous Indian youth, dressed like an English gentleman and barely able to speak in public. Although physically weak and unimpressive, Gandhi had already demonstrated a certain stubborn resolve. He had resisted the community headman who forbade him to go to England. He dressed like an English gentleman and had tried to learn dancing and ape English ways, but he had also remained true to his oath not to touch wine, women, or meat during his stay in England. He was learning a certain independence from the pressure of both the Indian and the English cultures.

Gandhi arrived back in Bombay only to learn of the death of his mother. His brother, anticipating a great income from Gandhi's law practice, had allowed household expenses to mount, in part by introducing English dress into the family. Gandhi could not develop a practice in Bombay and the family soon had to move to Rajkot where work was easier to find. Here he soon became disgusted by the petty intrigues of the town and when he received an offer to represent a firm from Porbandar in South Africa, he accepted, glad of the opportunity to escape India.

In Durban he was met by Abdulla Sheth, a partner in the firm, but even before leaving the boat, he sensed from the glances of the people a certain cold curiosity about this "coloured" barrister who dressed like an English gentleman. He was also stung by the lack of respect with which Abdulla Sheth was treated by Europeans who knew him. Arrangements were soon made for him to travel to Pretoria to represent the firm of Dada Abdulla and Company in court. A first-class seat was booked for him on the train, but when a passenger arrived in first class and saw that Gandhi was a "coloured" man, he left to return with officials who demanded Gandhi accept a van compartment. Gandhi refused, showing his first-class ticket, but was told he must leave anyway. He continued to refuse and was finally pushed off the train at Maritzburg by a constable, his luggage was thrown after him.

It was winter and extremely cold in the higher region around Maritzburg. Gandhi spent the night in the station shivering, determined not to face further insults by asking for his overcoat from his luggage. During the long night, he contemplated the prejudice and discrimination in South Africa. He rejected returning to India as cowardly and determined to remain in South Africa and fight color prejudice. He had already faced humiliating situations with the English in India, but it was perhaps this incident on the train and the cold night in the Maritzburg station that became the turning point in his career, strengthening his resolve for events to come.

Gandhi purchased a berth at Maritzburg and traveled to Charlestown, where he was forced to take a coach to Johannesburg and travel outside with the driver. The "leader" of the coach, as the white man in charge was called, at first gave up his usual position beside the driver to Gandhi, but later decided to smoke and spread out a dirty piece of cloth on the footboard for Gandhi. He resisted this final insult. Gandhi said if he could not remain beside the driver, he would go inside with the other passengers where he belonged.

> As I was struggling through these sentences, the man came down upon me and began heavily to box my ears. He seized me by the arm and tried to drag me down. I clung to the brass rails of the coach-box and was determined to keep my hold even at the risk of breaking my wristbones. The passengers were witnessing the scene—the man swearing at me, dragging and belabouring me, and I remaining still. He was strong and I was weak. Some of the passengers were moved to pity and exclaimed, "Man, let him alone. Don't beat him. He is not to blame. He is right. If he can't stay there, let him come and sit down with us." "No fear," cried the man, but he seemed somewhat crestfallen and stopped beating me. He let go my arm, swore at me a little more, and asking the Hottentot servant who was sitting on the other side of the coachbox to sit on the footboard, took the seat so vacated.[11]

Gandhi had achieved a victory of sorts in this struggle against South African racism. As a child he had been pained by the suffering of his father and the fasting of his mother. He had been cowed into obedience by his guilt. Now he was discovering as an adult that even the white coach leader could be influenced by the moral pressure of the other passengers and his own stubborn resistance. However, Gandhi's resistance was more than mere nonviolence. The Hottentot who quietly took his seat on the footboard was nonviolent as well. Gandhi refused to combat force with force, but he managed to mobilize moral pressure against the coach leader by telling him firmly that he was in the wrong and refusing to be dislodged from his seat without a struggle. In short, he had forced his opponent into overt violence against him. In this way, he made the lines of battle clear. It was a tactic he would use again and again in his struggle. He had already sent a telegram to the general manager of the railway from which he had been ejected at Maritzburg, describing his treatment and obtaining assurance of future safe travel. When he arrived in Sanderton he sent a long letter to the coach company agent describing the incident and the leader's threats to take revenge. He was assured that on his further journey he could have a seat inside the coach with the other passengers. Gandhi was learning to get the maximum mileage from each incident.

The Application to Politics

On his arrival in Pretoria, Gandhi found he had few immediate duties with the firm. Sheth Tyeb Haji Kahn Muhamad, the opponent in the suit with Dada Abdulla and Company, was a leading figure in the community and a relative of Sheth Abdulla. Gandhi was still intensely interested in making changes in the status of Indians in South Africa and he sought out Sheth Tyeb to help him arrange a gathering of Indians to present them with a picture of their condition. He wanted them to forget caste and regional differences and unite against the oppression of the South African authorities. It was his first public address and, though he was frightened and uneasy, he was now armed with a moral cause which gave him a sense of purpose. His speech came off well and he arranged for regular meetings of this kind. He was soon acquainted with everyone in the Indian community of Pretoria, and he began to teach them some of his principles of *Ahimsa* (nonviolence). But he was also groping for a larger idea, it was not enough to refuse to use physical violence. *Ahimsa* could only be successful if the self were purified of hate and the desire for revenge. Then and only then could the individual practicing *Ahimsa* remain calm and serene. Only then could he be sure that nonviolence would not degenerate into violence.

An important step in this discovery was made during his work on the suit for Dada Abdulla. The costs of the court and the lawyers' fees were mounting, and Gandhi realized that both sides would lose if the case could not be settled out of court. His approach to Sheth Tyeb (Abdulla's opponent) with the purpose of unifying the Indian community was surely no accident. In his autobiography Gandhi tells us that he sought out Tyeb because he was a community leader.[12] He makes no mention of how he handled his employment at the time as one of the attorneys for the opposition to Tyeb. Obviously, it would be helpful to establish friendly relations with Tyeb if he intended to bring him into the arbitration process. Since he was already working with Tyeb on uniting the Indian community, he had some credibility as a friend and another basis for meeting and talking with him.

This procedure of making a friend of an actual or potential enemy and, at the same time, pushing his friends to the limits of their endurance, was to become one of Gandhi's ongoing characteristics. Gandhi managed to push both sides to arbitration. The case was presented to the arbitrator and Dada Abdulla won. But Gandhi's work was not yet finished. Sheth Tyeb could not possibly pay the whole amount without bankruptcy and dishonor. Gandhi now argued the case for his opponent to Dada Abdulla, insisting on payment by moderate installments. He was finally successful and the installments were spread over a long period so as to make the burden on Tyeb less severe. "My joy was boundless," says Gandhi, "I had learned the true practice of law."[13] What he had learned in fact was a way of harmonizing his practice of law with his own personality and his general philosophy of life. He was later to make it one of the principles of *Ahimsa* not to institute a court case against an opponent, for the very suggestion of a demand for punitive damages, even in money, was for him a form of violence.

The Committment

Gandhi's experience in South Africa represented the beginning of his movement of nonviolent resistance or, as he later called it, *Satyagraha*. Gandhi read the work of other writers and was deeply impressed by the work of Tolstoy.[14] At the beginning he was merely spreading his ideas, encouraging others to resist oppression, trying to organize the Indian community by merging internal differences into the larger goal of freedom for all. His work began as a sideline to his primary profession of attorney. When the case for Dada Abdulla was finished he returned to Durban to make preparations for his journey to India. But friends urged him to stay in South Africa, they needed his legal knowledge and organizational skills.[15] He agreed to stay long enough to draft a petition against a franchise bill, but he became progressively more deeply involved in South African problems and remained twenty years.[16]

As one examines the documents he generated at this period—his letters to the newspapers, his endless petitions to the authorities at every level, his pamphlets and advertisements which have been brought together in his *Collected Works*—one is struck by his tremendous burst of creative energy. Gandhi was always an active, energetic person, but now his energy was focused on a single goal and we begin to see his full potential for the first time.

The surface appearance of this behavior is self-sacrifice for the good of others. But it is evident that Gandhi did not feel this way about his activity. Throughout his life he had already shown a strong tendency to forego sensual pleasure—not because he was lacking in sensuality but because he derived some other vaguely defined pleasure from the act of sacrifice. It made him feel virtuous. This thrill of his own personal goodness had a decidedly sensual quality in itself. It excited him and gave him a special kind of pleasure. Now this sacrifice was combined with something else—a sense of community, a vast group of people combining their efforts to overcome injustice. This sense of involvement, of touching the lives of others, of speaking—as Trotsky was later to remark—"from out of a warm cavern of human bodies,"[17] became an additional element in the excitement.

On his way through the Transvaal by coach he had hung onto the rail and refused to take a seat on the foot board voluntarily until the leader lost heart in his beating under moral pressure from the other passengers. As his work continued he came to minimize his formal legal activity and concentrate on words and acts designed to arouse a similar sense of guilt in the British populace as a whole. As a child he had been extremely vulnerable when his mother used this technique on him. She could make him feel terribly guilty when she fasted. However (and this is crucial to his approach) he never sensed her desire to dominate him or to force him into a particular behavior through guilt. His memory of his mother was always one of her sacrifice because of her love for him. As a result he was always watching his own behavior, and that of his followers, to avoid the impression of moral blackmail. He felt that if his sacrifice was conducted with hatred in his heart, this hatred and anger would be felt by his opponent and his effort would fail.

Ahimsa

Much has been said about Gandhi's self-realization through sacrifice, his politeness, his agreeable, friendly manner and the sweetness of his disposition. While none of this is untrue, it is important to remember the comments by Pyarelal regarding his "iron will" and the way he "enforced military discipline and clockwork regularity" on himself and those around him. There is no doubt, from Pyarelal's long biography, that others learned to fear Gandhi—not in the sense that one fears a physical beating—but with a deeper terror, a terror of the soul. Gandhi impressed his followers with an almost god-like perfection. To fall out of favor with him was to feel that one was "damned" in the most profound moral sense of that term. Gandhi held no formal religious position, but he held the power of a pope. While there was never a formal excommunication, his threat was all the more severe in that one could never be sure he had not wronged the leader in some way. All gifts, all service to him were "voluntary." Yet to cause him suffering, to give him pain, became the greatest of sins among his followers. Therefore, once one was caught within the orbit of his magnetism, service was no longer voluntary. If one came to believe, as many did, that Gandhi was a true saint, that he was the final arbiter of good and evil, there was no salvation outside his service and no escape from a terrible sense of unworthiness if one wronged him, even if such a wrong was due to neglect or inadvertence.

Even a delay in agreement with him, by exhausting his energies or his time, could make one feel guilty—not that Gandhi showed his impatience or his anger. He handled all objections by further discussion. He left it to others to recognize that time was running out, that they were using up the energies of this great man, and that he might have to work much harder in the following days if they did not give in and agree with him. His method of dealing with an expected £6 subscription to the movement by a wealthy host is typical of this approach.

> On one occasion . . . the situation was rather difficult. We expected our host to contribute £6, but he refused to give more than £3. If we had accepted that amount from him, others would have followed suit, and our collections would have been spoiled. It was a late hour of the night, and we were all hungry. But how could we dine without having first obtained the amount we were bent on getting? All persuasion was useless. The host seemed to be adamant. Other merchants in the town reasoned with him, and we all sat up throughout the night, he as well as we determined not to budge one inch. Most of my co-workers were burning with rage, but they contained themselves. At last, when day was already breaking, the host yielded, paid down £6 and feasted us. This happened at Tongaat, but the repercussion of the incident was felt as far as Stanger on the North Coast and Charlestown in the interior. It also hastened our work of collection.[18]

Gandhi avoided explicit threats or commands in the enforcement of his authority. He bullied others by his sweet persistence, his refusal to yield, his unwillingness to drop a subject until he had his way. Yet there was never a cloying sweetness about him. He managed to avoid the impression that he was insincere, that he really wanted to strike someone or that he was restraining his anger with great difficulty. The absence of anger—the genuine, unfeigned absense of anger—was a central aspect of his approach. This became the core of *Ahimsa*, his own brand of nonviolence.

Gandhi believed in the elimination not the suppression of anger. Whether he was able to accomplish this completely in himself we do not know. Erikson suggests that there was much violence in Gandhi's nonviolence. Indeed, Gandhi admitted the general philosophical truth of this statement on more than one occasion, i.e., that there is "much violence in non-violence" in the general sense, but not that he harbored impulses of anger or violence.[19] Nevertheless, he cautioned his followers against moral blackmail and he believed that a nonviolent movement could not be successful unless the participants had examined their hearts and eliminated all hatred for the enemy.

The Struggle against Anger

Gandhi did not achieve *ahimsa* in a single step. He struggled many years with his own anger, particularly when his wife and children became part of his life once again. After three years of work in South Africa, Gandhi asked leave in 1896 to go home to India for six months and return with his wife and children. By the time of his return his reputation was well established in both the Indian and white communities. A crowd of whites beat him and pelted him with sticks and stones.

He took refuge in the home of a friend and, finally, when whites surrounded the house, in the police station. Gandhi refused to prosecute his assailants although the secretary of state for the Colonies had cabled a request for such action.

He was now faced with the problems of running a household and educating his children in addition to his public work. He believed a public school education would not be satisfactory for his children and undertook to educate them himself—an activity for which he did not really have the time. All his children eventually resented this lack of a public school education to some degree, particularly his eldest son Harilal, who finally broke away from Gandhi altogether.

Gandhi determinedly refused all gifts and money which were offered.

> What right had I to accept all these gifts? Accepting them, how could I persuade myself that I was serving the community without remuneration? . . . . One of the gifts was a gold necklace worth fifty guineas, meant for my wife. But even that gift was given because of my public work, and so it could not be separated from the rest. [20]

But Kasturbai did not see things that way. They had nothing in reserve. They had children and should make some provision for their welfare. Gandhi had carefully prepared the children and, under his instruction, they all agreed to give up the jewels, insisting with their father that they would not need them. Kasturbai was insistent.

> "You may not need them," said my wife, "your children may not need them. Cajoled they will dance to your tune. I can understand your not permitting me to wear them. But what about my daughters-in-law? They will be sure to need them. And who knows what will happen tomorrow. I would be the last person to part with gifts so lovingly given."
>
> And thus the torrent of argument went on, reinforced, in the end, by tears. But the children were adamant. And I was unmoved.
>
> There were pointed thrusts and some of them went home. But I was determined to return the ornaments. I somehow succeeded in extorting a consent from her. [21]

As Gandhi suggests, it was largely through a kind of extortion rather than willing consent that he forced his wife to go along with the ideal of self-sacrifice. When her life was at stake, he was willing to leave the decision with her, but otherwise he believed it was his duty to *help* her on the way toward self-actualization. His desire to instruct his wife was so strong that it led to occasional lapses from his vow of nonviolence. One of these instances involved his desire to instruct her in doing the work of the untouchables. She balked at cleaning the chamber pot of a Christian clerk who would not, at first, clean his own. Gandhi then cleaned the pots himself.

> She could not bear the pots being cleaned by me, neither did she like doing it herself. Even today I can recall the picture of her chiding me, her eyes red with anger, and pearl drops streaming down her cheeks, as she descended the ladder, pot in hand. But I was a cruelly kind husband. I regarded myself as her teacher, and so harassed her out of my blind love for her.

> I was far from satisfied by her merely carrying the pot. I would have her do it cheerfully. So I said, raising my voice: "I will not stand this nonsense in my house."
>
> The words pierced her like an arrow. She shouted back: "Keep your house to yourself and let me go." I forgot myself and the spring of compassion dried up in me. I caught her by the hand, dragged the helpless woman to the gate . . . with the intention of pushing her out. The tears were running down her cheeks in torrents, and she cried: "Have you no sense of shame? . . . I have no parents or relatives here to harbour me. Being your wife, you think I must put up with your cuffs and kicks? . . . Let us not be found making scenes like this!"
>
> I put on a brave face, but was really ashamed and shut the gate. . . . Today I am in a position to narrate the incident with some detachment, as it belongs to a period out of which I have fortunately emerged. I am no longer a blind infatuated husband. I am no more my wife's teacher. [22]

As Gandhi suggests, there were outbursts of physical aggression and anger before he was able to manage his life and his own behavior so as to exercise moral control over others. In fact, it was probably as a result of his frequent contact with the "demon" of violence within himself that he developed his considerable sophistication in the practice of nonviolence.

Return to South Africa

Gandhi returned to the practice of law in India, promising to return to South Africa if needed. A cable asking for help soon called him back, and he agreed to go as soon as he could be supplied with funds.

A significant change after his return to South Africa was a new emphasis on the simple life and a determination to end the pretense of being an English gentleman. After reading John Ruskin's *Unto This Last,* he decided to live a life of labor and service and founded a communal farm on twenty acres near Durban. His followers baked their own bread and washed their own clothes. He planned to abandon the private practice of law and devote his life to public service, but he could not immediately discontinue his practice in Johannesburg. At Phoenix, he founded and largely prepared a magazine, *Indian Opinion.* He began to perform all his own services, even cutting his own hair and washing his own clothes. In 1908 he and some followers were jailed for resistance to the Asiatic Registration Act. It was his first term in jail. The prisoners were denied salt and curry powder and expected to finish their last meal before sundown. On his release he voluntarily adopted these same restrictions on his own eating habits.

Gandhi had been interested in the work of Tolstoy for several years and had written him many letters as "a humble follower." In jail he had further opportunities to read Tolstoy's works. In 1910 Gandhi's friend Herman Kallenbach gave a large tract of land (1100 acres) near Johannesburg to the *Satyagraha* movement; Gandhi called the gift Tolstoy Farm. Here he began a series of experiments in dietetics, particularly fasts in which he consumed nothing but water. He encouraged others, particularly the children, to join him in a communal fast, and he was profoundly impressed by the spirit of comraderie that developed among them. He felt fasting benefited him both physically and morally.

It was here that he used fasting as a form of discipline for two misbehaving children. [23] He later applied it in the political world as well. It was in his relationship with children and in the ashram life generally that Gandhi developed his techniques for testing himself and controlling others. He had already decided upon a vow of celibacy, but proving that he could restrain himself with his wife was not enough. He was later to develop the more exquisit torture of sleeping beside the naked bodies of young girls in his ashram. In his later years he was often seen in the company of attractive young girls who would massage him, support him while he walked (particularly when he was weak from fasting), or share his bed at night. This behavior may have been more than self-testing; perhaps he enjoyed tempting himself and may have derived a certain unconscious sensual pleasure from toying with the former objects of his desire.

He also put temptation in the way of others by sending boys and girls to bathe together in a spring. But he watched them like a hawk and when one of the young men made fun of the girls, he conceived the unique punishment (for the boy?) of shaving the heads of the two girls he had teased. His skill in arousing guilt was phenomcnal, for no possible punishment of the boy alone would have produced the desired effect. In all probability, he was also punishing the girls for their presumed provocative behavior.

To India Again

Throughout his long struggle in South Africa, Gandhi never lost sight of his goal of driving the British from India and instituting Indian self-government. But he was concerned first with the oppression of Indians by other Indians. In 1914, on the eve of World War I, Gopal Krishna Gokhale requested he return to India via England. Gandhi believed Indians, who had been indirectly participating in British violence by receiving British protection, should now support the British war effort. He urged them to organize an ambulance corps. Complete *ahimsa,* he argued, was not possible, for existence in society always involves *himsa.* He who cannot stop or resist the war may take part in it, while striving to free his people from war as a long-range goal.

However, while this was his overt reasoning, there seems to have been another basis for Gandhi's decision. Gandhi believed in loyalty and saw himself as a British subject. His followers complained that he was going against his own principles in attempting to recruit them for military duty, but Gandhi believed the British Empire to be one of the most democratic world powers. He admired the freedom which was possible for British subjects. His goal was not to destroy the British Empire, but to raise the Indian people to full appreciation of and participation in British democracy.

Therefore, his first goals on his return to India were to improve the lot of Indian labor, and to abolish the caste system and the great differences dividing rich Indians from their poorer fellows. On February 4, 1916, he addressed the opening of a school at Benares, founded by Mrs. Annie Besant, in which he told a gathering of British and Indian notables some of the defects of the Indian people: their love of luxury, their undemocratic ways, their perpetual filth. He pointed to the hypocrisy of elegant jewel-bedecked maharajas who only talked about the relief of Indian poverty. Cries from the audience demanded he sit down and he caused such a commotion that he was not able to finish his speech. It was this urge to get the Indian people to look first at themselves and their own imperfections, before thinking of expelling the British, that aroused so much conflict between himself and others also devoted to Indian home rule.

Gandhi needed to gain support from other Indians, particularly the wealthy and influential. How was he to handle the problem of co-optation—the greatest potential danger to all revolutionaries? How does one who hopes to lead labor accept a gift from a wealthy industrialist? How does a democrat handle support from a king? Rousseau faced this problem by refusing all gifts from everyone, friend or enemy although he was not really successful in this effort. He needed the help of others and frequently accepted gifts from people if he believed he could trust them not to try to influence him. Other revolutionaries have sought support through their organization alone, rejecting aid from the government, those connected with big business, or other external powers. Gandhi accepted all support, but made his greatest demands on his friends and supporters. The individual who presented Gandhi with a gift usually found that, far from making him vulnerable to influence, it only stimulated him to further demands. Gandhi reasoned that anyone who made a contribution to his cause must believe in what he was doing. A believer might also be interested in action or further financial sacrifice. If behavior was inconsistent with avowed belief, Gandhi was quite prepared to point this out.

Sheth Ambalal Sarabhai, one of the leading mill owners of the Ahmedabad region, delivered 13,000 rupies to Gandhi's ashram at a time when Gandhi was desperatly in need of help. He did not identify himself; he simply delivered the money and drove away. But it was not long after this that Gandhi, at the invitation of the Sheth's sister, took the side of the workers in a strike against all the mill owners of the region. In a long struggle Gandhi finally began a fast, ostensibly to purge himself for allowing the workers to express anger and to prevent possible violence, but it was the indirect (and supposedly unintended) pressure of this fast on the mill owners that finally brought them to an agreement. Gandhi was not unaware that the mill owners (and particularly his friend Ambalal) were concerned for his life. He considered this a serious flaw in his strategy, but he continued it anyway until his objective was achieved. Erikson[24] has examined this incident in depth as one of the central crises in Gandhi's development. While it was certainly his first major political incident, the use of fasting as a means of controlling others was already one of his basic skills.

Violence is Nonviolent

It was shortly after his Ahmedabad fast that Gandhi began serious recruiting for the British. His rationale was the same as in the Boer War; India was part of the British Empire. But another factor moved him into the recruiting conflict. He had always been uncomfortable with the English term "passive-resistance," to describe *Satyagraha*. For Gandhi *Satyagraha* was a form of active courage. As a child his many fears made him feel unmanly. Overcoming fear became the primary test of his manhood. While he could joke of his spinning as woman's work and often described himself as though he were a woman, these were all metaphorical expressions. In reality, his manhood was exceedingly important to him, but it was centered in a single virtue, courage. He was not troubled in the least by a suggestion that he was as sweet and loving as a woman, but he could be deeply hurt and angered by any suggestion that he lacked courage. There is no doubt that, in his own mind, courage was associated with masculinity. Women were protected by men. While he admired courage in women, he did not expect it and the lack of courage was "effeminate."

On June 22, 1918, in an appeal for enlistment, Gandhi argued that he was defending the masculinity of the Indian people by his drive for recruitment.

> There can be no friendship between the brave and the effeminate. We are regarded as a cowardly people. If we want to become free from that reproach, we should learn the use of arms.
>
> Partnership in the Empire is our definite goal. We should suffer to the utmost of our ability and even lay down our lives to defend the Empire. If the Empire perishes, with it perish our cherished aspirations.
>
> .... The foregoing argument will show that by enlisting in the army we help the Empire, we qualify ourselves for swaraj [home rule], we learn to defend India and to a certain extent regain our lost manhood. . . . If Gujarat wants to save herself from the reproach of effeminacy, she should be prepared to contribute thousands of sepoys. [25]

What is the source of this conflict and of Gandhi's apparent inconsistency? It is my belief that Gandhi was undergoing a change in his attitude toward the morality of violence. Previously he had battled for Indian freedom in South Africa and he had sought to improve the attitude of Indians toward their fellow Indians. He had supported the goal of *swaraj* (Indian home rule) for years in the Congress party, but he was now preparing himself to drive the British out of India. An attitude of strict nonviolence had been his policy, but could *swaraj* be achieved by nonviolence alone? I realize I am putting words in his mouth, for Gandhi never allowed himself to contemplate his own participation in violent acts against the British. But it seems to me that he was toying with the possibility that such an open fight might be necessary at some future date. How else can we explain his desperate effort to rationalize killing as a form of *ahimsa*? On July 17, 1918, in a letter to Hanumantrao, he said:

> ... that all killing is not *himsa*, that sometimes the practice of ahimsa may even necessitate killing and that we as a nation have lost the true power of

killing. It is clear that he who has lost the power to kill cannot practice non-killing. Ahimsa is a renunciation of the highest type. A weak and effeminate nation cannot perform this grand act of renunciation, even as a mouse cannot be properly said to renounce the power of killing a cat. . . . I see more clearly that we shall be unfit for swaraj for generations to come if we do not regain the power of self-defense. This means for me a rearrangement of so many ideas about self-development and India's development. . . .[26]

The more resistance he encountered, the more Gandhi extended himself until his recruiting drive occupied all his time. But despite his best efforts he was getting nowhere. His depression began to grow and in a letter to C. F. Andrews he poured out his feeling of discouragement and his growing conviction that the Indian people were perhaps, after all, a weak and cowardly people, unfit for self-rule.

My difficulties are deeper than you have put them. All you raise I can answer. I must attempt in this letter to reduce my own to writing. They just now possess me to the exclusion of everything else. All other things I seem to be doing purely mechanically. This hard thinking has told upon my physical system. I hardly want to talk to anybody. I do not want even to write anything, not even these thoughts of mine. . . . When friends told me here that passive resistance was taken up by the people as a weapon of the weak, I laughed at the libel, as I called it then. But they were right and I was wrong. With me alone and a few other co-workers it came out of our strength and was described as satyagraha, but with the majority it was purely and simply passive resistance that they resorted to, because they were too weak to undertake methods of violence. . . .[27]

In a letter to Maganlal Gandhi on July 25, 1918, the conversion seems complete. Gandhi, who laughed at consistency, now made the supreme effort to be consistent. Instead of saying that there are circumstances where violence is necessary and proper, he described situations where violence is nonviolence.

To be sure, I have felt, in all seriousness, that Swaminaryana and Vallabhacharya have robbed us of our manliness. They made the people incapable of self-defense. . . . The love taught by Swaminarayana and Vallabh is all sentimentalism. It cannot make one a man of true love. . . . I had not fully realized the duty of restraining a drunkard from doing evil, of killing a dog in agony or one infected with rabies. In all these instances, violence is in fact non-violence. . . . In the same way our offspring must be strong in physique. If they cannot completely renounce the urge to violence, we may permit them to commit violence, to use their strength to fight and thus make them non-violent. . . .[28]

Gandhi believed that people became ill because they did not take care of themselves. Acting against one's inner voice and eating improper foods were both important factors in his concept of illness. During his recruiting campaign, he lived on peanut butter and lemons, developing a severe case of dysentery, his first serious illness. He sought to cure himself by fasting and he refused all medicine. Doctors advised milk and he refused this as well, because of the cruel manner in which cows were milked. His nervous system seemed shattered. He was depressed and he became convinced he was going to die. At last Kasturbai suggested goat's milk and he relented on this occasion, although he was later bothered by this breach of his vow never to take milk. He recovered slowly. Gradually his failure as a recruiter and the British refusal to grant Indian independence led Gandhi to drop his efforts to make British soliders of the people of India.

The Outbreak of Violence

During the war British acts of oppression such as the arrest of the Ali brothers (two Moslem leaders); Mrs. Annie Besant; the Indian statesman, Tilak, in 1918; and the silencing of the Indian press made it increasingly clear that India was to be treated as a subject colony. After the war, Sir Sidney Rowlatt issued a report recommending a continuation for India of many of the wartime measures. The report was issued March 18, 1919, and that night Gandhi had a dream in which he conceived the idea of a nationwide hartal, a suspension of all economic activity and a general program of civil disobedience. After his long period of support for the British war effort, he now reversed himself and began a long campaign against the British government. He set March 30, 1919, as the beginning of his hartal.

Everywhere the *hartal* seemed a great success and Gandhi was encouraged by the enthusiasm he observed and the warmth with which he was greeted by the crowds. He was once again a major popular figure. But in Delhi British officers were attacked. There were riots, stones were thrown, streetcars derailed, buildings burned, and weapons captured. Gradually the violence spread to Bombay and even to Ahmedabad. Finally, on April 18, Gandhi told his people the entire campaign had been "a Himalayan miscalculation" and he ended it. He concluded that it was foolish to launch such a campaign before the people were properly trained in civil disobedience.

What was the reason for such a major miscalculation? Again, I am inclined to attribute it to Gandhi's ambivalence about violence. He was angry at the British and eager to strike a blow for Indian independence as soon as possible in answer to the Rowlatt commission. He was so eager that he risked violence to let them know his power. But once he saw the effect of his move in actual bloodshed and loss of British lives, he relented and called off the campaign.

Unfortunately, the violence was now out of control, particularly in the Punjab where the British had mistakenly tried to keep him out because of their fear that he might foment violence. In Amristar, a city of 150,000, the two leaders who might have controlled the population were arrested. A mob raged through the street and several British citizens were beaten to death. Order was restored only by Gandhi's forebearance in the face of the British repression that followed. In 1920 he was again disillusioned with British promises, and at last decided that complete independence from the British Empire was the only possible goal. He became president of the All India Home Rule League in August; with the death of Tilak, he also became leader of the Congress party. In December Gandhi was once again ready for a national program of noncooperation and he announced a resolution for making *swaraj* the goal of the party in a national convention in Nagpur.

Sir George Lloyd, the governor of Bombay, had already observed the violence that sometimes followed Gandhi's preaching of nonviolence. He was convinced that Gandhi was a devious rabble rouser who planned a violent revolt under the cloak of nonviolence. Gandhi described his movement as calling for the overthrow of the government, saying he was "legally seditious." He asked for no quarter and expected none. He had declared war on the government and predicted it could not last long. His original goal was to establish home rule within a year of his resolution. All of this tended to reinforce the government impression that if he was not violent himself, he might easily stimulate others to acts of violence. He was arrested once again, tried at Ahmedabad on March 18, 1922, and sentenced to six years, but was released in February 1924 following an appendectomy.

On January 1, 1930, he declared the independence of India. In March another spectacular incident occured. Gandhi was jailed when he announced his intention to make salt in opposition to British law. His followers then attempted the same thing and were brutally beaten by the police. Skulls and testicles were smashed by police clubs, and the area was soon littered with hundreds of bodies.

In 1935, Gandhi felt it necessary to sever all connections with the Congress party. He was still friendly with the members individually, but the restraints on his behavior, which were developing from his policy of nonviolence, made it difficult to interact with them on a day-to-day basis. He was not yet prepared to ask them to follow the difficult path he was devising for himself. Thus he gave up his seat and even his membership in the party. He often attended Congress Working Committee meetings, but only as an advisor.

The Quit India Movement

Gandhi resigned his leadership in the Congress party, but he still held a firm grip on the politics of the nation. In 1936, he consented to Indian Congress party participation in the elections for the provincial and central legislatures, relaxing his total boycott on cooperation with the British government. He was still a popular figure among the people, but there was more resistance to his nonviolent approach among the leaders of the Congress Party. Subhas Chandra Bose called for an armed revolt against Great Britain. Congress itself used its police power during strikes and religious riots. Jawaharlal Nehru, president of the Congress for 1936–37 and a close friend and admirer of Gandhi, disagreed sharply with him on the use of police and military power. When the Nazi army invaded Poland in September 1939, Lord Linlithgow, the viceroy, summoned Gandhi for a conference. Gandhi agreed to lend his moral support to the war effort but refused any recruiting. Both Nehru and Gandhi became increasingly concerned by the growing hostility against the British. They determined on a program of resistance to British rule as the only way of restoring Indian manhood. Nehru saw it as essential for creating in the Indian people the spirit of armed resistance to the Japanese. On August 7, 1942, Nehru and Gandhi jointly proposed a demand for the British to "Quit India." On August 8, the Quit India resolution was passed at an All-India Congress Committee meeting in Bombay.

Revolution

In all revolutionary struggles there is frequent deception on both sides. The more a struggle purports to be nonviolent, the greater the need for deception. A major government with military firepower at its command will not relinquish power easily, though the use of power may be disguised. A policeman may beat up a native, but fail to report the incident because he knows the police chief, while secretly approving the policy "to keep the little buggers in line," does not want to *know* about it. A nonviolent leader of the rebellious population may have friendly conversations with those engaged in violence. He may verbally disapprove of what they are doing, but nevertheless understand the extremity of their anger and smile at them benevolently. Much can be said in a smile.

Violent revolutionaries will not discuss planned assassinations, the storage of bombs and guns, or their efforts to derail trains in the presence of a saintly mahatma. They are not being secretive. It is only that they know he does not approve of such things and it would be insulting to discuss them in his presence. The mahatma, for his part, knows these fellows have all sorts of nasty things on their minds, but it would be improper to ask them about specific plans to harm anyone. This knowledge would obligate him to try to stop the violence. He might even feel compelled to betray them to the police; therefore it is better *not to know*.

Formerly Gandhi believed that *ahimsa* was not possible unless practiced without anger. Later he seemed to accept the fact that a great program of nonviolent resistance and civil disobedience requires a resolve, a determination, even an anger, on the part of the population. They must have their consciousness raised in regard to the injustice of their oppressors. They must be seething with indignation if they are to persist in a long program of resistance. Perhaps the indignation required by a nonviolent leader is greater than that of a violent leader. The latter needs only a few willing hands committed to destruction; the former requires a wide network of angry and restive people. In a sense, both are working for the same goal. The violent leader gains much sympathy from angry but nonviolent supporters who are quite willing to hide him when he is fleeing from the police. Further, he can recruit from the nonviolent when their relatives have been killed by the police or when some nonviolent protest is met with official brutality.

Like Kropotkin and Tolstoy, Gandhi was sympathetic to those revolutionaries involved in violent acts. He knew that many members of Congress had deliberately planned violence in the event of his arrest. He was under frequent criticism from individuals such as Jayaprakash Narayan, a socialist leader who admired him and whose people had been aroused by Gandhi's first acts of resistance, but who frequently urged him to abandon nonviolence for real, genuine struggle. Gandhi reminded Narayan that all factions of the party were at war with the British. He pointed out that Narayan's methods, quite legitimate in themselves, were detrimental while a nonviolent struggle was in progress.

In his speech to the AICC on August 8, he authorized all Indians to act on their own if he were arrested, but he "trusted" them to act nonviolently, knowing the many "black sheep" in their midst. He gave them the mantra, "do or die," and added "let every man and woman live every moment of his or her life hereafter in the consciousness that he or she eats or lives for achieving freedom and will die, if need be, to attain that goal." Thus while he continued to instruct his followers in nonviolence, his slogans, his suggestion that it was each person for himself if the leaders were arrested, and his call to "do or die" seemed very like a general's call to physical conflict. Knowing many members of Congress were inclined toward violence, and having talked and argued with them on a friendly basis, without effect, he must have known what would follow his arrest.

The next day Gandhi, Nehru, and several other members of Congress were arrested. Violence erupted all over India. Rioters attacked police, destroyed communication facilities, and killed British officials. Several cities and small towns fell entirely into the hands of the rebels. Gandhi continued his protest against British policy from jail. He said nothing of the violence of the Indians, feeling that since he had been jailed he could no longer be responsible for it.

On August 14, 1942, he wrote to the Viceroy, Lord Linlithgow, telling him that the British government had precipitated the crisis. "The precipitate action of the Government leads one to think that they were afraid that the extreme caution and gradualness with which the Congress was moving toward direct action, might make world opinion ever round to the Congress as it had already begun doing, and expose the hollowness of the grounds for the Government's rejection of the Congress demand."[29] In short, Gandhi suspected the British of deliberately provoking violence to make the Indians look bad. Perhaps this was really the way he felt, or perhaps it was his answer to the government resolution (which he quoted in this same letter) accusing the Congress party of deliberately planning and fomenting violence. Gandhi called this "a gross distortion of reality," adding that "Violence was never contemplated at any stage."[30]

Clearly, the attitude of Gandhi and the Congress party to the British government was now not the same as his earlier attitude toward the mill owners in the Ahmedabad strike. He had a genuine friendship and love for the mill owners and he was on terms of equality with their leaders. He sought to avoid making any statements or issuing any leaflets that portrayed the mill owners as evil or acting in bad faith. The open anger of the letters between Gandhi and Linlithgow became increasingly obvious; Gandhi insisted he had no violent intentions while Linlithgow reminded him that he was in charge and violence had occurred.

Francis G. Hutchins observes in his study of Gandhi's role in the Quit India movement that on many occasions Gandhi seemed to countenance the use of violence.

> Gandhi anticipated and implicitly sanctioned—both before and after the fact—the mass outbursts which followed the arrests of August 9. His initial comment, when informed of their extent, was an expression of surprise that they had not been more severe.[31]

Gandhi did not approve of planned *intentional* violence, but he was very sympathetic to impulsive violence provoked by outrage. But driving the British out of India had necessitated winding up the people like a coiled spring, and the line between hanging on or losing control wore very thin.[32]

In his letter of January 29, 1943, Gandhi seemed more than ever at one with the ideas of Tolstoy and Kropotkin regarding the "innocence" of violence provoked by those in power. He reminded Linlithgow that the violence followed the "wholesale arrest of principal Congress workers. . . . But you throw in my face the facts of murders by persons reputed to be Congressmen. I see the fact of the murders as clearly, I hope, as you do. My answer is that the Government goaded the people to the point of madness."[33]

Since Linlithgow refused him the "soothing balm" needed for the relief of his pain, he must resort to the law prescribed for *Satyagrahis*—a fast according to capacity. The fast would last twenty-one days and begin on 9 February. In a further exchange of letters, Linlithgow talked about everything else but Gandhi's intended fast. In every reply Gandhi reminded Linlithgow of his stated intention to fast.

Gandhi's fast would not be for disappointment in the violence committed by his followers, but for British failure to admit mistakes and quit India. Gandhi's letters also imply a threat; he does not want to fast until death, but the twenty-one days he proposes could easily lead to death in a man of seventy-three. Gandhi and Linlithgow both knew the people of India were worked up to a fever pitch of excitement. Gandhi's death during his fast could unleash undreamed-of mayhem and violence.

Linlithgow's answer to Gandhi on February 5, 1943, revealed the great distance between the style of thought in the two men. Gandhi's letters contained a logical form, which he no doubt used to communicate with the British. Trained in British law, he knew how to prepare a legal brief. He spoke of "evidence," "facts," "proof," but he really pleaded for understanding and love. He seemed to say to Linlithgow, 'Please! I am pleading with you. If you love us, as you claim to do, let us be free. If you persist in this domination, our love will turn to hate. I don't want it to happen. I want to be your friend, but my people come first.' Linlithgow, while he may have been aware of this undertone of feeling in Gandhi's letters, did not rule the British Empire. He could respond only to the logical content, not only because he was powerless to decide things on a personal basis, but because he was British.

Gandhi's character was such that he could not possibly have engaged in secret and explicit plans for violent acts against the British. On the other hand, there must have been a tacit understanding, certainly an awareness, that such plans were under way and that his arrest could trigger an outbreak of violence.

Gandhi spent at least twenty years patiently constructing a time bomb in full view of the British. He showed them all the parts; he had nothing up his sleeve. In fact, he no longer had any sleeves, nor any secrets, to hide. The British watched him work, but they did not fully understand what he was doing. He was such a jolly and friendly craftsman. He had such a mischievous sense of humor. When the last bolt was in place and he slowly pulled back the trigger, he smiled in satisfaction. The British were horrified by the result and first sought to disconnect the mechanism. When it blew up in their faces, Gandhi was deeply saddened. He tried to explain to them that he meant no harm. If they had backed away from the bomb and quit India, he could have defused it and no one would have been hurt. If the British still refused to quit India, Gandhi had many bombs in his armory. If they were shaken by the first explosion, he was now preparing a twenty-megaton fast that would blow the British to kingdom come.

Gandhi, of course, did not think in these terms. Once he had taken a vow he was fond of saying, "I am helpless." A vow, once taken, could not be broken— otherwise a vow had no meaning. Still, a vow was not a threat. Gandhi could never really perceive himself as a threat to anyone, particularly not a violent or physical threat. But to Linlithgow the threat was very physical. The smoke and carnage had not been cleared away from the last blast and here was another on the way. He was much more "helpless" than Gandhi, a mere soldier in the trenches. He could have refused to fight, but this was unthinkable to a man of his training and sense of empire. He tried instead to explain to Gandhi the violent nature of his proposed fast.

> I would welcome a decision on your part to think better of it, not only because of my own natural reluctance to see you wilfully risk your life, but because I regard the use of a fast for political purposes as a form of political blackmail (himsa) for which there can be no moral justification, and understood from your own previous writings that this was also your view.[34]

Linlithgow was right. Gandhi had already disavowed a fast "against" his opponent. He had even been troubled by the "grave defect" that he was threatening the mill owners in his Ahmedabad fast, even though he was actually fasting to discipline his own followers. But now there was not even a pretense that he was fasting for any other purpose than to threaten the British. In his reply February 7, 1943, Gandhi was outraged that Linlithgow should set himself up as an authority on *ahimsa*. Gandhi stood by his previous writings, but he wondered if Linlithgow could have read them. Most of all, he was offended by Linlithgow's remark that he was taking "an easy way out." This was, to a *Satyagrahi*, "an invitation to fast."[35] As to the reasons for his fast, Gandhi remained unclear except to say that it was not an act of political blackmail; "it is on my part meant to be an appeal to the

Highest Tribunal for justice which I have failed to secure from you. If I do not survive the ordeal I shall go to the Judgment Seat with the fullest faith in my innocence. Posterity will judge between you as a representative of an all-powerful Government and me as a humble man who has tried to serve his country and humanity through it."[36]

There is little point in trying to interpret Gandhi's statement as to the "meaning" of his fast. He was clearly in a struggle for power with Linlithgow and he was determined to fast. In the last analysis Gandhi always scorned mere logical consistency. He believed he could hear the inner voice of truth and this was more important than consistency.

The question of a fast, then, had nothing to do with whether it was consistent or inconsistent with his teaching. It was his only remaining weapon. Further, it was a weapon that required great courage to use. Courage and manhood had always meant more to Gandhi than logic, even perhaps more than being proven morally right. Linlithgow had, in effect, called him a coward in his taunt that a fast would be the "easy way out." He would show this fine British gentleman whether or not the fast was an easy weapon to use, and he was determined to make his opponent feel the sting of it, or perish in the attempt.

Thus Linlithgow or, in reality, Winston Churchill and the British Empire finally forced Gandhi to draw his sword. He had raised it before but always muted in its scabbard. The words like "truth," "ahimsa," "nonviolence" were written upon the scabbard, as though to disguise the purpose of the thing within. Only once before, in the strike at Ahmedabad, had the gleam of steel been visible. Now the old warrior turned for his last battle and the sword came out. The useless cover with its words of disguise fell to the ground, and the gleam of steel was there for all to see. The fast became a naked weapon of power and Gandhi was charging full tilt toward the British lines.

The Last Struggle

Whether Gandhi could last the twenty-one days was doubtful. He began his fast on February 10, 1943, and within days was visited by doctors who announced that his condition was rapidly deteriorating. Indian officials began resigning from the viceroy's council. Letters and telegrams poured in from all over India demanding Gandhi's release. Indian leaders arrived in person with protests. A crowd gathered around the palace of the Agah Kahn at Yeravda, where Gandhi was kept prisoner.

On February 15, massage was tried on Gandhi to keep him going, but his heart action was becoming feeble. On the 17th two more resignations were presented to the viceroy by council members. On the 18th Gandhi was no longer talking. On the 19th a nonparty conference of representatives from all over India met in Delhi to urge the government to release Gandhi immediately. On February 20 Gandhi was worse, spending his time in bed and in silence. On February 22 he was much worse, troubled by nausea, with an almost imperceptible pulse. The police and military assembled their weapons and took their positions. But the next day Gandhi showed some improvement; his nausea disappeared and he was able to take water. On March 3 at 9:30 a.m. Gandhi broke his fast amid the songs and excitement of the crowd.[37]

By his decision to fast for twenty-one days and not to the death, Gandhi made it possible for both the British and himself to save face. On the other hand, if God had wanted to take him during those twenty-one days, he was prepared to be the instrument of God's wrath against the British. It gave him full scope for his anger. If he recovered, he would be at peace once more.

The British remained adamant during the fast, but the slow pressure of a restive populace mounting against them shook their nerve. They slowly lowered their guns in relief, but they knew Gandhi could do it all over again on some other issue if they did not make plans for leaving India.

The end of the war and the successful conquest of totalitarianism made British domination of the Indian people more odious to both countries. Further, the great strain on the British people and their armed forces during the war made the thought of further military struggles in India unacceptable. But it was Gandhi's fast in 1943 that really broke the back of British rule. They had met his resolute will head-on, and they knew he would never tire in the struggle. Many more negotiations over the details and arguments of partition were to come, but the basic issue was decided.

On May 6, 1944, Gandhi was released from prison, but other Congress leaders were held until June 1945 by an act of Lord Wavell, the new viceroy. The long struggle between the desire of the Moslems under Mohammed Jinnah for a separate nation and Gandhi's strong desire for a united India now began. In the end, Nehru and the other Indian leaders accepted partition. On February 20, 1947, Prime Minister Clement Attlee announced that Great Britain would quit India not later than June 1948 and Lord (Admiral Louis) Mountbatten would be the last viceroy for India.

The transfer of power did not come easily. Many riots erupted, particularly in the Punjab where Hindu-Moslem antagonism was particularly strong. Gandhi was grieved by this fighting between two major groups from whom he had drawn his friends all his life. He spent much of his time condemning Hindu brutality to Moslems, even though he was frequently warned in person, by mail, and by telegram not to condemn his "own people." Within India, Gandhi had no separate group that he called his own.

Death

Gandhi's persistence in his religious beliefs, while refusing to be identified with any one religious group, aroused the antagonism of many Hindus. A group of young men, who had witnessed the shooting of Hindus in the Punjab and who were angered by Gandhi's demands of recompense for Hindu atrocities with no comparable demand from the Moslems, resented his influence and feared he would weaken the position of all Hindus. Gandhi was aware that this group might assassinate him, but on January 13, 1948 he commenced a fast in Delhi to obtain redress against the injury to Moslems in that city. He remarked, "I do not want to die . . . of a creeping paralysis of my faculties—a defeated man. An assassin's bullet may put an end to my life. I would welcome it. . . .[38]

Trotsky, who was suffering from high blood pressure at the end of his life, made a remarkably similar statement before his assassination. Both men may have wished for the end. Both feared a slow decline of their faculties.

The end came for Gandhi on January 30, 1948, at the age of seventy-nine, as he walked toward the wooden platform on the New Delhi prayer ground. A thirty-five year-old Brahman, Nathuram Vinayak Godse, a member of the dissident group of Hindus sworn to kill Gandhi, elbowed his way through the crowd and fell to his knees a few feet in front of the mahatma. He fired three shots, striking Gandhi in the abdomen and chest. "Hey Rama" (Oh God), cried Gandhi as he fell to the ground. His followers cradled his head in their arms and carried him to his room in Birla House, but he was dead before he arrived.

The Problem of Power and Nonviolence

The problem of leading a revolution and remaining nonviolent is brought into sharp focus by the case of Gandhi, because he was set upon a course of both nonviolence and victory over a military power. It is possible to remain nonviolent when one is only leading sporadic protests against government injustice. But when one tries to dislodge a formidable military power like the British Empire from a nation the size of India, it seems to me that violence or the threat of violence is inevitable.

I do not believe it diminishes the quality of Gandhi's achievement to say that his actions were very physically threatening to the British, whether he conceived them in that light or not. I find myself in agreement with Lord Linlithgow that, when it came to a choice between the strict principles of *Satyagraha* and a fast "against" the British, Gandhi chose the latter. After all, his goal in life was, first of all, to drive the British out of India. Being a good *Satyagrahi* was very important, but it was clearly in second place. It was his chosen method of attack, but he was not a man to become obsessed with a method or with the issue of consistency. When the crisis of choice arrived, the courage of combat was a more important virtue to him than the principle of *Satyagraha*. There is no doubt in my mind that Gandhi would rather be remembered for his courage than for his moral goodness.

Even if it had not been for his threatening fast, the total thrust of his mobilization of the people, the emotional content of his call to "do or die," and the extent to which he worked closely with other more violent members of the Congress party makes it clear that Gandhi forced the British out of India, in part, by the physical threat that he might lose control of the masses or that he might die in a fast after he had worked them into a white heat of anger.

In the last analysis it becomes difficult to distinguish between physical and moral strength. Gandhi sought moral strength; he sought the love and respect of the Indian people of all faiths; he sought to make the people aware of the injustice of their condition and raise their moral indignation. He believed that this indignation would eventually convince the British of the injustice of their position and force them to leave India for moral reasons. One could contrast this attitude of Gandhi with that of the British and say that the British, who were concerned with physical force, left India because they were afraid for their lives. But this interpretation is not strictly true either. The power of an army comes from its weapons, but also from its morale, as we Americans have learned to our dismay in Vietnam. Even the hard-nosed professional soldier must believe that his cause has some element of justice or he cannot continue to fight with the same fervor. The impossible moral position of the British in India began to infect the soldier and the viceroy, finally working its way back to the seat of empire itself. The British quit India, in part, out of a physical fear for their lives, but they quit primarily because they were defeated morally by one of the world's greatest experts in the use of moral force.

NOTES

1. E. Victor Wolfenstein, *The Revolutionary Personality: Lenin, Trotsky, Gandhi* (Princeton: Princeton University Press, 1971), 76.

2. Ibid., 76–77.

3. Erik H. Erikson, *Gandhi's Truth: On the Origins of Militant Nonviolence* (New York: W. W. Norton, 1969), 402–03.

4. Shri Pyarelal, *Mahatma Gandhi*, vol. 1 (Ahmedabad: Navajivan, 1965), 12.

5. Mohandas K. Gandhi, *An Autobiography: The Story of My Experiments with Truth* (Boston: Beacon, 1957), 27.

6. Ibid., 27.

7. Pyarelal, *Mahatma Gandhi*, 192.

8. Ibid., 192–93.

9. Gandhi, *Autobiography*, 31.

10. Wolfenstein, *The Revolutionary Personality*, 87.

11. Gandhi, *Autobiography*, 114.

12. Ibid., 125

13. Ibid., 134.

14. Ibid., 137–38.

15. Ibid., 139.

16. Ibid., 140.

17. Leon Trotsky, *My Life: Leon Trotsky* (New York: Grosset and Dunlap, 1930), 295.

18. Gandhi, *Autobiography*, 150.

19. Erikson, *Gandhi's Truth*, 368–76.

20. Gandhi, *Autobiography*, 220.

21. Ibid., 221.

22. Ibid., 277–78.

23. Ibid., 342.

24. Erikson, *Gandhi's Truth*, 70–110.

25. Mohandas K. Gandhi, *The Collected Works of Mahatma Gandhi*, vol. xiv (Ahmedabad: Navjivan Trust, 1965), 439.

26. Gandhi, *Collected Works*, vol. 14, 485.

27. Ibid., 474–78.

28. Ibid., 504.

29. Mohandas K. Gandhi, *Selected Works of Mahatma Gandhi*, edited by Shriman Narayan, vol. 5 (Ahmedabad: Navajivan, 1968), 269.

30. Ibid., 270.

31. Francis G. Hutchins, *India's Revolution: Gandhi and the Quit India Movement* (Cambridge: Harvard University Press, 1973), 279.

32. Ibid., 203.

33. Gandhi, *Selected Works*, vol. 5, 286–89.

34. Ibid., 294.

35. Ibid., 295.

36. Ibid., 298.

37. D. G. Tendulkar, *Mahatma: Life of Mohandas Karamchand Gandhi*, vol. 8 (Bombay: Vithalbhai K. Jhaveri and D. G. Tendulkar, 1953), 244–49.

38. Pyarelal, *Mahatma Gandhi*, vol. 1, book two, 202.

Chapter 6

KARL MARX:
Romantic Origins

The Aggressive Revolutionary

Until now we have directed our study to those revolutionaries with gentle dispositions and trusting attitudes toward others. Some, such as Rousseau, had a distinctly submissive, even a masochistic, approach to human relationships. Others maintained a position of equality or even leadership among their friends, while openly courting punishment from the authorities. They were proud of their suffering and seemed to gain a certain satisfaction from it.

With Karl Marx the picture changes sharply. Marx was an aggressive and domineering personality in most of his relationships (although his children did not see him in this light). Like the theorists of revolution who preceded him, he looked forward to a society that would be governed by a new position for the working person. But unlike many who saw this change coming about through education (Tolstoy, Sun Yat-sen) or through a new style in human relationships with authority (Rousseau, Kropotkin, Gandhi), Marx believed that actual participation in revolution was the only means of bringing about this alteration of consciousness on a mass scale. It was only in the process of revolution that the revolutionary class could rid itself of the prerevolutionary consciousness.

The young Karl Marx exhibited a vision of sacrifice and martyrdom but he gradually lost his joy in suffering when he saw the pain that his way of life inflicted upon his family.

Childhood and Youth

Karl Marx was born in the ancient Roman town of Trier in the Rhineland, on May 5, 1818. Karl was the oldest living son among nine children, his older brother having died the year after Karl's birth. He had an older sister, Sophie, and two other surviving younger sisters. The other children died in childhood of tuberculosis.

Karl's father, Heinrich, was the son of the rabbi of Trier, and his mother, Henrietta, was the daughter of a Dutch rabbi. Despite this strong Jewish background, there is little evidence of a sense of Jewish identification in either Karl or his father. Heinrich left his parents early in his career. He became a

Protestant in order to practice law and escape the state restrictions against Jews in this profession.[1] At the time of his baptism, he changed his name from Heschel to Heinrich. David McLellan[2] describes him as a liberal attached to the ideas of the eighteenth-century French rationalists.

Karl Marx was also baptized a Christian. In his early compositions on religion, such as his school leaving examination at the local high school,[3] young Karl did make a number of references to the special virtues of Christianity, as opposed to the earlier stoic philosophy and the harsh theory of duty of the "heathen peoples."[4] However, this was in the context of a special paper on religion. When he had an opportunity to choose his own topic, he selected "Reflections of a Young Man on the Choice of a Profession." Here his concept of God was a more vague and pietistic "Deity." This early essay revealed the intensity of what was to become the major goal of his life—his desire to help humanity. This goal had a strong "religious" element. Jerrold Siegel felt Marx was drawn to the life of the intellect as a life of sacrifice.[5] Youthful idealism and the striving for personal virtue are striking features of this essay by Marx:

> History calls those men greatest who have ennobled themselves by working for the common good. Experience regards as most happy the one who has made the most people happy. Religion itself teaches that the ideal being, after whom everyone aspires, sacrificed himself for mankind and who would dare to disavow such pronouncements?
>
> If we have chosen a situation in which we can most of all work for mankind, burdens cannot depress us because they are only sacrifices for all. Then we experience no petty, limited egotistic joy, but our happiness belongs to millions, our deeds will live on quietly, but always influential and the shining tears of noble men will fall on our ashes.[6]

While his father encouraged Karl in his early striving for personal virtue, the romantic attachment to a life of sacrifice was stimulated by the Baron Johann Ludwig von Westphalen, a close friend of the family. Although he was an important figure in the local government of Trier, the Baron was more interested in books than in government. His own son, Edgar, was not much of a scholar and rather a disappointment to his father. When he discovered the sharp intellect and the eagerness to learn in young Karl, he took a special interest in the boy. The two of them went for long walks together discussing literature, politics, and romantic poetry. Like Karl's father, the Baron was a liberal. He was well-read in Goethe, Schiller, Lessing, and the socialism of Saint-Simon. It was perhaps in these early conversations and his subsequent readings that Marx developed his strong desire for heroic sacrifice. His favorite figures were Don Quixote, Faust, and, above all, Prometheus. In his doctoral dissertation, which he dedicated to his "dear fatherly friend, Ludwig von Westphalen," he concluded the preface with the statement, "Prometheus is the noblest saint and martyr in the philosophical calendar."[7] Marx had already developed a deep skepticism toward all religions, but his reverence for saints and martyrs remained undimmed.

But it was not only the saintliness of Prometheus that Marx emphasized in his preface, he also noted his hero's hatred of gods. This aspect of Prometheus reveals the emergence of a second, more diabolical, element in Marx. Robert Payne stresses Marx's identification with Lucifer and points to the destructive theme in his poetry. He describes one of Marx's early poems, "The Player," as that of a satanic violinist who, "is clearly Lucifer or Mephistopheles, and what he is playing with such frenzy is the music which accompanies the end of the world. It is a thoroughly unpleasant poem. . . ."[8]

Payne captures the diabolical element in Marx but seems to have missed the duality of Marx's character. Marx was both creative and destructive. He derived a sadistic pleasure from attack, from the merciless, step-by-step, verbal dismemberment of his enemies. He was prepared to destroy the capitalist system and he could take a genuine delight in contemplating this destruction. But he also saw himself as a saint and martyr who sacrificed himself for the poor, the weak, and the helpless. We are reminded here of Carl Jung's finding that in order to achieve completeness, man must develop to the full his capacities for both good and evil.

If Marx was attracted to destruction, he was equally aroused by any stimulating idea. His greatest pleasure was having his mind in a state of full excitement, and he was fascinated by the idea that he could excite others or frighten them with words and ideas. In his "Notebooks on Epicurean Philosophy," he used three vertical lines in the margin (an unusual degree of emphasis for him) to highlight the following quotation: "The climax of thought (in regard to pleasure) is discovering exactly those questions (and those questions related to them) which cause the greatest fear [*Ängste*] in the mind."[9]

Marx, given his temperament and tastes, seemed destined to clash with the calmness and routine of conventional morality. A number of his early poems suggest that he sensed this coming conflict from the beginning of his intellectual development. It is as though he had drunk some poison that made him forever different and apart from others. He must end his own life or destroy the world. Here is one example among many.

Feelings . . .

I am caught in endless strife,
Endless ferment, endless dream;
I cannot conform to Life,
Will not travel with the stream

Heaven I would comprehend,
I would draw the world to me;
Loving, hating, I intend
That my star shine brilliantly . . .

Worlds I would destroy forever,
Since I can create no world,
Since my call they notice never,
Coursing dumb in magic whirl . . .[10]

Another element in this early poetry is longing for love, a great overwhelming and dramatic love for which he would give his life. The love poems have the same world-destroying force as his other poetry. Almost without exception, the hero (and sometimes the heroine as well) dies at the end. There is great tension, bloodshed, and misunderstanding for the hero. His love is fulfilled only in death.[11] The cause of death varies, but it is always violent: suicide, poison, conflict.[12] Sometimes the hero dies without any apparent cause except the extremity of his emotion.

Karl and Jenny

The desperation and hopelessness of these love poems is better understood if we recall that Marx saw himself as a misunderstood outcast of society, one who could find no comfort or compatibility in the ordinary woman. Only someone very special would do, someone who shared his own iconoclastic views, someone attracted not only by his heroism, but by the demon within him. In this respect he was indeed fortunate, for the Baron von Westphalen had a daughter, Jenny, four years older than Karl, who adored her father and who had been deeply influenced by the same romances and political ideas that Karl and her father had relished together. Jenny became a close friend of Sophie, Karl's older sister, and was soon introduced to Karl. At first they were playmates, but the friendship gradually ripened to love.

Karl both attracted and frightened Jenny. He had a similar effect on his sisters. He charmed them and bullied them at the same time. He loved Jenny fiercely, but he doubted that any woman could long remain with an outcast from society. He identified himself as an outcast from his early years, perhaps, in part, because he did not belong to either the Jewish or the Catholic community. He was constantly torn by doubts about Jenny. Could her undoubted love for him last in the face of what she might have to endure? If he lost her, there would be no other like her. She was unique, as though trained for him by her father. Tortured by these fears, he accused her of losing interest and demanded more attention. He doubted she could continue to love him and remain faithful.[13] She did her best to reassure him, but she was upset by his anger and always afraid he might do something desperate and dramatic. Their courtship was a stormy one, complicated by Karl's imminent departure from Trier after his graduation from the local high school to study at the University of Bonn. Before he left, Jenny and Karl arrived at an understanding that they would be married as soon as he was established in a profession.

Marx began his studies at the University of Bonn in 1835. He was already predisposed toward the romantic outlook and soon imbibed the atmosphere around him. He joined a "poetry club" in which the discussion centered as much on socialism as poetry. The club had connections with other organizations considered subversive by the government, and was under constant police observation. He also joined a tavern club composed primarily of students from Trier.

Members of the tavern club frequently engaged in street fights and duels with young Prussian aristocrats of the Borussia-Korps. Karl was wounded over the left eye in one of these duels. He took to carrying a pistol and was arrested in Cologne when it was found in his possession. The authorities in Cologne sent word of his arrest to the university, and Karl was close to expulsion for several weeks.

All of this activity disturbed his father. After two semesters at Bonn, it was decided Karl should move to the University of Berlin where an interest in science dominated the academic life, standards were more severe, and dueling was frowned upon. Before his departure he returned to Trier where he and Jenny became formally engaged.

The continued separation was a severe strain on both Jenny and Karl, as well as on Karl's father who tried to serve as an intermediary. Their letters indicate frequent misunderstandings accompanied by doubt, insecurity, and longing. Jenny had been raised with the traditional attitudes toward virginity, but she was also a warm-hearted and very emotional young woman and she was torn by conflict over his passionate declaration. In a letter she tells him:

> A girl's love is different from that of a man, it cannot but be different. A girl, of course, cannot give a man anything but love and herself and her person, just as she is, quite undivided and forever. In ordinary circumstances, too, the girl must find her complete satisfaction in the man's love, she must forget everything in love. But Karl, think of my position, you have no regard for me, you do not trust me. And that I am not capable of retaining your present romantic youthful love, I have known from the beginning, and deeply felt, long before it was explained to me so coldly and wisely and reasonably. Oh, Karl, what makes me miserable is that what would fill any other girl with inexpressible delight—your beautiful, touching, passionate love, the indescribably beautiful things you say about it, the inspiring creations of your imagination—all this only causes me anxiety and often reduces me to despair. The more I were to surrender myself to happiness, the more frightful would my fate be if your ardent love were to cease and you became cold and withdrawn.[14]

Jenny had an unusual intelligence and perception, but she believed she had only one thing she could offer Karl—her body. If she offered it too soon, he could grow tired of her before their marriage. She worried that she had not given enough and she was afraid she might give too much. She wanted to read, to expand her knowledge, not only so Karl would be proud of her, but for her own inner development. But Karl unsettled her so that she could not read through a page without her mind wandering all over the place so she forgot what she was reading. What did he think of her? He was so brilliant. His mind flashed from one idea to the next, tearing aside the veil of convention and seeing the world as it really existed. Why could she not tell him some of her thoughts? How could he love such a scatterbrain? The awful part of it was that she could laugh and tease with some of the men her father invited to their home, but she felt tongue-tied when she tried to talk to Karl. He was so dreadfully passionate and serious that she was afraid to be flippant with him.[15]

She was also fearful that Karl, with his passionate temperament, would rush into the arms of some other woman or that, in despair from his unfulfilled love, he would bring about some great calamity. Karl did nothing to allay these fears. If anything, he accentuated them. The poems he sent to her were filled with the yearning of a hero expiring for love, or they were violent, mad declamations against the heavens, the gods, and all who held power.

When Karl was away Jenny would sometimes turn to his father for advice. Before the approval of her family was obtained, Heinrich had to pass on Karl's letter to Jenny. Heinrich advised her to the best of his ability. He urged her not to take Karl's ravings too seriously and warned Karl that he did not fully realize the extent of Jenny's sensitivity and the degree to which he could upset her. But Karl enjoyed frightening others, even, perhaps especially, such "good" people as his mother, his father, Jenny, and their friends. He did not really want to make them fearful, but he did enjoy dominating others and fear was an important element in all his relationships. Any "right" that he was to uphold must be one worthy of a struggle and those who loved him must face the dangers along the way.

So he frightened Jenny and she could not help betraying her fear to his father. But she immediately tried to reassure Heinrich as soon as the older man became aware of it. Jenny loved Karl, in part, *because* he frightened her. She called him *"Schwarzwildchen,"* not only because he had a dark complexion and black hair, but because she was excited by his diabolical characteristics. She teased and goaded him with suggestions of her own thoughts about him, which he thought he knew but which, she assured him, he would really learn about after they were married. [16] In other letters she became even more suggestive, remarking that she really did not want to thwart his "wicked intentions" *(boswilligen absichten),* and if he were close to her she could not help but yield to him. [17]

Nowadays we would call Karl Marx a male chauvanist, but Jenny played into his fantasies perfectly. They were both products of a culture that regarded true masculinity as a kind of fierce, almost sadistic, domination and true femininity as pleasure in submission. Jenny's fears of Karl were, then, partly play-acting. She knew that he liked to play bully-boy and she delighted in gasping with wonder at his bold ideas and trembling at his anger. Later, when he was the terror of Europe and in frequent danger of arrest, she could not understand why the authorities were so cruel and unjust to him. Certainly, he was a devil in his way, but a charming devil, and all of his efforts were directed toward the good of humanity. For Jenny, at least in the early days of their relationship, the diabolical element in Karl was not diabolical at all, but a kind of mischevious sexiness.

In his letters from the university, Karl alarmed his father by his open confession of his high expectations and his sudden, world-shaking despair. He had a strong desire to enlist the sympathy of others and to play the fallen hero. He would plunge into work, exhaust himself and then become ill. Heinrich was angered by what he called Karl's "sickly sensitivity."[18] He believed that men might undergo distress and agony but should not take pleasure in such suffering. This was a kind of self-indulgence and self-pity unworthy of a man.

He had no doubt of Karl's ability but he was concerned by the boy's sensitivity and "self-love." Karl would plunge into grief over imaginary troubles, and seemed to long for some great calamity so he could suffer heroically. While Heinrich knew his son had a tendency to exaggeration, he could not escape being caught up occasionally in Karl's melodrama.

Heinrich's letters urged Karl to be strong, but tender; to have a pure, human heart, but to abolish all sickly sensitivity. A man should protect and comfort the weak, but show no weakness himself. He would only frighten those who depend on him and relied on his strength if he let them see his moments of grief and his "shattered heart." Heinrich sought to model Karl after a Prussian image of masculinity—the image he presented to the world. To find pleasure in suffering or to seek suffering as a way of life was a form of self-pity, a sickly sensitivity from which the youth was expected to recover. For the outside world, then, Marx adopted the stance of a fighter. In a parlor game called "Confessions," which he played many years later, he gave the following account of himself (abbreviated):

Your favorite virtue	Simplicity
Your favorite virtue in man	Strength
Your favorite virtue in woman	Weakness
Your chief characteristic	Singleness of purpose
Your idea of happiness	To fight
Your idea of misery	Submission[19]

To accept suffering as his lot, to "submit" to it, was weak and feminine. To be a man was to attack. Many accounts of Marx place him in this combative stance. Karl Schurz described him as follows:

> Marx's utterances were indeed full of meaning, logical and clear, but I have never seen a man whose bearing was so provoking and intolerable. To no opinion which differed from his own did he accord the honor of even condescending consideration. Everyone who contradicted him he treated with abject contempt; every argument that he did not like he treated either with biting scorn at the unfathomable ignorance that had prompted it, or with opprobrious aspersions on the motives of him who advanced it. I remember most distinctly the cutting disdain with which he pronounced the word *bourgeois* . . .[20]

One could count numerous similar descriptions by people who knew him as a public figure or a co-worker, for he could be equally virtriolic with those who opposed capitalism but disagreed with him on the tactics of the moment. However, there was another side to Marx. His father had urged him to be strong, but he had openly displayed his own affection for his son, even though he regarded it as "weakness." He wanted Karl to be tough, but also capable of tenderness toward loved ones. To a large extent Marx managed to live with this dual image of masculinity. He could be gentle with women and children, and even other men who acknowledged his superiority. He was extremely indulgent with his own children, and they seemed to have had no fear of him. While he was trying to work on *Capital* in his study, his children would harness him as a horse and "whip him up," as part of their games. He was like a lion who would let his own cubs maul him about, but was constantly wary and suspicious if a strange male entered his territory. Marx took the world for his territory and all males were potential aggressors.

Rebellion

In the fall of 1836, Karl set out for Berlin University, pained by his departure from an ailing Jenny and somewhat unsettled by the thought of unknown professors and students awaiting him. He plunged into his studies and had little contact with his fellow students. Gradually he developed an acute anxiety about his direction in life and his own ideas. He seemed lost, unable to pull things together. Suddenly, everything fell into place and he acquired a new way of looking at the world. Marx regarded this period as a turning point in his life. It represented, in some respects, a resolve to harden himself against weakness and sensitivity according to the wishes of his father. But it was also a rebellion against the older man, another outbreak of the kind of extravagant sensitivity Heinrich despised, and it ended with the enthronement of another father-figure, Georg Wilhelm Hegel, the guide to his future. Marx described the incident and the events leading up to it in a long letter to his father written over a year after his arrival in Berlin. It was a letter that he must have known would be upsetting to Heinrich in many ways. It is full of projects that have been undertaken and abandoned. It paints the picture of a youth pushing his intellectual studies to the point of illness and drifting into intellectual disorder, tendencies Heinrich had warned him against more than once. But it is also a very long letter in which he opens his mind completely to his father, shares all his ideas with him, invites his criticism, and begs to come home.[21]

This incident has many of the elements that Abraham Maslow has described in his concept of the "peak experience." Marx was filled with a kind of "madness," an ecstacy; but unlike Rousseau, who wept tears of joy over a similar experience, he could not simply give himself up to his feelings and thoughts. He was angry at being delivered to the "enemy," which is the way he regarded Hegel at the time. It was characteristic of Marx that he fought anything that threatened to control him and remake his life along different lines. He had a passion for control and domination. If there was a change to be made, he wanted to make it himself. Yet the sense of conversion, of being forced to give up his will to some higher consciousness, is evident in his account and, even though he reacted to it with anger, there was also apparently an outbreak of the kind of universal love that made him want to embrace every loafer in Berlin.

Marx had reached a crisis in his identity. He was disturbed by his own disorganization. A way of looking at life that seemed to make sense one day was all wrong the next. He was not sure what he was to stand for and what he would believe. Hegel was in vogue at the time, but Karl's conversion represented more than the mere acceptance of a popular hero. His attraction to the philosopher had a strong emotional component; something in Hegel pulled Karl like a magnet. It was Hegel's quality of perceiving things as a whole, of taking the largest possible world-view of all problems that Karl admired and aspired to achieve himself. Always contemptuous of minor conflicts and superficial problems, Marx's early essays and youthful poetry reflected his belief that his battle must be of major import, unconcerned with the narrow and parochial problems of a region. It must be a battle for the whole world or the very soul of humanity.

Marx was striving for the godhead, seeking to emulate Prometheus. But instead of snatching fire from the gods, he would perform some gigantic feat with his intellect, something to shake the earth and the heavens. To achieve this Olympian stance it was necessary to surpass all wisdom that smacked of a national or a cultural bias. Marx was always seeking some deeper, more profound understanding of some phenomenon that had a ready explanation in the academic and intellectual world of his time. Hegel seemed to provide the style and the approach for this task.

The Lure of Politics

Marx's relationship with Jenny continued throughout his struggle for his own identity. Jenny gained considerable maturity while Karl finished his work at the university and her parents further considered her marriage. She grew confident of Karl's love for her. Her letters were filled with hope, with descriptions of her love for him and her efforts to expand her own mind through further education.

Marx obtained his doctorate in April 1841 from the University of Jena, where he sent his thesis to avoid the longer process in Berlin. At first, he hoped to obtain a position as a lecturer, but he was disillusioned when his friend, Bruno Bauer, was fired from his teaching position for his unorthodox ideas. Marx's own liberal ideas soon led him to political activity and finally to journalism. Meanwhile, both Karl and Jenny were anxious to be married. His awakening interest in politics had brought back some of Jenny's old fears for her *"Schwarzwildchen."* She was afraid he would do something wild that would destroy not only his relationship with her parents, but also his own chances for a career.

After the death of his father in 1838, Karl and his mother did not get along well. He wanted money to marry and begin his career in journalism. His mother, angry at his refusal to take a government job or look for a university appointment, would not have him use good money to support a radical journal. She stopped his allowance and prevented him from receiving his share of his father's estate.

Through the influence of his friend Moses Hess, a communist of the French school, Marx began to write for the *Rheinische Zeitung*. When the alcoholism of the editor became a serious problem, Marx was given the job. He proved to be a sharp critic and a capable writer. When the paper was accused of communism because of the articles of Hess, Marx denied the charges and criticized communism as a philosophy. When the paper was suspended because of its liberal stand, he developed a plan with Arnold Ruge to work on a new journal which, at Marx's urging, was called the *Deutsch-französische Jahrbücher.* It was to be published in Strasbourg where Marx hoped to get some French contributors and develop a journal that was truly international in its scope and viewpoint. Marx was an internationalist before he became a communist. He was not sure just what he wanted to say, but he did know that he wanted to say it to the world. To do this, he needed a journal with an international following. He also wanted the widest possible range of ideas represented and he sought contributions from Moses Hess, the sentimental communist, Bakunin, the anarchist, and from a number of socialist writers.

The Jewish Question

Marx was anxious to start the new journal, for his position as one of the editors would enable him to marry Jenny. In March 1843 he wrote to Ruge concerning the intensity of his love and his anger at being prevented from marrying Jenny. [22] The chief opposition within Jenny's family came from her stepbrother, Ferdinand, who held a government post in Trier. The opposition within his own family came from his mother, who had felt snubbed by the von Westphalens after Heinrich's death and who was still withholding the funds Karl needed for a wedding.

Jenny had finally reconciled herself to Karl's political activity, but she was still deeply tied to the Rhineland and felt uneasy about the plan to publish the new journal in Strasbourg. Again, the fear arose that Karl might be doing something irrevocable that might cut them off forever from their friends, family, and homeland. In a letter from Kreuznach she remarked:

> This evening I had a tiny little idea about Strasbourg. Would you not be forbidden to return home if you betrayed Germany to France in this way, and is it not possible that the Liberal Sovereignty will also instruct you: "Emigrate then or remain away, if you are not comfortable in my states." Well, that is all, as I have said, just an idea, and Father Ruge will probably know what should be done, especially when a private little bird like this lurks in the background and comes out with a separate petition. [23]

But the decision was worse than she had feared. Marx and Ruge finally determined that Paris would be an even better location for their new journal; it was a genuinely international city and a place more likely to yield contributors. The decision to leave the Rhineland ended Jenny's resistance; she prepared herself for the inevitable separation from family and friends and soon professed herself as uncomfortable with the bourgeois life as was Karl.

The family resistance to their marriage continued on both sides. When Karl and Jenny were finally married in a Protestant ceremony in Kreutznach, June 19, 1843, the only family members present were Jenny's mother and brother Edgar.

Karl began his editing and writing for the *Deutsch-französische Jahrbücher* from Kreuznach where he remained for a while after the marriage with Jenny and her mother. He and Jenny finally arrived in Paris in October 1843 when Jenny was four months pregnant.

In November 1842, Bruno Bauer, Marx's friend from the Doctor's Club in Berlin, had written an article on the Jewish problem in the old *Deutsche Jahrbücher.* For several months, Marx, now a confirmed atheist, had been preparing some notes of his own on the same topic. As editor of the new *Deutsche-französische Jahrbücher* in Paris, he decided that a lengthy review of Bauer's work would be the best way of bringing out his own views on the subject. In an earlier article for the *Rheinische Zeitung,* he had become occupied for the first time with economic issues while defending those who had been prosecuted for "thefts" of dead wood from the land of the wealthy. He was already deeply identified with the poor and the oppressed. In his reply to Bauer's article, Marx demonstrated one of his most significant characteristics as a writer. He sought to look at his subject from the largest possible view. What was the world-significance of the Jewish question, in the light of history, politics, and human freedom? Bauer, he felt, had taken a rather narrow approach in terms of the persecution of the Jews. But what did the Jew signify for society? How did he fit into the total socioeconomic picture? In answering these questions, Marx was clearly influenced by the anti-Semitism of his time. But it is significant that he centered his attack on one particular element of the Jewish stereotype: the accumulation of capital. His identification with the poor, in his article on the theft of wood, had already placed him in a position of strong hostility to those who had money, were clever in manipulating money, and were greedy for more money.

In his article, "On the Jewish Question," he linked together Jewishness and moneymaking as common threats to social justice.

> We are trying to break with the theological formulation of the question. For us, the question of the Jews' emancipation is transformed into the question: what specific *social* element has to be overcome in order to abolish Judaism? For the capacity of the present-day Jew to emancipate himself is found in the relation of Judaism to the present day world. This relationship necessarily results from the special position of Judaism in the modern enslaved world.
>
> Let us consider the real worldly Jew, not the *Sabbath Jew,* as Bauer does, but the everyday Jew.
>
> Let us not seek the secret of the Jew in his religion, but let us seek the secret of his religion in the real Jew.
>
> What is the worldly basis of Judaism? *Practical* need, self-interest.
>
> What is the worldly cult of the Jew? *Huckstering.* What is his worldly God? *Money.*
>
> Very well! Then in emancipating itself from huckstering and from money, and thus from real, practical Judaism our age would emancipate itself. [24]

Though there is clearly anti-Semitism here, Marx is doing more than merely repeating the anti-Semitic cliches of his time. He is attempting to show that this same kind of huckstering has become the social style for the modern world. The

Jew, he says, has emancipated himself, not by acquiring money, but because money has become, through his influence, a world power. The Jew, then, is already emancipated, in the sense that Christians have become Jews.[25]

Since the question is not really theological, why bring the Jew into the argument at all. Having made his point, why does he not go on to examine the role of money in the modern world? He seems to have a special need to worry that bone of Judaism and its special relationship to money.

> Money is the jealous god of Israel, before which no other god may exist. Money degrades all the gods of mankind—and transforms them into commodities. . . .
> Money is the alienated essence of man's work, and this alien essence dominates him and he worships it.
> The god of the Jews has been secularized and has become the god of this world. The bill of exchange is the real god of the Jew.[26]

Anti-Semitism in the Jew has often been regarded as a form of self-hatred.[27] However, we cannot simply assume that this dynamic applies to Marx. He was baptized a Christian, his father having converted to Christianity before his birth. While he cannot have escaped the anti-Semitism of his time, his own Jewish identification—as well as that of his father—was never strong. It is not as though he sought to curry favor from the dominant majority by turning against an earlier, childhood identification of himself as a Jew. Marx was never afraid of being different. One could almost say that Marx *invited* the hostility of the dominant majority. Further, he did not really set out to avoid any association with the Jewish community. When the head of the Jewish community in Cologne visited him in March 1843 to ask for his help in preparing a petition for the Jews to the provincial assembly he was quite willing to do it, "no matter how much I dislike the Jewish faith."[28]

The Jewish stereotype has many facets. A person motivated by self-hatred would avoid this stereotype *in all its aspects*. Intellectualism has been both praised and condemned as a Jewish trait. Jews are called learned and scholarly by their friends and bookish and hair-splitting by their detractors. The same is true of internationalism as an aspect of the Jewish stereotype. People who approve of this trait call it cosmopolitanism and worldly sophistication. Those who disapprove refer to it as a lack of loyalty, unpatriotic behavior, even immorality. The Jews are "the people of the book," and Marx accepted his own bookishness, freely admitting that one of his favorite occupations was "bookworming."[29] The same was true of his internationalism. It was a point of pride with him that he saw things from a world perspective and not from the narrow confines of a religious doctrine, or from a national or cultural viewpoint. He was not concerned that his internationalism might be described as "Jewish" because of his background.

But his attitude toward money and money manipulation was different. This, he felt, *was* a Jewish trait and *not* an aspect of himself. If a non-Jew pressed him hard for a debt he was annoyed at the *person*. If he became entangled in a financial conflict with a Jew or even a person of Jewish origin like himself, the whole matter took on a different meaning for him. His sudden anger at Ferdinand Lassalle, whom he called a "Jewish-nigger" in a letter to Engels, [30] is a good example of this attitude. Lassalle made a display of his money which Marx could barely tolerate, but he also attached too many strings to a proposed contract when Marx asked him for a loan, and then finally reneged altogether.

What is the source of this peculiar and intense anger at the Jew as a manipulator of money? Certainly the European culture of his time provides much support for such an attitude. But Marx seemed to feel, in some way, that it was his own discovery. He had taken possession of it as though it formed an important element in his own development.

In the earliest exchange of letters between Heinrich and Karl, one is struck by this conflict over the management of money. Karl seemed determined to place himself in a state of financial crisis. His father insisted that he keep a record of expenditure and prepare a budget. Karl accepted his father's advice in most areas of his behavior, but in this one he defied him. However, the defiance was never open. Unfortunately, most of Karl's letters to his father are missing. But the one that is available, along with his father's replies to it, strongly suggests that, while Karl sometimes complained about the pressure from the older man, he never implied that his father was wrong or unjust. Instead, he ignored all financial questions until he reached a crisis. Throughout Karl's years at the university, Heinrich always warned his son about the need for saving, frugality, and caution in money matters. Again and again we find, in the letters from the elder Marx, the statement that the funds for the month have already been spent; he can send no more. Karl should keep a record, make a budget, keep accurate accounts.

In his letters to his father, Karl spoke of his plans, his ideas, his sleepless nights, his dreams, and the torment in his soul. For pages, he jumped from one topic to another and back again without order or sequence, in a manner that irritated his father. He did not confront Heinrich directly on the issue of money. Instead, he responded by spending it and by a few irregular and inaccurate remarks in regard to his budget and his expenses. At times the replies of Heinrich seemed to epitomize that despised figure of Marx's later writing, the petty bourgeois. After a lengthy letter in which the young Marx poured out his ideas, feelings, and plans, Heinrich responded with directions for reducing the cost of postage on such bulky mail.

> If you send bulky letters by ordinary post, they are very expensive. The last one cost a taler. Parcels sent by express post are dear too, the last one also cost a taler.
>   If you want to write a great deal in future, then write on all possible sorts of subjects so that what we hear is much and varied. Let it mount up to form a parcel and send this by the luggage van. Do not be offended at this little remark about economy. [31]

But Karl *was* offended, although his dependent status made it difficult for him to complain directly at the time. Heinrich's last letter to him (with the exception of a brief postscript) contains the reminder that, "On one point, of course, transcendentalism is of no avail, and on that you have very wisely found fit to observe an aristocratic silence; I am referring to the paltry matter of money, the value of which for the father of a family you still do not seem to recognize. . . . Thus we are now in the fourth month of the law year and you have already drawn 280 talers. I have not yet earned that much this winter."[32]

His father's anger brought no known retort from Karl and no attempt at reform. In his leaving certificate from Berlin University (in 1841) three years after his father's death, there is the notation that he had been a good student, but had been sued for debt several times.[33] Despite the frequent interchange and discussion between Karl and his father, there is no indication that he was able to confront Heinrich on the issue of money management—either by protest (if he felt such protest justified) or by self-discipline (if he agreed with his father's complaints).

In fact, in later life he seems to lean over backward to avoid any resemblance to this despised trait of his parents. When Karl married Jenny, she received a gift of money from her mother. Karl and Jenny left the money in an open chest on the table. Anyone who called was invited to take what they needed; the chest was soon empty.[34] This incident occurred almost five years after the death of his father, but Karl was still reacting against what he regarded as Heinrich's stinginess and he was still feeling Henrietta's tight control of money. It was as though Karl was saying, 'I am not a money-hungry Jew like my parents. Money means nothing to me.'

Both Karl's parents aroused his antagonism about money management. While we have few of her letters, Henrietta Marx may have been more tight-fisted with money than Heinrich. Certainly this was a role she played in Marx's adult years. Marx's extravagance and his inability to manage money may have been a reaction to his mother's efforts to make of him a good Jewish boy, who managed his money and took care of his mother. She was the more Jewish member of the family in her interests, her late religious conversion, her use of Yiddish, and her closeness to her parents. Marx's reaction against "Jewish" money management may have been in large part a desire to stamp out those aspects of his mother that he found and despised in himself. It is possible that Karl was denying her role in his life when he linked Judaism with money-grubbing, but not with the intellectualism and internationalism that were characteristics of his father.

NOTES

1. David McLellan, *Karl Marx: His Life and Thought* (New York: Harper and Row, 1973), 4–8.

2. Ibid., 8–10.

3. Karl Marx and Friedrich Engels, *Werke*, vol. 1, supplement (Berlin: Dietz Verlag, 1968), 598–601.

4. Ibid., 598–601.

5. Jerrold E. Siegel, "Marx's Early Development: Vocation, Rebellion, Realism," *Journal of Interdisciplinary History* 3 (1972), 475–508.

6. Marx and Engels, *Werke*, vol. 1, supplement, 594.

7. Ibid., 263.

8. Robert Payne, *Marx: A Biography* (New York: Simon and Schuster, 1968).

9. Marx and Engels, *Werke*, vol. 1, supplement, 27.

10. Karl Marx and Friedrich Engels, *Collected Works*, vol. 1 (New York: International Publishers, 1975), 525–26.

11. Ibid., 570.

12. Ibid., 23.

13. Ibid., 695–97.

14. Ibid., 595–96. This letter was first published in Russian.

15. Ibid., 696–98.

16. Ibid., 698.

17. Marx and Engels, *Werke*, vol. 1, supplement, 644.

18. Marx and Engels, *Collected Works*, vol. 1, 674–75.

19. *Reminiscences of Marx and Engels* (Moscow: Foreign Language Publishing House), 268. From a manuscript by Marx's daughter, Laura.

20. McLellan, *Karl Marx*, 453. From *The Reminiscences of Karl Schurz* (London, 1909).

21. Marx and Engels, *Werke*, vol. 1, supplement, 3–8.

22. Marx and Engels, *Werke*, vol. 27, 417.

23. Marx and Engels, *Werke*, vol. 1, supplement, 644–45.

24. Ibid., 372.

25. Ibid., 373.

26. Ibid., 374–75.

27. Gordon W. Allport, *The Nature of Prejudice* (New York: Doubleday, 1958), 147–49. See also Kurt Levin, "Self-Hatred Among Jews," *Contemporary Jewish Record* 4 (1941): 219–32.

28. Marx and Engels, *Werke*, vol. 27, 418.

29. *Reminscences of Marx and Engles*, 250–51. From the notes of Marx's youngest daughter, Eleanor.

30. Marx and Engels, *Werke*, vol. 30, 257.

31. Marx and Engels, *Collected Works*, vol. 1, 666.

32. Ibid., 692.

33. Ibid., 704.

34. *Reminiscences of Marx and Engels*, 279. From a memoir by Franzisca Kugelmann.

Chapter 7

KARL MARX:
The Antagonism to Capitalism

The Break with Ruge

When Karl Marx and Arnold Ruge began to work together in Paris, a growing difference soon appeared between them. Although he had spent a period of confinement in the fortress of Kolberg and was refused a university post because of his support for a free Germany, Ruge was a man of independent means. He was respectable, polite, meticulous about his personal appearance, and even something of a prude. Marx remained the unkempt, disorderly, and debt-ridden scholar. He would become so absorbed in books and ideas that he ignored the world around him, including his study and his own personal appearance. He liked rich, highly seasoned food, caviar and black cigars. He would buy the things he wanted when he had the money, going without food, if necessary, when his funds were exhausted. His work habits were irregular. He would sometimes take off during the day and then work far into the night, sleeping in his clothes on the couch in his study and getting up to work again in his rumpled attire. His books lay about his study on tables and chairs, half-open, marked-up, with the corners of pages turned down. He smoked incessantly and dropped matches wherever he used them. His study was filled with forgotten pipes and half-smoked cigars.[1]

When Marx and Ruge joined a live-in community with other writers, as they did briefly in Paris, it seemed inevitable that their life-styles would clash. Moreover, Ruge's wife was a quiet domestic woman, quite unlike the lively, vivacious, and well-educated Jenny Marx. An open break occurred when Marx announced that he was a communist. This appears a rather sudden change from his article in the *Rheinische Zeitung* in which he would not even concede a "theoretical reality" to communist ideas,[2] but we also know that Marx had already been attracted to communist ideas through his association with Moses Hess. If one reads between the lines of his letters and articles on this subject, he appears to be interested in developing a *better form* of communism, rather than rejecting it entirely. Even in his early statement in the *Rheinische Zeitung,* he only opposed communist ideas *in their present form (Gestalt).* He did not simply dismiss these ideas, but proposed a thorough criticism through which he could examine them in more depth. Marx regarded the communism of his time as too confused, soft, and sentimental. He was really searching for something more radical and challenging. We must also remember that, in his newspaper article, he was speaking for publication and may have been wary of declaring himself openly as an exponent of a doctrine that was considered such a menace by the Prussian state.

In Paris he came in contact with a wide variety of writers and activists. Heinrich Heine visited Karl and Jenny daily for a time. He also met Louis Blanc and other French socialist writers. He talked with Proudhon and Bakunin—both of whom he later opposed. He may have precipitated the break with Ruge to escape all further strictures on his thought and writing, giving himself an opportunity to develop his own ideas.

The Meeting of Marx and Engels

"Jennychen," the first child of Karl and Jenny, was born May 1, 1844. She was rather sickly at first and Jenny visited her mother in Trier to show the child to her family and consult a doctor. It was during her absence that the historic meeting between Marx and Friedrich Engels took place.

Marx and Engels had met briefly once before, but at that time Engels was closely associated with the *Freien,* a group of Marx's former Berlin colleagues with whom Marx and Ruge had broken. Their first meeting did not come off well. Engels had been looking for direction and wanted to talk to everyone. His meeting with Moses Hess, shortly after his abortive visit to Marx, won him over to the cause of communism. On his second meeting with Marx, Engels was passing through Paris when Marx was alone looking for companionship. Engels' work was known to Marx. He had previously written several articles for the *Rheinische Zeitung* which Marx had admired. The two men talked for hours and enjoyed each other's company. They were struck by their complete agreement on so many important issues and decided on a collaboration that was to last the remainder of their lives.

They were of strikingly different temperaments and habits. Marx was a family man. When they had met in Berlin, Marx was a student at the university and Engels was a military cadet, proud of his appearance as a soldier. In a letter to his sister, he talked at great length about the colors, the piping, the shoulder straps, the shiny buttons, and the effect he created when he sat down in the front row at a poetry reading.[3]

Engels never lost his concern for his appearance and the effect it might have on the ladies. Among his friends, he gained a reputation as a womanizer, and had a number of affairs. He resisted marriage but for many years kept a mistress, Mary Burns, although the word "kept" is hardly appropriate as Mary worked to support herself. Engels was called "General" by his friends because of his interest in military strategy (the name was actually initiated by Marx's family). Paul Lafargue draws this picture of Engels in his middle years:

> Engels was as methodical as an old maid. He kept everything and registered it with the most scrupulous exactitude. . . . He worked quickly and without effort. In his large, well-lighted studies, whose walls were lined with bookcases, there was not a scrap of paper on the floor, and all the books were in their places with the exception of a dozen or so on his desk. The rooms were more like reception rooms than a scholar's study.
>
> He was just as particular about his appearance: he was always trim and scrupulously clean, always looking as though ready to go to a parade. . . . He was economical as far as his personal needs were concerned and incurred only such expenses as he deemed absolutely necessary, but his generosity toward the Party and his Party comrads when they applied to him in need knew no bounds. [4]

Unlike the relationship with Ruge, this difference in temperament and habits did not interfere with the relationship between Marx and Engels. Engels was profoundly impressed by Marx's education and intellect. He regarded Marx as a genius almost from their first meeting and looked up to him as to a father or an older brother. He copied some of Marx's mannerisms, particularly in his writing style, and developed some of the sarcasm and invective already evident in Marx's correspondence. But he was more than an imitator. Marx recognized in him an intelligence and a facility for expression that was far beyond his years and flattered the younger man by proposing that they write a book together.

While Marx and Engels were preparing their collaboration, Jenny was visiting in Trier. She still loved pretty clothes and it was important for her, as a source of personal pride, to keep up appearances. She had the same mercurial disposition that Karl found so attractive when he first met her. She would become radiant over the sight of a new cloak and Karl loved to buy things for her. She had an unlimited faith in his ability and she was sure he would turn the world upside down. But, as she was capable of a kind of ecstatic joy, she could also be plunged into despair by bad news or by a continued shortage of money. The financial pressures on them had begun to mount and, as Jenny left Paris for Trier to visit her mother and seek help for her sickly child, she had already developed certain fears about her future.

Jenny tried to put on a brave front. She had a new velvet cloak, a feathered hat, and a fine coiffure. For the first time, she felt that she looked more elegant than any of the visitors who called on the family. Jennychen began to improve with the help of a doctor and a wet nurse. But something about the stability, the flatness, and the changeless quality of life in Trier bothered her. Callers were impressed by her elegance, but kept talking about the importance of a steady income. They wondered how Karl was doing and if he would not perhaps finally accept a university post or a government job.

In Paris, surrounded by Karl and his friends who talked of the revolution as though it could begin any day, she had a sense of the great ferment in society, the imminence of change. She knew that Karl would help to bring about the crisis. She was sure he would also be a leader in the society that followed. But now that she was back home in Trier, it seemed that nothing had changed after all and no one really expected anything momentus to happen. Could she be wrong? Perhaps this great upheaval of society would come about more slowly than she had imagined. Oh, these asses (one of Karl's favorite words), couldn't they see the earthquake coming? But perhaps Jenny also wondered how long she could hold out in the face of this crush of convention, for she called out in her letter, "Oh, Karl, what you are going to do, do it soon."[5] It was as though she were asking him to destroy the conventional world before it engulfed her completely. Perhaps she sensed, in some way, the trials she was about to face, the long struggle ahead that would sap her strength, her youth, her health, and her sanity. The vague, ominous fears about their future, that she had felt before they were married, seemed to come back to her now that she was away from him. She felt that she might be punished some day for her attitude of confidence and cockiness toward the middle-class people of Trier. But in the end she brightened with her usual volatility and gave him a humourous critique of his writing style.[6]

New Economics

In Paris, Karl was indeed hard at work in his effort to shake the foundations of society. But he was not one who could dash off several pages in an hour, nor would he mount the barricades for a foolish and sudden attack against a society that was not ready for change. His approach was the slow, methodical, step-by-step preparation of a case against the capitalist system. He must have all the evidence first. The adult Karl Marx was a rare and peculiar combination of traits. He had the mind of a scholar and the fiery anger of a street fighter. He would not leave an idea until he felt that he understood it completely. He was an omnivorous reader, a self-confessed bookworm, swallowing everything he could get his hands on, preparing copious notes and sharpening his thinking by writing his own reaction to the things he read. He had already developed a high regard for the historical perspective and he was convinced that the revolutions of the past had failed because the people were not conscious of their rights and their power.

Too many writers, he thought, had merely reacted to events, to aspects of the system. When the event had passed, the cause was forgotten. What was needed was a comprehensive view of the whole unjust system—how it began, how it was perpetuated, and where it was leading. He must show that the injustices in Trier and Berlin were the same as those in Paris and London. He must go beyond the merely local incident and demonstrate the interrelationship of oppressive acts throughout the world. He must show the foolishness of overthrowing the government of one nation, when one was unprepared to overthrow all capitalist systems everywhere.

There were two important sources for these early works of Marx: his readings on economics and philosophy and his own emotional life. From April to August of 1844, Marx did most of the work on his "Economic and Philosophical Manuscripts," a title given to a collection of manuscripts which were never completed and not published until 1932. The importance of these manuscripts lies in their revelation of Marx's early thinking about economic and philosophical problems. These manuscripts reveal a Marx who was deeply concerned with humanism and moral questions. In his emphasis on man's *alienation* from himself, from the products of his labor, and from his fellowman through the process of capitalism; he initiated a theme that was to be found in a number of existentialist writers. This alienation came about, said Marx, because the capitalist had complete control over the means of production, including the utilization of labor. As a result, the object produced by the worker, which contained, in essence, his labor, was no longer his own. It could be stored by the capitalist and sold in the future, in competition with the worker's own labor. Thus the more the worker produced, the less he could possess. His labor, in the form of this object of his work, now stood as an *alien being,* a power independent of him.[7]

The manuscripts contained a developing philosophical embodiment of Marx's personal life-style. They were, in part, a justification for his own refusal to join the traditional society. Many of his early conflicts with his father had to do with his inability to handle money. He could never save it and was frequently forced to write desperate letters to his father long before a new supply of funds was due to arrive. In his Paris manuscripts Marx began to develop a rationalization for this behavior. It was characteristic of him that his approach to this problem took the form of an attack on saving rather than a justification of spending. Some of his lines sound like a belated answer to the scolding letters of his father—an answer he could not give while the old man was alive.

> Political economy [*Die National ökonomie*] the science of *wealth* is, there-fore, at the same time, the science of renunciation, of starvation, of *saving* man the *need* for fresh *air* and physical *activity.* This science of a wonderful industry is, at the same time, the science of *asceticism.* Its true ideal is the *ascetic* but *usurious* miser and the *ascetic* but *productive* slave. Its moral ideal is the *worker* who brings part of his wages to the savings bank. . . . Self-renunciation, the renunciation of life and all human needs is its principle theme. The less you eat, drink, buy books, go to the theater, the ball or the pub, think, love, theorize, sing, paint, fence, etc., the more you *save* and the *greater* becomes your treasure, which neither moth nor rust will devour, your *capital.*[8]

Clearly, this is a one-sided argument. It is possible to save a little and still enjoy the theater, painting, reading, etc., but for Marx (in 1844 when these man-uscripts were written) there was a dichotomy between saving and the full cultural and emotional development of man. Some of this was, of course, a matter of emphasis. He was reacting against the excessive working hours of the indus-trial state and the attempt to justify this human privation through the morality of work and saving. But there is another element in the emotional quality of his writing. Saving meant self-alienation. It was an all-or-none proposition. It was either human riches and human values or the dead, dry, dehumanizing life of capitalism. Here the more personal element crept into his discourse. These early manuscripts also reveal an attack on the capitalist that bears a close resemblance to his earlier article on the Jewish question.

> No eunich flatters his despot more abjectly or seeks by more infamous means to stimulate his dulled capacity for pleasure in order to solicit some favor for himself, than does the eunich of industry, the entrepreneur, to solicit for himself a few pieces of silver, to charm the golden birds out of the pockets of his dearly beloved Christian neighbors. (Every product is a bait with which to entice the substance, of the other person, his money. Every real or possible need is a weakness which will bring the fly into the glue trap—general exploitation of man is a bond with heaven, a side from which his heart is accessible to the priest, so every need is an opportunity under the guise of good fellowship. . . .) The entrepreneur accommodates himself to the most depraved fancies of the other, plays the pimp between him and his needs, awakens unhealthy appetites in him and lies in wait for every weakness, so that he may claim the cash for this service of love.[9]

Whenever we discover such vehemence, we are justified in suspecting that the description has a highly personal meaning for the theoretician. This was clearly the case in the Marxist image of the capitalist. In such passages, the Jewish stereotype can be more openly displayed because it is no longer Jewish. Marx can speak of the capitalist flattering and enticing his victim, stimulating his sensuality and greedily snatching a few pieces of silver, because he no longer consciously associates these characteristics with his parents or with his early concept of Jewishness. It is no longer the Jew, but the capitalist, that he hates.

The anti-Semitism of Marx has so often been used as a political weapon against his ideas that it is important to see his position in clear perspective. Eric Fromm[10] has pointed out that Marx's early essay on the Jewish question has often been distorted and deliberately mistranslated (as "A World Without Jews"). It has been advertised as the source of the anti-Semitism of both Hitler and Stalin. This is a deliberate attempt to discredit Marx by associating his name and his ideas with a repressive and discredited dogma. On the other hand, I cannot agree with Fromm when he says, "To designate Marx as an anti-Semite is nothing but cold-war propaganda."[11] Marx's essay on the Jewish question was larger than the mere description of the role of the Jew. It concerned the nature of human society, covering both religious and political freedom. Nevertheless, the anti-Semitic elements in it are unmistakable. His letters also contain a number of anti-Semitic remarks, notably his attack on Lassalle.

For those who admire Karl Marx, either for himself or his works, his anti-Semitism is a source of considerable embarrassment. But I don't believe we can clean it up by trying to pretend it did not exist. Anti-Semitism was an element in much of the liberal and socialist thinking of his time and he did more than just accept it. He wanted to show that he understood the real defects of the Jew more profoundly than anyone. While Marx seemed to make it a central issue in his article "On the Jewish Question," he dropped his particular animus toward the Jews and selected capitalism as his target. Capitalism was a larger, more general, more menacing demon for him to tackle. In his own later work he made no attempt to link the ideology of capitalism with Jewish origins. From time to time he let go a few sly barbs at the "Jewish" nature of money, but these statements are extremely rare. They are essentially side remarks, and no longer form the central feature of his argument.

We have seen that Marx, although he despised the Jewish religion, could also come to the aid of Jewish organizations when his help was requested. He was not above the anti-Semitic slur, but he did not fit the modern image of the Jewish anti-Semite: one who tries to save his own skin by a cowardly attack on "those other Jews." Marx both loved and hated the Jews as he both loved and hated his father and mother. This was an important element in his political development, but it was not the only—or even the most important—source of his political ideas. It would be a gross oversimplification to maintain that the entire structure of Marx's theory of capital is "nothing but" a product of his youthful anti-Semitism arising out of the conflict with his parents. His background partly accounts for the emotional impact that economic issues had upon him. It does not explain his genius or the mature development of his theory. Marx's anger toward his mother and father and his hatred of what he regarded as "Jewish" money-hunger served as the stimulus for the development of his ideas on capital, but he was soon to leave these ideas far behind in his study of the historical development of capitalism. Although he never disavowed his earlier work on the "Jewish Question"—he was not one to disavow anything he had written—he never returned to it. His mature works do not reflect any essential relationship between capitalism and the Jew.

My own study of the significance of his Jewishness for Marx is quite different from that of Jerrold Siegel,[12] who seems to link the Jew with the proletariat in Marx's thinking, making him a champion of the disenfranchised Jews. However, Saul Padover,[13] like myself, seems to regard "The Jewish Question" as Marx's repudiation of his own Jewishness. He also offers at least a suggestion that it was an attempt to curry favor with Christian anti-Semites, a point on which I have raised doubts.

Marxist Communism

We have already noted that the communism of the French school did not appeal to Marx. While he had lost all belief in a god, he was still looking for some one thing, some absolute good that would solve all the problems of the world. This characteristic was evident in him from his earliest writing. Marx and the other young Hegelians had rejected the religious aspects of Hegel's philosophy, but they were still looking for something all-encompassing. In the course of writing his "Economic and Philosophical Manuscripts," he clarified his thinking about communism. He adopted the word, but his communism would be something more than the mere negation of private property. He made a distinction between this "crude communism"[14] and a more positive appropriation of capitalist wealth for the total development of humanity. His communism would represent the final form of all political development. It must encompass the world and answer all the problems of humanity. This, at least, is the way he saw it during the time of his Paris manuscripts.[15]

There was always a lag between Marx's ideas and an open publication of his views. He had an urge to develop his idea into a great comprehensive work, but he would not rush—nor be rushed—into a hasty expression until he had done the necessary research.

Marx believed that the proletariat would not be ready for action until it had a fully developed consciousness, which could emerge only from a thorough understanding of the phenomenon of capitalism. How could this come about? Marx felt he could communicate this understanding to the worker through a series of pamphlets and articles and finally through a master work that would present it as a whole. He would outline the historical development of capitalism and show the central role of capital in the exploitation of labor. He would form workers associations to discuss these ideas. Only after these organizations were formed would real action be possible. The revolution, when it finally emerged, would not result from a sudden impulse of anger or a small group of opportunists, but from a broad education of the masses, based on a full understanding of class antagonisms.

The Paris manuscripts, when first undertaken, were probably designed to be this master work, but Marx soon realized that he needed much more information and the manuscripts were never finished. Characteristically, Marx felt that a comprehensive development of his philosophy required reading everything he could find on the subject and examining each element from every possible angle. Every idea led to another and he would sometimes stay up for several nights in a row thinking, writing, and reading.

His attendance at workers meetings finally led Marx into a deep involvement with a secret society of German workers called the League of the Just. Both Marx and Engels were invited to join this group, but they refused. The conspiratorial atmosphere troubled them, for the League was not opposed to sending groups of revolutionaries back into Germany to attempt *putsches*. In 1839 they had helped to organize an uprising in Paris which, because it did not have broad support among the people, was put down by the National Guard. Karl Schapper and Heinrich Bauer, two of the leaders of this group, were imprisoned and then deported to London. The communism supported by the Paris branch of the League was that developed by Wilhelm Weitling. Weitling preached brotherly love, the union of mankind, and the development of a "perfect" society. Marx first admired Weitling's book, *Mankind as It Is and Ought to Be;* but as his own ideas developed, he became increasingly critical of the sentimentality and the semireligious aspects of Weitling's style. He finally came to regard Weitling's doctrine as vague, nebulous, and lacking in class consciousness. Marx worked best when he was on the attack and roused by anger at the stupidity of his opponents. Only when he had developed a full head of steam could he set forth his own ideas. While this warm-up was necessary, it meant that he gave undue prominence to the ideas he attacked. *The Holy Family,* one of the early works authored with Engels, was one of the worst examples of this approach. It was long and tedious. Later he would learn to eliminate some of his criticism of other writers and deal directly with his own ideas.

The Evolution of Theory

Engels was out of Paris before *The Holy Family* was finished. He left Marx to struggle with the manuscript while he returned to Barmen to work in the family business. Here he came into disagreement with his father, particularly when the young and enthusiastic Friedrich published his views in a communist paper on which he worked with Moses Hess in nearby Elberfeld. The Chief Prosecutor made inquiries about him, but he dismissed this with a confident assertion that no one would bother him as long as he was quiet about his activities. Moses Hess warned him that they were both under investigation, but Engels was sure that Hess was only seeing a phantom.[16] In early 1845 he learned that the police were planning to arrest him and he finally fled the country.

Meanwhile, Marx was also under investigation in Paris. He had managed to avoid directly antagonizing the French, but the Prussian government was outraged by his articles in *Vorwärts* and pressure was brought to bear on the French to close the journal and expel its writers. On January 25, 1845 an order was issued by François Guizot, the French Minister of the Interior, expelling Marx, Ruge, Heine and other leading contributors. Marx left for Brussels; Jenny remained behind to sell their furniture and linen; arriving in Brussels a few days later. Marx took a small house in the Flemish section of the city. Engels rented the place next door, and Moses Hess and his wife moved next door to Engels.

Jenny was pregnant when she arrived in Brussels. Remembering her difficulty with the first child, her mother, Caroline Von Westphalen, sent her own maid, Helene Demuth (Lenchen or Nim, as she was called by the family), to look after Jenny. Karl and Jenny could not afford a servant, but Lenchen became a member of the family and an important source of strength for both of them. She was only twenty-five when she arrived, but she soon proved to be not only a help to Jenny but a good household manager who was careful with money. She helped them economize and often used her own savings when they were destitute. According to Wilhelm Liebkneckt, she was one person Karl could not bully and when he had "stormed and thundered so that nobody else would go near him, Lenchen would go into the lion's den. If he growled at her, Lenchen would give him such a piece of her mind that the lion became as mild as a lamb."[17]

Lenchen was a plain woman but not unattractive. Several men became interested in her. However, her loyalty to the Marx family was such that she remained with Karl and Jenny for the rest of their lives. She became very close to Karl. She would insist that he stop writing long enough to eat his meals and she took care of him like one of the children when Jenny was away. This relationship soon became one of close personal attraction. Neither Karl nor Lenchen has left any written record of their feeling for each other, but it may be that her affection for Karl prevented her from developing a close attachment to any other man.

In the summer of 1845 Jenny's pregnancy was well advanced and she left for her mother's home in Trier where their second child, Laura, was born in September. In July, Marx and Engels went to Manchester, England for six weeks to research Marx's book on economics. This was soon abandoned in favor of a more general review of history and social criticism called "The German Ideology," in which Marx outlined the materialist approach to history and described the historical stages through which society evolves in its inevitable path toward communism. This part of the book was brilliant, but Marx, again, spent too much time disposing of his critics and the ideas of other writers. His own ideas were lost in a giant work devoted to picking at the use and misuse of words and often to facetious ridicule. Although he could never publish the work as a whole, he had certain sections privately printed in order to put his ideas into circulation.

NOTES

1. Paul Lafargue, *Karl Marx: The Man* (New York: New York London News Co., 1947), 14–15.

2. Karl Marx and Friedrich Engles, *Werke*, vol. 1 (Berlin: Dietz Verlag, 1968), 108.

3. Marx and Engels, *Werke*, vol. 2, supplement, 490–91.

4. *Reminiscences of Marx and Engels* (Moscow: Foreign Language Publishing House), 87–94. From Paul Lafargue's "Reminiscences of Engels."

5. Marx and Engels, *Werke*, vol. 1, supplement, 649.

6. Ibid., 650.

7. Marx and Engels, *Werke*, vol. 1, 345–46.

8. Marx and Engels, *Werke*, vol. 1, supplement, 549.

9. Ibid., 547.

10. Karl Marx, *Karl Marx: Early Writings*, edited and translated by T. B. Bottomore, with a new Foreword by Erich Fromm (New York: McGraw-Hill, 1963), iv-v. From the Forword by Erich Fromm.

11. Emil L. Fackenheim, *God's Presence in History* (New York: New York University Press, 1970), 57–79. Fackenheim refers to Fromm's statement as "a piece of apologetic dishonesty for which there is no excuse." However, it seems to me that Fackenheim carries the argument of Marx's anti–Semitism to the other extreme when he says, ". . . in view of the enormous influence of Marx's thought for well over a century, it is not far-fetched to connect this nineteenth-century slander either with twentieth-century Soviet antisemitism, or with the compulsive anti-Zionism, which bedevils even the noncommunist left" (p. 57). Anti-Semitism has not been a central feature of Marxist doctrine, as it was clearly a central aspect of Hitler's ideology. Marx's essay, "On the Jewish Question," is today a relatively obscure and seldom read document in the legacy of communism. While anti-Semitism exists in the Soviet Union today it is not justified on theoretical grounds by reference to the early works of Marx. Quite the opposite was true of the Nazi regime in

Germany which attempted to justify anti-Semitism by an elaborate theory of racial superiority and inferiority.

12. Jerrold Seigel, *Marx's Fate: The Shape of a Life* (Princeton: Princeton University Press, 1978), 144–45.

13. Saul K. Padover, *Karl Marx: An Intimate Biography* (New York: McGraw-Hill, 1978), 166–68.

14. Marx, *Early Writings*, Bottomore, ed., 154–55.

15. Ibid., 155.

16. Marx and Engels, *Werke*, vol, 27, 6.

17. *Reminiscences of Marx and Engels*, 117. From the "Reminiscences of Marx" by Wilhelm Liebkneckt.

Chapter 8

KARL MARX:
Revolution in Theory

The Eve of Revolution

From the day of their marriage, Karl and Jenny had difficulty managing money, but in 1846 they began to experience the kind of grinding poverty that would be a part of their life together. An economic crisis struck that year with the failure of the corn and potato crop over much of northern Europe. In France and England industrial depression was followed by financial crisis. In October the Marx family moved to Ixelles, a suburb of Brussels where they could find less expensive quarters; Karl's son Edgar was born there in December 1846. A small child with bright, deep-set eyes, he was called "Musch" (from the French *mouche*) or "Little Fly" because of his size. He soon became the favorite of his father, who had long wanted a son. In his early years Musch had few illnesses and seemed stronger and more vigorous than his sisters.

Jenny found life in Brussels very difficult, but she hoped that the severity of the depression and the financial crisis would discredit the governments in power. This feeling was strengthened by her conversations with Karl and with Engels, both of whom believed that financial panics served as a prelude to revolution.

Marx was in increasing conflict as he saw the revolution approaching. He was developing a comprehensive theory of social and political change but he needed a single document that would summarize his ideas in simple, direct phrases and he needed an organization that would support and spread his views. His ideology could not yet be summed up by a single, immediately recognized term. He called it "communism," but this was a word already in wide use throughout Europe. If he had simply called himself a communist and began to advocate his ideas, he would be surrounded by a crowd of conflicting speakers, each preaching his own brand of communism. Before Marx, "communism" was understood to describe an organization or community in which goods were held in common.

Marx created a new meaning for the word "communism." So successful was he in putting his own brand on the word that the old meaning has vanished from common usage. To this day, people living in communes in capitalist societies would not consider calling themselves "communists," although such a designation would have been quite appropriate before Marx took possession of the word.

We currently regard communism as a form of state socialism under the dictatorship of a single party or class—the proletariat. But for Marx the term represented a body of theory and a group of tactics which could not be encompassed by this single concept. Marx did not invent the elements of his doctrine, but he organized and synthesized them into a general theory. The idea of a dictatorship of the proletariat originated with François Babeuf. But Babeuf believed that this dictatorship could be achieved through a conspiracy and a seizure of power. Marx insisted that the support of the masses was necessary for a successful revolution and this was not possible without the fully developed consciousness of the working class.

Why did Marx engaged in such a monumental struggle to take possession of the word "communism," when he differed so sharply with other communists? Why could he not simply invent another word to distinguish his own ideology clearly and avoid further confusion? The answer rests in his fascination with his own demonic image and in his desire to appropriate the rich historical connotation that the word communism already carried. Babeuf and others had been instrumental in teaching a primitive communism to the leaders of the old Commune of Paris. This commune became the great voice for workers' equality in the French revolution and was regarded as the first "workers' republic" in history.

Thus the word, "communist," and the red flag[1] were important symbols for Marx. Unlike "socialism," which had a mild, gradualist connotation, "communism" already terrified the crowned heads of Europe. For this very reason no other word would do for the ideology of Karl Marx. It is not surprising that this revolutionary in the realm of ideas, who never led an insurrection or fired a shot in battle, was to hurl syllables and phrases against the words of his opponents. With a sharp and biting sarcasm, he attacked the opposition in public and private meetings. With a barrage of criticism, he led a communist correspondence committee to explode the ideas of other communist writers and speakers. And with a final charge, he hurled his own manifesto upon the world, declaring himself the official spokesman for world communism.

The Communist League

Throughout 1846, 1847, and early 1848, Marx and Engels sought to expand their Communist Correspondence Committee into an international party. They contacted Karl Schapper, one of the leaders of a branch of the League of the Just in London, and proposed that a congress be held to iron out differences in their views. Another leader, Moll, visited Marx in Brussels to establish a meeting date. The Central Committee of the League was now in London and the conference was to be followed by a public manifesto outlining the doctrine of the League. The meeting was held June 2–9, 1847. Engels participated but Marx could not attend,[2] being overwhelmed, as usual, by financial problems. He sent Engels a letter in May complaining that both Hess and Bernays owed him money, asking for help in collecting his debts.[3] He had allowed himself to be bled by a physician and the wound had festered instead of healing. His arm was still very weak at the time of writing.[4]

The minutes of the meeting indicate that the League already had branches in many of the major cities of Europe and a representative was sent to the United States.[5] The meeting was a major step forward for the ideas of Marx and Engels. While some of the policies were agreed upon in advance, Engels' presence undoubtedly helped to provide a clear statement of their position. The League was renamed *The Communist League* and the slogan, "All men are brothers," was changed to "Proletarians of all countries—Unite."[6] In keeping with this change, the followers of Weitling were purged from the Paris branch of the League. Although now a much smaller group, the communists in Paris were more unified.

The old League had been a secret, conspiratorial organization, but Marx and Engels opposed conspiracy. They believed it impossible to educate a large mass of people in secret and without mass support a revolution would fail. However, constant surveillance by the government and the threat of infiltration by a police spy or an *agent provocateur* made some secrecy necessary. The resulting compromise was a secret society of "circles" and large "communities"[7] which supported front organizations or open educational societies in which the members of the secret society played a prominent role.

The antagonism to all religions and to Judeo-Christian morality was a feature that shaped both the theory and the tactics of the Marxist brand of communism. In Engels' "Communist Confession of Faith"[8], religious beliefs are specifically rejected. In their correspondence with Gustav Köttgen, Marx and Engels indicate that communists will "have no truck with any tedious moral scruples,"[9] referring to Judeo-Christian morality. Actually both men were exceedingly moralistic in their beliefs, their behavior, and in their style of condemnation. They also opposed the notion of a "personal" morality which exists separate from the needs of the party. A good communist should do what is necessary to further the aims of the revolution. The idea of a merely personal goodness, the desire to build one's personal virtue was regarded as a form of vanity and egoism. In a similar manner, the need to live well or to support one's family could not be used as justification for the use of party funds. The morality of the communist was that of sacrifice: the sacrifice of himself, his family, and his egotistic idea of a purely personal virtue to the needs of the party.

Revolutionary Agitation

By the fall of 1847 a revolution had begun in Switzerland. In 1845 the Catholic cantons had united into a separatist confederation, the Sonderbund. Their purpose was to preserve the church, prevent the secularization of monasteries, and maintain a conservative government. But the radical cantons united against them. In July 1847 the Sonderbund was dissolved by fiat and by November the radicals were on the march. The revolution had a distinct religious flavor, but the Holy Alliance had begun to falter. England refused to support the more conservative faction and sent an emissary to the radicals. Prince Metternich sympathized with the conservatives, but failed to intervene. The result was a new, more liberal constitution for Switzerland. This break in the unity of the great powers was fatal and revolution soon spread to Italy where the Bourbon king of Naples was overthrown and a republic proclaimed.

Marx, who was acutely conscious of world affairs, sensed a new movement against repression that would touch all the advanced nations of the world. Fearful that he may have already delayed too long by insisting on ideological purity before joining the League, Marx brought the Brussels Correspondence Committee into the Communist League in August.

In the November meeting Marx and Engels were victorious. The overthrow of the bourgeoisie was clearly designated as the aim of the League[10] and Marx was given the responsibility of developing a manifesto which openly declared the principles of communism to the world. He now had the mandate he wanted.

On reading the *Manifesto of the Communist Party,* one has a strong sense of the emotional release it must have provided for Marx. He had been tied up in knots with his thoughts and he had great difficulty putting them on paper in any coherent form. His propensity for detailed criticism had trapped him too many times in lengthy and arid expositions which buried his major ideas. But now he felt himself the representative of "communism," and the impending revolution gave an additional urgency to what he had to say now with the utmost boldness.

Jenny's *"Schwartzwildchen"* appears in this work. The man who delighted in his own demonic image had now taken possession of that marvelous and terrifying word with which he would frighten all Europe. In the introduction he took special pleasure in the terror he will bring forth by finally showing the true face of communism.

> A spectre is haunting Europe—the spectre of communism. All the powers of old Europe have entered into a holy alliance to exorcise this spectre: Pope and Czar, Metternich and Guizot, French radicals and German police-spies. . . .
>
> Two things result from this fact:
> I. Communism is already acknowledged by all European Powers to be itself a Power.
> II. It is high time that Communists should openly, in the face of the whole world, publish their views, their aims, their tendencies, and meet this nursery tale of the Spectre of Communism with a Manifesto of the party itself.[11]

But the communism of Marx also satisfied his noble idea of himself as a Prometheus who brings fire to humanity and who threatens the gods, or those, who like gods, seek to rule the world. The word "communism" was a sword which he would use to advance the cause of the underpaid and underprivileged. Declaring his opposition to the profit system and demanding the forceful overthrow of capitalist society throughout the world, Marx concluded with his now famous call for an international union of workers.

> The Communists disdain to conceal their views and aims. They openly declare that their ends can be attained only by the forcible overthrow of all existing social conditions. Let the ruling classes tremble at a Communistic revolution. The proletarians have nothing to lose but their chains. They have a world to win.
>
> WORKING MEN OF ALL COUNTRIES, UNITE![12]

The *Manifesto* was published in London on the eve of the revolutions that swept over Europe in 1948–49. While little noticed at the time, it was to become a major political document, making a name for Marx with both the radical Left and the police as the leading figure in world communism.

No "communist party" existed at the time the *Manifesto* was written. The Communist League represented Marx's claim to speak for world communism. Although it had a widespread organization with branches in many major world cities, it was still a secret organization and not a political party which openly sponsored candidates. Presumably, Marx hoped the *Manifesto* would represent a major step in the creation of a political party and that it would reach others who accepted the principles of communism and wanted to form such a party.

The Revolutions of 1848

Marx was already under observation by the police in Brussels when the revolution broke out in Paris in 1848. He immediately wrote to the new Provisional Government asking for cancellation of a previous order expelling him from France. Ferdinand Flacon replied for the new government by hailing him as "Good Loyal Marx" and inviting him to the new French Republic, an asylum for all friends of liberty.[13] Marx and Engels may have hoped for and even expected a genuine workers' revolution in 1848, but it was soon clear to both of them that this was not to be the character of the new revolution. The tricolor was everywhere. The red flag of the workers' revolution flew only on the Hotel de Ville, that old symbol of the far Left in France. In early March, several other attempts were made to raise the red flag over public buildings, but Lamartine, a leader of the liberal bourgeoisie, worked for a compromise in which a red rosette was placed on the tricolor and universal suffrage became a part of the liberal platform.

Marx and Engels were off to Cologne, Germany where they founded a new revolutionary paper the *Neue Rheinische Zietung,* and published a pamphlet on the demands of the "communist" party in Germany. An order for Marx's expulsion, because of his articles and paper, drove him to Paris and Engels joined the revolutionary forces in Baden as a soldier. Soon the faltering revolution in Paris forced Marx to leave for London. A pregnant Jenny remained behind until Marx could find a place for her. Once in London, he worried that Engels would be shot for his revolutionary activity, and he urged him to come to London as well.

With the suppression of the revolution in the German states and in France, both French and German refugees began to arrive in London. Engels took up residence in London and briefly tried his hand at journalism. Unable to make a living, he finally contacted his father and sought a reconciliation. His father arranged a position for him with the firm of Ermen and Engels in Manchester, but he continued his correspondence with Marx and the other refugees in London. The refugees talked and wrote a great deal, but they were read mostly by each other. They tried to convince themselves that a new European revolution was about to break out at any moment. Marx and Engels were caught up in this fervor and gave support to these hopes. But there was another, almost unspoken element in their writing: a sense that the great opportunity had passed and there was nothing but hard work ahead.

Like Rousseau in his later years, Marx, who was only thirty-one when he arrived in London, had already begun to develop a certain bitterness toward his work and a sarcastic attitude toward his own political writings as well as those of his fellow refugees. In Marx's case, this led to a string of scatological references. He frequently referred to his work as "my shit" or "my crap." In a letter to Engels he said, "One issue of my crap [dreck] has arrived here."[14] In closing a communist meeting: "I have adjourned the shit indefinitely."[15] After asking Engels' opinion on the theory of David Ricardo he concluded, "Because I have bored you with this shit I am sending the enclosed package of letters . . . to cheer you up."[16] Regarding the progress of his work: "I am far enough that in five weeks I should be finished with the whole economic shit. . . ."[17]

On other occasions he could be more relaxed and genuinely humorous, as when he told Engels: "Now I have a whole load of emmigration drivel to send you, and if you know of a farmer in your neighborhood who can use the droppings [guano] of these clean birds for fertilizer, you can do business."[18] At times one has a strong feeling that Marx was repelled not only by his own work but by the products and commodities he must study in order to develop his theory: "In fact, of course, this 'productive' worker cares as much about the crappy shit he has to make as does the capitalist himself who employs him, and who also couldn't give a damn for the junk."[19] At times money and commodities are seen as filthy and having the repulsive odor of feces. In one of the rare passages of *Capital,* in which Marx also gives vent to his anti-Semitism, he remarks, "The capitalist knows that all commodities, however scurvy they may look, or however badly they may smell, are in faith and in truth money, inwardly circumcised Jews, and what is more, a wonderful means whereby out of money to make more money."[20]

Rousseau developed such a neurotic fear of his own work and the work of other political writers that he was afraid to open a book on the subject. If he did open the book, he would catch himself and slam it shut suddenly so he would not "become hooked." Rousseau had turned away from his political writings because he could not face the possibility of his own loss of innocence—the possibility that his motives might not be entirely pure. Marx's attitude toward his work was decidedly different. He was determined to finish the task he had set for himself.

His early youthful vision of communism as true humanism, the answer to all the problems in the world, no longer inspired him with the same enthusiasm. But he sustained himself by his anger against the inhuman working hours and the brutal enforced labor of children that he saw around him. The violent, almost ecstatic energy of the *Manifesto of the Communist Party* was to give way to a hard, plodding determination. Much of the joy had gone out of his work, but Marx forced himself to continue for the next twenty years by the sheer intensity of his will. Toward the end of his work on *Capital*, he sent a reply to Siegfried Meyer, a German-American socialist.

> Why I never answered you? Because I was perpetually hovering on the verge of the grave. Therefore I had to use every moment in which I was capable of work in qrder that I might finish the task to which I have sacrificed my health, my happiness in life and my family. I hope this explanation requires no further supplement. I laugh at the so-called "practical" men and their wisdom. If one chose to be an ox one could of course turn one's back on the agonies of mankind and look after one's own skin. . . .[21]

The London Period

Not only did Marx fail to look after his own skin, but his preoccupation with his work caused him to neglect the welfare of his family. He spent much of his time in London working in the British Museum, far from the daily crises that Jenny often had to face alone with the children. Jenny firmly believed that Karl should be free to do his important work and that it was her responsibility to isolate him from trivial bourgeois cares. She felt guilty when he was pulled away from his writing by a family crisis, but she could not handle their poverty alone.

Marx was busy collecting money for the refugees in London and for a new revue he had founded, *Neue Rheinische Zeitung—Politish-Oekonomisch Revue*, which was published in Hamburg. His scruples would not permit him to use any of these funds for the support of his family, no matter how desperate their circumstances. Once the *Revue* was published, he hoped to gain some funds from the subscriptions. Clearly, much of his bitterness toward his work arose from the suffering he observed in his own family, knowing that the money he was collecting and spending on aid to refugees and political propaganda might have gone to help his wife and children. Throughout his period in London, Engels supplied Marx with money, although, in the beginning, he was never able to send enough. He responded to urgent requests for £2 or £4 whenever he could, but not until he became well established in Manchester was he able to send regular sums to Marx.

Jenny knew that Karl did not manage money very well. She went along with his extravagance in their youth, but he continued to spend money on excursions with friends or a tour of the local pubs. He seemed to have no awareness of the need to conserve their meager resources. When they arrived in London he rented a flat in Chelsea which was beyond their means. Here Jenny gave birth on Guy Fawkes

Day to their second son Heinrich, or Foxchen as he was called by the family in memory of the great conspirator. Soon afterward they were evicted from the flat and Jenny gave vent to her feelings in a letter to Joseph Weydemeyer. As one of the few letters from her in which she goes into detail regarding her domestic situation, it is worthy of a lengthy quotation.

> My husband has been almost suffocated by the petty cares of the bourgois life and in such an upsetting manner that the whole energy, the whole quiet, clear, sure, selfconsciousness of his being was necessary to keep him upright in this daily, hourly struggle. . . .
>
> I came to Frankfurt to pawn my silver, the last that we had. In Cologne I had to sell my furniture because I was in danger of losing my linens and all that I have. My husband went to Paris when the unfortunate era of the counterrevolution began. I followed him with my three children. We had barely gotten adjusted to Paris when we had to leave (even to me and my children no permission was given to stay longer). I followed him again across the ocean. In a month our fourth child was born (Heinrich Guido). You have to know London and the conditions here to know what that means. Three children and the birth of a fourth. For rent alone we had to pay 42 talers a month. All this we were able to pay out of our own money, but our small resources were empty when the *Revue* started. In spite of promises money has not come in except in small amounts so we are in a most painful situation.
>
> I shall describe to you just one day of this life just as it was, and you will see that perhaps few refugees have gone through anything like it. As wet nurses here are beyond our means I decided to nurse my child myself in spite of continuous terrible pains in the breast and back. But the poor little angel drank in so much worry and stifled misery that he was always sickly and was in terrible pain day and night. Since he came into the world he has not slept a single night, two or three hours at most. Recently he has had violent convulsions, too, so the child wavers constantly between a miserable life and death. In his pain he sucked so hard that my breast was chafed and cracked and the blood often poured into his trembling little mouth. I was sitting with him like that one day when suddenly our landlady came in. We had paid her 250 talers during the winter and had an agreement that we would give the money later, not to her but to her landlord, who earlier had a bailiff's warrant against her. She entered and denied the contract, demanded the £5 we owed her and as we had no money at the time (Naut's letter came too late), two bailiffs came and gathered together all my little possessions, linen, beds, clothing and everything, even the cradle of my poor children, the best toys of my daughters, who stood there weeping pitifully. They threatened to take everything within two hours—I would then have to lie on the floor with my freezing children and my sore breast. Schramm, our friend, hurried to town to bring help for us. He got into a cab, the horses lurched forward, he jumped out of the carriage and was brought to the house bleeding, where I was moaning with my poor shivering children.
>
> We had to leave the house. It was cold, rainy and dull. My husband looked for a place for us. No one would take us when he spoke about our four children. Finally a friend helped us. We paid our bill and I quickly sold all my beds to pay the pharmacist, the baker, the butcher and the milkman who were upset by the scandal of the bailiff and suddenly came rushing forth with their bills. The sold beds were taken to the entrance and loaded on a cart. Then what do you think happened? It was some time after sunset. It was

against English law. The landlord rushed up to us with constables, claiming there might be some of his belongings among the things and we wanted to leave the country. In less than five minutes there were more than two to three hundred persons loitering around our door, the whole mob from Chelsea. The beds were brought in again. They could not be delivered to the buyer until after sunrise the next day. When we had sold our belongings we were in a position to pay every last bit we owed. I went with my little darlings to the two small rooms we now occupy in the German Hotel, 1 Leicester Street, Leicester Square, where for £5½ a week we found a humane reception.

Forgive me dear friend that I have described just one day of our life here. It is indiscrete, I know but my heart was running over tonight into my trembling hands and I had to pour out my heart to one of our oldest and truest friends. Do not believe that these petty cares have crushed me. I know only too well that fighting is not isolated and especially that I still belong to the chosen ones, the lucky ones, since my dear husband, the staff of my life, is still at my side. [22]

Marx now had four children: little Jenny, Laura, Edgar, and now the frail Foxchen, the little wormlet as Jenny called him, who was born amid their turmoil and real poverty in the Soho district of London. Marx was overwhelmed with his efforts to organize a worldwide communist movement and to keep up with his theoretical work at the same time. By writing to Weydemeyer and others and by making visits to relatives in search of funds, Jenny hoped to take some of the burden from Karl. In August 1850 Foxchen was ill and the family was desperate for money. Jenny, although unwell herself and pregnant with her fifth child, left her children in the care of Lenchen to go to Holland and seek help from Karl's uncle. But the old man, still suffering from the effects of the revolution on his business affairs, did not look kindly on revolutionaries. He gave her nothing; Karl, if not famous, was rapidly becoming notorious. Jenny also sought help from her own relatives, but they too may have felt unable to aid her without giving hope and support to the man who would destroy them.

Jenny's anxiety about Foxchen was not misplaced. Shortly after their move to 64 Dean Street in Soho, Marx wrote to Engels on November 19, 1850 that the "little powderconspirator" had died that morning through one of the sudden convulsions that had frequently visited the sickly child. Jenny was "completely beside herself" and Marx asked his friend to write a few lines to give her some consolation. [23] It was becoming increasingly apparent that Jenny's grief was more than a mere reaction to the death of her son; it was the manifestation of another, more somber aspect of her personality. In the course of the years that followed she was to have several long periods of depression, each of which lasted for several months. She certainly had abundant cause for despair, but she would also have sudden changes of mood: feverish gaiety followed by a relapse of depression when a new crisis emerged.

Jenny still helped Karl with his work as much as possible. She served as his secretary, copying his illegible scrawl and dealing with the creditors whenever she could. She also sent requests for money to his colleagues and to relatives on both sides of the family. On March 28 she gave birth to Franziska, her fifth child. At this point Jenny collapsed. In a letter to Engels, Marx remarked that Jenny's sickness was due more to domestic concerns than to anything physical. He had to discontinue his work to deal with the tradesmen, who were dunning him with their bills, and to look after his sick wife.[24]

Jenny was developing a growing anger at Karl's inability to feed and care for their family, but she also felt guilty about expressing this anger openly. She had already made up her mind that Karl was a great genius and she had decided that it was an honor to do her part in this great work by copying his manuscripts and writing letters for him. But this loyalty and quiet service was to be tested many times by the suffering of her children and by other blows to her self-esteem which made her wonder if she was really part of a great cause or only another victim.

One such blow was the birth of a son to Jenny's maid, Helen Demuth, in the summer of 1851. There is no documentary evidence that Jenny ever discovered Karl was the father of this child, but she could not have isolated herself completely from the rumors current at the time. Many of the letters between Jenny and Karl and between Marx and Engels were destroyed, probably by Engels and Helen Demuth (Lenchen) when they were going over Karl's letters and papers after his death.[25] But the existence of this new male child was a great source of frustration for both Jenny and Karl. The previous March, when Franziska was born, Karl had very much wanted another son.[26] Now he had a son he could not acknowledge. The one thing he feared most was the loss of Jenny's love and he knew that taking the child into his home would drive Jenny from him.

Engels, who had assumed so many of Karl's burdens, was persuaded to accept paternity of Helen's child, named Friedrich after his "father." Apparently, rumors circulated regarding Friedrich's paternity; Jenny may or may not have believed them. She makes only an oblique (possible) reference to this incident in her autobiography: "In the early summer of 1851 there occurred an event which I shall not touch upon further although it brought about a great increase in our private and public sorrows."[27]

Her misery was intensified by the death of Franziska little more than a year after her birth. She came down with a severe case of bronchitis on Easter 1852. Marx was himself plagued by everything from hemorrhoids to boils. In 1853 he was close to death with an attack of the liver illness that killed his father. In 1855, Eleanor Marx, the last of his children, was born. The family named her Tussy. In March of that year, while his youngest child was ill, Musch, his favorite and his only remaining male child, developed serious gastric pain. Marx cancelled a proposed visit to Engels, sitting up every night with his sick child. On April 6, Musch died in his father's arms.[28] Marx was devastated. The whole place seemed gloomy and abandoned and everything reminded him of Musch. Said Marx, "I have been through all kinds of bad luck but only now do I understand real disaster. I feel broken down. Fortunately, since the funeral I have had such severe headaches that I haven't been able to think, hear or see. With all the terrible torment that I suffered in these days the thought of you and your friendship has always held me together, and the hope that we still have something worthwhile in this world to do together."[29] After the funeral, Marx and Jenny left for Manchester to visit Engels, but they were not yet in a position to move permanently from Dean Street.

After the death of Musch, Karl burrowed more deeply into his work and, despite his acute sensitivity to the suffering of the masses, developed a certain insensitivity to the suffering of those close to him. More and more he complained of Jenny's inability to act as his secretary. When Engels wrote to him in 1861 that Mary Burns, his mistress of twenty years, had died, he replied with a few sentences of condolence and continued with a long description of his financial problems, closing with an urgent request for more money. Engels reply was so cold that it seemed the lifelong friendship of the two men was about to end, but Marx hastened to repair the damage to the best of his ability. For sometime afterward, however, there was a distance between them.

The Final Years

The First International was founded in 1864. Marx was the leading figure in it and it absorbed much of his time and prevented him from completing his work on *Capital.* The International achieved its greatest influence during a series of conferences in Europe between 1867–69, although by this time it had lost much of its influence in England. Bakunin, the anarchist, began a series of arguments with Marx in his own struggle to dominate the International and various European governments began a systematic persecution of the organization.

In the *Civil War in France 1870–71,* Marx issued one of his most important addresses. It is one of his finest works, rich in historical insights but full of drama, as though written in the heat of battle. It ran through three editions and sold 8000 copies, a large sale in those times for a document of current commentary. It helped to brand the International as one of the greatest threats to the established governments of Europe.

But Bakuninist opposition was already rising in the various branches of the organization. In 1870 a separate anarchist section opposing Marx's ideas had been set up in Geneva. In 1871 this conflict was partly resolved, but in 1872 at the last full meeting of the International the division was even more apparent. The Bakuninists were expelled, but with the transfer of the General Council to New York, the International was effectively dead, though it lived on into 1873.

In the last years of his life, Engels was able to supply Marx with more funds. Karl and Jenny had a house of their own; their daughters married, except for Eleanor who was interested in the theater and engaged in an intermittent affair with a journalist of whom Marx did not approve. *Capital,* volume I, was first published in 1867; but with the International dead, Marx did not seem able to work effectively on volumes II and III. He and Jenny were both frequently ill during the last decade of his life and he had the energy for only a few brief polemics. He was often so sick he had to give up beer for weeks on end. In 1881 Jenny Marx died at age sixty-seven from a cancer of the liver that had plagued her for years. Karl never really recovered from her death and was further crushed by the death of his daughter Jenny in 1883, at age thirty-eight, apparently also of cancer. He returned to London from the Isle of Wight where Lenchen (Helen Demuth) cooked for him and nursed him until he died of bronchitis on March 13, 1883 at the age of sixty-four.

The Inhibition of Aim

Masochism has been described as an inhibition of aim. In social masochism we are not referring to an inhibition of the sexual aim, but to an inhibition of masculine power-striving. In Karl Marx there can be no doubt about the inhibition of his striving for power *through money*. In fact, his sense of helplessness and inadequacy in relationship to money persisted throughout his life. He developed a relationship with Engels in regard to money which was similar to the one he had with his father. He managed to involve himself in one financial crisis after another. In each crisis he called out desperately to Engels for help and the latter never refused him.

But what of the other aspects of power? Marx had a positive mania for leadership. In political matters he would tolerate no opposition. His fellow communists soon found that they must submit to his direction or become his enemy. Engels, who supported Marx financially, became his disciple in politics. There was simply no other way to relate to Marx in the realm of ideas. It is almost as though he compensated for his masochism in one area by a kind of imperious domination in other areas of his life.

Still it is possible that if we look carefully at the area of politics we will find an inhibition of aim in this area as well. Marx's avowed aim was revolution against the capitalist society. However, by the very nature of his approach he seemed to be saying he was not ready to assume full power. Three characteristics combined in him to inhibit the immediate physical expression of his aggressive impulses: (1) his fascination with a complete wholistic understanding of the subject in depth, (2) his internationalism, which made him hold back revolution in any one country, (3) his love of books, words, and ideas.

Masochism and the Dynamics of Delay

We have noted that the dynamics of masochism is closely linked to the experience of delay in gratification. The pleasure associated with this delay is that of anticipation of the final satisfaction. Reik has described this element of delay and its resemblance to the child who saves a special favorite morsel for the end of his meal. But in the process of delay this favorite sweet is sometimes not consumed at all. In social masochism the "final" satisfaction is the release of all the angry and destructive impulses, the disgrace and perhaps even the death of the oppressor.

Hence the tendency to an indefinite delay in social masochism. The humiliated person remains in disgrace and contents himself with the fantasy that someday, perhaps even after his death, he will be rehabilitated.

In the case of a successful revolutionary theorist, it is possible to have one's cake and eat it too. One can strive for the success, for the victory of one's *theory*, even if the actual revolution remains unrealized. One can create a revolutionary organization, produce propaganda, and achieve a certain eminence for one's ideas without actually engaging in armed combat. It is as though each of Marx's traits of character combined to produce the maximum effect. His search for completeness, for the most profound explanation, required that he read everything, thus producing a delay of theory development but a more profound and detailed theory. His internationalism led him to refuse any result that could not be applied everywhere. All of these qualities involved delay, but they also brought about an expansion and penetration of the revolutionary theory to all aspects of society. Thus for Marx the delay served not only to prolong the excitement but to expand the total thrust, the power of the revolutionary impulse. This delaying action is even more successful when it is an essential ingredient in the theory itself. One is delayed, then, not only by the necessity of completing one's theory, but the theory itself contains a justification for further delay. Just as the purpose of delay in masochism is to increase the final pleasure, so the justification for delay in Marx's theory is designed to increase the overwhelming power and force of the final revolutionary outbreak. By delaying minor revolutionary discharges in one nation after another, Marx built up such a head of steam for his revolution that it should have occurred simultaneously in all nations. The final outbreak would be so overwhelming that nothing could stop it. It would encompass the world.

This, of course, is the revolution in fantasy. In reality, revolution took a rather different course. Yet one cannot observe the twenty foot high pictures of Marx and Engels during a Russian celebration in Moscow's Red Square or in the streets of Peking without a feeling that Marx has indeed achieved the final satisfaction he desired. He is still hailed today as the prophet and creator of revolution. He has achieved revolutionary immortality.

Theory or Action

For a man who is still regarded as the world's most influential revolutionary, it is a strange anomaly that many activists of his time had their doubts as to whether or not Marx was really a revolutionary at all. The explanation for this controversy is to be found in Marx's own internal conflict, based on the dynamics of masochism we have already discussed.

Such misunderstanding (and it was, in part, a misunderstanding) was inevitable, given his position. For Marx was striving to master both theory and practice at the same time. The professional critics regarded him as unprofessional, too much concerned with social realities. Many of the professional activists, on the other hand, regarded him as too theoretical and divorced from real human suffering. How could he spend his time spinning out ideas when there were real enemies to attack? Was he actually suggesting that the revolution be delayed when there was not a moment to lose?

Marx felt that he must follow his own sources in the development of his ideas. His theory of historical materialism implied that the proletariat would come to power through a series of inevitable stages of historical development. First the older aristocracy, the landed gentry, would give way to the bourgeoisie who had created the power of capital. When the bourgeoisie had developed commerce and industry to the fullest extent, the proletariat would be pulled together in large working groups for the economy of factory operation. In such groups they would be easier to organize and enlighten. But all capitalist governments understood the danger of a workers' revolution. If a revolution took place before the consciousness of the worker was fully developed, it would merely provide an excuse for repression. Even if the workers should succeed in a temporary seizure of power, other reactionary governments would come to the aid of the old regime as they had done in France. It was for this reason that premature *putsches* were dangerous. If revolution were delayed until the full development of class-consciousness, this full awareness of workers would prevent their use as soldiers by capitalist regimes to crush a workers' republic.

In Marx's time, as today, workers were still intensely nationalistic. They had been taught that they were Frenchmen, Englishmen, Germans, or Italians and that their interests were represented by their government which sought some economic or military advantage over another government. If France prospered or increased its military power, the French worker believed that he was prospering *in opposition to other workers*. He must learn that his interests were not those of his country but of his class. He should not be in opposition to other workers but to the capitalist system—wherever it was found.

The idea was certainly revolutionary, but it was somewhat complex for those who wished to rush into the streets and begin the revolution at once. Had Marx been a mere academic scholar who set down his ideas without leaving his study, his work might never have gained the reputation and influence it finally achieved. But he was an avid writer of articles and short pamphlets and he always maintained, with the help of Engels and other friends, a formidable correspondence. Further, he was constantly placing himself in situations where he could engage in discussion. In his attendance at meetings of workers' associations he encountered those who disagreed with him or challenged him to clarify his ideas. He was a lion in public debate. Some men become incoherent when they are angry; they lose their train of thought and blurt out things they do not mean. For Marx, anger was a source of inspiration. It seemed to stimulate his intellect. His mind became clear and he would bear down on his target with a fine precision, taking his opponent's words and using them against him, tearing apart the ideas of his adversary and, at the same time, bringing forth his own with clarity and directness.

However, despite his eloquence in public debate and his skill as a speaker,

Marx was never able to resolve this conflicting image of himself. Was he a "mere" theoretician or a "real" practicing revolutionary? His strong interest in theory and in the criticism of criticism made him an easy target for those who believed that all theoretical work was a form of cowardice—a retreat from the "real" word of action. His position was further complicated by the fact that the theory he was developing was one which called for a necessary inhibition of action. When a man calls for revolution and then adds, "But not yet! We must first prepare our consciousness," he may easily be accused of vacillation or even a complete lack of interest in the workers and their "real" daily problems.

In his own mind, Marx was clear on this point. Theory was essential to practice. One could not lead a revolutionary movement without some basis for justifying one's acts. There must be some theory of the way society should be, to form a basis for criticism of society as it is. And surely this theory must be developed prior to action.

Marx welcomed attacks from conservative politicians, the censor, or the police. These were his enemies from whom opposition was to be expected. But he could not understand those on the Left who implied or openly stated that he was an armchair revolutionary who had no real feeling for the suffering of the workers. In one form or another he was subject to this kind of attack throughout his life from Weitling, Bakunin, Goltschalk, Lassalle, and others. Marx was always deeply angered by these attacks and, although he sometimes suffered the private insinuations of Lassalle in silence, he could be aroused to a table-pounding fury when he received such a slur in public from Weitling.

While the accusations were often misguided and short-sighted, they clearly struck an exposed nerve in Marx. They were not only an attack on his manhood, for he was proud of his role as an active fighter for revolutionary causes, but they hit upon a crucial aspect of his personality that was in direct conflict with his more active organizing work. Marx was indeed in love with words. He delighted in puns, in playing with sentences, in inverting ideas to see how they would sound, in scrounging about for a new concept, in "bookworming," and in discovering the real meaning behind the meaning of what someone had said. Chiasmus was one of his favorite devices. Sometimes he could use it in a sharp, sarcastic, and devastating manner that would decimate any opponent in a single phrase, as in his answer to Proudhon's book *The Philosophy of Poverty* which he called *The Poverty of Philosophy*. But there were other times when the urge to reverse an idea seemed to dominate his thinking.

Reik has commented on the role of reversal, contradiction, and irony in masochism with particular emphasis on the paradoxes of Jesus. What Reik has said of paradox is equally applicable to the chiasmus of Marx.

> The paradox contradicts traditional opinions, turns them upside down, in order to see what they look like. Furthermore, it contains an element which as yet has not been sufficiently appreciated and which codetermines its genesis and formulation. Whoever coins paradoxes unconsciously anticipates the impressions of his listeners, their opposition to his assertions,

maybe even their mockery, and this very anticipation leads him into a specific formulation. Thus the paradox contains an attack on generally accepted ideas; however, in a sense it enjoys the attack of the others, even of the future listeners, by anticipation, and by this very anticipation assumes a character of intentional absurdity. One has the impression that the speaker makes mock at himself, yet knowing exactly how and why, remains in command. What he really mocks at is the anticipated argument of his enemies. [30]

The anticipation of ridicule was a central element of Marx's work. But unlike many of the gentle revolutionaries, Marx loved to use ridicule as a weapon as well. In fact, one of his greatest weaknesses was his tendency to become caught up in what his opponents had said, looking about in their works for juicy quotations that he could dissect with his incisive wit, spending much time and energy to skewer each misuse of a word, to locate every trace of false sentimentality.

There may have been more than just pleasant associations that attracted Marx to theory. Knowing what we do about the young Karl's intense willfulness and his anger when opposed, the strong letters from his father, the criticism of his spending, and the demand that he keep accurate and orderly records must have aroused his anger, even his hatred. Karl also loved his father. This love and his very real dependency on his father made it difficult for him to express his anger openly. His father constantly reminded him of his hopes for his son and how deeply he would be hurt if Karl disappointed him. This must have aroused a strong fear of hurting his father and a guilt regarding his anger and his destructive feelings. There is no record of an open break between father and son. However, it is not difficult to imagine a young Karl anticipating the day when he would be finished and could give the old man a piece of his mind. That day never came, for his father died before he finished his work at the university.

The one area in which Karl could struggle with his father was the realm of social theory. Here he could advance his ideas, dispute with his father, and even receive encouragement. The hope of eventually resolving this conflict in the realm of theory may have been a factor in his attraction toward Hegel's notion of a thesis, antithesis, and synthesis. [31] His own ambivalence toward his father must have been intense, but the Hegelian approach seemed to promise a resolution to this ambivalence, this thesis-antithesis, in a final synthesis which would resolve the conflict without destroying either. Further, it allowed the disagreement to remain on an intellectual level where the elder Marx had found conflict quite acceptable. Marx, then, avoided open physical conflict with his father by struggling with him in the realm of ideas. He may well have thought that someday he must engage in a real fight to achieve his independence, but the theoretical struggle represented a means of delaying this final clash.

It is not surprising, then, to find that the theory he developed was a call for warfare against his father's class but a warfare that must be delayed until the appropriate time, and his own rebellion against his father was delayed until after the old man's death. Death did not resolve the problem, but the ambivalence about his father was projected onto an entire class, the bourgeoisie. On the one hand, the bourgeoisie were tyrants, bloodsuckers, and money grubbers; but on the other hand, they were overthrowing the old feudal system and bringing about the changes that would permit the rise of the proletariat. Therefore, it was pointless to attack the bourgeoisie until their work was finished. They were useful. In fact, they were the only ones who could bring about the necessary changes in society.

We have said that Marx was right in regard to the importance of the theory he was developing and its power to change the world, but this does not mean that his theory was an accurate reflection of the inevitable historical development of society. Lenin and Trotsky and later Mao were to demonstrate that it was not necessary to wait for the full development of the bourgeois class in order to bring about a communist revolution. In fact, communist governments were first established in the more backward, semi-feudal nations of the world and not the fully developed capitalist states as Marx had predicted. This would suggest that at least such aspects of Marx's theory as the ambivalence about the bourgeoisie, their usefulness, their evil character and, most of all, the necessity for delay in attacking them developed from his personal needs.

It is not at all clear that his theory would have been better or more persuasive had he correctly seen the true historical outcome. When we speak of "personal needs" influencing a person's thinking, one has the impression that these are nonrational aspects which detract from his clear view of reality. But an important personal need for Marx was complexity and depth in his ideas. He had a passion for the integration of various fields of knowledge. It was important to his own intellectual self-actualization to develop a theory that could only be understood through a knowledge of history. He managed to weave his personal ambivalence toward the bourgeoisie into a logical structure that was complex, rationally consistent, and fully integrated with the known history of his time. Like a Pythagorean solution, it was a thing of intellectual beauty. As such it contained a persuasive power that survived its failure to predict world events. Further, it was based on a methodology that proved more enduring than the theory itself.

The Role of Suffering

In the face of the real agony of Jenny and Karl Marx and the unbelievable working conditions of nineteenth-century industrial society against which Marx was fighting, a certain discomfort must haunt anyone who tries to explain his behavior in terms of a "need for suffering." Clearly, many of Marx's problems stemmed from the suffering inherent in any determination to combat the established order of society. One could say with as much veracity that he suffered because of his courage or his high moral principles, which made it impossible for him to charge for his speeches to workers groups and which made it necessary for him to refuse Lassalle's offer to open a public subscription to publish his work on economics.

Seemingly, his acute sensitivity to the suffering of others made it impossible for him to "be an ox" and save his own skin while watching young children working ten-hour days under brutal conditions. To describe Marx's life, work, and theories as "nothing but" the product of his moral masochism is truly a distortion of reality. The injustice of his times and the conditions against which he battled were real problems and he played a significant role in changing the world.

Yet if we review the pattern of his life, it is apparent that his financial crises began to develop long before his interest in politics. Both McLellan and Padover have demonstrated that Marx's actual income from his writing and support from Engels was sufficient to provide an adequate living if he had managed the money with care. His early poetry and his identification with Prometheus make it clear that he was bound to enter some adventure that would involve him in personal torment. And Jenny, instead of being frightened away by his poetic excesses, his self-punishing study habits, and his general propensity for heroic sacrifice, found him charming. The very "sickly sensitivity" which angered his father attracted Jenny. Evidence suggests that in addition to her own feminine masochism in relation to Karl's domineering personality Jenny was also intrigued by the thought of Karl suffering heroically or perhaps severely wounded for some noble cause. The following is from one of her early letters to him in their courtship days.

> So, sweetheart, since your last letter I have tortured myself with the fear that for my sake you could become embroiled in a quarrel and then in a duel. Day and night I saw you wounded, bleeding and ill, and, Karl, to tell you the whole truth, I was not altogether unhappy in this thought: for I vividly imagined that you had lost your right hand, and, Karl, I was in a state of rapture, of bliss, because of that. You see, sweetheart, I thought that in that case I could really become quite indispensable to you, you would then always keep me with you and love me. I also thought that then I could write down all your dear, heavenly ideas and be really useful to you. All this I imagined so naturally and vividly that I continually heard your dear voice, your dear words poured down upon me and I listened to every one of them and carefully preserved them for other people. You see, I am always picturing such things to myself, but then I am happy, for then I am with you, yours, wholly yours. . . .[32]

In Jenny, too, we can see that the sadistic fantasy lurked behind the most overt expression of her awe and delight at Karl's domination. She admired him and wondered at his greatness and her own unworthiness, but this very discrepancy in her picture of their relationship made her sometimes long to reverse things, to have him helpless, completely dependent, and unable to escape her. This fantasy also contained a certain ecstatic bliss in his suffering itself, as though the fallen hero had a special charm for her. The suffering seemed to make his work more noble and she, by giving herself to it, became noble also. Perhaps this element in their relationship was one of the factors that held her by his side throughout all the terrible years of poverty and sacrifice.

The Creature of Contradictions

We have observed in the young Karl Marx several seemingly contradictory trends. Completely dependent on his friend Engels as far as money was concerned, he dominated Engels and all his other friends in the field of politics. His refusal to take money for his political work and his mismanagement of money left him in acute poverty, a degree of suffering that he did not have to endure and which seemed to have within it a strong element of masochism. On the other hand, his stormy, dominating temperament, his biting sarcasm, and his delight in tearing apart the works of his opponents through a caustic critique suggest a sadistic side to his character.

Combative in the field of politics, he was gentle, patient, and tolerant with his children. He loved his wife and children deeply and it hurt him to see them suffer. Yet he continued his life-style of poverty despite the death of his son—due in large measure to his inability to pay for adequate food and medicine—and the increasing mental and physical illness of his wife. Why was he unwilling to make any concessions in his struggle? His youthful dream of sacrificing himself for humanity and his adult ambition to save the oppressed people of the world suggest a man obsessed by the search for personal virtue, an individual determined to become a living saint; but his fascination with the diabolical qualities in himself, his contempt for religious people, his bold proclamation of his own atheism, his delight in frightening the authorities with his ideas, and his need to be thought of as dangerous suggest a man who sought a demonic image. The *real Karl Marx* cannot be understood without an appreciation of these contrasting desires and the ambivalence about himself and his role in society that followed him to the end of his life.

NOTES

1. The red flag was originally used by the French monarchy as a symbol that martial law had been declared. But on July 17, 1791, the government raised the red flag and Lafayette ordered his troops to fire on a mob. The result was the massacre of the Champs de Mars in which hundreds of people were killed. The next year the people marched with their own red flag declaring material law against the government. In the revolution of 1848 the bourgeois republicans sought to bring back the French tricolor as the symbol of revolution, but various workers'organizations hoisted the red flag. From this point the red flag was the symbol of revolution, generally a workers' revolution. At first, both anarchists and communists used it, but communists finally appropriated it for their own and anarchists used the black flag.

2. Karl Marx and Friedrich Engels, *Werke*, vol. 27 (Berlin: Dietz Verlog, 1968), 27, 80–83.

3. Ibid.

4. Ibid.

5. Karl Marx and Friedrich Engels, *Collected Works*, vol. 6 (New York: International Publishers, 1975), 589–600.

6. Ibid.

7. Ibid., 633–37.

8. Ibid., 103.

9. Ibid., 56.

10. Ibid., 633

11. Ibid., 481.

12. Ibid., 519.

13. Ibid., 581.

14. Marx and Engels, *Werke*, vol. 27, 150.

15. Ibid., 156.

16. Ibid., 162.

17. Ibid., 228.

18. Ibid., 320.

19. Karl Marx, *Grundrisse* (New York: Vintage, 1973), 273.

20. Karl Marx, *Capital: A Critical Analysis of Capitalist Production*, vol. 1 (New York: International Publishers, 1967), 154.

21. Karl Marx and Friedrich Engels, *Selected Correspondence* (Westport: Greenwood, 1942), 219.

22. Marx and Engels, *Werke*, vol. 27, 607–10.

23. Ibid., 143.

24. Ibid., 226–27.

25. David McLellan, *Karl Marx: His Life and Thought* (New York: Harper and Row, 1973), 271–72. When Eleanor Marx discovered she had a half brother, she located him and began writing to him. Robert Payne has collected some of these letters.

26. Marx and Engels, *Werke*, vol. 27, 228. Marx wrote to Engels, "My wife, unfortunately had a girl and not a boy. What is worse she is still suffering."

27. Robert Payne, *The Unknown Karl Marx: Documents Concerning Karl Marx* (New York: New York University Press, 1971), 126. From the autobiography of Jenny Marx.

28. Marx and Engels, *Werke*, vol. 27, 443.

29. Ibid., 444.

30. Theodor Reik, *Masochism in Modern Man* (New York: Grove, 1941), 344.

31. A thesis, antithesis, and synthesis are themes implicit in Hegel's works and have been noted by numerous commentators, although Hegel does not use these terms himself.

32. Marx and Engels, *Collected Works*, vol. 1, 696–97.

Part 3

VICTORY WITHOUT POWER

Introduction

In Part II we examined the lives of men who regarded themselves as revolutionaries, but who held back from active revolutionary combat because of nonviolent inclinations or an absorption in theoretical development as a precursor to revolution. In this section we will deal with those revolutionaries who had no apparent hesitation about launching an actual revolution, but who were reluctant to take up the problems of ruling a country. This is clear in the case of Trotsky and Guevara. It is less obvious with Sun Yat-sen.

While there are various reasons for this hesitation, all three men shared a moral revulsion to post-revolutionary administration and rule over the masses. All three seemed more interested in the moral education of the people than in the practical matters of governing a nation. They displayed a need to continue the sense of internal "psychological" change within the people, to keep alive the sense of newness and excitement of revolutionary ideas, to continue the awakening of "revolutionary consciousness." Trotsky even prepared a pamphlet which he called *Permanent Revolution,* suggesting a revolution which never ends in administration, but continues to inspire a ferment in the minds of people all over the world.

There is, of course, no neat break from one revolutionary type to another. Robert Lifton has described Mao Tse-tung, years after the supposed administrative success of his revolution, launching a new "Cultural Revolution" in an attempt to recapture that lost psychological sense of being in the process of a grand new awakening. Mao apparently felt that his revolution was losing its momentum and, more important, its youth. Lifton has described the Cultural Revolution as a search for "revolutionary immortality."

This is the mysterious quality for which all our revolutionaries are searching. They want not a mere revolutionary "happening," but they want to place the stamp of *their* personality and *their* ideas on that happening. Arguments with fellow revolutionaries are seldom concerned with who will have the most physical power, but rather, who will be remembered as the most radical and the most rebellious of all. Marx was most stimulated when he could diminish the boldness or the revolutionary importance of an opponent. It was a great joy to him to dissect the "dead" and "tame" ideas of other innovators, who regarded themselves as unusual or shocking, and show that they were mere sheep in wolves clothing. The ideas of others represented some tampering with the system, some correction of local abuse, some Sunday-school pronouncements about moral reform. He and he alone was the true world-shaker. When his ideas were fully developed they would change the very basis for human perception.

But Marx, too, became lost, from time to time, in administrative detail. He had no nation to govern, but he had the Internationale which finally became a vast unwieldy machine that he could no longer control. Even in the smaller Communist Correspondence Committee and the Communist League he was impatient with the slow process of administrative machinery. He was frustrated by efforts to keep the refugees of the 1848 revolutions working together in London. Engels described him, when he edited the *New Rheinische Zeitung*, as a dictator by general consent. He was at his best in the world of thought, when his ideas were so compelling and his personality so charismatic that he charmed others into following him. He was truly magnificent when his indignation was aroused by some vague shuffler of ideas such as Weitling, who, he felt, sought to arouse the people without giving them a coherent program or a meaningful plan of attack.

The men in Part III of this study differ from those in Part II in their need for action. They wanted not merely a coherent plan of attack, but the physical aspect of revolutionary action. They wanted to bring about real structural change in the government and they had no reservations about violence. At the same time they had a passion for *moral* leadership, for inspiring the *minds* of people. They required a constant feeling that the people understood and believed in what they were doing. They could not exercise power *over* the people, but wanted to feel they were acting *with* the masses. For these men, an important aspect of this contact with the people was their own sense of opposition to power. The notion of the maintenance and consolidation of power, secret machinations to secure their own personal ambitions, was repugnant to them. They needed to feel a deep identification and ongoing contact with the people; to maintain this feeling, some kind of opposition to power was necessary.

In the Introduction to this book I stressed the dual nature of the sado-masochistic personality and the accusation that some rebels had become tyrants after assuming power. However, I have also noted that, while the rebel and the tyrant are both sado-masochists, their values are markedly different. The personality of the rebel is such that he cannot become a classical tyrant; he will not drop his identification with the common people and build a system based on a stratification of classes, a hierarchy of power with himself at the top. Nor will he seek the trappings of power and a luxurious style of living. Still, after revolutionary victory comes a need to put down those who opposed the revolution. In the ruthlessness of his attack on "counter-revolutionaries," the revolutionary leader may display the repressed, sadistic aspect of his personality. While he may strive to avoid such a position of power because of discomfort with this sadistic side of himself, he may, once he sees his role as inevitable or a product of his "duty," take to it with a fervor which shocks his old comrades. However, it is moral reform that remains close to his heart. He would rather convert than destroy an enemy. He would prefer to trust, rather than be on guard against betrayal. While he may lead the revolutionary armies or accept a temporary role as administrator, he must, at last, return to the more romantic role of opposition. It is only in the final section, the successful revolutionaries of Part IV, that we will see a sublimation of this rebellious spirit in favor of administration, control, and the unrestrained use of power.

Chapter 9

SUN YAT-SEN:
The Eclectic

Personality

As already suggested in the study of Gandhi, it is not always easy to make a distinction between violent and nonviolent revolutionaries, for all forms of nonviolent revolt put a certain coercion and pressure on the adversary. Also, some individuals, such as Kropotkin, speak openly of the need for violent revolt early in their careers, but become increasingly nonviolent as they continue to examine the morality of revolution. Some, such as Gandhi, condemn violence in any form, whether used by the oppressed or the oppressor. Others, such as Kropotkin, condemn violence, but cannot find it in their hearts to condemn violent *individuals* who have attempted to assassinate an unjust ruler.

Sun Yat-sen also represents an interesting combination of violent and non-violent tendencies in one individual. Sun had a gentle and agreeable personality, but from his early years he manifested a stubborn and peculiar kind of defiance toward all authority, including religious authority. Like Rousseau, he would do almost anything for a person who urged him in the name of love, but he was angry and resistant toward any pressure of obligation. Like all of our nonviolent revolutionaries, he was trusting, sometimes too trusting, of those who wanted to make peace with him or who came to him in friendship. Like Tolstoy and Gandhi, he was a vegetarian.

Sun's autobiography is concerned almost entirely with his plans for China and his revolutionary activity. We must turn to other sources to find something of his personality. Justice Paul Linbarger remarks, "I have known Sun to help men who were frauds and do it merely because he felt sorry for them."[1] "If there was any weakness in Sun," he said, "it is the weakness of forgiveness."[2] Upton Close describes him as being as gentle and forgiving as a child.[3] In regard to his trust, his wife Ching Ling said, "What I admire most in my husband is his utter unselfishness and believing in the best of every person he meets—he never suspects anyone of wrong intentions."[4] Tai Chi-Tao calls him "a saint of Chinese civilization who has inherited its past and created its future."[5] Dr. James Cantlie describes Sun as one of the most welcome visitors to his home for "children and servants alike conceived a deep regard for him; his sweetness of disposition, his courtesy, his consideration for others, his interesting conversation and his gracious demeanor attracted one toward him in an indescribable fashion. . . ."[6] How did such a gentle soul manage to lead a revolution? Most observers maintain that Sun led others through his "moral force"[7] by example and not by command. But in the last analysis, most charisma is indefinable. Dr. James Cantlie, in telling of his own trips to Macao to help Sun in surgery describes this quality of leadership.

> . . . he performed important operations requiring skill, coolness of judgement, and dexterity. . . . Why did I go this journey to Macao to help this man? For the reason that others have fought for and died for him, because I loved and respected him. His is a nature that draws men's regard towards him and makes them ready to serve him at the operating table or on the battlefield; an unexplainable influence, a magnetism which prevails and finds its expression in attracting men to his side. [8]

The Youthful Rebel

We know little of the background of Sun Yat-sen, not even the day of his birth, although November 12, 1866, is usually chosen. He was born of peasant parents in Choyhung, the "Blue Village" of south China, thirty miles north of the Portuguese colony of Macao. Not much is known of his parents. Perhaps the one significant characteristic of family members was their propensity for travel. His father's two brothers had died seeking gold in California and Sun's older brother had left for Hawaii at an early age to engage in foreign trade. Aside from this, we know little of Sun's very early years, for his autobiography omits much of his early life. Paul Linebarger has presented many stories of the early life of Sun Yat-sen similar to those described by Rousseau and Tolstoy, but the source of these tales is questionable. We see the young Sun Yat-sen confronting river pirates who robbed a man of the village and resolving to bring law to China. We see him standing up bravely to the Manchu agents sent to confiscate the property of three brothers in his town. However, the phraseology and the adjectives used in these tales have the quality of a Parson Weems. Little Sun Yat-Sen is always brave and manly, always speaking out for justice when no one else dares. Linebarger did interview Sun, but, by his own admission, he found Sun a bit too modest and had to "supplement" his information by interviewing others. "Because of the various sources from which the subject matter is drawn, it has been found difficult to organize the narration so that extraneous material, repetition and hero-worship should not affect the biographical data."[9] This difficulty is compounded by the fact that Linebarger seldom tells us whether a particular story comes from a relative, a friend, from Sun himself, or from Linebarger's own surmises. For this reason I have made little use of the Linebarger book.

When he was twelve years old, Sun's brother Ah Mei arranged to bring him to Hawaii for a visit that was to last several years. Here he was educated in the

Christian school Iolani. Sun, who had been born a Buddhist, was soon deeply impressed with the Christian doctrine. Iolani was a British school, but he learned much there of the American Revolution and American freedom. He seems to have associated the ideas of Christianity with British and American democratic ideals. He saw Christianity as a religion of progress opposed to primitive and superstitious idolatry. His brother became increasingly concerned by Sun's enthusiasm for Christianity. At age sixteen, when he finally asked permission to become a Christian, his brother refused. He had evidently not given much attention to the effect of Sun's education and was profoundly shocked by his brother's request. He blamed himself for Sun's corruption and wrote immediately to his parents asking that the boy be sent home. The father, in writing to the older brother, said, "I will take this Jesus nonsense out of him when he comes home."[10] Before he left Hawaii, Sun received the second prize in English grammar and also carried away an English Bible.[11]

After his return home, he met a friend, Lu Hao-tung, whose family was visiting his area. Lu had traveled widely with his family, had learned English, and was already a Christian. It was from Lu that Sun learned some of the details of the Taiping Rebellion in which the leader was influenced by Christianity and organized revolutionary religious services which emphasized the destruction of idols. This behavior was an important influence on Sun and his friend. The two boys determined to strike their own blow against idolatry. According to Lyon Sharman's account, Sun and Lu went to the local temple with some of their friends where Sun spoke of the error of idolatry. "He climbed up, seized the hand of the central image and broke off its finger; he almost mutilated one of the other images."[12] The mere neglect of the local idols was supposed to result in sickness and death, but Sun remained unscathed, much to the horror and amazement of the other boys.

This was a revolutionary step on Sun's part, a break with the traditions of his family. Both Gandhi and Sun seem to have been attracted to the beliefs and practices of Westerners, particularly British and Americans, in the early stages of their development. But Gandhi decided the best way to drive the British out of India was to become more devoutly Indian in both religion and culture.

Sun's initial resentment was not directed toward a specific foreign influence in China, but toward the Manchu government which he saw as the tool of all foreigners and a source of enslavement to the Chinese. Sun's early contact with Western foreigners was more positive and he evidently tried to be more like them in order to overcome China's oppressors, but here we are missing certain vital elements in his early life. His *personal* identification was clearly with a nonviolent, trusting, essentially loving personality. We might suspect that this was his mother, but there is no solid evidence on which to base this assumption. However, the influence of his later years induced him to rebel against the beliefs and traditions of his family. His breaking of the finger on the idol was an aggressive act of defiance against his father. But the aggression was displaced. He attacked not his father, but the god of his father, a being supposed to be even more powerful. Clearly, Sun was rebelling not only against the potential threat of his father, but against all efforts to immobilize and subdue him.

As a result of his misconduct, Sun had to leave his native village; his father was no doubt relieved to see him go. Sent to Hong Kong to further his education, he applied at the Christian school and within a year entered Queens College. His father died within that year and it was probably after his father's death that he accepted the offer of Dr. Hager, a missionary from the American Board of Commissioners of Foreign Missions, to be baptized as a Christian.[13] Sun married during his first year at Queens College. His family probably insisted upon it as a last desperate effort to keep him from the dangers of foreign influence. His bride, a member of the Lu family, was a traditional woman who remained with her husband's family in Choyhung where Sun only saw her when he came home for the holidays.[14]

In his early years at Queens College, Sun took his conversion to Christianity quite seriously, making attempts to convert other Chinese and to sell Bibles. For him Christianity was not merely a new religion, but a form of political liberation. Certainly, Christianity in its teachings is no more violent and aggressive than Buddhism, but Christians represented to Sun the powerful and aggressive Westerners and their culture. While his own personality remained very much like that of other nonviolent revolutionaries, he gradually conceived a policy of violence against the Manchu Empire. This attitude developed slowly, only after his proposals for reform failed to get a hearing.

He began his medical career at the Canton Hospital school in 1886–87; his childhood friend Lu Hao-tung was also a student here and the two young men frequently discussed the possibility of a revolution against the Manchus. In his further studies at the medical school in Hong Kong he found three other friends with whom he would talk about his plans for revolution. But he was also active in his efforts at reform. In 1893 he made a trip to the north to see Li Hung-chang, the viceroy. Sun had certain proposals for the modernization of China that he wanted to put before the old man who was known to have considerable influence with the Manchu regime. But Sun and his friend were unable to see the viceroy. In his own account of this incident, Sun placed little emphasis on the reform elements in his proposal. His trip north was "to see how stable the Tai-tsing dynasty might be."[15] During this period he organized the Prosper China Society which was essentially a reformist organization designed to study progressive methods for the modernization of China.

Sun had little to say about his own interpersonal relationships with his family and even with his first wife. His early marriage was imposed upon him; it was simply another means of bringing him face-to-face with his reponsibility to family and Chinese tradition. Either by accident or design, a bride was chosen for him who was very conservative and who opposed most of his revolutionary plans. Sun says very little about his wife but it is clear that they had little in common. She soon moved to Hawaii to live with his brother's family and here she too became interested in Christianity. This may have been a belated attempt to achieve some understanding and closeness to her husband. Sun's brother dropped much of his opposition to Sun's Christian conversion and contributed to Sun's Prosper China Society when Sun went to Hawaii to enlist the help of Chinese, English, and American friends.

In Honolulu Sun received a letter from his friend and admirer Charlie Soong, an Americanized Chinese who had come to Wilmington, North Carolina in 1880. Charlie urged him to return to China and take advantage of the difficulties China faced in the war with Japan as an ideal way to foster revolution. Charlie Soong was essentially an American with strong capitalist aspirations, but never lost his interest in China and frequently urged Sun to visit the United States to raise funds and propagandize for the revolution.

The Revolutionary

Following his friend's advice, Sun traveled over China making plans for his revolution. The defeat of China by Japan was finalized in the treaty of Shimonoseki, April 17, 1895. The humiliation following this defeat was used by the revolutionaries as a basis for building a strong, free China which could overcome future adversaries. Sun disguised his revolutionary movement as an agricultural society and began making plans for the capture of Canton. They smuggled guns from Hong Kong and recruited members both there and in Canton. However, a consigment of 600 pistols disguised as casks of cement was discovered when one of the casks was accidently broken in shipment. Seventy people were arrested and three of Sun's trusted friends were executed. He cut off his queue (pigtail), grew a moustache, and left China for the Philippines. His new attire made him look Japanese and allowed him later to travel to Japan and establish additional foreign contacts for his Chinese revolutionary movement. He also spent much time in the United States raising funds and lecturing on the coming revolution in China. On passing through London, he was captured and imprisoned in the Chinese Embassy. Had he not been rescued through the efforts of his friend, Dr. Cantlie, he would probably have been deported to China and executed. The story of his imprisonment and escape was filled with the kind of suspense and excitement that captures the imagination of reporters. It made all the London papers and Sun became famous overnight as a notorious Chinese revolutionary. The experience did much to aid his fund-raising efforts in England and the United States.

Throughout this period Sun was doing both intense theoretical and practical work. He was reading the works of Jean Jacques Rousseau, Thomas Jefferson, Henry George, and Karl Marx. He incorporated his own brand of revolutionary socialism and land reform in his *San Min Chu I*, written in 1898. Unlike Fidel Castro who had his Guevara and Lenin who had his Trotsky, Sun Yat-sen had no major theoretician to whom he could delegate the task of building the moral force of the revolution. But perhaps there was a reason for this absence of a strong intellectual force outside Sun. Both Trotsky and Guevara had a strong personal need to be the chief *moral* authority for the revolution. Sun was perhaps too deeply involved in this goal to allow anyone else to assume primary responsibility. He was more willing to relinquish his administrative and military power than he was to give up his moral authority. The same was true of Gandhi, who resigned from Congress but who retained his moral influence over his followers.

In 1900 Sun attempted to take advantage of the Boxer Rebellion and install his own revolutionary movement in China. He was not allowed to land at Hong Kong, so he sent emissaries to direct the revolution in his place. One of his close associates, Yamada, a Japanese revolutionary, was captured and executed. The 1900 affair was the second defeat of the revolution, but Sun felt that progress had been made toward "China's gradual awakening from sleep."[16] Still, he saw himself as engaged in a long struggle which would probably not be victorious until after his death. Not until 1905, with the creation of his United League (*Tung Meng Hui*), an international revolutionary organization, did he begin to believe that revolution could be accomplished in his lifetime.[17] Sun continued to propagandize for the Chinese revolution among Chinese, Japanese, and Occidentals throughout the world. His United League was a loosely organized society which developed its own revolutionary army, an army that often acted independently of Sun and sometimes without his knowledge. In 1907 Sun and his colleagues (then in Tokyo) were unable to join a revolt in Pinli because they did not hear of it in time. This revolt, too, was crushed.

When the revolutionaries finally controlled southern China through a revolution resulting in the capture of Wuchang, Sun was traveling in South America and the United States on one of his many fund-raising and propaganda missions. He immediately concluded that the international status of the revolution was a matter of life and death and that it was essential that he depart for London to secure English support. Even with the internal military situation in China at a crisis, Sun's broad world view of revolution (shared with Trotsky and Guevara) predominated. This is not to say that Sun was at all unrealistic in his attitude. China was at that time dominated by six Western powers. The international situation was even more important than in the Russian Revolution and certainly as critical as in the Cuban Revolution. Significantly, even when the newspapers prematurely titled him president of the new Chinese republic, Sun felt there were other competent leaders who could direct the revolution within China. The one thing that must be done and which he alone could do was to secure the world situation.[18]

News of the attack on Canton reached him in New York and he sent a telegram to Governor Chang Ni-isi suggesting he surrender the city to avoid bloodshed. In England he tried to block payment of the English loan to the Manchu government and sought to prevent Japan from helping the dynasty. In France he met with the opposition parties and gained their support for his republic. He finally arrived in Shanghai thirty days later, at the time of the peace conference between north and south China. He was elected provisional president of China in 1912, although the north was still in the hands of the Dowager Empress. Sun merged his own revolutionary party with several others to form the Kuomintang—the National

People's Party. In order to secure the resignation of the Empress and unite all China, he worked out an agreement with Yuan Shih-kai, commander of the army of the north, that he (Sun) would resign his new post as president of the Chinese republic in favor of Yuan.

Return to Revolution

In the fall of 1913 Yuan suppressed the Kuomintang and tried to rule China by force. Sun began another uprising, but was forced to flee to Japan and go into hiding for a time. In 1909 Sun's brother and wife had returned to China from Hawaii. After her husband was elected president, she went to Nanking, but fled to Macao with her child, probably at Sun's insistence, when the new uprising began. Here she became a convert to Christianity and was given work by one of the missions as a Bible woman, teaching the Gospel in Chinese homes.[19] What was happening to her is not clear and Sun gives us no account of her. It would seem that she admired her husband and was striving to follow some of his ideas. However, by the time she had fully discovered the "revolutionary" aspects of Christianity, Sun had gone beyond religion and into politics. The lack of close personal contact made it difficult for her to interact with his rapid changes on a daily basis, although she bore him a son and a daughter.

In Tokyo, Sun worked with his friend Charlie Soong, who had been the treasurer of his short-lived revolutionary movement and who had fled with him. Charlie's daughter E-ling worked for a while as Sun's secretary, but she soon married H. H. Kung, an ardent revolutionary with strong political ambitions. E-ling was replaced as Sun's secretary by her sister Ching-ling, who had graduated from Wesleyan College in Macon, Georgia. Already an enthusiastic revolutionary thanks to her father, she was much more politically sophisticated and better educated than Sun's wife. At this time, Sun's wife is said to have moved to Japan and, at the urging of her husband, given her consent to a separation. Sun married Soong Ching-ling in Japan on October 25, 1915.[20]

Though considerably younger than her husband, Ching-ling had in many respects been prepared by her father for such a man. She accepted Sun's guidance without the questions and conflicts experienced by Kasturbai in her efforts to follow Gandhi. Gandhi was never successful as his wife's teacher; she was still very much ashamed of being in jail at the time of her death and she wondered why Gandhi wanted the British out of India when there was plenty of room for everyone. Still, he did bring her along in his political development with some reluctance on her part. Ching-ling was a college graduate and a widely traveled woman before she met Sun. His attraction to this young, vibrant woman is not surprising. For Sun, religion was no longer an integral aspect of his revolutionary ideology.

Sun found allies in Japan, for south China was an important source of trade for the Japanese. They sought to maintain a policy of strict neutrality, but they were not opposed to sheltering a possible future president of China from his enemies.

In Tokyo, Sun began forming a more tightly organized party in which the members were to take an oath of loyalty to him personally. The Japanese offered their support and Sun eagerly accepted. A volunteer Japanese force was provided along with funds and rifles. Yuan, meanwhile, had obtained much support from other foreigners: loans from Great Britain and advice from the United States in the form of a constitution, giving Yuan supreme power, drafted by Professor F. J. Goodnow of Johns Hopkins.

Sun has often been criticized for the naiveté with which he accepted Japanese aid and for his assumption that the Japanese were motivated by friendship for his movement. But all allies on either side gave their support with the hope of gaining power in China. Sun simply took his support from a nation that had long been an enemy of his people. Yuan made things much easier for his enemy by offending public taste when he revived the splendid ceremonies of the imperial regime and prepared for his own coronation. Revolts broke out all over China and some of Sun's old revolutionary comrades returned from abroad to give him support. Yuan died in disgrace on June 6, 1916; Sun could now rule, at least in the south. He formed a comittee of revolutionary leaders at Canton to develop policy, but to his great surprise was consistently outvoted. He was not an astute politician and did not know how to maneuver people. He soon returned to Shanghai to write.

Throughout this period Sun moved back and forth, from active revolutionary leadership to retreat and further theoretical activity. He blamed himself for his failure to awaken the masses of Chinese people and often to convince his own colleagues, who regarded him as too theoretical and idealistic. In reflecting on this problem, he remarked:

> At first it seemed as if I, as the leader, would be able very easily to give effect to the programme. . . . If I had succeeded in achieving this, China would have found her place amongst the family of nations and would have entered the path of progress and happiness. But, unfortunately, the Revolution was scarcely completed when the members of our party unexpectedly turned out to be of a different opinion from myself, considering my ideals too elevated and unattainable for the reconstruction of modern China. . . . Therefore it turned out that my programme had less chances of being realized when I held the post of President than when I was leader of the Party which was preparing the Revolution.[21].

When he speaks of himself as "president," he is obviously referring to the early period when the old regime was first overthrown, but the disagreement over his leadership continued throughout his life.

San Min Chu I

Sun was never a skillful writer but he was a good speaker and he wrote during a period of revolution in Chinese writing which emphasized writing as one speaks. Many of Sun's lectures were taken down and published in a book called the *San Min Chu I* (Three Principles of the People) in which he outlined some of his beliefs and plans for China. He read Rousseau's *Social Contract* and warmly advocated his ideas on democracy.[22] He also read the theories of Marx and admired the lucidity of his thought as well as his socialist ideas.[23] However, while he saw Marx as an excellent guide, he did not believe China could make use of his methods.[24]

The principles of communism and the Communist party itself could be useful influences in China if they were adapted to the special conditions of China and not followed in a slavish and automatic manner as though the words of Marx were gospel.[25] This was what Sun believed, but he was not a practical politician. He needed a means for "awakening" the people of China and in 1920, when the first Soviet representatives contacted him, he encouraged them to send advisors. In this same year he was again able to return to Canton as "President of China" due to the influence of his followers in Parliament, but this presidency consisted only of Kwangtung Province. All attempts to retake the north failed. In 1922 a new revolutionary army under the leadership of Li Yuan-hung captured Peking and Sun Yat-sen was invited to come north and help plan a new China. But Sun was now fifty-six and somewhat wary of dealing with the practical men on revolutionary committees; he refused. His colleague Chen was outraged by his refusal and attacked the presidential palace. Sun fled with a few loyal officers (among them Chiang Kai-shek) to Shanghai where he issued a manifesto calling for universal suffrage, a check on militarism, and the development of industry. Chen attacked all these ideas as too idealistic.

In 1924 Sun called troops to his aid and defeated General Chen. He became once again generalissino and chief executive of south China. Chiang Kai-shek became his chief of staff. He sought aid and support from the West, but most foreign powers supported his opponents in the north. As a result, he sent Chiang Kai-shek to the Soviet Union to study military organization and began to cement his own contacts with the Soviets. Sun died in early 1925 at the age of fifty-nine and Chiang began a growing estrangement with his Russian advisors. In 1925 he seized power and expelled all communists, including Mao Tse-tung (director of propaganda for the party and the only formidable ideologist), from the revolutionary party of the Kuomintang. It became a crime punishable by death to be a communist or communist sympathizer. From this point on the Kuomintang ceased to be an ideological organization for raising revolutionary consciousness but became more and more a military power.

Both Chiang and Mao claimed to be the true inheritors of the mantle of Sun Yat-sen. Both, of course, could make some claim to this position. Sun had made his closest friendships with Western leaders and he admired Western philosophy, but he had also come to recognize the importance of soviets as actual revolutionary units to raise the consciousness of the masses. In many respects he was a more creative thinker than either Chiang or Mao and he would probably have devised his own blend of sovietized democracy. However, in his absence China was faced with the difficult choice between a corrupt and self-indulgent Chiang and an ascetic self-sacrificing Mao who promised hardship and struggle on the road to communism and national independence.

On November 12, 1956, over twenty years after Mao Tse-tung was elected chairman of the Soviet Republic of China and began his famous Long March which was to end in the victory of Chinese communism over the forces of Chiang Kai-shek, celebrations were held all over China to honor the birth of Sun Yat-sen. In his speech on this day Mao remarked:

> Let us pay tribute to his memory, for his steadfast struggle against the Chinese reformists in which he took a clear cut stand as a Chinese revolutionary democrat in a period preparatory to the democratic revolution in China. . . . We completed the revolution left unfinished by Dr. Sun; we have developed it into a socialist revolution, which we are now in the course of completing. [26]

The Role of Moral Masochism

In the life of Sun Yat-sen we would be hard pressed to find instances in which he deliberately courted suffering or took pleasure in his own suffering. While he must have known he would be punished for breaking the finger of an idol, this act from his childhood lacks the essential elements of masochistic provocation (at least in the details available to us). We have already noted Reik's description of the masochistic rebel as one who follows a "Promethian model" in his defiance of the gods. [27] In this respect Sun Yat-sen seems to fit the pattern, but rebellion in itself does not constitute moral masochism. Sun, in his own account of himself, does not provide us with examples from his childhood in which he admired the suffering of Jesus.

We find only a faint echo of sado-masochism in Sun's tendency to alternate between a struggle for military domination and his frequent revulsion from this role to one of moral leadership. One of the best Western sources on Sun, Lyon Sharman's *Sun Yat-sen: His Life and Its Meaning*, seems to attribute his frequent failure in power to his autocratic rule and to his tendency to overreach himself in his vision for a union of all China. While she often attributes this tendency to the autocracy inherent in the ancient Chinese culture, she seldom attempts to explain his periods of retreat, except as a failure to get the full autocratic control he desired. [28]

While I fully accept Sharman's account of Sun as an autocrat in his behavior, one has only to read his works to discover his moral beliefs were in the direction of democracy. One is reminded of Rousseau's writings about democracy, but Rousseau also showed a tendency to become autocratic when dealing with rebels against his own ideas and in his efforts to manage children. Sun, like Rousseau, sought a character for himself of perfect sweetness and justice to others, but he was frequently angered by what he regarded as the stupidity of his fellow revolutionaries who felt his democratic ideals were too advanced for China. Unfortunately, we do not have any good first-hand accounts of his meetings with his colleagues, but he must have been torn between the desire for a posture of sweetness and accommodation and the urge to beat democracy into their heads with a club. Thus we find him, on the one hand, struggling to gain complete and undisputed control of all China, north and south; and, on the other, retiring from political life to write, study, and teach the people.

His own writings give the impression of a man who sought democracy for China, a man who was influenced by Jefferson and Rousseau, who admired Marx, but who did not accept the need for a dictatorship of the proletariat or class warfare. Clearly, Sun regarded himself as one who sought power only to bring about a moral change in the Chinese people. He had a need similar to that of Gandhi to retreat from politics, to write and think, to create a revolutionary consciousness in the people which would be the best defense against a return of the ancient Chinese imperialism. The following is from his memoirs:

> In the second year of the Republic, Yuan-Shih-Kai united the whole country, and I went on working, without occupying myself with politics: but when he brutally murdered Sun-Chiao-Jen, could I remain passive? Without having a single soldier at my disposal, I declared the necessity of fighting Yuan-Shih-Kai. . . .
>
> The spirit of revolt was sown by me in the people so effectively that it was sufficient for the Restoration to show its face for it immediately to be rebuffed by the efforts of the whole people. From all this it can be seen that I renounced the Presidency, not for fear of the power of Yuan-Shih-Kai, but because I could not carry out the tasks of revolutionary reconstruction. [29]

This task of revolutionary reconstruction had to do with the democratization of China, not only from the standpoint of administrative reforms, but, more deeply, in the minds of the people.

We see here the first glimmering of the notion of revolutionary consciousness, an idea that was enunciated by Marx but which was to be carried to its more extreme and sometimes unrealistic forms by Ché Guevara and Mao Tse-tung. It was a belief that the mind, the thinking, and the attitudes of a people could be so profoundly transformed that they would accept no government that did not follow the principles of the founder. It was a belief that revolution could change the basic *morality* of an entire people, could change even their personalities and their capacity for compassion for others, for the poor and the disadvantaged. To a certain extent, of course, this is true, but it is also true that the people tire of sacrifice, of high moral principles, that jealousies and private desires arise. There are moments when, under the inspiration of a Sun Yat-sen or a Ché Guevara, the working man will finish a day of toil in the fields and come home to volunteer his labor to build a road. At other times, when his children are complaining of hunger and his wife tells him the roof leaks, he thinks "to hell with the revolution." If he is allowed to slip back into this mode of private concern for the nuclear family, the revolution is lost, even though it may have achieved a military supremacy over the countryside.

This desire to exercise a moral authority over his people and to create in them a special revolutionary virtue was clearly a continuous and dominant urge in Sun. Education and training were vital aspects of any government transition. [30] In Mao

Tse-tung, as we will see later, the administrator and military leader were at first dominant, only to give rise later to a fear that he had failed to bring about the required moral change and that China might slip back into a capitalistic imperialism after his death.

But for Sun, the urge for a moral reform was so dominant that it often interfered with his military ambitions and his administrative control. We find him stressing education as the only means for overcoming the "slave psychology."[31] The state, he said, was merely a vessel to hold the hearts of men and state policy was a reflection of psychological factors.[32]

Despite our failure to find clear evidence of masochism in the childhood and life history of Sun, he provides certain similarities to the revolutionaries we have already studied. The sweetness of his personality, his conviction that the revolution will triumph through the virtue of its people, and his general emphasis on moral reform as more important than political and military changes all suggest a certain kinship with the first revolutionaries we have examined.

Sun consistently described himself as a failure, yet he is even today one of the great heros of the Chinese Revolution. This, too, fits with the image of the moral masochist who is content to regard himself as a failure in the present if he can envisage himself as vindicated at some later date, and future generations visiting his tomb pay him honor and respect.

NOTES

1. Paul Linebarger, *Sun Yat-Sen and the Chinese Republic* (New York: Century, 1925), 255.

2. Ibid., 254.

3. Upton Close, *Eminent Asians* (New York: Appleton, 1930), 16.

4. Grace T. Seton, "The Great Leader of China," *American Review of Reviews* 67 (June 1923): 634.

5. Wang Chi-sing, *The Foundations of San Min Chu I in the Chinese Culture* (Shanghai: Kuo Hsueh Press, 1927), 3. From the Preface by Tai Chi-tao.

6. James Cantlie, *Sun Yat-Sen and the Awakening of China* (New York: Fleming H. Revell, 1912), 57.

7. Linebarger, *Sun Yat-Sen*, 57.

8. Cantlie, *Sun Yat-Sen and the Awakening of China*, 31.

9. Linebarger, *Sun Yat-Sen*, ix.

10. Henry B. Restarick, *Sun Yat-Sen: Liberator of China* (New Haven: Yale University Press, 1931), 17.

11. Lyon Sharman, *Sun Yat-sen: His Life and Its Meaning* (Stanford: Stanford University Press, 1968), 10–14.

12. Ibid., 19.

13. Ibid., 19–21.

14. Ibid., 23–24.

15. Sun Yat-sen, *Memoirs of a Chinese Revolutionary: A Program of National Reconstruction for China* (New York: AMS Press, 1970), 187.

16. Ibid., 199.

17. Ibid., 203.

18. Ibid., 221–22.

19. Restarick, *Sun Yat-sen*, 128.

20. Ibid., 129.

21. Sun Yat-sen, *Memoirs of a Chinese Revolutionary*, 5–6.

22. Sun Yat-sen, *San Min Chu I* (Chungking: Republic of China, Ministry of Information, 1943), 173.

23. Ibid., 373–77.

24. Ibid., 382–83.

25. Ibid., 427–41.

26. *Dr. Sun Yat-sen* (Peking: Foreign Language Press, 1957), 9–11.

27. Theodor Reik, *Masochism in Modern Man* (New York: Grove, 1941), 157.

28. Sharman, *Sun Yat-sen*, 214, 351.

29. Sun, *Memoirs of a Chinese Revolutionary*, 126–27.

30. Ibid., 133.

31. Ibid., 136.

32. Ibid., 138–43.

Chapter 10

LEON TROTSKY:
The Internationalist

Background

Karl Marx had begun to see the decline of Tsarist Russia in the last years before his death, and in 1885 Engels was in correspondence with Vera Zasulich, a founder of one of the first Marxist groups in Russia. But Marx was far from making a direct application of his theory of historical materialism to Russia. In a letter written toward the end of 1877 he cautioned against a too wide and general application of his theory. He pointed out that events which are strikingly analogous but which take place in different historical surroundings may lead to very different results.[1] Lenin and Trotsky were soon to demonstrate the truth of this statement.

Childhood

On October 26, 1879, Lev Bronstein (Leon Trotsky) was born, the fifth child of a Jewish farmer on the estate of Yanovka in the southern Ukraine. Like the father of Karl Marx, the older Bronstein was unconcerned with religion and did not attend the local synagogue. Lyova's (diminutive of Lev) mother was more attached to Judaism and would not travel or sew on the Sabbath. Lyova regarded his father as the more intelligent and sensitive member of the family. He was quieter and gentler with the children than the mother, who would sometimes lose her temper without reason or vent her fatigue on the children. In his own account of his early years, the adult Trotsky described his family as one without displays of tenderness.[2] His mother and father were away from the children all day working in the fields, they had a close comradeship with each other but not with their children. Nevertheless, he gives several examples in which he was shown affection by his parents. When he fell from a shovel and began to cry he was picked up and kissed by his mother.[3] After the adults had tolerated much foolishness on the part of Lyova and his sister, they would "pat and kiss me" and put him to sleep in a feather bed.[4] We will soon discover other incidents in which they showed even greater solicitude and concern about his hurt feelings.

Lyova was not taught Yiddish as a child and when he was sent to stay with relatives in Gromokla, where he went to school for a short period, he was out of

touch with his schoolmates and could not understand his teacher. He was repelled
by the dirt and the hovels of the Jewish settlement and attracted toward what he
came to regard as the more civilized behavior of the gentile community. Even as a
young child he was attracted to those people who seemed to him more cultivated
and educated and it is not surprising that shortly after his return from the Jewish
school, he was impressed by the arrival at Yanovka of his cousin Monya (Moissey
Filippovich Schpentzer). Monya was twenty-eight when he came to Yanovka and
Lyova noticed that his mother always gave his cousin the best cuts of meat, asked
how he enjoyed his food, and inquired as to his favorite dishes. He was a city youth
from Odessa and his learning impressed everyone. He taught the young Trotsky
many things: how to hold a glass, how to wash, how to pronounce certain words,
and the medicinal value of fresh milk. He also had a strong influence on the social
attitudes of the impressionable child.

> When the overseer once struck a shepherd with a long knout because he had
> kept the horses out late, Monya grew pale and hissed between his teeth,
> "How shameful!" And I felt that it was shameful. I do not know if I would have
> felt the same way if he had not made his remark—I am inclined to think I
> would. But in any event he helped me to feel that way, and this alone was
> enough to instill in me a lifelong sense of gratitude.[5]

It was shortly after this that Trotsky went to live with Monya's family in Odessa
where he went to school and began to receive a more sophisticated city education. The Schpentzer family was affectionate with the young Lev and Monya
encouraged him to read and provided him with the works of Tolstoy, Pushkin, and
Nekrassov.

The Sweet Pain

The first incident in which we see in Trotsky the kind of moral indignation that
was evident in other revolutionaries is in his expulsion from the school at Odessa.
He was accused of leading the other students in howling at one of the teachers.
Trotsky argued that he participated but was not an instigator of the howling. He
was deeply upset by his expulsion, but he could not show much emotion. "I did not
cry. I merely pined."[6] He was later readmitted to school in the third grade. He
maintained that the emotional release of feelings in which he flung himself on the
bed and wept over his sense of injustice, occurred over a year later in the fourth
grade when he was fourteen years old. However, in his autobiography this
incident appears on the page following his expulsion. It may have been a delayed
response or perhaps it occurred at an earlier point, closer to his expulsion, and
Trotsky exaggerated his stoicism over the event. In either case the feeling
associated with his ecstatic experience is strongly colored by a sense of injustice,
a certain "sweet pain," and a deliberate prolongation of the suffering, suggesting
it was pleasurable. The end of Trotsky's account follows.

> He [Trotsky] came home with a buzzing head, with painful music in his
> temples. Dropping the kit on the table, he lay down on the bed and, hardly

realizing what he was doing, began to weep into the pillow. To find an excuse for his tears, he recalled pitiful scenes from books and from his own life, as if to feed the furnace with fresh fuel, and wept and wept with tears of spring longing.[7]

Trotsky concluded his description of his school life with the remark that the injustice he experienced at school, contrary to its direct purpose, sowed "the seeds of enmity for the existing order. Those seeds, at any rate, did not fall on barren ground."[8]

It is always difficult to find the point of origin for such feelings. The "sweet pain" of knowing that he had been unjustly treated may have originated much earlier in some experience with his parents, some incident that he failed to mention in his autobiography and for which this later event is only a screen memory. Trotsky separates this incident of his "sweet pain" from all other events of that period. It seems to come upon him without cause, as though it related to some event in the distant past and is now experienced, once again, in connection with a current experience.

Wolfenstein's study of Trotsky suggests a possible origin of this feeling. Wolfenstein also mentions Trotsky's remark that his parents were not tender with him but that they were close with each other.

> In this passage Trotsky practically screams out his grievance: *I was ignored and unloved, even the cattle got more attention than I did and what love was displayed was between my parents—I was excluded!* This is the cry of the lonely child, trying hard not to blame his parents, but hating them for their lack of solicitude just the same.
>
> The grayness in Trotsky's young life was the color of loneliness, of feeling unloved. . . . His mother's absence, moreover, exacerbated Trotsky's relations with his father. It is hard enough for a child to accept the father's relationship with his mother in circumstances where the mother is at home with the children; where the mother is not home explicitly because of her bond with the father (where all tenderness is between mother and father, as Trotsky noted), then the tension between father and son becomes almost overwhelming.
>
> . . . If, additionally, the father is generally kind and indulgent, as Trotsky's father appears to have been, the relationship is infused with ambivalence, with love and respect for the father on the one hand, resulting in the internalization of the father's moral standards, and hate for him on the other—which, when combined, result in pervasive feelings of guilt and anxiety.[9]

Thus in Trotsky, the initial sadistic and destructive impulse toward his father was inhibited by guilt. From Reik's description of the dynamics of masochism, we would expect Trotsky to find some way back to the love of his parents through suffering, some "sweet pain" to draw him close to them again.

Trotsky returned every summer to his father's farm, but now he saw the environment in the light of his growing education and his liberalized views developed in the Schpentzer home. He reports an incident on one of these summers in which his father had taken possession of a peasant's cow that had wandered into his fields and eaten some of his grain. The peasant who owned the cow was following his father begging to have his cow returned.

> The scene stirred me to my very marrow. The genial mood I had carried away from the croquet court with its fringe of pear-trees, where I had routed my sisters with flying colors, instantly gave way to a feeling of intense despair. I slipped past my father into my bedroom, and falling flat on the bed, gave myself up to tears, despite my status of a boy of the second grade. . . . Mother came from the mill—I could recognize her voice at once; the sound of plates being prepared for dinner came through, and I heard mother calling me. . . . But I did not answer and went on weeping. Tears were beginning to yield a sense of blissful pleasure. Then the door opened and Mother bent over me.
>
> "What's the matter, Lyovochka?"
> I made no answer. Mother and Father whispered something to one another.
> "Are you upset about the peasant? But we gave him back his cow and we did not fine him."
> "I am not upset about that at all," I answered from under the pillow, painfully ashamed of the cause of my tears.
> "And we did not fine him," Mother said again with emphasis. It was Father who had guessed the cause of my sorrow and told Mother. Father noticed much in passing, with one quick glance. [10]

This scene may have occurred prior to his expulsion from school, as the young Lyova was still in the second grade (the grade from which he was expelled) when it occurred. It raises, once again, some doubts about Trotsky's statement that his parents were strict with him and showed him little tenderness. It seems to describe a scene in which the parents feel guilty because they have in some way hurt the feelings of their little son. They are contrite; they come to him and explain themselves, asking for his forgiveness. He is pleased by his power over them, but also somewhat embarrassed. Like the incident of Trotsky's ecstatic feelings after his expulsion from school, this incident has the same combination of suffering and extreme pleasure. But surely this is not the first incident of its kind. The father has already learned to know, from observation, what it is that has upset his son. Clearly, this is a learned behavior, based on incidents that occurred earlier in the child's life, possibly those in which Lyova himself was unjustly punished and took pleasure in the knowledge of his own virtue and the repentance of his parents.

Regardless of the events that preceded this experience with the peasant and his cow, it is clear that at this point in his life the young Lyova had already learned that he could have a powerful influence on his parents by being "hurt," particularly if his *feelings* were hurt.

Unlike Rousseau, we do not find Trotsky connecting his sympathy for the peasants with an "eternal hatred of oppression." In Trotsky's case the oppressor was his father, whom he loved and respected. It was only the injustices he experienced in school that he could clearly link with his "enmity for the existing order." Yet the feelings are similar. The experience with the peasant and the example of Monya may well have prepared the way for his later attitude toward the school and the Russian monarchy.

His first serious contact with political questions occurred at the age of seventeen in Nikolayev, a time Trotsky regarded as the turning point of his youth. He was lodged with a family while attending the local school and the sons of the landlady attempted to draw him into political discussions, expressing some of their Marxist views. Trotsky at first replied with disdain, but finally "The ideas filling the air proved stronger than I, especially since in the depths of my soul I wished for nothing better than to yield to them."[11] Trotsky remarks that his "consciousness" was receptive to such ideas, being filled at the time by vague feelings of social protest. What did these feelings consist of? "Sympathy for the down-trodden and indignation over injustice—the latter was perhaps the stronger feeling."[12] The transformation was now almost complete. The feelings of tenderness and sympathy for the oppressed were being replaced by the stronger feelings of anger against the oppressor. But there was also, mixed with this desire to fight injustice, a revulsion toward the backwardness, the primitive conditions, and the ignorance that characterized the Russia of his times. Thus Trotsky emerged into adulthood with the feeling that the working man should rise against his masters and against the Tzar, but he was sure that the way to this revolution lay in intellectual enlightenment of the masses.

Intellectualism and the Dynamics of Delay

Reik has insisted that the basic aim in masochism is one of revenge and destruction. The masochistic fantasy is really a cover for basic sadistic desires. Thus, the desire to suffer while working for revolution would seem a perfect blend of both the overt masochistic fantasy, with the sadistic aim also conscious, but delayed. One *submits* to self-imposed suffering, to the discipline of a revolutionary movement with the thought that "someday" one will gain full power and be able to punish and dominate the enemy.

However, in order to sustain this fantasy, delay is essential. The basic sadistic impulse, which was probably directed toward the father or possibly both parents, is restrained by guilt. Therefore, one cannot merely rush out to make a physical attack on some government figure. One must have the *feeling* of conducting an attack without actually incurring the responsibility for such an act. The building of a theoretical structure for revolution and the gradual organization of activist groups serves this purpose.

The *method* by which one delays the final outburst of revolutionary furor will depend on other factors in the life history of the individual. Trotsky was strongly attracted by foreigners and foreign cultures because he considered them more advanced than the primitive society of Russia. This may well have been a product of his initial antagonism to the narrowness and parochial attitudes that he attributed to the Jewish community of Gromokla. His initial desire for involvement in the larger, more cultured gentile community was finally expanded into a kind of revolutionary internationalism, a belief that the more advanced and enlightened ideas, the more forward looking and revolutionary ideas could be found outside the primitive and culturally backward environment of Russia.

This was not an uncommon attitude. Many of the wealthy and better educated Russians had escaped to Paris, Berlin, or even London where they might find more discussion and intellectual stimulation than in Moscow or St. Petersburg. Marxism was, of course, one of those dreaded foreign ideologies that was both mysterious and attractive to rebellious and intellectual Russian youth such as Trotsky. However, it seemed that Trotsky must first combat every new idea before he could yield to it. He was initially repelled by Marxism because it seemed to be a completed system. He was attracted to theoretical work himself and thought he might develop his own revolutionary ideology, not only because of his growing interest in all intellectual matters, but because he was already habituated to the notion of a period of delay before revolution, and delay required some justification.

It was inevitable that Trotsky would finally succumb to the ideas of Marx. In order to attack the theory he must first understand it and he soon found Marxist theory quite complex and not easily mastered. This stimulated his intellectual curiosity. It required time to understand the theory, but time that could always be justified on the grounds that one was actively preparing the revolution by reading and studying. Further, the theory had its own built-in justification for delay. One could not build a workers' state until the conditions were right. Russia had a relatively powerless and undeveloped bourgeoisie. Therefore, it was necessary to prepare for the development of the bourgeoisie before a communist revolution would be possible.

In this discussion I have tried to show how the *personal needs* of Trotsky led him to adopt a Marxist position, but the historian and the professional revolutionary will certainly object that there was a rational basis for Trotsky's ideological development. Delay was not only justified by theory; it was justified by reality as well. Communists in Russia did not have the strength to attack the government when Trotsky began his work. It was necessary to organize, to create a disciplined body of followers, to present them with a rationale for their behavior, to keep them in line and avoid a premature and abortive *putsch* against the government. Unlike Marx, Trotsky was involved in the planning and execution of a revolutionary uprising. He was one of the actual leaders of the final insurrection in 1917, while Lenin was in hiding. How, then, can we describe his behavior as motivated by masochistic needs? It is only when we view the full development of Trotsky's political career, including his later abdication of power and his refusal to recognize the threat posed by Stalin, that we can make a judgment on this point. It is also necessary to remember that all behavior is overdetermined. There is no single cause of each step in the development of the individual, but a multitude of conflicting and often contradictory pressures. Unlike the sexual masochist, Trotsky's entire life was not dominated by a single, highly personal, instinctual aim. Masochism was a powerful element in his dynamics, but he also reasoned about events and their consequences. When the moment of crisis arrived he was quite capable of overcoming his private instinctual needs for a heroic effort, only to relapse into a subordinate position after the success of the revolution.

Further, Trotsky was attracted to Marxism by other aspects beyond its justification for delay. We have already noted its intellectual depth. It was an international theory which emphasized the need to develop the consciousness of workers throughout the world. It was therefore, by implication at least, a more powerful idea than any that had gone before, for it encompassed not just a national revolution but world revolution. It is not surprising that the young Trotsky, already an incipient internationalist, should be attracted by an idea that suggested foreign travel and contact with other cultures as inherent and necessary parts of one's revolutionary activity.

Provocation

In Trotsky, then, we find an individual whose personal psychodynamics were very similar to those of Marx. He had the same intensely rebellious attitude combined with a strong scholarly interest. He both identified with his father and sought to overcome him. He was restrained by a sense of guilt from an immediate attack. He also showed the same tendency to generalize these feelings toward authority as a whole: first toward his early school authorities and finally toward the government.

However, moral masochism involves not merely the preparation for the fight against injustice, but also an ongoing need for a sense of personal virtue. The masochist has learned from earlier life experiences that suffering and struggling for others is accompanied by a strong feeling of being right, an immediate sense of the justice of his cause.[13] Merely preparing for a revolution by developing an ideology, preaching to revolutionary groups, or publishing open criticism of the government is insufficient to excite one's sense of personal virtue if unaccompanied by punishment. Some actual physical contact must be made with the cruelty of the oppressor. The revolutionary discovers that punishment is pleasurable only if it gives him a sense of his own virtue and the knowledge that in the end he will be proven right. In the case of Trotsky, as in that of many of our other revolutionaries, his masochism seems congruent with his life goals. He operated his provocation so successfully that we can no longer tell the difference between masochism and courage.

Trotsky was jailed during a series of mass arrests of suspected revolutionaries in 1898. He spent a long period of complete isolation in Kherson Prison; he could communicate with no one, was half-starved, had no change of underwear, no soap or water for washing, and was eaten by lice. He used the time for reflection, writing, and, when possible, studying Marxist theory. When he was transferred to a Moscow prison, he heard of Lenin's new book, *The Development of Capitalism in Russia,* and in the comparative freedom of this new environment he was able to read it. Prison stimulated his ingenuity and he devised new means of communication with the prisoners, passing his notebooks on ideology back and forth. He staged several protests, once persuading his fellow prisoners to go on a hunger strike to demand the release of juvenile prisoners to their parents. In Moscow he staged another demonstration against the solitary confinement of a prisoner who failed to take off his cap for the governor of the prison. Like Marx, he had that combination of tenderness toward those close to him and absolute ruthlessness toward the enemy. Isaac Deutscher has given this account of his character during his prison period.

> Harsh and defiant toward authority, or, as he himself would have said, towards the class enemy, he was warm-hearted and even sentimental with his comrades and their relatives. The convicts were allowed to receive their relatives twice a week. After these visits Bronstein [Trotsky] showed a moving tenderness not only to his own girl [Alexandra Sokolovskaya] and future wife . . . but to all the other women who came to see their husbands and brothers; he charmed them with his chivalry. The women usually took home the men's linen, but Bronstein refused to benefit from such comforts, washed and repaired his own linen, and mocked at revolutionaries so ensnared in bourgeois habits and prejudices as to burden their womenfolk with such work. . . . So much was he remembered for the warmth of his friendship that years later his friends, who had in the meantime become his opponents, were puzzled by his ruthlessness in the revolution and in the civil war.[14]

From all accounts Trotsky seemed to enjoy his imprisonment and learned to adjust to it as part of the long process of delay necessary for final victory. If confinement gave him a sense of virtue, it also stimulated his energy. One wonders if such a character trait is not essential to a revolutionary in the early stages of preparation. Who else could endure the long periods of disgrace and privation? Who else could hold out so long against discouragement and actually seem to thrive on punishment? In his first exile at Ust-Kut "life was dark and repressed," the house full of cockroaches and the woods so infested with midges that they had bitten a cow to death. While the scenery was beautiful, Trotsky scarcely noticed it. "I was studying Marx, brushing the cockroaches off the page."[15] Indeed, his intense intellectual energy seemed to sustain him while many of his fellow prisoners and fellow exiles went mad or committed suicide. "In all the big exile colonies there were graves of suicides. Some of the exiles became absorbed in the local populations, especially in the towns; others took to drink. In exile, as in prison, only hard intellectual work could save one. The Marxists, I must admit, were the only ones who did any of it under these conditions."[16]

After Trotsky's second arrest following the abortive revolution of 1905, Julius Martov advised all the defendants to plead their case with moderation, but Trotsky persuaded his fellow prisoners into taking the most defiant and provocative stance. The revolutionaries, he insisted, should make no effort to conceal their actions but actually use the prisoner's dock to state their principles.[17] His prison cell became a library; he read all the latest news and opinion while he prepared his speech. "I feel extremely well, I sit and work and am quite sure that nobody can arrest me."[18]

The Sudden Eloquence

Like Rousseau, Trotsky seemed galvanized into life and gifted with a sudden eloquence when he moved toward politics. Like Gandhi, he emerged from a shy and awkward youth to become a great motivator of crowds. In speaking of his "natural inclination," Trotsky described a person quite different from the political infighter and speechmaker. "I must say that, by natural inclination, I have nothing in common with seekers after adventure. I am rather pedantic and conservative in my habits. I like and appreciate discipline and system. Not to provide a paradox, but because it is a fact, I must add that I cannot endure disorder or destruction. . . . The desire for study has never left me, and many times in my life I felt that the revolution was interfering with my systematic work."[19] But in this same description of his own personality, he makes it clear that the revolution stimulated the emergence of some of his character traits. "I cannot deny that my life has not followed quite the ordinary course. The reasons for that are inherent in the conditions of the time, rather than in me. Of course, certain personal traits were necessary for the work, good or bad, that I performed. But under other historical conditions, these personal peculiarities might have remained completely dormant, as is true of so many propensities and passions on which the social environment makes no demands."[20]

Trotsky began to speak at workers meetings and write for *Iskra*, one of Lenin's early revolutionary journals. It was in this work that he made his first impression on Lenin. Deutscher describes some of these early essays.

> The distinctive mark of his early contributions to *Iskra* lies not so much in originality of ideas as in the force of the emotional current that runs through them, in the passionate character of his revolutionary invocations, and in the almost dramatic vehemence of the invective he poured out on Russia's rulers and on socialism's enemies.[21]

His early speeches had the same quality. Lenin and Martov made use of his debating skills at the second Congress of the Russian Social Democratic party in London. In this Congress, he "played a leading role . . . in the momentous split between Bolsheviks and Mensheviks."[22]

> Contemporaries have described the first sudden and irresistible impact of his oratory, the elan, the passion, the wit, and the thunderous metallic voice, with which he roused audiences and bore down upon opponents. This appears all the more remarkable as only a few years before he could only stammer in blushing perplexity before a tiny, homely audience and as he had spent most of the time since in the solitude of prison and exile. . . . This is one of those instances of latent unsuspected talent, bursting forth in exuberant vitality to delight and amaze all who witness it.[23]

Many of our revolutionaries seem transformed in an almost mysterious way by the experience of social protest. It awakens some dormant aspect of themselves which had not expressed itself before. We are reminded of Rousseau's sudden discovery of his own capacity, which he describes in his *Confession*.

> This was the origin of my sudden eloquence, and of the truly celestial fire

which burned within me and spread to my early books, a fire which had not
emitted the tiniest spark in forty years, because it was not yet kindled.

I was truly transformed; my friends and acquaintances no longer recognized me. I had ceased to be that shy creature, who was shamefaced rather
than modest and who had not the courage to show himself or even to speak. I
had ceased to be a man who was put out by a joking word and blushed at a
woman's glance. Bold, proud and fearless, I now carried with me wherever I
went a self-assurance which owed its firmness to its simplicity. . . . The
contempt which my deep reflections had inspired in me for the customs, the
principles and the prejudices of my age made me insensible to the mockery of
those who followed them; and I crushed their little witticisms with my
observations, as I might crush an insect between my fingers. [24]

This sudden change from shyness to eloquence in both Rousseau and Trotsky
is quite striking. Gandhi tells of a similar change, but he does not place the same
emphasis on suddenness. Reik has described this process in masochism. The
masochist has a strong need for a public display of his misfortunes and his
condition. But in the process, the meaning of this display changes from sub-
missiveness to the defiance which underlies all masochism. Shyness and sub-
missiveness change to defiance and rebellion. In the social masochist the hidden
rebellious impulses can be released because the masochist feels he is fighting for
others, not for himself. Completion of this transformation may mean more than
the mere sublimation of a masochistic impulse. Rousseau was electrified by a
transformation of his character; Trotsky was changed in a different way. At the
height of his ecstacy in mass meetings, he was fused with the crowd.

My audience was composed of workers, soldiers, hard-working mothers,
street urchins—the oppressed under-dogs of the capital. Every square inch
was filled, every human body compressed to its limit. Young boys sat on their
fathers' shoulders; infants were at their mothers' breasts. No one smoked.
The balconies threatened to fall under the excessive weight of human bodies.

I made my way to the platform through a narrow human trench, sometimes I was borne overhead. The air, intense with breathing and waiting,
fairly exploded with shouts and with the passionate yells peculiar to the
Modern Circus. Above and around me was a press of elbows, chests and
heads. I spoke from out of a warm cavern of human bodies; whenever I
stretched out my hands I would touch someone, and a grateful movement in
response would give me to understand that I was not to worry about it, not to
break off my speech, but keep on. No speaker, no matter how exhausted,
could resist the electric tension of that impassioned human throng. They
wanted to know, to understand, to find their way. At times it seemed as if I
felt, with my lips, the stern inquisitiveness of this crowd that had become
merged into a single whole. Then all the arguments and words thought out in
advance would break and recede under the imperative pressure of my
sympathy, and other words, other arguments, utterly unexpected by the
orator but needed by these people, would emerge in full array from my
subconsciousness. On such occasions I felt as if I were listening to the
speaker from the outside, trying to keep pace with his ideas, afraid that, like
a somnambulist, he might fall off the edge of the roof at the sound of my
conscious reasoning.

> Such was the Modern Circus. It had its own contours, fiery, tender and frenzied. The infants were peacefully sucking the breasts from which approving or threatening shouts were coming. The whole crowd was like that, like infants clinging with their dry lips to the nipples of the revolution. [25]

One can make a number of symbolic interpretations from Trotsky's rich metaphoric expression: his identification of speaking with nurturing, his acceptance of the role of "mother" of the revolution with the infants (his listeners) clinging with their dry lips to *his* nipples. But it is important to note the source of this stimulation as well. Something about an expectant mass of humanity excites him. There is the prospect of welding them together into a moving force for social change. Here the sense of his own identification with the group is very apparent. He speaks from a "warm cavern of bodies." He has been, in effect, incorporated by the crowd; he is part of them. He loses his identification as a separate individual and hears his own words as though he were one with the audience. Therefore, he knows what they need to hear; further, he knows what they need in general and he can speak for them. He has incorporated the group into himself.

In a civilized individual it is impossible to distinguish those aspects of pleasure in group association which are purely instinctual from those which are learned. The original biological base has been covered with a heavy layer of culture, of learned attitudes. But the sense of ecstasy in Trotsky's account has such a strong physical content that one is inclined to suspect that the source is instinctual. There is considerable basis for describing his feeling as libidinal and relating his account to a kind of sexual ecstasy. However, we may be dealing with another drive quite as strong as hunger, thirst, and sexual appetite. It may provide a physiological reward similar to sexual release, but it may be dependent on different sensory and hormonal sources. I am speaking, of course, of the gregarious or community instinct in humans, the pleasure in mutual purposeful association.

The Encounters with Lenin

We have already followed Trotsky through his initial rebellion against the ideas of Marx and his final submission. For Trotsky, this submission was always possible if his antagonist was perceived as another Promethean battling against those in power. But before he would submit he must be won over intellectually. A similar process was repeated with Lenin. Initially, Trotsky had a strong intellectual and, literary affinity for Parvus (A. L. Helphand). He was attracted by the latter's internationalism and views on Russia. In the initial conflict between the Bolshevik faction of the Communist party, headed by Lenin, and the Mensheviks, Trotsky sided with the latter. The Mensheviks had the greatest influence in the beginning and soon took over *Iskra*.

While the initial split between Bolsheviks and Mensheviks was related to Lenin's desire for a more closed party organization as opposed to the more open formula of Martov, the basis for the split really seemed to be a clash of personalities and a feeling that Lenin wanted to dominate the party. However, the Mensheviks were essentially the party of compromise with the liberals and reformers, while Trotsky was clearly a revolutionary. He soon realized that he was ideologically much closer to Lenin. Nevertheless, he continued to oppose him and directed much personal invective at Lenin during this period.[26]

In his initial attraction to revolution, Trotsky wanted to rebel against all formal discipline including the discipline of a revolutionary movement. The rebellious feeling was paramount and he had not yet reached the point where he himself would see the need for party discipline and centralized control. He charged Lenin with 'substitutism.' Lenin's approach would lead to a party that would substitute itself for the working class; then the private caucus would substitute itself for the party; then a central committee would substitute itself for the caucus; and finally a single dictator would substitute himself for the central committee.[27] At this time such a charge had no basis, but it was characteristic of Trotsky that, in his youthful rebellion, he had a prescience pointing to an important future defect in the party which he would one day encourage and help to implement.[28]

Gradually Trotsky's differences with the Mensheviks became more apparent. They fully expected the coming Russian revolution would be led by the liberal bourgeoisie. For Trotsky, it became increasingly apparent in 1905 that the proletariat was the only class capable of forming a provisional government. Parvus and Lenin, both still in exile at this time, agreed with him. It was at this period that the first council of workers (or soviet) emerged from the demands of workers during a printers' strike in St. Petersburg. The communists at first regarded the soviet as a potential rival to their party, and it was not until November of 1905 that Lenin urged his followers to cooperate with the soviets.[29]

Trotsky appeared at the soviet in October, after his return from Finland. He represented the Mensheviks in the soviet, but when the Tsar, frightened by the sudden and growing power of the soviet, offered a constitution, Trotsky warned a large crowd of workers and students that the promise of the Tsar was a mere paper that could be torn to pieces the following day. With this, he proceeded to tear up the manifesto of the Tsar before the eyes of the crowd.[30] He rose to a position of power within the soviet and soon held the Menshevik faction of the party under his sway. He was finally arrested when the police disbanded the soviet, but this basic organizational structure of 1905 was later to be reconstituted in the successful revolution of 1917.

Permanent Revolution

In prison the Menshevik leadership advised the revolutionaries to organize their defense on strictly legalistic lines, but Trotsky urged a position of outright defiance. He wanted to use the trial as a chance to state the case for revolution. In this he found himself again in agreement with Lenin and the Bolshevik Central Committee. Once again, Trotsky did some of his best intellectual work in prison.

His experience with the St. Petersburg soviet convinced him that organizations of this kind could form the basis for the workers' power in the next revolution, and he outlined this thesis in his *History of the Soviet* in which he urged the formation of such workers' councils all over the country.[31]

Lenin was impressed by his position and made several attempts to win him over to the Bolshevik faction, but for the time Trotsky remained critical of both groups. He still believed that he could unite both factions of the party.

Trotsky's realization that the bourgeois class in Russia was incapable of leading a revolution and his active preparation for a workers' revolution in the immediate future represented a distinct departure from classical Marxism, but it was congruent with the reality of his times. In line with the anticipated success of the workers' revolution, Trotsky began work on a reinterpretation of Marxism which he called *Permanent Revolution*.[32] This was certainly his most important work of this period. While he agreed with the Bolshevik view that the bourgeoisie was incapable of leadership in the coming revolution, he went beyond them in insisting that the revolution would end in a socialist government. In this respect he also disagreed with the prognosis of classical Marxists who felt that socialism would be achieved first in the more "advanced" or fully developed and industrialized Western countries. To those who objected that he was deviating from the historical prognosis already laid down by the master, Trotsky replied:

> Marxism is above all a method of analysis—not analysis of texts, but analysis of social relations. Is it true that, in Russia, the weakness of capitalist liberalism inevitably means the weakness of the labour movement? Is it true, for Russia, that there cannot be an independent labour movement until the bourgeoisie has conquered power? It is sufficient merely to put these questions to see what a hopeless formalism lies concealed beneath the attempt to convert an historically-relative remark of Marx's into a suprahistorical axiom.[33]

While Trotsky was attracted to the theory of Marx because of its intellectual depth and its rationale for delay of the revolutionary process, he was not so rigid as to cling to this theory in the face of the reality he saw developing ahead of him. The evil could be overthrown, not merely in his own lifetime, but in the immediate future. If our assessment of Trotsky's psychodynamics is correct, this departure from classical Marxism was in conflict with his own masochistic need for an undefeated and more powerful adversary against whom he could continue his ongoing struggle in the role of a less powerful but more virtuous rival. How could he maintain his role of underdog at the head of a victorious workers' revolution? While he speeded up the timetable for a socialist revolution in Russia, he pointed out that such a revolution would be unstable and weak in a world of powerful social democratic parties and would incur the hostility of world reaction. The only hope to save such a revolution was to make it permanent, or international, in scope.

> Left to its own resources, the working class of Russia will inevitably be crushed by the counter-revolution the moment the peasantry turns it back on it. It will have no alternative but to link the fate of its political rule, and hence,

the fate of the whole Russian revolution, with the fate of the socialist revolution in Europe.[34]

Thus Trotsky, even in his revision of Marxist theory, still delayed final victory. He still saw himself on the side of the weak against the strong and the poor against the rich. Even in his rebellion against the Marxist idea of the primacy of a bourgeois revolution, Trotsky reinforced the internationalist element in Marxism and made it absolutely essential to the survival of the new and relatively weak government of Russia. It is interesting that both the theory of Marx and the revised theory of Trotsky contained a justification for prolongation of the revolutionary struggle. For Marx, it was the necessity for a bourgeois stage of the revolution that prevented an immediate victory. For Trotsky, it was the weakness of the workers' government that necessitated further struggle with the help of an international workers' organization. In both cases, this aspect that prolonged the struggle proved to be the part that was a product of personal needs, for historical events have shown that this prolongation was not really necessary.

On the other hand, neither Marx nor Trotsky was flying in the face of reality. In the larger sense in which both men conceived their theories they were essentially correct. The failure in prediction was limited to specific cases. In the perspective of world history, bourgeois revolutions and bourgeois governments have preceded proletarian revolutions. In fact, it was Marx's clear demonstration of this fact and his prediction of an eventual proletarian revolution that stimulated Lenin and Trotsky to try to bypass the bourgeois phase altogether. By predicting the future, Marx gave others the tools to change it. In the case of Trotsky's revised theory, he was correct in regard to the *tendencies* he saw developing and wrong only in terms of the outcome. The Russian peasants *did* finally turn their backs on the revolution and had to be appeased for many years with the NEP (New Economic Policy). Even this approach failed and they were finally crushed by the totalitarian methods of Stalin. The bourgeois governments of the world *did* try to launch a counter-revolution in Russia, but they too failed in their efforts. Trotsky himself was instrumental in frustrating these efforts when he undertook the task of developing the Red Army.

The Rebel within the Party

To say, then, that Trotsky had a "need" for the role of underdog may be correct, but it is not conclusively demonstrated by his theory of permanent revolution. For he had not misperceived reality nor had he deliberately refused to accept a position of power. In fact, in his statement that the workers should seize power and accept the responsibility for forming a socialist government, he is actively seeking a position of power. This would seem, at first, to be in direct conflict with his need for the role of underdog.

But we have already seen that, within the communist movement itself, Trotsky had already placed himself in the position of rebel against a very powerful adversary, Lenin. Despite Lenin's many efforts to enlist Trotsky in the Bolshevik faction and despite his own increasing agreement with both the theory and the strategy of that faction, Trotsky maintained his position of rebel. Further, he had isolated himself from the Mensheviks, his only possible base of power, and had castigated Lenin with statements that seemed to make reconciliation impossible. He had indeed isolated himself from power within the communist movement while, at the same time, calling for an assumption of power by the movement itself. He had emphasized to the maximum his capacity for rebelliousness and defiance while insuring that he would not need to assume the role of leader should his efforts prove successful.

Union with Lenin

For many years the Second International seemed to embody the hopes of all those who looked for a worldwide alliance of workers in support of socialist governments, but the Second International collapsed with the beginning of World War I and the sudden upsurge of German nationalism. Many ardent socialists throughout Europe called for workers to support their national government and fight the enemy. Trotsky was forced to break with his old friend Parvus, the leading German Marxist writer, when he declared his support for the German government. Lenin immediately called for an abandonment of the Second International and the creation of a true world socialist movement in a purified Third International. In this he was, once again, in agreement with Trotsky who, in his *War and the International*, had described the decline of German socialism and called for a rebirth of the labor movement. At the same time Trotsky felt called upon to make a final break with the Menshevik faction which was still holding out the hope of a reunion with the old German socialists and which was opposed to a Third International.

All of these circumstances brought Lenin and Trotsky closer together and, when an international conference of socialists was called at Zimmerwald, Switzerland on September 5, 1915, they cooperated in support of an international socialism and described the betrayal of the socialist parties in the famous Zimmerwald Manifesto drafted by Trotsky. However, Lenin's group wanted to go still farther. He called for a civil war of workers against their governments in order to put an end to the war of nationalism. At this conference an international committee was elected which was later to form the Third International.

In France, Trotsky published a small but militant Russian paper *Nashe Slovo* (Our Word) which, due to pressure from the Russian embassy, finally led to his expulsion from France and indirectly to his deportation to New York. It was here that he heard of the rising in Petrograd and after a period of detention in Nova Scotia, arrived in the Russian capital on May 4, 1917, to find the Tsar overthrown and a provisional government led by Aleksandr Kerensky in power. Lenin had already returned from exile and he had carried on a struggle against the right wing of the Bolshevik party which still insisted on a necessity of the bourgeois phase for the Russian revolution. Lenin and the Bolshevik party were now fully in agreement with Trotsky's position, not only in regard to his belief in an immediate worker-led socialist government, but with his views on international revolution as well. Trotsky, even though he had taken the leadership in developing the theory of revolutionary action now associated with the Bolshevik party, had really no party of his own. He was always too revolutionary and too far left for the Mensheviks, and he opposed the Bolsheviks because he failed for many years to recognize the valuable qualities in Lenin. Therefore, he was forced to assume a subordinate role to Lenin in the revolutionary party. Was he "forced" to assume this position or did he really want to play the role of Engels to Lenin's Marx? Certainly, he struggled hard for and achieved *intellectual* leadership. In this respect he is more comparable to Marx than Engels. But now we are talking about a real revolution and not merely the dominance of a theoretical position. Trotsky managed, in the very process of intellectual domination of his party, to arrange for his subordination to Lenin in the sense of actual command. Lenin had seen the wisdom of Trotsky's more international position, especially in his prediction of a victory of the workers' party and an immediate installation of a socialist government. But in all these areas he had made Trotsky's position his own and, while certain members of his party accused him of abandoning his own position for that of Trotsky's, Lenin finally managed to direct his party into this new theoretical approach without relinquishing his position of leadership.

Lenin immediately offered Trotsky and his friends positions of leadership within the Bolshevik party and on the editorial staff of *Pravda*. Trotsky still held out for a time, demanding a change in the name of the new party and still hoping to unify Bolsheviks and Mensheviks. But soon the Mensheviks openly rejected him at public meetings and he made no further attempts to form an alliance with them.

After the abdication of the Tsar, the Provisional Government was unstable, but the Bolsheviks were a minority party and could not yet move to seize power. Lenin, who had arrived in Moscow on a sealed train provided by the German General Staff, was accused of being a German agent. Fearing arrest and execution by the Provisional Government because of this accusation, he went into hiding. Meanwhile, the Bolsheviks had achieved a majority in the Soviets. While both Lenin and Trotsky were prepared for insurrection at this time, Lenin believed the Bolshevik party should lead the insurrection in its own name. Trotsky, on the other hand, believed the revolution should be directed through the Soviets and he was confident that the Bolshevik majority would carry the day. Under the banner of the Soviets, Trotsky saw the insurrection as a broad representative act of the workers. As Lenin could not appear publicly, Trotsky's plan was the one which was finally carried out, but he worked closely with Lenin until the government was finally in the hands of the Bolsheviks. [35]

The Refusal of Power

Following the victory, Lenin immediately proposed that Trotsky head the new government as "Chairman of the Soviet of People's Commissaries" on the grounds that Trotsky was head of the Petrograd soviet which seized power. But Trotsky refused, proposing Lenin's name, and his proposal carried.[36] Concerning his own role in the new government, Trotsky remarked, "Strangely enough, I had never even given a thought to it; in spite of the experience of 1905, there was never an occasion when I connected the question of my future with that of power."[37] This attitude is characteristic of the professional rebel. While he can often see himself leading a protesting crowd, the vision of himself in a position of power makes him uncomfortable and he tends to repress such ideas. Now that victory was complete, Trotsky wished to "retire behind the scenes for a while."[38] To Lenin's insistence that he at least take over the commissariat of the interior, Trotsky replied that his Jewish origin might prove a barrier to such a position. Lenin scoffed at this reasoning and almost lost his temper, but Trotsky was adamant.

In reality it was not really his Jewishness that served as a barrier to his acceptance of the post but his internationalism (which is often associated with Jewishness in the mind of the provincial politician). Local or even national problems repelled him with a kind of "moral nausea."[39] He found he could not concentrate on local problems but was not really in a position to take action on the international scene, aside from issuing a few proclamations. Somehow, he wanted "to develop the October revolution further, extend it to the entire country."[40]

While Trotsky was probably wrong in assuming that his Jewishness would be used against him by his enemies directly after the revolution, it was his internationalism that was later to be held up to him during the period of reaction as a kind of Jewish trait, a too intellectual cosmopolitanism, a lack of sympathy for local problems and for the soil and people of mother Russia.[41] This is one of the many ironies of revolutions in general, and the Russian Revolution in particular. Some of the old revolutionary values, such as internationalism, were turned around to carry a connotation just opposite of their original significance.

Following the humiliating Treaty of Brest-Litovsk and the increasing pressure of the German Army on the eastern front, Trotsky agreed to accept the enormous task of building a Red Army capable of repelling the various bourgeois powers. In this his administrative skills achieved a brilliant success.

In November 1918 the Treaty of Brest-Litovsk was annulled with the fall of the Austro-Hungarian and German Empires, but the Right Social Revolutionaries assembled a government at Samara on the Volga under the protection of the Czechs and Admiral Kolchak's White Guards. As a result, Trotsky was engaged in a protracted civil war, not only with Kolchak and his forces but with General Denikin who grouped his troops along the Don. Trotsky organized the Red Army under a single command and when the Czechs seized Samara, he ordered a compulsory conscription of workers. He followed each battle in detail, personally criticizing, demoting, and promoting commanders. Meanwhile, he had to contend with criticism from within the party where Stalin already opposed his handling of the southern front.

It seems that once the revolution was successful, different individual qualities in the leaders became important. The intellectual, the theoretician, the one who gained satisfaction from suffering and deprivation was no longer needed. The new structure of the Bolshevik party favored those with an active impulse for power, an immediate urge to dominate, a more hedonistic temperament, those with less need for personal virtue and therefore fewer scruples about the means they used to achieve party leadership. We will observe that some of the personal qualities and interests which led to Trotsky's success in the initial stages of the revolution proved detrimental to his survival in the later stages.

But, in the interim, Lenin was in power and his own revolutionary background was essentially that of asceticism and personal sacrifice. He urged Trotsky into a role that he could accept, people's commissar for foreign affairs.

The Rise of Authoritarianism

Trotsky and Lenin, despite their expectation of a worldwide revolution, now found themselves leading the only communist nation in the world. The abortive communist rising in Berlin had been crushed and revolutionary movements in England and France had been suppressed. Lenin still hoped for a rising in Europe and Trotsky had a positive horror of isolation from the cultural and industrial centers of Europe. He knew this would make the economic struggle of the new Soviet Republic that much more difficult. For a while, an abortive attempt was made to carry the revolution abroad with the newly organized Red Army. This began with an invasion of Poland described as an attempt to assist Polish communists. It was a position that Trotsky resisted from the beginning but which he felt obliged to endorse for the sake of party unity. Trotsky at last insisted on peace with Poland and an end to the attempt to spread communism by the sword. Lenin backed him. Peace was finally concluded with the Red Army at the gates of Warsaw.

Trotsky was essentially an idealist. His sure hand in the administration of the Red Army was based, in large measure, on his capacity for self-sacrifice and his ability to inspire that sacrifice and devotion in others. For his outstanding leadership and his inspirational defense of Petrograd he was awarded the Order of the Red Banner. But with the cessation of the civil war, the Soviet administration was now faced with the enormous task of mobilizing the peasants to produce food and the workers to produce manufactured goods.

How could this be accomplished without the help and support of European allies? Trotsky believed it could be done with the same kind of sacrifice that had built the Red Army. In fact, he advocated the militarization of labor, compulsory work crews designed to accomplish the rapid socialization of all Russia. In his review of Trotsky's policy and the authoritarian way in which he tried to force the peasant and the worker to produce with the same discipline that he used in the army, Deutscher remarks:

> At the very pinnacle of power Trotsky, like the protagonist of a classical tragedy, stumbled. He acted against his own principle and in disregard of a most solemn moral committment. Circumstances, the preservation of the revolution, and his own pride, drove him into this predicament. . . . Yet in acting as he did, he shattered the ground on which he stood.[42]

In this application of such extreme authoritarian methods, Trotsky revealed a side of himself that was not yet apparent. Perhaps this is one of the reasons he refused a position of power after victory. He may have sensed that his own need for continuous sacrifice was no longer congruent with the spirit of a victorious Bolshevik party. The Red Army was the only place in the new regime where sacrifice and discipline were still appropriate. This need arose from the severe conditions of the civil war. Once the war was over, he was faced with the more mundane acts of food production and manufacture, certainly vital to the survival of the regime, but less dramatic and heroic.

While the old Bolsheviks in the party supported Lenin, they did not like Trotsky. He seemed too quick to change and altogether too willing to take a position in direct opposition to current party policy. Trotsky was always taking chances with ideas, refusing to take a safe position and seeming to care nothing about building his base of power within the party. He neglected to reassure the old guard by convincing them that he was not part of a clique or special interest group. This behavior seemed to threaten them even more, partly because the role of the perpetual rebel was carried on with such brilliance, but also because in his refusal to seek allies and behave in a predictable manner he seemed to everyone to be a member of the opposition.[43]

Trotsky and Stalin

Lenin had already proposed Stalin for the party's general secretary in April 1922, and he now proposed Trotsky for deputy chairman of the council of people's commissars. Trotsky refused and thus annoyed Lenin who had hoped to have Trotsky as his deputy. Stalin had long burned with a resentment toward Trotsky. Their enmity dated back to policy struggles during the battles with the White Guards, but it was aggravated by Trotsky's rather obvious contempt for Stalin's ideas and intellect.

Stalin had meanwhile consolidated his position within the party and began to attack Trotsky in the Politbureau, claiming he had refused to be a deputy to Lenin because he sought some larger power. He soon had both Leo Kamenev and Gregory Zinoviev aligned with him in the Politbureau in opposition to Trotsky. Trotsky remained aloof. He seemed unaware that the opposition to him was mounting and he refused to recognize the possibility of succession, by anyone, to the power now held by Lenin.

It has never been confirmed just when Lenin had his first stroke. He was very ill in July, 1921, and had retired from many party activities. The bell on his phone was removed and replaced by a light so it would not disturb him. Toward the end of September his health was clearly failing. There was no public communication from him for long periods. He was surely the victim of at least one stroke during this period.

Lenin had grown disillusioned with Stalin. The latter's attempt to turn Rabkrin, the workers and peasants inspectorate, into his private police disturbed him. Also, he was angered by his own slowness in realizing the extent to which Stalin was crushing the rights of Georgians and Ukrainians in the interests of administrative centralization. On December 23 and 25, he dictated his last message to the party. In it he spoke out forcefully against the suppression of the small nationalities, with an unmistakable reference to Stalin as the "coarse brutish bully" who was seeking to centralize all of Russia in the manner of the Tsars.[44] Finally on March 5, shortly before his death, Lenin, who had obviously developed an increasing concern about where Stalin would take the revolution, called upon Trotsky to undertake the defense of the Georgian deviationists before the Central Committee. He urged Trotsky to proceed vigorously against Stalin, to trust no "rotten compromise" Stalin might propose and, most important, to give him no warning of the attack.[45] But Trotsky's temperament was such that he could not follow these instructions. He warned Stalin, through Kamenev, that he would not demote Stalin if the latter would change his policy toward the smaller nationalities. He warned him that if he did not accept these terms he would publish the text of Lenin's final remarks. Stalin accepted this compromise immediately and agreed to reword some of his statements regarding the nationalities. During this period Lenin suffered another stroke. Although he lived for another ten months, he was without speech and paralyzed most of the time. Meanwhile, Trotsky helped the Central Committee (dominated by Stalin, Zenoviev, and Kamenev) suppress Lenin's final remarks. There was no vigorous defense of the rights of the small nationalities and no attack on Stalin. In covering these events, Deutscher remarks:

> Hindsight makes Trotsky's behavior appear incredibly foolish. This was the moment when his adversaries were taking up positions; and every one of his steps was as if calculated to smooth their way.
>
> It seemed to Trotsky almost a bad joke that Stalin, the wilful and sly but shabby and inarticulate man in the background, should be his rival. He was not going to be bothered about him, he was not going to stoop to him or even to Zinoviev; and, above all, he was not going to give the party the impression that he, too, participated in the undignified game played by Lenin's disciples over Lenin's still empty coffin. Trotsky's conduct was as awkward and preposterous as must be the behavior of any character from high drama suddenly involved in low farce.[46]

Trotsky's refusal to protect himself was certainly due to overconfidence and unwillingness to engage in a petty power struggle on the eve of Lenin's death. But were there other reasons for his refusal to protect himself? We have already seen him refuse positions of power on at least three occasions: his refusal of the chief position in the party, in deference to Lenin; his refusal of the position as head of the commissariat of the interior; and his refusal of the position of Lenin's deputy in the Central Committee. Was this not another refusal of power, this refusal to "lower himself" by struggling with Stalin? And was it not because of his prefer-ence for the position of outsider and leader of the opposition? Certainly, this was the net result of his refusal. For Stalin consolidated his power and placed his own men in important positions at all levels of the party. Trotsky, instead of looking to his own position, continued to call for party unity and this meant, of course, support of the Central Committee now dominated by Stalin, Zinoviev, and Kamenev. When the Georgians came to Moscow to protest, he failed to support them. When the leaders in a workers' movement were arrested by the GPU, he offered no objections. However, despite his loyalty to the party, he began to have frequent clashes with the triumvirs (Stalin, Zinoviev, and Kamenev). Finally, when Zinoviev tabled a motion to change the composition of the Military Revolu-tionary Council over which Trotsky presided, he was deeply hurt and resigned in protest from every position he had in the party. "He asked to be sent abroad 'as a soldier of the revolution' to help the German Communist party to prepare its revolution."[47] But the triumvirs prevented his departure and refused to accept his resignation.

While Trotsky had supported the ban on inter-party factions, he was distressed when Felix Dzerzhinsky actually proposed the Politbureau declare that it was the duty of every party member to denounce to the GPU people who opposed the official leadership. In a letter of October 8, 1923, he criticized this proposal somewhat indirectly and renewed his criticism of the economic policy of the triumvirs. On October 15, forty-six prominent members of the party also issued a statement critical of this policy, declaring that the country was threatened with economic ruin. They also protested against the ban on inner party groupings. In all of their proposals they probably acted with Trotsky's knowledge if not his actual support, but he denied this.[48] This group was the nucleus of what later became known as the Opposition or the Trotskyist Opposition.

Perhaps Stalin's most effective attacks on the Opposition were his opportunist policies which veered now to the right and now to the left, often taking a position almost identical to one Trotsky had proposed and hinting, indirectly through other parties, that he might be willing to make peace with members of the Opposition if they would admit that they had been wrong in fighting him. This approach produced a number of defectors discouraged by their long isolation.[49] But once welcomed back in the party, the defectors were imprisoned or executed one by one. Trotsky and Trotskyism became a rallying point for all those communists morally opposed to Stalin's regime. But only those with a strong spirit of martyrdom similar to Trotsky's could or would endure the punishment and privation inherent in such a stand.

   Meanwhile Trotsky himself was sent into exile, first to Alma Alta in the
farthest reaches of the country and finally to Turkey. Stalin carefully organized a
system of patronage in which he nominated his own allies as regional or local
secretaries. He was cautious in avoiding any antagonism to other party members
during his attack on Trotsky, but he attacked them in small groups when Trotsky
was defeated. After victory he demanded a complete humiliation and recantation
of the victim's former political beliefs. Trotsky was almost alone in his refusal to
recant. Finally, Stalin resorted to the rewriting of history to prove to future
generations that Trotsky was a counter-revolutionary. But all of this did not quell
his fears that someday Trotsky might come back and push him from the seat of
power. He resorted to the murder of thousands of enemies whom he imagined
were Trotskyists. Through it all, Trotsky, hounded from one country after
another, continued writing against Stalin. Perhaps his most famous analysis of
the Stalinist regime was *The Revolution Betrayed* in which he fully exposed what
he described as the Soviet Thermidor, the period of reaction and reversal which
follows revolution.

Above It All

Trotsky did not have the natural reserve of Lenin. He had strong personal
feelings about others and his statements and speeches always bore the stamp of
his personality. Yet he believed that it was proper for him to remain above
personal animosity, to avoid seeking power for himself, to seek the victory of
communism in the abstract, regardless of who carried the banner. He was
intensely egotistical about his own abilities, yet he strongly desired that leadership in the party should not depend on his special genius. He was always in doubt
as to the role he should play in guiding the party. Therefore, he was in perpetual
conflict between an attitude of aloofness and "objectivity" about events and one
of deep personal and even partisan feeling. His autobiography and his diaries
reflect this conflict. His story of his own life is rich in personal detail and feeling
during the early years, but it seems to freeze into an objective account of events
and "reasons" for his actions after he becomes a communist. We hear of his
marriage to Aleksandra Sokolovakaya as an afterthought. They were working
together and marriage naturally followed. It was good for the cause. Did he love
her? He makes no mention of this. In a similar manner we hear of his separation
from his first wife and his marriage to Natalia Sedova. Trotsky was deeply
attached to his children but he tells us little of his feelings. Even his diaries contain
impersonal intellectual responses to an event, a book, or a newspaper article.
His opposition to Stalin was based strictly on Stalin's policy, but for a man with
Stalin's ideological "flexibility" this was an empty effort. One could not really
oppose Stalin's policy of the moment unless one raised the issue of his frequent
changes of policy, that is, his character. Trotsky believed he should not make an
issue of personalities. What happened to this or that person was not important.
Only the cause of communism was important. When a comrade was murdered,

he regreted the loss but he showed a certain impatience when others wanted to examine the details. Personal details were not important; murder was murder. The fact was important but not the personality. Each individual was to be considered on his own merits, not his connections, his relatives, or the recommendations of his friends.

Stalin took the opposite position. Every relative or friend of Trotsky became an object for persecution. His son Lyova, who worked for the Trotskyist party in Paris, was murdered by one of Stalin's assassins. His daughter Nina died at Alma Alta and his second daughter Zina committed suicide in Berlin at the age of thirty, after a desperate effort to become part of her father's political life. Trotsky refused to make use of her in the mistaken belief he could protect her. Perhaps the most unbearable blow was the arrest of his youngest son Sergei who had ignored politics all his life. A gymnast in his youth, he had finally developed an interest in science. He had an opportunity to leave Moscow with his father, but he loved his work at the Technical Institute and both father and son had thought he would be safe if they did not correspond. In the spring of 1935 Trotsky learned of the arrest of Seryozha (Sergei) shortly after he discovered that his first wife Alexsandra had been taken from her grandchildren, with whom she was living in Leningrad, and sent to Siberia.

Trotsky was himself frequently forced to seek a more secure refuge. Turkey was so close to the Soviet border and Soviet influence, so with the help of friends he fled to Norway, but he was not allowed to stay. Finally, with the assistance and support of Diego Rivera, he fled to Mexico. However, throughout his long battle against the persecution of Stalin and the assassination of his friends, he tried to maintain an open attitude of trust towards strangers until they proved themselves dangerous. Even when he felt suspicion toward someone, he felt obliged to treat him with courtesy, to concentrate on his ideas rather than on his own immediate physical danger.

When one of Stalin's assassins, pretending to be a convert to Trotskyism, called on him in Mexico to ask for help with an article he was writing, Trotsky invited the man into his study even though he was already suspicious of him. Trotsky felt excessive suspicion would cut him off from others and make him a prisoner in his own home. He bowed his head over the desk to read the article and the assassin buried an axe in his brain.

The Holding Back and Letting Go of Anger

When his life is described in this manner—an account of the bare facts of his rise to power, his refusal of position, and finally his loss of power—one gains the impression that Trotsky was just too nice a fellow to make a good revolutionary. But this is not true. In his initial attacks on Lenin he was vitriolic and it was Lenin who exercised restraint in his hope that he could later win over Trotsky for the party. In his great and moving speeches against the Tsar there is an audacious, almost an outrageous, attack on the principles of old-fashioned 'decency.' During the revolution of 1905, in his speech rejecting the Tsar's manifesto, he showed with unmistakable clarity that he had no need to be nice or polite to anyone in authority.[50]

Later, in his zeal to support the revolution during the civil war, he proposed and carried out plans for the conscription of workers. Under his direction and supported by Lenin, the state, instead of withering away, moved to a position of total control of the working class. He supported first the total rule of the Bolshevik party as the only party and then a ban on factions or opposition groups within the party. In many respects he helped to shape the tools that Stalin was later to use against him. He proposed and supported these totalitarian methods because he felt the party was threatened with destruction, but he supported them nonetheless.

While he was often polite and friendly with those who offered help, he was quite capable of turning on them his most vitriolic criticism if he felt betrayed by them. When he sought refuge in Norway, he was at first polite and friendly with members of the Norwegian government. But when it was clear to him that Norway intended to expel him, he told Trygve Lie that he was committing a crime. When Lie extended his hand for a final reconciliation, Trotsky refused. It seems that Trotsky could give full vent to his anger *only when he was absolutely sure that he was faced with an enemy more powerful than himself.* A powerless enemy was beneath his contempt and if someone professed to agree with his principles, he was inclined to be trusting. His belief in revolutionary solidarity was always more important to him than his own life. It was this belief that inhibited his full condemnation of Stalin, even from exile.

But once he knew his enemy, Trotsky was a terror. Nothing could shake him. For one who must be so careful not to be unfair to anyone or accuse anyone unjustly, the knowledge that he had clear and final proof against an opponent released a terrible energy in him. At last he could fight without any hesitation or doubt.

This was his feeling during the October revolution when he could release his full fury against the Tsar. This was his attitude when sent into exile and able to lead the opposition against Stalin. But Trotsky tended to hesitate until it was too late, to give his enemy too much time to show his colors. He had to be sure, absolutely sure, that he was justified in his attack. In the October revolution, with Lenin prompting him from the wings, he made no such mistake. In his battle with Stalin, he delayed too long and he failed to heed Lenin's warning. In the final battle of his life he was also too much concerned with justice for his opponent. His assassin, "Jacson," had already revealed himself in many ways. He had made several previous visits and, in one of these, he actually sat on a writing table above Trotsky's head while the latter read a draft manuscript for an article. Throughout the interview he remained with his hat on and his coat clutched to his body. After the session Trotsky returned with renewed suspicion and told his wife Natalya that he did not want to see Jacson again. But he relented. He suspected Jacson was a fraud and an imposter, but he did not yet know his purpose and he had no proof. When the assassin returned with the typed copy of his article, Trotsky agreed to see him. It was not until that fatal day in Coyocan when Jacson brought the axe down on his skull that sixty-year-old Trotsky finally knew his enemy. Only then could the full fury of his anger come forth; once again he was too late. Jacson the assassin gives this account of Trotsky's last battle.

> 'I had put my raincoat . . . on a piece of furniture,' 'Jacson' testifies, 'took out the ice axe, and, closing my eyes, brought it down on his head with all my strength.' He expected that after this mighty blow his victim would be dead without uttering a sound; and that he himself would walk out and vanish before the deed was discovered. Instead the victim uttered 'a terrible, piercing cry—I shall hear that cry all my life,' the assassin says. His skull smashed, his face gored, Trotsky jumped up, hurled at the murderer whatever object was at hand, books, inkpots, even the dictaphone, and then threw himself at him . . . a furious struggle went on in the study, Trotsky's last struggle. He fought it like a tiger. He grappled with the murderer, bit his hand, and wrenched the ice axe from him. The murderer was so confounded that he did not strike another blow and did not use pistol or dagger. Then Trotsky, no longer able to stand up, straining at his will not to collapse at his enemy's feet, slowly staggered back. When Natalya rushed in, she found him standing in the doorway. . . .
>
> (Natalya): 'What has happened?' I asked. 'What has happened?' I put my arms around him. . . . Calmly, without anger, bitterness or sorrow, he said: 'Jacson.' He said it as if he wished to say: 'Now it has happened.' We took a few steps and slowly, aided by me, he slumped down on to a mat on the floor.'[51]

The Suicide Motive

This, it seems, is the way it all happened. Trotsky restrained himself out of a sense of fairness and could strike only when he knew his enemy. But there remains one additional consideration. Why did he insist on seeing Jacson even when he had told Natalya not to admit this man again? He was already suspicious. Why did he bow his head for the axe? Obviously, we cannot climb inside his mind to find out, but there remains one document which may cast further light on his behavior. His death occurred Tuesday, August 20, 1940, but in March of that same year he had written the following testament.

> The nature of my illness (high and rising blood pressure) is such—as I understand it—that the end must come suddenly. . . . If the sclerosis should assume a protracted character and I should be threatened with long drawn out invalidism . . . then I reserve the right to determine for myself the time of my death. The "suicide" (if such a term is appropriate in this connection) will not in any respect be an outburst of despair or hopelessness . . . but whatever may be the circumstances of my death I shall die with unshaken faith in the communist future. This faith in man and in his future gives me even now such power of resistance as cannot be given by any religion.[52]

Did Trotsky bow his head to the assassin's axe because he felt the end was near anyway? Was there a part of him that needed to provoke the enemy into showing his face, to make him strike the final blow? Was his last act a deliberate search for a martyr's death? Clearly he did not have much longer to live in any event. Like Ché Guevara, he may have sought one final battle, to die the combative death of a revolutionary.

NOTES

1. Karl Marx and Friedrich Engels, *Selected Correspondence* (Westport: Greenwood, 1942), 354–55.

2. Leon Trotsky, *My Life: Leon Trotsky* (New York: Grosset and Dunlap, 1930), 17.

3. Ibid., 3.

4. Ibid., 15.

5. Ibid., 42.

6. Ibid., 70.

7. Ibid., 72–73.

8. Ibid., 77.

9. E. Victor Wolfenstein, *The Revolutionary Personality: Lenin, Trotsky, Gandhi* (Princeton: Princeton University Press, 1971), 55–56.

10. Trotsky, *My Life*, 82.

11. Ibid., 98.

12. Ibid., 96.

13. Theodor Reik, *Masochism in Modern Man* (New York: Grove, 1941), 88.

14. Isaac Deutscher, *The Prophet Armed: Trotsky 1879–1921* (New York: Random House, Vintage, 1965), 41.

15. Trotsky, *My Life*, 125.

16. Ibid., 126.

17. Deutscher, *The Prophet Armed*, 146.

18. Ibid., 147. Quoted from Sverchkov, D. *Na Larie Revolutsii* (Leningrad, 1925).

19. Trotsky, *My Life*, xix.

20. Ibid., xvi–xvii.

21. Deutscher, *The Prophet Armed*, 67.

22. Ibid., 69.

23. Ibid.

24. Blanchard, William H., *Rousseau and the Spirit of Revolt* (University of Michigan Press, 1967), 71.

25. Trotsky, *My Life*, 295–96.

26. Deutscher, *The Prophet Armed*, 93.

27 Ibid., 90.

28. Ibid.

29. Ibid., 125–26.

30. Ibid., 128–44.

31. Ibid., 145–49.

32. Leon Trotsky, *The Permanent Revolution and Results and Prospects* (New York: Pathfinder, 1978). This book contains the original statement of the theory first published in *Results and Prospects*, published in 1906, as well as the later restatement, *The Permanent Revolution* published in 1930.

33. Ibid., 64.

34. Ibid., 115.

35. For the details of this struggle and transformation see Deutshcer, *The Prophet Armed*, 57–324.

36. Trotsky, *My Life*, 339.

37. Ibid.

38. Ibid., 340.

39. Ibid.

40. Ibid., 341.

41. Isaac Deutscher, *The Prophet Unarmed: Trotsky 1921–1929* (New York: Random House, Vintage, 1959), 258–59.

42. Deutscher, *The Prophet Armed*, 486.

43. Deutscher, *The Prophet Unarmed*, 34–35.

44. Ibid., 71–72.

45. Ibid., 90.

46. Ibid., 93.

47. Ibid., 111.

48. Ibid., 113–15.

49. Ibid., 409.

50. Deutscher, *The Prophet Armed*, 128–29. Quoted from Trotsky's *Die Russische Revolution* (1905), 93–96.

51. Isaac Deutscher, *The Prophet Outcast: Trotsky 1929–1940* (New York: Random House, Vintage, 1963), 504–505.

52. Leon Trotsky, *Trotsky's Diary in Exile* (Cambridge: Harvard University Press, 1958), 166–67.

Chapter 11

CHÉ GUEVARA:
The Romantic Revolutionary

Identification with the Underdog

Ernesto Guevara de la Serna was born June 14, 1928, of an aristocratic family who had been major Argentine landowners for several generations. His father Ernesto Guevara Lynch was an easygoing, well-educated, but impractical fellow who acquired his wealth through inheritance and marriage, and then lost much of it through bad investments. Most sources agree that the rebel in the family was Ché's mother Celia de la Serna. She is described by Daniel James as a "flaming rebel through and through who combined with her rebelliousness a fierce independence, an unwavering stubborness, a keen intelligence and a sharp tongue."[1]

Ché's father also had liberal political views. He encouraged the young Ernestito to mingle with the poorer classes and to help in the grape harvest. Ché developed a pride in looking like a working man and throughout his life showed a remarkable lack of concern for his personal appearance. He once arrived at a children's birthday party at the swank Sierra Hotel looking unkempt. A little girl reacted by saying, "Why did they let in the shoeshine boy?" Ernesto started swinging. His father was called in to put an end to the commotion, but instead joined his son, assailing the "rich bastards" who had ganged up on Ernestito with his walking stick until both father and son were thrown out by the hotel staff.[2]

This combative attitude was only one side of Ché's identification with the underdog. From his early years, he had a strong sympathy for the weak, the poor, and for animals. On the death of his dog he organized a funeral and gave an emotional speech broken with sobs. In his last year at medical school he climbed a pipe, despite protests of neighbors, to rescue a sparrow caught by the wing between tiles on the roof.[3] One of his first interests after his medical training was the treatment of lepers, the most outcast and despised among the ill. (Gandhi and Sun Yat-sen also treated lepers.) On one of his travels with a friend, he had a fit of rage when he came across some starving children on a large United Fruit plantation.[4] What was the source of this acute, painful sensitivity to the suffering of others?

His parents may have provided an example in their sensitivity to his own suffering as a child. Ché had severe asthma from the age of two and his parents left their home in the more humid region of Rosario to seek the higher and drier climate of Alta Gracia in the province of Cordoba where the family doctor had told them their child's health might improve. Celia blamed herself for her son's asthma as she had taken him swimming on a very cold day when he had his first attack.[5]

There was a physical and hereditary basis for Ché's asthma. His mother and his daughter were troubled by the same illness. It improved in high, dry climates and was much worse in humid, tropical areas. However, Celia's guilt about her own responsibility for Ché's illness may have had some basis for there is a definite relation between Ché's asthma attacks and episodes of strong emotion. The intensity of her anxiety about his condition and her protectiveness may well have aggravated his attacks. His asthma was so severe he could not attend school and his mother served as his tutor as well as his nurse. In his biography of Ché; Daniel James has portrayed the character of this relationship with his mother, her emotional as well as her political indoctrination. Ché's freedom was restricted; he missed some of the pleasures of early childhood, particularly the opportunity to go to school and play with other children. At the same time, he received special treatment within his family and this aroused the jealousy of the other children who would often tease and torment him. The result was a child acutely conscious of his difference from others, who also felt cheated and deprived because of his asthma.[6]

While Ché hated the aristocracy, his first love was the beautiful and aristocratic María del Carmen Ferreyra, or Chichina, as she was called by her family and friends. He showed this same partiality for aristocratic women when he met Aleida March during his adventures in Cuba. This desire to be poor and dirty himself while developing a relationship with aristocratic women is understandable when we consider Ché's relationship with his mother. She was always the aristocrat in the family, but she took a special interest in her underdog son. Even in his affair with Hilda Gadea, we will find Ché looking for a woman who was above him in some way, able to take a benevolent attitude toward him.

Ché never tried to minimize the social differences between himself and Chichina. In fact, he exaggerated the differences. He sometimes entered her home in ragged and soiled clothes with uncombed hair. He would hold up his trousers with a piece of rope.[7] This certainly put off the other members of her family, but Chichina was evidently at an age of rebellion against her father and her attentions to such an opposite character as Ché aroused her father's anger.

James records Chichina's reminiscence of those days: "He fascinated me. His obstinate look and irreverent nature. His sloppy dress made us laugh and, at the same time, feel a little ashamed."[8] Perhaps this was his goal, for Ché took pride in being dirty. Sometimes it was almost a fetish with him. Ricardo Rojo describes his "monumental unconcern about his slovenly appearance" as he entered the bar of the Sucre Palace in La Paz, Bolivia, the most luxurious hotel in the city.[9] On another occasion he won a bet with his friends by making his underwear, stiffened with dirt from the road, stand by itself.[10] We are reminded of the holy men of India who took pride in a kind of masochistic self-neglect. Ché made special efforts to appear in the most elegant surroundings in dirt and rags to remind others of the immorality of their needless luxury while the poor were dirty and starving.

Asthma and Oppression

Ché's feeling for the oppressed was related to his own experience as an asthmatic. Hilda Gadea, his first wife, provides a revealing account of the association, in Ché's mind, between the oppression of asthma and political oppression.

> During the first days of our marriage, Ernesto was very worried about a patient at the hospital whom he called "Old Maria." Very moved, he told me about her condition, an acute case of asthma. His interest was so strong that I almost felt jealous of that woman; she was on his mind almost all the time. Every morning he rushed to see her. . . . One day he said very sadly that Old Maria might possibly die that night. He went to the hospital that evening to be at her bedside, helping to do everything possible to save her. The effort was in vain; that night the old woman died of asthmatic suffocation. She was a very old woman, extremely poor. . . . She had been a washerwoman all her life, her years sad and hard. For Ernesto she was representative of the most forgotton, the most exploited class. . . . When he departed on the *Granma* I found a notebook of poems in the suitcase that he left with me. One of the poems was dedicated to Old Maria. It contained his promise to fight for a better world, for a better life for all the poor and exploited. [11]

Thus, Ché's political attitudes as an adult were shaped not only by the opinions of his mother, but also by his own personal feeling of being a victim of injustice, a victim of this strange affliction of unknown origin which restricted his freedom to move, to breathe, and which even threatened his life. He was a beautiful child, tender and delicate, with an unusual capacity to inspire pity in others, but he received no reward if he indulged in self-pity. At an early age he was taught to be tough, to struggle against his illness, to engage in sports despite his handicap. Thus he learned to avoid the open cry for love and tenderness, but when he was overcome with an attack of asthma his parents showed their concern and their sympathy for him.

He became interested in medicine in an effort to combat his own condition. His specialty was allergy. But he also sought to escape the immediate sense of his own weakness by getting away from home. Whenever he could leave medical school, Ché spent his time traveling around South America. It was on one of these tours after his graduation that he met Hilda Gadea and developed a relationship similar to the one he had with his mother. Like his mother, she was strong-willed, stubborn, and had decidedly left-wing political opinions. She took a protective attitude toward him, paying his rent and loaning him money. She was an ardent communist and she introduced Ché to Fidel Castro who was preparing for a return to Cuba on the *Granma* to begin his long struggle against the Batista regime. But it was Ché's asthma that seemed to cement his relationship with Hilda. In describing their relationship, she remarked:

> He told me about his illness; he had suffered from asthma since he was three years old. Thereafter, I always felt a special concern for him because of his condition. . . .[12]
>
> Months later Ernesto informed me that they (his friends) used to tease him about me and my interest in him, although up to that time it was only intellectual and political. But it's true that I had a special consideration for Guevara because of his asthma. . . .[13]
>
> Two days later Ernesto called me at the office to tell me that he had not been able to come to see me the day before because he had been ill, and that the asthma attack would last several days. . . .
>
> His room was upstairs but in spite of his illness he was waiting for me in the downstairs hall. It was the first time I had seen him or anyone else suffering from an acute attack of asthma, and I was shocked by the tremendous difficulty with which he breathed and by the deep wheeze that came from his chest. I hid my concern but insisted that he lie down; he agreed that it would be better, but he couldn't climb the stairs and refused to accept my help. He told me where his room was and asked me to go up and bring him a syringe that was ready to use. . . . I did as he said and watched him as he applied an injection of adrenalin.[14]

Finally, Ché managed to get to his room and lie down.

> Trying to conceal how much I had been touched by all this, I conversed about everything and anything, all the while thinking what a shame it was that a man of such value who could do so much for society, so intelligent and so generous, had to suffer such an infliction; if I were in his place I would shoot myself. I decided right there to stick by him, without, of course, getting involved emotionally.[15]

Despite her professed desire to keep the relationship on an intellectual level, Hilda was already deeply involved. Her main concern was really to avoid being hurt, for she was older than Ché and rather unattractive. But Ché appreciated her care and a strong reciprocal feeling developed between them. They were married and Hilda gave birth to a daughter before Ché left on the *Granma* with Fidel for the Cuban revolution.

Tough and Tender

Ché Guevara was a peculiar combination of toughness and tenderness. Like Lenin, Trotsky, and Marx, he was noted for his tenderness toward children, fallen comrades, and the underdog, but he was capable of an absolute ruthlessness toward anyone he regarded as an oppressor. As a child and as a young man he often demonstrated a similar ambivalent image. Ché's father regarded him as bold, reckless, a natural leader, although "timid." Neighbors often described him as a daredevil who would take chances with his life to overturn foolish beliefs. Others described him as sweet, reserved, even withdrawn and introverted.[16] He had a desire for independence but a longing to be loved and protected. Hilda Gadea seemed to sense this conflict in him. She fed his intellectual interests with her own knowledge of Marxism. She looked after him by loaning him money and mothering him in his illness. This same contrast between toughness and softness was noted by people who met him for the first time as an adult.

Hilda Gadea:
Guevara had a commanding voice, but a fragile appearance.[17]

I.F. Stone:
He was the first man I have ever met that I thought not just handsome but beautiful. With his curly reddish beard, he looked like a cross between a faun and a Sunday-school print of Jesus. Mischief, zest, compassion and a sense of mission flashed across his features during our interview.[18]

Richard N. Goodwin:
From a distance . . . the slightly stocky, erect man in fatigues, with his untrimmed beard, had seemed rugged, even tough. Now, as I looked at him across a distance of a few feet, his features seemed soft and slightly diffuse, almost feminine.[19]

Like Gandhi, Ché gave much credit to books for the development of his sense of belonging to a human community. As a youth he was interested in older boys and their ideas. Alberto Granados, who was at the university when Ché was in high school, remarks that he and his friends were impressed with Ché's intelligence and depth of knowledge and thus he was allowed to hang around with the university students. Says Granados, "I made much use of his father's library. Ernesto was the main reader and I was in second place. . . . There is no doubt that from childhood he had an intellectual sense that permitted him to distinguish himself in all aspects of life."[20] However, despite his intellectual interests Ché was not a good student. He would study with great intensity when he became interested in a subject, but he was often bored by assignments. He was at his best when he became emotionally involved with a subject.

He was particularly inspired by the poetry of Pablo Neruda. He would read poetry for hours and learn it by heart, reciting it later to his friends in a voice filled with emotion. Hilda Gadea reports that he could still quote extensively from Neruda when he was in Guatemala. The poetry of Neruda is filled with striking images of a suffering humanity and a strong sense of injustice. Neruda entered politics to become a senator and finally a communist. His career as a senator ended in exile because of his protests against corruption in Chile. Some of his poems, particularly *The United Fruit Co.*,[21] are directed against exploitation of South America by United States capitalism.

Ché had read widely from revolutionary writers, particularly Marx and Lenin, and he hoped to become the theoretician of the Cuban Revolution. Certainly, he had a profound influence on Fidel Castro. He was regarded by the Cuban revolutionary leadership as the intellectual and publicist of the revolution, but his theoretical work, if it was ever begun, did not survive him. Daniel James has pointed out Ché's nihilism and his resemblance to Nechayev, the Russian terrorist. His principal work, *Guerrilla Warfare*, like his *Message to the Tricontinental* contains this strong element of the romance of total destruction. In Ché Guevara, more than any revolutionary writer, we find this particular combination of a belief in virtue and a professed love of mankind combined with a strong advocacy of armed insurrection and a preaching of hatred for the enemy.

From the beginning of the guerrilla struggle in Cuba, Ché experienced conflict between his roles of doctor and soldier. He excelled in guerrilla training and was at the head of his class.[22] By the end of the first battle in Cuba at Alegria de Pio, it was clear that his primary role would be that of soldier of the revolution. In the battle all but fifteen of the eighty-two expeditionaries were killed and the survivors had to pick up their supplies and move on. Ché remarked, "I had before me a field pack filled with medicines and a case of ammunition—the two were too heavy to be carried together; I took the case of ammunition, leaving behind the field pack."[23] Thus the crucial decision was made under the pressure of a forced choice, even though Ché knew he might need the medicine to fight his own private battle against asthma. In fact, he had already experienced a severe asthma attack during the battle. From this point, Ché directed his principal efforts to the guerrilla campaign—serving as a doctor when not actively engaged in battle—and was finally appointed *Comandante* by Castro.

This dual role of doctor and revolutionary fighter expresses well the "tough and tender" image that was to follow Ché throughout his life. Even his lectures on guerrilla warfare are interspersed with comments on treating a wounded enemy with care and respect and making sure a wounded companion is never left to the mercy of enemy troops.[24]

His Internationalism

As *Comandante*, he had left the role of doctor far behind. In fact, as he became less concerned with the technical aspects of medicine, he showed an increasing involvement with the moral aspects of the revolutionary movement. Like Trotsky, he was always deeply concerned with the moral justification for revolutionary action and this led him inevitably toward revolutionary theory. Had he taken upon himself the primary role for the direction of a revolutionary movement, his capacity to stand aside and observe what was happening would have been impaired. Like Trotsky, he was always deeply attached to the international aspects of revolutionary ideology. It seemed to him that fighting in a revolution not in his own country there was a certain detachment from narrow self-interest. This detachment, this refusal to help himself or even a country closely connected to his own origin, was extremely important to Ché. It seemed to make his cause more universal and hence more justifiable. There was clearly a strong romantic element in this revolutionary morality. With Ché, we make the complete circle back to the romanticism of Rousseau. In his "Message to the Tricontinental," his last public speech, this blend of romanticism and internationalism is presented as a kind of universal revolutionary morality. Like Trotsky, he saw revolutionary internationalism as an indirect way of saving his own country, but as we read the words of Trotsky we cannot escape a feeling that it is the *internationalism* of the revolution that is important and not its potential effect on Russia. This feeling is even more evident in Ché's "Message to the Tricontinental." In fact, one has the feeling he has lost sight of Cuba as a separate entity altogether.

> And let us develop a true proletarian internationalism, with international proletarian armies; let the flag under which we fight be the sacred cause of redeeming humanity so that to die under the flag of Vietnam, of Venezuela, of Guatemala, of Laos, of Guinea, of Colombia, of Boliva, of Brazil—to name only a few scenes of today's armed struggle—will be equally glorious and desirable for an American, an Asian, an African, or even a European.
>
> Each drop of blood spilled in a country under whose flag one has not been born is an experience for those who survive to apply later in the liberation struggle of their own countries. . . .
>
> We cannot elude the call of this hour. Vietnam is pointing it out with its endless lesson of heroism, its tragic and everyday lesson of struggle and death for the attainment of final victory. . . . And if we were all capable of uniting to make our blows more solid and infallible . . . how great and how near the future would be! . . .
>
> Whenever death may surprise us it will be welcome, provided that this, our battle cry, reach some receptive ear, that another hand be extended to take up our weapons, and that other men come forward to intone our funeral dirge with the staccato of machine guns and new cries of battle and victory.[25]

It is this romantic element that has such a strong appeal to the young people of today. The heroic image of the revolutionary fighter, wounded, suffering for humanity, and struggling to raise the symbol of revolution aloft in his last effort so that some other hand can grasp it and carry it forward to victory. The image of the dying hero who gives his life for all of us is indeed the image of Christ on the cross dying for all so that all humanity may be saved. It is this romantic notion of suffering and self-sacrifice that forms the psychological basis for both religious and revolutionary masochism.

However, it is clearly more than the product of a private personal need. I have emphasized, in the lives of revolutionary leaders, some of the personal experiences that shaped their masochistic orientation. But we have come a long way from the sexual masochist described by the Freudian psychoanalyst. Revolutionary and religious leaders may indeed be shaped and stimulated by certain masochistic experiences in early childhood, but their success depends on an appeal to something more universal in all humans.

Revolutionary Morality

All major revolutionaries who strive for more than a mere seizure of power or palace coup, look for some moral justification to motivate their followers. They recognize that the satisfactions of the full stomach, which follow victory, are short-lived. There must be some ideology, some shared belief, but more than that, some *feeling* of oneness that unites one's followers. Without this, the most charismatic leader cannot have more than a temporary effect. To achieve this sense of unity there must be an element of self-denial, particularly in the initial stages of a revolutionary movement. For it is a basic psychological truth that one only gains a sense of oneness with others by a reduction of one's immediate sensual gratification. This is not altogether inconsistent with Maslow's statement that a sense of universality and oneness with humanity is based on a prior satisfaction of one's more basic sensual needs. [26] For in either event, the pressure of sensual needs has been diminished, either because they have been satisfied or because they have been transcended.

However, while the romantic-moralist has a powerful psychological influence on idealistic youth throughout the world, he is often less able to assume a position of leadership in his chosen country once revolutionary victory has been achieved. As a devout moralist, he continues to believe that others can be motivated by moral incentives. He expects them to continue to make sacrifices for the revolution. In his "Socialism and Man in Cuba," Ché wrote:

> If a man thinks that in order to dedicate his entire life to the Revolution, he cannot be distracted by the worry that one of his children lacks a certain product, that the children's shoes are in poor condition, that his family lacks some very necessary item, beneath this reasoning the germs of future corruption are allowed to filter through.
>
> In our case we have maintained that our children must have, or lack, what the children of the ordinary citizen have or lack; our family must understand this and struggle for it. [27]

But Ché's family did not understand, and his wife would not struggle for it. Ché was now married to the beautiful Aleida March, whom he had met while she was working with a women's committee in the Sierra Escambray. Like many another guerrilla fighter she had shared the rigors and the sacrifices of his campaigns, but now she wanted to enjoy the fruits of victory. While he did not complain of her publicly, it does not take much reading between the lines to see that Aleida began to subvert his efforts when he asked her to continue her sacrifices after victory. Enrique Altuski describes Ché's behavior when someone complained of a food shortage during a long meeting.

> . . . and he said that this was not so, that in his house they ate reasonably well. Half seriously, and half in jest, I told him, "Maybe you receive an additional ration." The next day he called us to tell us, "It was true, until yesterday we were receiving an additional ration." [28]

Ricardo Rojo gives an account of a direct exchange between Ché and Aleida when she called his office one day to ask for the use of his car to go shopping. "No, Alieda," Ché answered. "You know the car belongs to the government, not to me. You can't use it. Take the bus like everyone else." [29]

Nothing disturbed him more than suspicion that he might be getting special treatment or that he might appear to be getting special treatment because of his position of power.

Immediately after the victory of the revolution, his asthma was so severe that his doctors insisted he take a rest at the seaside resort of Tarara where Batista had built a group of luxurious homes for himself and his friends. When he was criticized for this in one of the popular Cuban magazines, he was deeply mortified and sent a note to the editor explaining why he had to rest in such a place. He was uncomfortable amid the manifestations of power or success. He could take the offensive only when he could see himself as oppressed or when he became the champion of the oppressed. The situation that was most likely to arouse his compassion was one in which he regarded another person or group as physically weak, wounded, ill, oppressed, or outcast.

Religion and Revolution

Ché, as a good Marxist, was also an atheist, but we have already noted in his "Message to the Tricontinental" the themes of suffering and dying for humanity and the "sacred cause of redeeming humanity" which have a decidedly moralistic if not religious significance.

Ché believed that he could motivate others through moral incentives. He felt if others could become aware of their relationship to a world community they would work and sacrifice without material rewards. In his "Socialism and Man in Cuba," he elaborated on this theme at some length. He spoke of "revolutionary consciousness" which for Ché meant an ongoing sense of being part of the larger human community, an expanded sense of self. Ché felt that all people were capable of this feeling at great moments of crisis in which heroic acts were performed. Somehow, he felt, Cuba would learn to make this feeling a part of everyday life.[30] It is the sense of isolation, this lack of awareness of one's relatedness to others that Ché substituted for the religious concept of original sin.

> To summarize, the culpability of many of our intellectuals and artists lies in their original sin; they are not authentic revolutionaries. . . . The new generations will arrive free of original sin. . . . It is not a question of how many kilograms of meat are eaten or how many times a year someone may go on holiday to the seashore or how many pretty important things can be bought with present wages. It is rather that the individual feels greater fulfillment, that he has greater inner wealth and more responsibilities.
> . . . Let me say, with the risk of appearing ridiculous, that the true revolutionary is guided by strong feelings of love. . . . Everyday we must struggle so that this love of living humanity is transformed into concrete facts, into acts that will serve as an example, as a mobilizing factor.[31]

Clearly, this was the kind of morality that motivated Ché in his own life. He gained a special pleasure from the feeling of helping others and from the sense of comraderie with the outcast and the poor. His work with the lepers gave him a sense of virtue, says Rojo, "Because the highest forms of human solidarity and loyalty arise among lonely and desperate men."[32] But not all members of the revolutionary government felt the same way. They insisted that material incentives had proved essential in the older communist countries and that men would work only if they received direct material rewards. In the end they proved to have a better understanding of the new Cuban man than did Ché. His efforts to bring about major increases in production through the award of medals, scrolls and personal recognition by the government proved largely ineffective. In fact, production declined decisively. Moral incentives had worked to drive Ché all his life, but they would not work on the multitudes.

Don Quixote

In his "Notes for the Study of the Ideology of the Cuban Revolution," Ché remarked, "The more uncomfortable the guerrilla fighter is, and the more he experiences the rigors of nature, the more the guerrilla fighter feels himself at home, his morale is higher, his sense of security greater."[33] Here he was speaking for himself. He accepted two positions in the victorious revolutionary government of Cuba: president of the National Bank and minister of industries. In both positions he was a dismal failure. He admitted some of his major errors in a discussion of the state of the Cuban economy,[34] but his description concerns errors of logic and errors of strategy. In fact, Ché was not comfortable in an administrative post. He found himself performing a function, working with production reports, plans, and figures. His role had always been to publicize, to inspire, and to fight for the revolution. He was comfortable traveling around the world telling others about the Cuban revolution but in Cuba he seemed at home only in the cane fields where he could feel a direct contact with the poor. Rojo describes him on one of these expeditions.

> I must confess that I thought the outing would follow a typical Latin American pattern: a minister or a president working in the sun, photographers doing a good job, a backdrop of authentic laborers at work, and the government man with a cool drink in the shade, talking about the latest news, surrounded by officials and newsmen. It wasn't that I didn't trust Guevara. Far from that, it was my own incapacity to imagine a situation different from the well-known pattern.
>
> We arrived at last. The trucks were parked . . . in an effort to do the job right [I] announced that I'd work without gloves or a shirt.
>
> "I can see you've never done this kind of work," Guevara slowly remarked. He was as smugly pleased as a kid waiting for his cocksure buddy to make an ass of himself. And that's what happened: I didn't know that the sugar cane throws off a microscopic powder that enters the pores and irritates and cracks the skin. After a short while I too asked for a long-sleeved shirt and elbow-length gloves.
>
> We worked without stopping from six-thirty A.M. to eleven-thirty A.M. By then the sun made work unbearable, and everyone took time out for lunch under an open shed. There was a general feeling of comraderie. . . . Guevara was beaming. His ideal seemed to have been achieved. A community of men and women drawn together by work, capable of performing in a remarkable manner, happily gathered together without false respect or sham differences.
>
> The work continued at the same pace from three o'clock to seven-thirty P.M.[35]

This is indeed a beautiful image: the great man, one of the leaders of the new Cuban nation, who never loses his personal contact with the people. But there is an uncomfortable feeling that this work in the cane fields provided Ché with an escape from the more difficult work at the Ministry. As the problems became more complex, as his economic and industrial policies began to fail, as his political differences with Castro became more pronounced, Ché spent more time in the cane fields. In March 1965, he sent a letter to his mother telling her he planned to cut sugar cane for a month and then perhaps gain some experience managing a factory. She was concerned. Had he been dismissed from the ministry? Why was he spending so much time cutting cane when so many others could do this job?[36] Cutting cane was undoubtedly both a form of penance for his failure as an administrator and an escape from the responsibilities which burdened him. He felt a sense of personal virtue only when he could have this immediate contact with the oppressed or when he could fight against a powerful oppressor with the odds heavily against him. Ché was conscious of this need. He expressed it openly in his farewell letter to his parents, referring to his heels on the flanks of Rosinante (the horse of Don Quixote) as he returns to the road, his lance under his arm.[37]

Much speculation has centered on the extent of the disagreement between Ché and Fidel Castro before his departure from Cuba. Clearly, they had begun to move in different directions. Fidel was developing an increasing reliance on the Soviet Union and showed a willingness to adapt Cuban economic goals to Soviet world plans, including a return to sugar as the primary crop. Ché was more interested in the underdeveloped nations of the world; he was a Maoist in speech and action, although he never identified himself as such.

But he also wanted to escape from his role as an administrator, and it is unlikely that Fidel had to exert much pressure on him. In his open criticism of the Soviet Union and his insistence that it use its resources to help underdeveloped nations, he had already taken a policy position in sharp contrast to Castro. He had to go and he was ready to go. There may have been some sadness about his own separation from the common sense of purpose they had shared, perhaps even some bitterness, as he unnecessarily renounced, among his other titles and positions, his Cuban citizenship. But there is no feeling of recrimination in any of his letters to Fidel or to his family. All the events leading up to his departure suggest that he was burning one bridge after another, making it impossible to turn back. He would go where he could feel the old thrill and excitement of combat against the rich and powerful on behalf of the poor. Fidel helped him with money, arms, and manpower. Ché began by commanding a small Cuban contingent in the Congo in support of the Kinshasa rebels. While his men fought well, Ché was disillusioned with the Congolese rebels and returned to Cuba in six months to begin preparations for a new adventure in Bolivia that was to prove his last fight.

The Struggle in Bolivia

He left Aleida behind, evidently without regret. There were already signs of conflict between them and Ché resented any suggestion that he should be responsible for "providing" for his wife and children. We have noted his sharp response to Aleida when she asked to use the government car. He took a similar position in regard to any suggestion that his wife or children should have special treatment; the revolution would provide for them. In his final letter to Fidel Castro he remarked, "I leave my children and wife nothing material, and I am not ashamed. I am glad it is so. I ask nothing for them, as the state will give them enough with which to live and be educated."[38] He would possess no one and he wanted no one making demands on him, either for time or for material support. Love he could give, but not always a personal love in his physical presence. His family had to be content with the knowledge that they were loved as part of a greater world community.

His most satisfactory relationship with a woman appears to be one in which she was fighting by his side against an oppressor. His closest relationship to Hilda Gadea was when the two of them were escaping from Guatemala after their support of the ousted Arbenz government. It was then that he asked her to marry him and go to Mexico. After the child was born, Ché was off to a revolution in Cuba. In Cuba his relationship with Aleida developed from their partnership as combatants against the Batista government. After victory she bore him four children, although their domestic life was interrupted by extensive traveling and much night work for Ché. Even before his departure for Bolivia, he had begun a relationship with the legendary Tania, who fought by his side in the jungle.

Tania has become a heroine to the Left because of her death in combat. She was actually a Soviet KGB agent sent to keep a watch on Ché because of his anti-Soviet statements and his claims that the Soviet Union was not doing enough to help the underdeveloped countries. Born Haydee Tamara Bunke Bider of German parents in Buenos Aires, November 19, 1937, her Argentine birth may have attracted Ché to her when he first met her in East Germany during one of his many trips abroad to establish relations with other communist nations. Daniel James maintains that she betrayed Ché to the Bolivian authorities, although the evidence is circumstantial.[39]

In Bolivia, the rebels suffered frequent and often severe shortages of food and water. Sometimes they had only lard for food and eating it made them sick. Uncooperative peasants failed to provide necessary supplies. On May 9, 1967, after eating only lard for several days, Ché reported: "I was feeling faint and I had to sleep for two hours in order to be able to keep on at a slow and staggering pace, the march thus being carried on. We ate lard soup at the first watering place. The people are weak and already there are some of us with edema."[40] There were also shortages of water that went on for days and at one point the men were so desperate they were drinking their own urine.[41]

The chief battle for Ché was the war with his asthma. Throughout most of the campaign they were in the humid lowlands that aggravated his condition. To make matters worse, enemy forces discovered the cave containing his medicine and other supplies.

On June 14, his thirty-ninth birthday (and also that of his daughter Celita, named after his mother), Ché reflected on his age and his future as a guerrilla fighter. [42] While he described himself as sound at the time, he may have sensed the first stirrings of his asthma, for within a few days he was riding a mule for the first time in the war. [43] On June 23, he admitted that "asthma is threatening me seriously and there is very little medicine in reserve." [44] From this point there are a series of notations about the severity of his asthma and Ché was not one to mention his physical problems unless they were severe.

June 24:   My asthma is getting worse.

June 25:   My asthma continues getting worse and now I cannot sleep well.

July 7:   My asthma is getting worse.

July 8:   I injected myself several times in order to be able to go on, ending up using a 1:900 adrenalin solution prepared for Collyrium. If Paulino has not fulfilled his mission (to get medicine) we will have to return to the Nacahuasu to get medicine for my asthma.

July 12:   My asthma was hard on me and those miserable sedatives are almost used up. [The term used here for 'sedatives' is *calmantes*, a more general word which probably refers to his anti-asthma pills.]

July 30:   My asthma bothered me a lot and I was kept awake all night. [45]

There were frequent exacerbations and remissions of his asthma until they reached the higher altitudes shortly before the final battle. In addition, he was removing ticks from his body, puncturing an abscess on his heel which prevented him from walking, and suffering the usual bouts of sickness and vomiting due to the erratic eating habits and sometimes putrid food they were forced to eat.

Ché often worried about his sickness, not so much in terms of his survival but because of the example of toughness and endurance he wanted to set for the other men.

On September 2 he first heard that Joaquin's group, including Tania, had been attacked and killed, but he was skeptical. As the reports continued to come in, he finally accepted the deaths of Joaquin and Negro, but he refused to accept the death of Tania even when Radio Cruz described the discovery of her corpse. [46]

The army was now closing in on him and there was little chance for escape, although he tried to lead his men out of the ambush. In retrospect there seems to have been a suicidal element in Ché's Bolivian campaign. He was no longer the youthful adventurer; he was almost forty, somewhat corpulent, and taking heavy doses of cortisone which gave him a "moon face." It is not clear whether he was still using cortisone in the jungle but, if he was, it would certainly account for his problem with edema. Cortisone causes the body to retain moisture in the tissues and produces an enlargement of the prostate gland, inducing frequent urination.

However, his asthma was also giving him trouble in Cuba and if he had remained at home he might have required hospitalization in another year or so. He may have decided to die with his boots on in one final battle that would end the working of his tortured lungs. He may also have hoped that his tough persistence in the face of his handicap would inspire his men to go on without him under new leadership. Perhaps he hoped to live out the final lines from his speech to the Tricontinental in which he spoke of falling in battle and raising his weapon to be seized by other hands that would carry on the fight. Image was important to Ché. He did not want the world to remember him as an asthmatic invalid dying in a hospital bed.

On October 8, 1967, at Quebrada del Yuro in a last fierce battle with the Bolivian forces, Ché fell with nine bullet holes in him. Captured alive, he was taken to the village of La Higuera, but died on the way. Before his death, he revealed his identity to General Alfredo Avando Candia, Commander in Chief of the Bolivian armed forces. "I am Ché Guevara," he said, "and I have failed."[47]

The legend of the heroic revolutionary fighter had reached such proportions at the time of his death, a death already rumored on numerous occasions, that the Bolivian Army made a special point of displaying Ché's corpse before the world press. With a certain bloodless indifference his body was placed on a large cement washtub in its canvas litter where the reporters crowded about taking notes and the photographers struggled for space to take a picture. It was as though the government wanted to show once and for all that the legend was dead.

But in his efforts to carry his revolutionary spirit throughout the world, Ché accomplished more by his death than he could have achieved by his continued existence in a worn body that even his will could no longer sustain. The picture of his corpse convinced no one. Revolutionary groups throughout the world raised the slogan, "Ché lives!" His more lifelike image soon appeared on posters in student dormitories and university halls. The picture that survived recalled the romantic tones of his speeches and his rugged persistence in the face of overwhelming obstacles. Just as Ché would not accept the death of Tania, revolutionaries throughout the world refused to believe the death of Ché. His spirit was invoked in every battle and his picture was carried on flags and posters in every protest march, particularly in Europe and the United States, the very heart of the capitalist world that he could not penetrate while he was alive.

NOTES

1. Daniel James, *Ché Guevara: A Biography* (New York: Stein and Day, 1970), 29.

2. Ernesto Guevara, *Venceremos: The Speeches and Writings of Ché Guevara,* edited by John Gerassi (New York: Macmillan, 1968), 4.

3. Ibid., 5.

4. Ibid., 10.

5. James, *Ché Guevara*, 32.

6. Ibid., 34.

7. Ibid., 55.

8. Ibid., 56.

9. Ricardo Rojo, *My Friend Ché* (New York: Dial, 1968), 25.

10. Rojo, *My Friend Ché*, 40.

11. Hilda Gadea, *Ernesto: A Memoir of Ché Guevara* (New York: Doubleday, 1972), 111.

12. Gadea, *Ernesto*, 3.

13. Ibid., 26.

14. Ibid., 28.

15. Ibid.

16. James, *Ché Guevara*, 34–36.

17. Gadea, *Ernesto*, 2.

18. Ernesto Guevara, *Guerrilla Warfare*, authorized translation, translated by J. P. Morray, preferatory note by I. F. Stone (New York: Random House, Vintage, 1969), viii. From the preferatory note by I. F. Stone.

19. James, *Ché Guevara*, 143–44. Quoted from the article by R. N. Goodwin in the *New Yorker* of May 25, 1968.

20. Manual Ebon, *Ché: The Making of a Legend* (New York: Universe, 1969), 15.

21. Robert Bly, ed., *Neruda and Vallejo: Selected Poems* (Boston: Beacon, 1971), 85.

22. James, *Ché Guevara*, 84.

23. Ibid., 89.

24. Guevara, *Guerrilla Warfare*, 36–37.

25. Ernesto Guevara, *Ché: Selected Works of Ernesto Guevra*, edited by R. E. Bonachea and N. P. Valdes (Cambridge: MIT Press, 1969), 180–82.

26. Abraham H. Maslow, *Toward a Psychology of Being* (Princeton: Van Nostrand, 1968). 71–114.

27. Guevara, *Ché: Selected Works*, 168.

28. Ibid., 20.

29. Rojo, *My Friend Ché*, 144.

30. Guevara, *Ché: Selected Works*, 159–61.

31. Ibid., 166–68.

32. Rojo, *My Friend Ché*, 17.

33. Guevara, *Ché: Selected Works*, 54.

34. Ibid., 137–48.

35. Rojo, *My Friend Ché*, 109–10.

36. Ibid., 172.

37. Guevara, *Ché: Selected Works*, 424.

38. Ibid., 423.

39. James, *Ché Guevara*, 205, 237–41, 285.

40. Ernesto Guevara, *The Diary of Ché Guevara: Bolivia: November 7, 1966–October 7,*

1967, the authorized text in English and Spanish, edited by Robert Scheer, with an Introduction by Fidel Castro (New York: Bantam, 1968), 110.

41. Ibid., 164.

42. Ibid., 125.

43. Ibid., 128.

44. Ibid., 129.

45. Ibid., 130–47.

46. Ibid., 171.

47. James, *Ché Guevara,* 8.

Part 4

THE SUCCESSFUL
REVOLUTIONARY

Introduction

Our last three revolutionaries, Castro, Lenin, and Mao, are all men who achieved revolutionary victory and who became chief administrators in the new regime. They found it necessary to subdue the impulse to perpetual revolution—at least long enough to consolidate their power. Mao's revolutionary urge broke out again in his later years. However, all three men probably struggled continually against the revolutionary impulse, the desire to overturn everything and begin again as an underdog and outsider. This impulse is ever present in the revolutionary, even one who has become the successful leader of a new government. If he is to retain this new position, reason must always struggle against the desires and pleasures of his developing years—the very desires and impulses which have led to such great rewards in the past. Fidel Castro represents a fascinating example of a successful struggle of this kind. We will find in him many of the characteristics of other revolutionaries, but he has managed, somehow, to integrate these characteristics into a style of administration and government.

Lenin and Mao represent more difficult cases. They were more stoic characters, reluctant autobiographers who felt that their personalities should have no bearing on the revolution. They stressed factual aspects of the oppressor and revolutionary inevitability. Mao's autobiography, given to Edgar Snow, has a mythological and self-conscious quality—as though he is presenting his concept of the proper development of a revolutionary, with occasional anecdotes to fill out the story. Both Lenin and Mao saw their behavior as a logical development from the circumstances.

Only Castro combines revolutionary success and administration with the imagery, the light-heartedness, and the feeling of continued rebelliousness characteristic of his early years. This may reflect some unique personality element or it may be due, in part, to his leadership of a small, developing nation which remains an underdog among the world powers. This position allows Castro the scope for continued struggle against oppressive forces, not only on the Right, but also against those on the Left who would make a satellite of Cuba.

The Wives and Children of Revolutionary Leaders

The approach of Castro, Mao, and Lenin toward their wives and children reflect the culmination of an attitude that we find in the earliest revolutionaries. Some form of love relationship was necessary for all of them but there was a constant struggle to subdue this private sexual and paternal need. In the early revolutionaries it is never under control. Lawrence found his private satisfaction by devious means. Rousseau took a mistress for his sexual needs, but his love of ladies of quality surfaced and interfered with his life and work. He was deferential to the nobility and, by turns, both obsequious and defiant to the grand ladies he loved. He was also jealous and possessive of his friends. But children had a special capacity to arouse the tyrant in him. If they were good, he was pleased to instruct them, but if they were naughty, he became angry and punitive. The idealized and calm image he presents in *Émile* does not fit his own behavior when he acted as a tutor to two unruly children. He disposed of his own children by giving them to a foundling home.

Marx seems to represent the opposite extreme from Rousseau. He married Jenny von Westphalen because he was "head over heels" in love with her and attracted to her mind and her personality as well as her body. He struggled to raise several children. An outrageous bully with other men, he was gallant with women and his children remembered him as affectionate, tolerant, and indulgent. He loved them with a fierce devotion and encouraged them to come into his study at any time to talk or ask questions. He was patient and attentive. He often abandoned his work to play with them and paid for it by spending the night at his desk, sleeping, for a few moments, in his clothes on the couch in his study.

Nevertheless, like Rousseau, he could not support a wife and children, although he had one of the most brilliant minds in Europe. The family diet was heavy in starches and they often ate nothing but potatoes, or missed meals altogether. They could not afford medical attention except in dire emergencies and at least two of his children died, in part, from malnutrition and lack of proper medical care. But, unlike Rousseau, he could not simply dismiss the needs of his family. While he was often sustained by the importance of his work, his emotional sustenance came from Jenny and his world would have collapsed without her. Jenny may have been a cyclothymic personality, with alternate periods of elation and depression. She could become ecstatic over a second-hand dress and sing in a beautiful voice during their period of poverty in London. She cheerfully copied Karl's works and took a special delight in her humble role in advancing the ideas of the great revolutionary. She had many discussions with him but was always as an obedient pupil, amazed at his profound insights. At other times she was overcome with sadness and distress by their living conditions and could no longer face the landlady and the tradesmen who came to their door about overdue bills. She would take to her bed for days and talk to no one. Two of her daughters committed suicide. There is some indication that tendencies to elation and depression are hereditary. The evidence for this is clear in manic-depressive psychosis, but Jenny was not psychotic although she was often incapacitated by depression.

However, Jenny's periods of depression were frequently reactions to an acute crisis in their circumstances and when she gave way Karl himself found the struggle difficult. This accounts for much of his bitterness and anger at society. He often said that he should never have married, but his wife and children were essential to him, despite his torment at their misery.

In Gandhi's life we discover more dimensions in a father's attitude toward paternal responsibility. Gandhi welcomed his wife and children into his larger family: the poor and disenfranchised of the world. When they all lived in a humble ashram on a restricted diet with no formal education for the children, he felt they had a healthier diet than the meat-eating diet of the Westerner or the elegant and spicy food of the wealthy Indian. His children, he said, were having a great educational experience by sharing in his work and needed no formal education. He would accept no gifts, even those given to his wife and when she protested he conspired with his children to convince her she was lacking in faith and conviction if she kept her jewelry. Under the pressure of the entire family she relented.

At first glance it would appear that while Rousseau avoided having a family and Marx cursed the capitalist system (and himself as well) for the misery of his family, Gandhi convinced himself and everyone around him that poverty was not misery but joy. One must not avoid it but rush into its arms. If one is denied shoes, he should give away his shirt as well. The one rebel in this paradise was his oldest son Harilal, who resented his lack of formal education. He was the only son as stubborn as his father. He refused to yield to Gandhi's subtle moral pressure to devote his life to public service and the two men clashed head-on. When Harilal realized that he would never be given what he wanted, he became determined to wound his father as deeply as possible. The deepest wound he could give was the destruction of his own moral character, and particularly his public image. This he accomplished through a series of thefts and bogus investment schemes. He was often drunk in public and he used his father's name to advertise himself. In 1925 Gandhi publicly dissociated himself from his son in a open letter in *Young India*. He described one of Harilal's schemes and warned others not to be taken in by him. Harilal continued his defiance by taking money from Gandhi's opponents to write articles exposing him. When his mother was on her deathbed, he arrived drunk and had to be removed from her presence. He later attended his father's funeral without being recognized and died penniless in a tuberculosis hospital in Bombay.

Thus even Gandhi could not escape the painful aspects of self-sacrifice. He would not admit his suffering and he encouraged his family to accept their poverty with a sense of pride, but Harilal refused the role his father had carved out for him and denied his father's moral superiority by showing the world what a corrupt son he had raised. He humiliated and degraded himself in a masochistic manner, but this too was a form of defiance against his father, for him, the greatest tyrant of all.

Tolstoy, too, represents a special case in the treatment of his family. He began his life as a count who could afford the best and he taught his family how to enjoy the good life. But as he grew older the luxurious life of the wealthy became more and more inconsistent with his chosen role of reformer. He began to haul manure, dig in the field, dismiss his servants, and empty his own chamber pot. He encouraged his children to ignore their opulent surroundings and some of them worked in the field with him. In the end he gave away everything: his home, his property, the royalties on his books. The person who suffered most from his sacrifice was his wife Sonia, who had lovingly copied all his works when he was the world famous novelist Count Leo Tolstoy, but who was finally driven mad by the sharp and completely unexpected change in her life-style to which she could not adapt and which she fought every step of the way. In the end Tolstoy could escape from luxury only by escaping from Sonia and his own estate. She watched him day and night with the fear of a fanatic. But he left in the middle of the night by train, suffering his last illness in a tiny stationmaster's house by the railroad station in Astaporo, where Sonia was denied permission to see him until near the end. Even then, she had to enter when he was asleep, gasping out her request for forgiveness and her words of love before being hurried out of the room by doctors. He never regained consciousness before he died.

In the case of Ché Guevara, who was married twice, and who died in the jungle fighting in a guerrilla band with his new girl friend Tania, we have a more routine attitude toward sacrifice. He had charmed Chichina by arriving with a rope around his trousers and he proved his courage to Hilda Gadea by refusing to give in to his attacks of asthma. But he kept a tight rein on aristocratic Aleida March's search for special privilege. Ché's attachments to women were intense but transitory. They tried to accept the fact that he belonged not to them, but to the revolution.

This also was the case with the wives of Lenin and Mao. There is a stolidness about both wives, as though they had repressed all feminine needs, just as their husbands had, at least partially, repressed their needs for moral leadership and for continued rebellion after achieving power. We know little of the family life of Lenin and Krupskaya. She knew the intimate details of his life, but has shown us almost nothing of their relationship in her wooden biography of him, which, to do her justice, was first published during the heavily censored reign of Stalin. Lenin and Trotsky were both firm advocates of the elimination of "woman's work" as a specialty, believing that both men and women should play an active political role. Trotsky, the emotional and expressive speaker, was also strangely quiet about his family life. We know of the agony he suffered when his children were murdered or persecuted by Stalin, but he has left no love stories, no sense of his family life. The sacrifices he made throughout the years of his persecution were painful but involuntary.

Of all our revolutionaries, only Castro had the misfortune to marry a wife who actually went over to the opposition, and here it would seem to be a thoughtless act of personal survival with little political conviction. Castro never married again and little is known about any further relationships with women. Like all the revolutionaries in the final section of this book, he kept his personal life as private as possible. Even those in Part III (Sun Yat-sen, Trotsky and Guevara) had begun to play down the role of the family. As we advance from Part I to Part IV, the family seems to play a less important role in the life of the revolutionary and the wife is increasingly submerged in the career of her husband. Perhaps this is one of the necessities of revolutionary power; the role of a professional revolutionary, accepted early in life, leaves no room for the special demands and private opinions of a wife and children.

The one thing that comes through very clearly from these lives is that the revolutionary wife must be prepared for sacrifice no matter how much she is loved. Unfortunately, she may not always know she is about to become the wife of a revolutionary. Sonia Bers married the world famous author and wealthy Count Tolstoy, never recognizing the future martyr. Being less prepared for what she was to face, she suffered most. Putlibai Gandhi was married as a child to a husband chosen by her parents and, while she protested all the way, she finally resigned herself to the life of sacrifice, perhaps because her expectations were not so high. As the revolutionary becomes conscious of his aims early in life, he is more inclined to look for a wife who is tough and ready for sacrifice and the wife is more likely to know what she is getting in her husband.

Chapter 12

FIDEL CASTRO:
Maximum Leader

Early Years

One trait which all our *successful* revolutionaries have in common is a certain guardedness about their private lives. While superficially quite open and willing to reveal their tastes and opinions, they manage to divert reporters and interviewers from the details of their early development or the more personal and idiosyncratic aspects of themselves. In this respect Fidel Castro is quite characteristic. Herbert Matthews, who probably knows him as well or better than any of the American journalists who have visited him, remarks, "Normally Fidel never talks about his family, his personal affairs, or his personal life, even with his closest associates. . . . Anyone working on the Cuban Revolution or on the life of Fidel has to be reconciled to the fact that he does not want to talk about himself."[1]

Fidel's father was Angel Castro y Argiz, an immigrant from Spain who arrived in Cuba without funds, but who soon became wealthy by buying land and growing sugar. He married a Cuban woman who bore him two children, Lidia and Pedro Emilio. On his estate, "Las Manacas," he also had an affair with a peasant girl, a Creole woman named Line Ruz Gonzalez who bore him three children, Angela, Ramon, and Fidel. After the death of his wife, Angel married Lina and they had four other children, Juana, Raul, Emma, and Augustina. Fidel Castro was born August 13, 1927.

Fidel, like Ché, was always closer to his mother. As he grew older he came to resent the power of his father and the manner in which he exploited his own peasants. Lee Lockwood speaks of one of the few occasions when Castro mentioned his father.

> Then, in a curiously detached voice, he begins to speak about his father. He had owned a large sugar plantation on the other side of the mountains. He had been a *latifundista*, a wealthy landowner who exploited the peasants. He had paid no taxes on his land or income. He had "played politics for money."[2]

But in estimating the size of his father's estate and the number of *caballerias* working for him, he gave a large figure which his brother Raul disputed. The two brothers argued briefly and finally Raul gave up and Fidel continued talking. There is just a suggestion here that, in the mind of Fidel, wealth and evil were equated and that, in retrospect, his father seemed larger, more influential, and more of an exploiter than he was in reality. Trotsky, Mao, Kropotkin, and Tolstoy were all distressed by the role of their fathers as wealthy exploiters. But only Trotsky's father seems to have been concerned by the opinion of his son and tried to assauge his tears and pain when he witnessed this exploitation.

There is no hint of any paternal sympathy from Fidel's father. Instead, one gets a rather severe picture of a patriarch who would rather put his son to work in the fields. If Fidel had not rebelled and threatened to burn down the house if he were not sent to school, he may have missed his education altogether.[3] His mother was evidently subservient to the father and accepted most of his attitudes. The father died in 1956 when Fidel was in Mexico. When, after his 1959 victory, Castro broke up and distributed the Manacas plantation as part of his agrarian reform movement, his mother and older brother, Ramon, were at first outraged. However, Lina retained affection for Fidel, despite her opinion of his politics. Once he had put Ramon to work on agrarian reform, Fidel finally won his mother over to a grudging acceptance of the revolution.[4]

That Attraction toward Dirt and Disorder

The records of his early schooling describe Fidel as an energetic, athletic charmer. The charismatic quality that he manifested as leader of the revolution and finally as premier of Cuba had shown itself very early in his school years. In the year book of Colegio Belén, a preparatory school in Havana that he attended in 1945, he is described as brave in defending the school flag, but one who knew how to "win the admiration and affection of all. . . . He has good timber and the actor in him will not be lacking."[5] One of the first things a young actor must do is find a role for himself. Fidel was not sure what he wanted to be. He determined to go on to the University of Havana to study law, sure of one thing: he would always take the side of the poor against the rich, the exploited against the exploiters. From the beginning, he developed a certain carelessness about his dress and appearance; or rather, he took great care to look unkempt and careless of his appearance.

His enemies later made a great point of his uncleanliness. Nathaniel Weyl has searched through anti-Castro papers in Miami and even interviewed Fidel's professors to substantiate his assertion that Castro was known as *bola de churre* ("grease ball") at the university and that his fellow students were repelled by his "filthy personal habits." For Weyl this is clearly sumbolic: "The cultivation of personal uncleanliness symbolizes a desire to defile on a much larger scale."[6] His uncleanliness as a student is a supposed reflection of a generalized desire to corrupt and defile Cuba and the world at large.

In line with his own bias, Weyl has made an error similar to Payne's discovery that Karl Marx had a diabolical element in his personality and in his identification. Like all the revolutionaries we have covered, Fidel had a real disgust for any form of luxury or status-seeking. The young actor was already devising his role and his costume. Dirt was his badge of identity, but it represented a search for virtue, not an effort to defile or an attraction to corruption.

Even his friends have noticed this trait in Fidel, but to them it is part of his charm, his informality, and his lack of affectation. Herbert Matthews describes him as a man who likes to shed the artificial restraints of society. His beard and fatigue uniform are merely devices or tools to set the atmosphere he wants to create around him. He sought this same informality in his early years long before his revolutionary triumph.

> The last letter in *Carta del Presidio* is written to his sister Lidia. It is about an apartment he rented for himself, Raul and two of his sisters. In it he writes of himself as being of 'a bohemian temperament and naturally disorderly' (poco ordenado). Then he adds: 'There is nothing more agreeable than having a place where one can throw on the floor as many cigar butts as one pleases without the subconscious fear of a maid who is waiting like a sentinel to place an ashtray where the ashes are going to fall.'[7]

While Castro was indeed "naturally disorderly," the adoption of a particular life-style based on disorderliness and informality is characteristic of many revolutionary leaders of the Left. We have noted a similar attraction to self-neglect in Guevara, Rousseau, Marx, and Tolstoy.

Marriage

Despite his identification with the poor, Fidel's first known love was Mirta Diaz Balart, the daughter of a wealthy Cuban family. The course of this early love had many similarities with Guevara's attraction to Chichina del Carmen Ferreyra. Mirta's family strongly disapproved of Fidel. It is not known if he arrived to visit her holding up his trousers with a rope, but he was already a member of a radical student organization at the University of Havana and the nickname "Grease Ball," which Weyl attributes to him, is supposed to have originated in his university years. Whether it was politics, dirt, or both that raised the antagonism of Mirta's family, their courtship encountered considerable difficulty. However, Mirta was a philosophy student at the university and there was plenty of opportunity for them to meet on campus. On October 12, 1948, Fidel and Mirta were married and a son, Fidel, was born to them September 15, 1949.

When Fidel was later imprisoned after his attack on the Moncada barracks, Mirta sought financial help, not from her father, but from the Batista regime through the intervention of her brother. When the minister of the interior announced publicly the dismissal of Mirta from her sinecure position, Fidel was outraged. He wrote to his wife telling her he could not believe that she had ever accepted money from Batista and he wanted to challenge his brother-in-law to a duel. But on July 21, 1954, he learned that the accusations were indeed true and that his wife was divorcing him, an action completed in December of the same year. His son was educated in Cuba and the United States, but apparently arrived back in his homeland in time to accompany his father on a tank during Fidel's victorious entry into Havana on January 8, 1959.[8] After this, his father took charge of the education of the young Fidelito. Herbert Matthews makes a casual mention of other women rumored to be part of Fidel's life, but "Two of his friends have said to me that he never really loved any woman except Mirta—which may be a case of romanticizing. He simply was not made for marriage; his life has been so bound up in his work that there is no room for a normal married life."[9] This was in 1969.

José Martí

Marx was strongly influenced by Hegel through the full development of germinal ideas that could have taken a markedly different direction in another theoretician. The influence of José Martí on Fidel Castro was more direct and specific through both his life and works.

José Martí (1853–1895) was not only the hero of Castro, but also the hero of the anti-Castro Cubans in Miami, who still conduct their annual José Martí parade. How can one individual serve as an inspiration to such disparate elements in a nation? To understand this it is necessary to grasp Martí's intense desire to free Cuba from Spanish colonialism, but, at the same time, his caution lest some new conquerer exploit Cuba. Thus he opposed both the casual interest of the United States in purchasing Cuba from Spain and the leadership of General Maximo Gomez, a former Spanish general born in Santo Domingo, who became commander-in-chief of the Cuban revolutionary army in the first and second wars for Cuban independence.

The intensity of Martí's patriotism may be related in part to his early deportation to Spain for revolutionary activity. He was sent to prison as a boy of seventeen for writing a long epic poem glorifying the Cuban revolution. In 1870, he was sent to the government quarries for backbreaking labor, but was finally pardoned and deported to Spain. He briefly visited Cuba only twice until he landed with a revolutionary force twenty-five years later. In the intervening years he became Cuba's foremost poet and writer. Although he completed his education in Spain at the Universities of Madrid and Zaragoza, he always regarded himself as Cuban and continued to play a role in all Cuban expatriot revolutionary groups.

Personal luxury, the accumulation of money, and oppressive power were the great signs of corruption for Martí. He was a true internationalist whose articles appeared in newspapers all over the western hemisphere from the United States (where he published in English) to the major nations of Latin America. Everywhere he sought to glorify those leaders who lived simply and denied themselves for their country, from the Puritans of the American Revolution to Simon Bolivar and Miguel Hidalgo y Costilla.

However, Martí was more than a mere patriotic writer. He was a poet and a romantic whose works read like Ché Guevara in those moments when Ché reached the heights of romantic ecstacy. José Martí sang the kind of heroic prose, the romance with death and self-sacrifice, that was made for the Latin temperament. His is the song of the Spanish matador transformed from the bull ring to the realm of politics.

In 1892 he organized the Cuban Revolutionary Party from seven Cuban patriotic clubs in New York City. He had long ago patched up his discord with Maximo Gomez, with whom he worked out the details of a plan for invasion of Cuba coupled with local insurrection. On April 11, 1895, he landed on the island, but on May 19 he died in combat before victory was achieved.

Castro and Martí

When Fidel began attending the University of Havana, the writings of Martí were enjoying a renaissance. The imperialism of the United States, only beginning in Martí's time, was now a dominant force in the Americas. But the thing that impressed Castro as he read Martí was the antagonism to corruption and greed, the search for personal honesty in government and, above all, the role of selflessness and sacrifice in the life of a revolutionary. Fidel determined he would seek nothing for himself, not even leadership. He would become a simple foot soldier in the revolution.

While Cuba was officially a sovereign state, the Cuban nationalists still regarded it as excessively dependent on the United States. Politics in Cuba had become corrupt and politicians used power as a road to personal enrichment while providing American businesses with Cuban governments friendly to their enterprises. A new Cuban aristocracy had risen from the ruins of Spanish power. The indifference to race which Martí had praised was certainly not characteristic of Cuba during Castro's youth. Blacks and mulattoes rarely achieved high positions in the government and they were barred from many social clubs and residential areas.

Castro's original idea of being a simple foot soldier in the revolution never materialized. He was a natural leader among the students and he soon became a member of the UIR, one of the more radical groups on campus. Frequent fights erupted between the UIR and MSR (a revolutionary socialist group) and at one time Fidel participated in a joint expeditionary force preparing to overthrow the Dominican Republic.

Fidel was one of the founders of a new radical but anticommunist political party, the Partido del Pueblo Cubano (PPC), also known as the Orthodoxos. He represented the more activist and revolutionary wing of the party, but he very much admired the leader, Eduardo Chibás, and followed him everywhere, frequently campaigning for him throughout Cuba. Chibás took a strong stand against graft and corruption but was unable to prove his charges and committed suicide as a defiant protest against the "government thieves."

Fidel was crushed by the suicide of his hero, but still believed he might run for Congress and find a platform from which to develop a more radical and revolutionary following. He prepared for the election of June 1, 1952, but on March 10, Batista seized power in a military coup. Fidel prepared a number of legal briefs attempting to challenge the new government in the courts. After several fruitless attempts he finally decided to organize an active revolutionary group to attack the Moncada military barracks and gain the arms and ammunition for a full-scale revolutionary movement.

Moncada

The Moncada attack took place on July 26, 1953, and is called by Fidelistas, "the mother of the revolution." A complete failure from a military standpoint, it was to have tremendous symbolic importance. As the leader of the attack, Fidel became the chief target of the Batista regime and the symbol of the Cuban resistance movement. While only three Fidelistes were killed in the attack, the government brutally tortured and executed prisoners: sixty-eight executed and thirty-two imprisoned. Fidel, fortunately, was captured by Lieutenant Pedro Sarria, who refused to send him back to the barracks, but insisted on a civil prison. Also, before his capture, Monsignor Enrique Perez Serantes had secured an agreement with the government that there would be no more killing of prisoners.

Every effort was made to deny him publicity. He was refused a courtroom trial on a claim that he was sick, although he sent a letter to be read in court saying he was not ill. His trial was conducted in a nurses' lounge at the Civil Hospital, where he made his famous speech, "History Will Absolve Me." The original speech has been eclipsed by a pamphlet that Fidel wrote in prison, with the same title, and which he smuggled out by writing between the lines of letters to friends. It was later published in 100,000 copies and distributed by friends all over Cuba. Castro was inspired by Martí, but his major revolutionary pamphlet lacks the broad sweep and international understanding that characterized the work of Martí. It focused on the defense of his actions at Moncada, but it also indicted the Batista regime. It was written when he was twenty-six years old after a university education directed primarily toward the law. For this reason, one finds in it the terse logical reasoning of a legal defense, a promulgation of proposed revolutionary laws, and a citation of the acts of injustice of Batista.

Everywhere in his speech one finds the influence of Martí. Cuba is described as "the country of Martí." He complains that he is denied the works of Martí in prison. His last paragraphs contain the hope that Cuba will be worthy of the apostle Martí. "He has not died. His people are rebellious, his people are worthy, his people are faithful to his memory. Cubans have fallen defending his doctrines. Young men, in a magnificent gesture of reparation, have come to give their blood and to die at the side of his tomb so that he might continue to live in the hearts of his countrymen. Oh, Cuba, what would have become of you if you had let the memory of your apostle die!"

> I conclude my defense, but I shall not end it as all lawyers for the defense do, asking for acquittal for the defendent. I cannot ask for acquittal when my companions are already suffering in the ignominious prison on the Isle of Pines. Send me there that I may share their fate. It is conceivable that honest

men should be dead or in prison when the president is a criminal and a thief!
... Condemn me, it does not matter. *History will absolve me!*[10]

Here is the young Fidel Castro, full of the spirit of Martí and the notion of self-sacrifice. Like many revolutionary leaders before him, he anticipated death rather than victory. His only hope was the thought that he might become part of some revolutionary spirit that would live after him in his people.

Victory and Power

I will not recount here the details of Castro's final release from prison, his persistent attempts to organize a revolutionary movement with the Orthodoxo party, his departure to Mexico to organize the *Granma* expedition, his landing with a ragged band of revolutionaries who were almost decimated on their arrival by Batista forces, his final organization of a guerrilla force in the Escambray Mountains and his victory over the Batista forces in early 1959. These adventures are covered in great detail (including the numerous skirmishes and Fidel's political infighting with the various urban guerrilla groups) by Rolando Bonachea and Nelson Valdes in their excellent introduction to the first volume of the *Selected Works of Fidel Castro,* entitled *Revolutionary Struggle.*[11]

We are interested here in the psychology of Castro. What lay behind his persistent refusal of post-revolutionary political and administrative power and yet his insistence that he and only he would lead the revolution? Various writers have suggested that his refusal of power was mere pretense, that he was always scheming for one-man rule of Cuba and that he planned a communist dictatorship from the beginning. More doubts have been raised concerning the ideological development of Fidel Castro than any other revolutionary leader. This may be because the word "communism" has a special, almost mystical meaning to North Americans and anti-Castro Cubans. To say that Fidel was "really" a communist from the beginning of his political career is like saying he was really Satan's child and only "pretending" to be democratic. Lionel Martin tells us Castro first used the word "socialism" in public only after the Bay of Pigs invasion attempt, but that the roots of his communist orientation can be found in his student years and in all his early speeches.[12] However, I find the evidence presented to be unconvincing.

While the Cuban communist party repudiated the Moncada raid as a futile *putsch*, they later accepted it as merely a step in Fidel's master plan. One would expect such a turnaround in a communist party once they had harmonized their differences with Castro. But Castro clearly exposed his "master plan" in "History Will Absolve Me," and there was no great rush of the communists to join him at that time.

The Refusal of Power

It is well documented that Castro refused political and administrative power on a number of occasions. The question remains, was it part of some secret, devious plan for a final dictatorship or was he really in personal conflict? There is no conclusive answer to this question. I am convinced that Fidel began his revolutionary career with an intense desire for personal sacrifice and self-abnegation.

Herbert Matthews, who interviewed Castro after his triumphant entry into Havana, recalls one of his earlier letters to Conte Argüero in which he insists that neither he nor his comrades harbor the slightest personal ambition. After victory he took a similar position. Matthews remarks:

> Curiously he had the same idea when he came down from the Sierra Maestra in triumph and entered Havana. He did not take the premiership at first. I remember a conversation my wife and I had with him at the time, in which he insisted that he would be content temporarily heading the armed forces and that then he would like to retire to the Sierra Maestra to develop it and to teach. This made no sense, but I do not believe these statements were his guile. They could be a case of his intelligence telling him that *caudillismo* and dictatorship ought to be avoided, while events and his own dominating character nullified this possibility.[13]

I believe Matthews is essentially correct in his assessment of Castro's motives. However, it was not only his intelligence that told him *caudillismo* should be avoided. Castro, like all our revolutionaries, had a deep revulsion to any image of himself in a clean white shirt, business suit, and necktie, giving orders on the administration of government. The limosine and the royal office of the executive made him uncomfortable. He was at his ease as outsider and critic. Like Trotsky, he would like to stand aside from the center of the new revolutionary government and "help it" with his criticism. This is perfectly consistent with the psychology of all the revolutionaries we have studied thus far. They may be extremely autocratic and jealous of power as an outsider (as was Marx); they want to be the *main critic* of the administration in power, but they are repelled by the stuffed-shirt atmosphere, the respectability, and the boredom which they associate with day-to-day administrative responsibility. Castro (like Marx) had a passionate desire for leadership, but (like Marx) he worked best when he had something to attack and when he could identify himself with the oppressed. Obviously, as president of Cuba, he could not retain this identify as the outsider and the underdog.

Much earlier in his campaign, Fidel had given some thought to the selection of a president for Cuba. He contacted Paul Chibás and Felipe Pazos, two respected Cubans in the Orthodoxo party, asking them to come to the Sierra for a conference. At the meeting Pazos suggested that the Cuban Constitution of 1940, which Fidel had sworn to restore, could be amended by lowering the age requirement so as to make it possible for Fidel to become president. Fidel would not have it, saying he had no political ambitions. He also opposed the idea of a weak president, with himself as prime minister, again insisting he had no political ambitions. Out of this meeting came the famous Sierra Maestra Manifesto of July 12, 1957.[14] The document, written by Fidel and edited by Chibás and Pazos, records Fidel's contempt for those who intrigue and maneuver for public power.[15]

The manifesto was essentially a call for unity among the various factions. The urban guerrilla movements and the Castro forces were to agree on a single leader who would not represent any one group. For his candidate, Fidel proposed Judge Manuel Urrutia Lleo, the man who, as a member of the Batista regime, had presided over the trial of the captured *Granma* expeditionaries and who had upheld the right of all Cubans to take arms against tyranny and oppression. He admired Urrutia's courage and impartiality.

Urrutia's Presidency

On January 1, 1959, Judge Urrutia was called to Santiago de Cuba by Fidel Castro to take office as president of the Republic. Almost immediately he became concerned by his isolation from all the powerful political organizations. Both Castro and Guevara had stepped aside, saying they wanted nothing. At first, Urrutia hoped to award posts to some of the sectors excluded from the government, but they all demanded nothing. "Fidel Castro," he says, "had made 'disinterest' fashionable and they could not easily go against the current."[16] In retrospect, Urrutia sees the entire maneuver as part of a Castro plot to seize control for himself. Castro, he says, erected obstacles to everything he wanted to do and then "took to the microphones to criticize the government and weaken its authority.[17] For his decisions, Urrutia had to meet with the Revolutionary Council of Ministers, a majority of whom were also part of Castro's 26th of July Movement. He had long been opposed to the gambling interests in Cuba which were always linked with traffic in narcotics and the corruption of officials. Under heavy opposition from the Council of Ministers (several members of which he believed were pressured by Castro) he finally succeeded in passing a law against gambling. He recommended giving compensation to casino employees for the loss of their jobs. But Castro went on television and publicly criticized the ordinance, saying, "From an air-conditioned office it was very easy to take bread from the mouths of Casino employees."[18]

Many agree with Urrutia that Castro's behavior in the early years was part of his long-range plan to take over the government. Even then, he was acting as a communist.

> This was one more move of Castro's toward acquiring total power, a move that revealed his totalitarian thinking. . . . Although Castro had hailed my independent vote in favor of the *Granma* expeditionaries and the revolutionaries of the November 30 uprising because it suited him at the time, he could not tolerate my voting independently in respect to the gambling law because communists cannot tolerate more than one way of thinking—their way.[19]

Urrutia offered to resign the presidency but the Council of Ministers persuaded him to stay.

What was really happening at this point? Fidel, like Trotsky and Guevara, wanted to step aside from the government once the revolution was victorious. He pictured this as a gesture of his own disinterest and humility. But he *did not* want to give up his role as champion of the oppressed. Just as he had struggled vigorously for complete control of the revolutionary movement, while demanding no political post, he now seemed to believe that he could retain the role of outsider. But his position had changed drastically since the revolution. All through his days in the Sierra Maestra he had been interviewed by reporters for the North American press who made of him an international symbol of the resistance to Batista. He was a natural politican and a charmer who had already come to symbolize the spirit of Cuba to both the North American and Cuban people.

While he still liked to consider himself a gadfly in the hide of the state, this role was no longer possible. In the eyes of Cuba and the world, he was the state. If he really wanted to give up this power, he would have to support the decisions of his nominee whether he liked them or not. The issue of communism in all this is quite beside the point. Fidel was a charismatic leader who had enjoyed his brief taste of power. He was opinionated, strong-willed, even dictatorial in his character. In the Sierra Maestra he was a lovable dictator; his men followed him with confidence because he seemed to know what he was doing. He could argue better than anyone else and if he did not convince them he charmed them into agreement. Already the notion of being a "Fidelista" (a loyal follower of Fidel) was taking hold in the Cuban people. He had only to stand before them in his fatigue uniform with his cigar protruding at a jaunty angle and they cheered him wildly.

The elements of one-man rule emerged in Cuba not because of communism, but because of the personality of Fidel and because of the heroic image he had attained in the minds of the Cuban people. The later adoption of the communist system emerged from several factors. Both his brother Raúl and Ché Guevara believed that opposition to North American imperialism was impossible without joining the communist block of nations. Castro's perpetual need to criticize wealth and power left him unsatisfied with any government except that of his own creation. If he could not be a gadfly in Cuba, he would make Cuba a perpetual gadfly to the self-satisfied capitalism of the United States. Where could he go for support in this cause? The only strong anti-capitalists were communists.

The Evolution of the New System

It seems to me that Castro's communism emerged slowly, and only after several attempts to live within the confines of the old Cuban Constitution. I do not believe he knew when he first began the 26th of July Movement that he would abandon this constitution. It is easy to look back and see how he moved always in that direction, but I doubt that it was part of a long-range plan conceived in his prison on the Isle of Pines or, as some have said, even before that—in his student days. I do not know if it was ever feasible, from an economic standpoint, to make Cuba into a successful capitalist nation, a competitor of the United States, and a center of international tourism. But it is clear, from the personalities and orientation of such men as Castro and Guevara, that Cuba could not follow the U.S. model in a search for bourgeois happiness. Once Castro took control of Cuba, it must become a land of struggle, a nation of underdogs, in which the accumulation of great wealth was looked down upon as a form of corruption.

In the initial stages of the Cuban revolution, Fidel not only identified with the underdog and outsider, but probably believed himself to be one as well. He had no administrative experience in government. He was tempted to seize the reigns of power, but he was fearful of making a complete mess of things. Urrutia mentions several occasions when he sought to resign after Castro became prime minister and began expanding his power. Castro asked him to remain, "saying that if he failed in his undertaking, I could again take charge of the policy of the revolutionary government." On another occasion, Castro sent his ministers outside with Urrutia to plead with him, one of them, Manuel Ray, saying, "Doctor, don't resign, for you are the Revolution's last hope."[20]

Says Herbert Matthews of this period:

> Fidel does have a convenient—almost innocent—capacity for self-deception. He was quite capable, with one side of his nature, of feeling that he could stand aside and, with another side, of being driven to seek and hold the primary place of power. Having taken the premiership, it was typical of him that he should have had the most widely optimistic ideas about what he was going to achieve.[21]

In July 1959 Castro was reported to have resigned and on the 17th he launched into a lengthy speech against Urrutia and his policies. Urrutia's fourth resignation followed, and the presidency went to Osvaldo Dorticos Torrado. Meanwhile, Fidel retained his position of prime minister. Dorticos remained in office throughout the changes of 1960, which included a redistribution of wealth and major land reform. No session of the national legislature occurred in 1960 and Fidel assumed greater and more absolute powers. All government action took place by decree, ratified by voice vote of gatherings of assembled citizens. No reference was made to a date when elections would occur and the old constitution seemed to slip slowly into obscurity.

Meanwhile, an active program of school building and housing developments for workers was undertaken. Agricultural cooperatives were established and new roads were built everywhere. In October, urban property, mines, and oil refineries were nationalized; much of this property was owned by foreign interests. In July the U.S. Congress authorized reallocation of the sugar quota, which determined the regular yearly purchase of sugar from Cuba. Castro called this move economic aggression, but it was now clear that he must make other alliances if Cuba was to survive. The Soviet Union provided advisors and a credit of $100 million, while some other agreements were made with east European states exchanging sugar for other goods. Both the Soviet Union and the People's Republic of China sent diplomatic missions to Cuba. Severe restrictions were placed on what could be taken out of Cuba when traveling abroad. By December, 40,000 Cubans had left for Miami. Cuba was moving toward socialism; the loss of

American support was inevitable. Clearly, Cuba must become part of the communist block of nations whether or not she formally adopted that ideology by name.

Counter-revolutionary movements began throughout Cuba with frequent acts of sabotage and minor military clashes. On January 3, 1961, President Eisenhower broke off diplomatic relations with Cuba. On January 12, Uruguay expelled the Cuban ambassador. President John F. Kennedy announced in April, in response to charges from Castro, that U.S. forces would not intervene in Cuba. But on April 17 the United States CIA-sponsored Bay of Pigs invasion cost hundreds of Cuban refugees their lives. On May 1 Castro proclaimed Cuba a socialist state.

In retrospect, it is clear that once Castro began to move toward socialism and a communist alliance, he had to move fast. Many vigorously anti-communist Cubans, both within and without Cuba, were ready to prevent his changes. Whether or not he used Manuel Urrutia as a cover for his intentions while he prepared the way for socialism, only Castro could tell us. But working in the shadow of the world's major capitalist power and still uncertain about the attitude of his own people toward socialism, he may well have felt that his risks of failure were high and that Urrutia could pull the country together in some way if he were decisively defeated. However, it is clear that the majority of Cubans were not prepared to oppose Castro, not even on the issue of socialism. No massive uprising occurred in Havana or anywhere else during the Bay of Pigs invasion, as the CIA had predicted. Today Cubans follow Castro not only for his ideology but for his qualities as a charismatic leader. Newsmen who visit him are impressed by the ease with which they travel anywhere in Cuba and ask any questions. Castro remains the same informal, charming conversationalist and he dominates the nation by an apparent general agreement. Most Cubans who have remained in Cuba are now "Fidelistas."

Fidel has since stated that he was a communist from the beginning of his career, that his actions were all part of a plan for the socialization of Cuba. But this statement was made after he was already an avowed communist and following the Bay of Pigs invasion. One must look at it with the same scepticism with which one takes all statements by politicians in power. Fidel no longer had any need or desire for support from the United States. He now wanted to win the respect and recognition of the Soviet Union. This so-called "confession" does not change the facts of his early history or development, although it has damaged his reputation for integrity.

NOTES

1. Herbert L. Matthews, *Castro: A Political Biography* (London: Allen Lane, Penguin, 1969), 19–20.

2. Lee Lockwood, *Castro's Cuba, Cuba's Fidel* (New York: Random House, Vintage, 1969), 16.

3. Matthews, *Castro,* 20.

4. Ibid., 18.

5. Ibid., 20–21.

6. Nathaniel Weyl, *Red Star over Cuba* (New York: Devin–Adair, 1961), 50–51.

7. Matthews, *Castro,* 34.

8. Ibid., 27.

9. Ibid.

10. Fidel Castro, *Revolutionary Struggle: The Selected Works of Fidel Castro, 1947–1958,* edited by R. E. Bonachea and N. P. Valdes, vol. 1 (Cambridge: MIT Press, 1972), 220–221.

11. Castro, *Revolutionary Struggle,* vol. 1, 1–127.

12. Lionel Martin, *The Early Fidel* (Secaucus: Lyle Stuart, 1978).

13. Matthews, *Castro,* 72.

14. Castro, *Revolutionary Struggle,* vol. 1, 99–100.

15. Ibid., 343–44.

16. Manuel Urrutia, *Fidel Castro and Company, Inc.* (New York: Frederick A. Praeger, 1964), 33.

17. Ibid., 34.

18. Ibid., 37.

19. Ibid.

20. Ibid., 38–39.

21. Matthews, *Castro,* 119.

Chapter 13

V. I. LENIN:
The Stoic

The Invisible Personality

Lenin is a revolutionary who has drawn a curtain over his childhood. While Castro tries to avoid talking about his private life, he loves to talk to reporters. He is a colorful personality and personal incidents often erupt out of his conversation, as though he cannot help revealing himself. Lenin, on the other hand, is often described as colorless. The few accounts of intimate friends reveal him as a man of strong inner feelings, who seldom showed emotion and who was even guarded in expressing an opinion until he had thought about it for days. Krupskaya, his wife, who, in her long biography of Lenin, reveals almost nothing of their personal life together, does mention his shyness and his "nerves." Lenin's method for handling a severe emotional upset was to withdraw. Sometimes he would spend a few days on the beach. At other times he would walk the streets all night or remove himself to the bedroom with the blinds drawn and his hands over his eyes.[1] It is almost humorous that his wife should mention his "ardour" that swept her off her feet, only in relation to one of his political articles.[2] Lenin had chosen a wife who matched his own discretion, his secrecy, and his one-sided devotion to the revolution. Like Trotsky his only occupation was that of professional revolutionary, but unlike Trotsky, he left no autobiography or diary and he lacked Trotsky's wide-ranging interest in world literature. He guarded himself against any pleasure which might distract him from his central purpose. He even denied himself the opportunity for martyrdom, first, by refusing the provocative stances taken by his brother and, second, by directing the revolution while hidden from public view in order to avoid arrest.

The Young Manhood of Lenin

We cannot locate in Lenin's childhood incidents which might have served to shape his adult attitude toward suffering and self-denial. He was born Vladimir Ilyich Ulyanov on April 22, 1870, the son of a Russian father, a schoolteacher and administrator, and a German mother. In early youth he developed a basic mistrust of others and a general attitude of caution and reserve. Wolfenstein relates this caution to the fact that Lenin was late to begin walking as a child. He learned by watching then doing. "This lack of impulsiveness was one of Lenin's characteristics throughout his life. Any new policy which Lenin put forward was always preceded by a long period of silent and absorptive gestation."[3] In this regard, he was very different from Trotsky. In fact, it may account for their style of interaction in which Trotsky would seize upon a new idea or a significant policy change only to find Lenin resistant. Yet Lenin frequently adopted Trotsky's position after several months of deliberation.

Both Lenin and Trotsky were disciplined in school for ridiculing a teacher. Trotsky was actually dismissed and pined over the incident. Characteristically, we know little of Lenin's reaction. Even the death of his father in 1886 brought little overt response from him. Lenin's brother Sasha was executed for revolutionary activity against the Tsar in May 1887. At the end of that year, Lenin, in his first semester at Kazan, was arrested for participating in a demonstration against the university inspector. Wolfenstein[4] has presented some interesting speculation on the development of Lenin's rebellious behavior, but we really have little material evidence, for Lenin never described his feelings. In fact, he seemed never to react to events at all. On the outside stoney and silent, Lenin would then suddenly erupt into action. He had little need to explain himself in personal terms. To be sure, he was later to develop a detailed theoretical justification for his behavior, but his need for the personal sympathy and love of others was minimal.

'Revolutionary Asceticism'

Bruce Mazlish believes that "revolutionary asceticism becomes more and more prominent and more and more functional as we move toward more modern, conscious, and professional revolutions."[5] However, for Mazlish, "revolutionary asceticism" encompasses more than the generally understood restraint of sensual appetite (self-denial for an ideal). It also includes a strong element of narcissism, an inability to love others, and a tendency to identify this self-love with an abstraction such as "the people."[6] The revolutionary ascetic is, for Mazlish, an ideal type to which any individual will only partially correspond. While Mazlish mentions the importance of masochism in the development of the attitude of self-denial, he points out that in the revolutionary ascetic the constellation of ascetic traits may "be present for different psychological reasons (e.g. hard work may be a sublimation rather than a masochistic punishment of the self)."[7]

The masochism described by Freud and Reik is characterized by a strong element of emotional display, a direct effort to enlist the sympathy of others. Reik has chapters entitled "The Demonstrative Feature" and "The Secret Meaning of the Display in Public" in which he stresses the need of the masochist to be publicly humiliated. Sometimes he describes the "silent suffering" of the masochist, but in such cases there is something conspicuous and obvious about the way he shows his suffering to others but never speaks about it himself.[8] We can find some of his tendency toward public display in all the revolutionaries we have covered *prior to Lenin*. Lenin's character is even more indicative of a person who has subliminated many of his masochistic needs. He is cautious, suspicious, self-contained.

Perhaps the example set by his brother helped to shape his character. Lenin admired his brother Sasha when the two of them were very young. But after the death of his father, Sasha engaged in an inept attempt to assassinate Alexander III and was quickly arrested. His mother was told that he could save his life if he recanted his beliefs, but he refused, saying, "I want to die for my country."[9] One of his comrades had escaped and when the court asked why he made no such attempt, he again replied, "I don't want to escape. I want to die for my country."[10] He made several attempts at his trial to show "the thought process which convinced me of the necessity to commit this crime"[11] and he described how the "vague dreams of freedom, equality, and brotherhood took shape for me in the strictly scientific forms of socialism."[12] The judge interrupted several times to warn him not to stray from the subject, but Sasha continued, "In the Russian nation you will always find ten persons who are so loyal to their ideas and who are so filled with the unhappiness of their country that it is no sacrifice for them to die on behalf of their cause."[13] Here we see in Sasha evidence of the overt masochistic motivation, the desire for death and martyrdom that is not evident in Lenin, particularly the emphasis on the moralistic attitude behind his actions.

In spite of his noble motives, Sasha was executed and the death of his beloved brother, following closely on the death of his father, must have had a profound effect on Lenin. It seemed to accentuate his natural tendency to be somewhat suspicious, guarded, and taciturn. Clearly, his brother's death demonstrated to Lenin the danger of hasty action and the futility of great moral pronouncements about love of country. It is almost as though Lenin reacted against this "display in public" which characterized the revolutionary behavior of his brother.

Even though he did not like to make a public display of his sacrifice, Lenin made self-denial a central feature of his character. He lived frugally, devoted his time to study and political activity, and even denied himself entertainment. His speeches and writings are devoid of flamboyance or literary flourish. Like Trotsky, he seemed to thrive in prison, giving himself over to reading and writing his political ideas. Speaking of Lenin's self-denial, Maxim Gorky writes:

> A man with an astonishing strength of will, Lenin had in the highest degree the best qualities of the revolutionary intelligentsia—self-discipline often amounting to self-torture, self-defacement; in its most extreme form to the renunciation of art, to the logic of one of Andreyev's heros: "Others have hard lives—it means that I also have to have a hard life."
>
> In the difficult year of famine of 1919, Lenin was ashamed to eat the food sent to him by comrades, soldiers and peasants from the provinces. When parcels arrived at his uncomfortable flat, he frowned, became embarrassed, and hurried to give away flour, sugar and butter to the comrades who were sick or weak through lack of food. . . .

> Personally undemanding, a teetotaller and non-smoker, busy from morning till night with complicated, difficult work, quite unable to take proper care of himself, he followed vigilantly the lives of his comrades. [14]

Gorky also remarks on Lenin's tendency to sacrifice emotional and artistic pleasure. There is a suggestion that he regarded such pleasure as a weakness.

> And then, narrowing his eyes and smiling, he added sadly: "But I can't listen to music too often, it affects the nerves, makes you want to say kind, silly things, to stroke the heads of the people who, living in a terrible hell, can create such beauty. Nowadays you mustn't stroke anyone's head, you'd get your hand bitten off, you've got to hit them over their heads, without mercy, although, ideally, we're against the use of force. H'm, h'm, our duty is infernally hard!"[15]

While Gorky's observations support the ascetic image of Lenin and his wish to sacrifice himself for others, Gorky seldom describes Lenin's extreme caution and suspicion. He was so fearful of arrest and execution that he remained in hiding throughout most of the October revolution until Trotsky had secured the victory. He was suspicious of everyone's behavior and motives. He subjected Trotsky to exhaustive questioning during the October days, fearful that Trotsky might fail to carry out an insurrection at the last moment. But in all of this behavior, there is no hint of false pride, bravado, or compensatory behavior. Lenin knew he had the courage to act in a revolution. He had no need to pose as the great leader by showing himself in public and risking arrest. He was not afraid of appearing fearful, which is, in itself, an unusual form of courage.

Self-Denial and Self-Neglect

According to Mazlish, Lenin embodied to an unusual degree the two aspects of the character he described as the "revolutionary ascetic," i.e. the leader with "few libidinal ties" and the "puritan" or self-denying attitude.[16] While it is true that these two traits were certainly important to his success, I wonder if Lenin's interest in revolution was not stimulated by a more openly masochistic and self-destructive aspect in himself, a side which he was later able to tame and redirect to the goal of revolutionary victory. I raise this speculation from the few clues we have from his personal behavior, but also because this seems a common characteristic among those revolutionaries who are both theoreticians and agitators. We can see a hint of this "self-torture" in Gorky's description of him. Krupskaya indicated that he had, at one time, almost resigned himself to the fact that a genuine revolution would not be possible in his own lifetime but could be accomplished only by future generations[17], again suggesting a willingness to sacrifice himself for some future goal. The disappearance of his stomach troubles in prison also supports this general picture of an individual who can welcome total domination by an oppressor under certain circumstances.

Bertrand Russell, who had an hour's conversation with Lenin, has described the extremely spartan surroundings of his study. To Russell he was surprisingly friendly and without a trace of *hauteur* or self-importance.[18] Russell advocated "free love" and was often accused of being a communist. Some of Lenin's followers, particularly his mistress Inessa Armand, also supported greater sexual freedom for women. Thus, not surprisingly, the notion of free love was often associated with Russian communism. But Lenin himself would have nothing to do with such distractions and he was concerned that Inessa's efforts to prepare a pamphlet on this subject might be misunderstood as "freedom from child-bearing" and "freedom for adultery."[19] Sex, for him, was reserved for the bedroom and he was not inclined to discuss it publicly. He was a Victorian in these matters as with all sensuality. In this regard he forms a striking contrast to Rousseau, who was raised in the prim and proper city of Geneva, but who overflowed with talk of love, romance, and sensuality, even while he fought against it.

While Lenin stressed simplicity in his living standards and was embarrassed by any show of luxury or sensuality, he was not embarrassed by power. In fact, he felt that his sacrifices gave him the right to direct others in the revolution. However, like the typical revolutionary of the Left, he retained his identification with the oppressed. Despite his ruthlessness and his occasional brutal remarks, he was not a rebel who became a tyrant once he achieved power. To the end he disdained the elegant dress, the luxurious surroundings, and the grand manner of the world leader.

Lenin and Revolutionary Consciousness

The term "revolutionary consciousness" has acquired several different meanings, but its principal function for the revolutionary leader is a kind of self-embodiment that will outlive his own short life. It is a representation of himself, as he views society, and it is created in his own personal style. For both Marx and Lenin this notion of revolutionary consciousness was closely related to theory. The idea must come *before* the action. The role of feeling is deemphasized and the role of deliberation and advance planning is raised to the utmost importance. In this regard Lenin was quite different from Trotsky, who often felt a romantic sense of oneness with the people and believed he would know what to do and say out of his enthusiasm of the moment.

For Lenin, the leadership of the intelligentsia and the control from above was central to any revolutionary movement. He had a horror of political spontaniety and would be a firm opponent of many new-left politicians whose slogan was "If it feels good, do it" (in both sex and politics). His famous pamphlet, *What Is To Be Done?*, comes down hard on the "slavish cringing before spontaneity."[20] If possible he was a more firm advocate of "the word before the deed" than was Marx. In his own account of the failure of earlier revolutionary movements he remarks, "Political consciousness was completely overwhelmed by spontaneity"[21] and he warns against the "infatuation with terrorism."[22] Here, of course, he meant terrorism as a form of political statement, which might well lead to the type of martyrdom suffered by his brother. Thus, in his theoretical work, as in his personality, he was an advocate of cautious planning prior to action and he was wary of those who would whip up the emotions of the crowd without adequate preparation. In this regard we are reminded of Marx's thundering denunciation of Weitling.[23]

NOTES

1. Nadezhda K. Krupskaya, *Reminiscences of Lenin* (New York: International Publishers, 1970), 86, 193, 198–99, 208.

2. Ibid., 232.

3. E. Victor Wolfenstein, *The Revolutionary Personality: Lenin, Trotsky, Gandhi* (Princeton: Princeton University Press, 1971), 41.

4. Ibid., 3–49.

5. Bruce Mazlish, *The Revolutionary Ascetic: The Evolution of a Political Type* (New York: McGraw–Hill, 1976), 11.

6. Ibid., 29.

7. Ibid., 32.

8. Theodor Reik, *Masochism in Modern Man* (New York: Grove, 1941), 72–83, 136–46.

9. Louis Fischer, *The Life of Lenin* (New York: Harper and Row, 1965), 10.

10. Ibid., 14.

11. Ibid., 15.

12. Ibid.

13. Ibid., 16.

14. Maxim Gorky, *Lenin, A Biographical Essay* (London: Morrison Gibb Ltd., 1967), 41–42.

15. Ibid., 45.

16. Mazlish, *The Revolutionary Ascetic*, 136–37.

17. Krupskaya, *Reminiscences*, 335.

18. Fischer, *The Life of Lenin*, 407.

19. Ibid., 79.

20. Vladimir I. Lenin, *What Is to Be Done?* (Moscow: Progress Publishers, 1973), 34.

21. Ibid., 37.

22. Ibid., 51.

23. A complete account of this table-thumping session in which Marx drummed Weitling out of the Communist League and repudiated his emotional expression of ideas without theoretical foundation is to be found in Paul Annenkov's *The Extraordinary Decade*, translated by Irwin R. Titunik (Ann Arbor: University of Michigan Press, 1968), 168–170.

Chapter 14

MAO TSE-TUNG:
The Return to Romanticism

The Embodiment of Others

Mao, like Lenin, gave us little autobiographic information of the type required for a psychological study. While Edgar Snow made a valiant effort to extract autobiographical information from Mao during a long interview for his *Red Star over China*,[1] Mao lacked the basic autobiographic motivation that drives the individual to remember those things about himself that are unique, even peculiar. Mao stands at the opposite pole from Rousseau in this dimension. While Rousseau examined his thoughts and his actions, as though each had occurred for the first time in himself, Mao was already deeply identified with the communist party at the time Snow met him and he considered most of the highly personal details of his life as extraneous events unrelated to the central purpose of his existence.[2]

Even in the story of his childhood rebellion against his father, he imposed the group experience of political revolt backward upon his individual life so that this experience became a mere copy of his later rebellion. "There were two 'parties' in the family," he tells Snow. "One was my father, the Ruling Power. The Opposition was made up of myself, my mother, my brother and sometimes even the labourer. In the United Front of the Opposition, however, there was a difference of opinion."[3] Snow mentions that Mao sometimes gave an amused smile when he used these political terms to describe his childhood, but it does indicate that he was unwilling to delve deeply into his personal feelings and preferred to present his childhood as a "typical" political drama. In his account of the development of strategy in dealing with his father, he *thinks* about his behavior and he notes the weakness and strengths of his opponent. When his father threatened, he negotiated. The struggle in the family is "dialectical." He learned by his father's response that he was more successful when he defended his rights by open rebellion. But this is all a logical process, like one clever general learning to outwit another. We cannot reach the little boy who is terrified of this powerful "rich peasant" and who feels a deep sense of personal injustice at being made to work in the field with the other laborers hired by his father.

Mao clearly developed an early identification with his mother and her concern for the oppressed. This may well have been intensified by the fact that the family was even more oppressed than the laborers on his father's farm. Speaking of his father, Mao said:

> He was a hot tempered man and frequently beat both me and my brothers. He gave us no money whatever, and the most meagre food. On the 15th of every month he made a concession to his labourers and gave them eggs with their rice, but never meat. To me he gave neither eggs nor meat. [4]

Thus we learn of Mao's subservient position and his personal suffering. He was an ardent physical culturist and he did not accept luxurious living. It seems that Mao, like most revolutionaries, had characteristics of both his mother and his father. His overt and obvious identification was with his mother and with the oppressed. But in his asceticism and his determination to live frugally, he was like his father.

He describes an incident in which he became very angry with a youth who had the temerity to discuss with his servant in Mao's presence the purchase of a piece of meat. Mao was so annoyed he would not see the fellow again. He condemned the youth because the subject of meat was too trivial to be discussed by serious-minded young men. [5] He did not place a strong overt emphasis on the need for personal sacrifice. In fact, the way Mao told the story, everyone was annoyed at the triviality of the young man. It was a group feeling.

This is the chief difficulty in understanding Mao as an individual. He saw himself as an embodiment of group feeling, a man who sensed what others needed and felt and acted for them. With Sun Yat-sen we have an opportunity to sense his conflicts, his personal doubts about himself, his feeling of being *different* from the other revolutionaries and his failure to convince them of some of his own idealistic goals. But in Mao's case, even in the later cult of Mao worship, he becomes different only in the sense of being *better*. He was idolized not for his individuality, but because he *was* China, the embodiment of the best of the Chinese people.

Revolutionary Romanticism

It is ironic that this leader who stresses the logical development of his strategy and the natural consequences of oppressive acts should have been born in south China, the center of romanticism and idealistic tales. Mao was born in the village of Shao Shan, Hunan province, in 1893. His schoolteacher was a stern taskmaster like his father, and both urged him to study the classics. But Mao developed an interest in the romance of old China, "especially stories of rebellions."[6] While his personality appears outwardly stoic and unemotional, he seems to have been deeply impressed by tales of heroism and romance, similar to those that excited the impressionable Rousseau. Mao persisted in his love of the romances, despite the punishment of his teacher and the criticism of his father and was "much influenced by such books, read at an impressionable age."[7] Like Marx, Mao was moved by strong romantic, even sentimental images in his childhood and, like Marx, he sought to present a more stoic, logical image as an adult.

In his early years there seems to be only one incident in which Mao stresses his *difference* from others. This is in regard to a food rebellion during the famine in Changsha. The rebels were beheaded and their heads displayed on poles. Most of the students sympathized with the rebels but "only from an observer's point of view." For the first time Mao indicates his own deep resentment at the injustice of the treatment of the rebels and his feeling that they were "people like my own family."[8]

While we can find this evidence of Mao's identification with the oppressed and his tendency toward a frugal ascetic way of life, there is never a hint, from his own account, that he learned to enjoy suffering or that he received some pleasure from personal sacrifice. But this is the sort of detail that a group-oriented person such as Mao would be likely to omit, i.e. his personal tastes, his private feelings, and his sources of sensual satisfaction.

Mao would certainly have to be prepared for suffering and sacrifice to endure a series of events such as those in the famous Long March. The Long March was Mao's personal response to the circumstances facing him at the time, but there is no evidence to suggest an excess of zeal for suffering and sacrifice in this behavior. He was pursued through much of his route by Chiang Kai-shek.

Revolutionary Immortality

While there is insufficient data for a psychological study of Mao as an individual, Robert Lifton[9] has examined some of his conflicts by tracing conceptual connections between individual and collective patterns in China. Lifton finds, in the Snow interview with Mao, evidence that Mao was contemplating his own death and that he was concerned with the possibility that the youth of China might fail to carry on the traditions of the revolution, that indeed they might negate the revolution entirely.[10] Lifton traces the development of the Red Guard, the Cultural Revolution, and the encouragement and direction that Mao himself gave to both. It was an indication of Mao's efforts to immortalize his own thoughts and the spirit of revolutionary fervor, to transform the will of the Chinese people, particularly the youth.

To a large extent the work of the Red Guard was destructive to the stability and productivity of China. Factories were smashed in order to destroy "old methods;" university professors were attacked to eliminate "old ideas." The romantic belief in the will of the individual and the notion that revolutionary zeal was the chief requirement for progress, even for technological achievement, were reborn. Lifton coined the term "psychism" to describe this phenomenon. The Chinese themselves, says Lifton, refer to this spirit as "revolutionary romanticism."[11] The vigorous stimulus that Mao gave to the emergence of this movement certainly suggests his strong attachment to the romantic images of his youth and his belief that this romanticism was, in itself, the essential element in revolutionary fervor.

But Lifton has outlined several examples to suggest that, instead of improving productivity, the psychism induced by Mao led to economic disorder. The attempt to substitute the building of backyard furnaces for steel factories proved ineffective. Technicians and engineers received their instruction from politicians and technical skill was downgraded. One can see a parallel here with the successful experience of the guerrilla who made up for his lack of sophisticated weapons by his zeal for the cause and his ability to live off the land, capturing the weapons of his opponent. But economic development is not the same as warfare. Ché Guevara was later to make a similar discovery when he tried to apply revolutionary zeal to the industrial problems of Cuba.

Social Masochism and Immortality

There is a psychological link between Lifton's concept of revolutionary immortality and the social masochism described by Reik, particularly Mao's demand for "sacrifice" during the Cultural Revolution. However, the personal element becomes increasingly difficult to discover. Part of this is due to Mao's reticence in discussing his personal life, but perhaps this very reticence—this lack of a need for private personal justification—suggests a change in the nature of the masochistic impulse, if indeed we can still describe this phenomenon as related to masochism at all.

Reik has associated the masochistic urge for immortality with the process of delay of gratification and with the social anxiety associated with masochism.

> The social anxiety he wants to get rid of is shifted from his contemporaries to those who come after him. The suspense is prolonged beyond his own life. The social anxiety has at first assumed the shape of the fear of death. In order to escape this powerful psychic pressure the masochist submits to still more suffering, postponing the satisfaction anew. He now expects it only after his death and anticipates it by phantasy. The ego recoils from the threat of complete annihilation, having transferred the expectation of imminent calamity to this terrible punishment of eternal destruction of his personality. By contrast, the certainty of continued individual existence after death appears as a premium.[12]

Mao's urge for revolutionary immortality may have been with him throughout his life, but the anxiety about the survival of his ideas developed later in his career. We find a similar phenomenon in Tolstoy, Trotsky, and Guevara. The quality of this concern for immortality as it appears in the later life of the individual seems distinctly different from the physical self-sacrifice of youth. There is a concern with one's words and ideas, a desire that one's morality of sacrifice should live on in some way through the mass acceptance of these ideas, but particularly as they are associated with one's name and personality.

This is evident in the case of Mao, whose little red book of quotations was developed during his lifetime as a kind of concrete entity to be carried by every individual. It was a way of immortalizing the thoughts of Chairman Mao—a part of Mao that would live forever and continue to inspire the party. In this drive for immortality there is, again, something beyond the mere postponement of gratification described in the social masochism of Reik.

NOTES

1. Edgar Snow, *Red Star over China* (New York: Garden City Publishing Company, 1939).

2. Ibid., 111–12.

3. Ibid., 114.

4. Ibid.

5. Ibid., 130–31.

6. Ibid., 115.

7. Ibid., 116.

8. Ibid., 118.

9. Robert J. Lifton, *Revolutionary Immortality: Mao Tse-tung and the Chinese Cultural Revolution* (New York: Random House, Vintage, 1968).

10. Ibid., 11–19.

11. Ibid., 56.

12. Theodor Reik, *Masochism in Modern Man* (New York: Grove, 1941), 334–35.

Chapter 15

BEYOND MASOCHISM

A Review of the Phenomenon

While the dynamic of masochism may play an important role in revolutionary behavior, there are limits beyond which it ceases to serve as a useful explanation. In many respects it helps to account for the form but not the content of revolutionary motivation. Masochism is primarily a negation, a denial of self-interest or at least a delay of gratification. Revolution is also a negation, a denial of the legitimacy of existing powers. But there is a positive moral aspiration in the revolutionary which cannot be contained in the idea of self-sacrifice alone. For the sexual masochist the aim is orgasm through a distorted form of gratification. For the revolutionary there is not only an inhibition of aim, but a change in the content of the drive. Yet it would seem that the libidinal energy of the masochistic impulse is frequently used and even reactivated in revolutionary behavior.

What causes the masochist to become a *moral* masochist instead of merely enjoying the suffering? We can see this change clearly in Rousseau when he receives the spanking from his uncle. The punishment is severe and painful and is for a "crime" he did not commit. Further, he is punished along with his cousin and the two boys feel a comradeship in their suffering. They feel a certain unity as a result of the injustice which they have both suffered and righteous anger replaces the sexual pleasure because (a) sexual feeling toward a man was abhorrent to Rousseau and (b) feeling and sharing righteous indignation was also pleasurable.

But to expect this sequence of events in the lives of all our revolutionaries would be expecting too much. It is important that the sexual feeling was never completely sublimated, but returned to haunt Rousseau several times in his life. There was then, a return of the repressed. This was true in T. E. Lawrence as well, although the sexual aspect of masochism seemed more homosexual than heterosexual. This sexual element in masochism seems closely associated with guilt, for we do not find the overt sexual masochism in our later, more successful, revolutionaries, either because it was never present or because it has been completely and successfully sublimated. If this is the case, they have either forgotten (repressed) this childhood masochism or they would prefer not to mention it.

We *do* find, in such intermediate types as Gandhi and Marx, an inordinate tendency to suffer or to take pride in their sacrifices for humanity. But this is a different phenomenon. Guilt has been changed to pride and there is no later emergence of the guilty aspect of suffering. Again, we cannot be sure it was ever present. It is clearly a moral masochism, but not necessarily a sexual masochism.

Trotsky's pleasure in speaking from the "warm cavern of bodies" returns to the second element in Rousseau's moral masochism, an unmistakably pleasurable sense of feeling at one with the community of the oppressed, but the feeling of guilt is not present. Trotsky felt both a part of the people and a nurturing leader of the people. He felt their intense hunger to know and believed he could give them what they wanted as they clung "with their dry lips to the nipples of the revolution." While Trotsky, as a child, often enjoyed weeping and got his way with his mother, and particularly with his father, through his tears, he wept over injustice and his reward was the reward of righteousness.

However, there are revolutionaries who do not fit neatly into the masochistic model. While they engage in ascetic and self-denying behavior, their behavior is not demonstratively masochistic; it is not deliberately provocative or self-torturing. It does not exceed the asceticism which is a necessary part of any disciplined, long-range revolutionary planning. We can see a consistent pattern of rebellion and risk, but we do not find, in their childhood or adult life, a real need for punishment and suffering. Such men are Kropotkin, Lenin, Castro, and Mao. This may be because their provocative behavior was justified by the cruelty of the state and their punishment, while not self-administered, followed as a consequence of their revolt. But at this point it becomes difficult to distinguish between masochism and courage. Did Lenin, Mao, and Castro rebel because they had focused on punishment or because they were outraged by injustice? We cannot find the answer to this question by looking at the lives of individuals alone. The realities of the world situation can have a decided influence on the actual manifestation of the masochistic impulse. In some historical periods the revolutionary leader finds himself in a society or a situation that is ripe for revolution. Crane Brinton has suggested that some societies block the progress of their more creative people and bring about an alienation of the intellectuals.[1] However the revolution itself may pass through several stages before it develops to full fruition. The alienated intellectuals provide a theoretical basis for revolt, a social myth on which others may build. Revolutionaries learn from each other and each may carry the process a bit farther. Marx provided a theoretical foundation on which Lenin, Trotsky, and Mao were to build, but Marxist communism provided only a set of general principles which each later modified in accord with the realities of the time.

We are left with a feeling that the ability to use suffering in a positive way is important for a revolutionary and that it may even be helpful to take pleasure in one's suffering. But, like the monks of old who were warned against taking too much pleasure in mortification of the flesh, the revolutionary must be prepared to drop the role of martyr after power is achieved, or face a loss of leadership. Further, suffering alone does not seem to be a sufficient motivation for the accomplishments we have described. There may have been some other positive urge to accomplish or create something for which these men were willing to risk their lives and endure possible suffering, even though suffering itself may have had little attraction for them. Perhaps this same positive urge exists in our other revolutionary leaders as well. Thus masochism may be a necessary but not a sufficient explanation for the behavior of Marx, Trotsky, Gandhi, Guevara, Rousseau, and even T. E. Lawrence.

Not for Myself

The term "self-sacrifice" does not seem adequate to cover the full range of activities of our revolutionaries. We are tempted to use a term more like "self-forgetful" and "group-oriented" or "mass-oriented." But then we are reminded of the self-importance and even self-aggrandizement of some of our revolutionaries and we recognize that the self may be very central to their considerations. It is not so much neglect of the self but the neglect of one's *material needs* that is striking in the revolutionary. While the revolutionary begins by giving these material things to others, in the long run it is not so much the material well-being of humans that concerns him but their minds, moral attitudes, and souls.

Lawrence did not want to hand freedom to the Arab people on a silver platter and then accept their gratitude. He wanted them to burn with his own excitement at the thought of a free and independent Arab republic. His assignment was merely to secure Arab cooperation in order to further British goals, but Lawrence was one of those people who had to believe in the moral justification of whatever he was doing. He therefore changed the goals from a mere British advantage to the noble cause of Arab freedom.

While an urge to suffer may explain Karl Marx's provocative personality and difficulties with money, it does not help us understand the lifelong effort of this intellectual to transmit his ideas, his goals, and the intensity of his aspirations to the working class. Marx was a decidedly different being from the worker he sought to educate. His mind wandered over the obscure heights while the worker was sunk in tedium, oppression, and poverty. Yet Marx was convinced that he could—that he must—shape this mass of unorganized wage slaves into a coherent, purposeful movement to change society. He had an urge to dominate this mass with his mind, much as he dominated Jenny, but he also wanted the worker to become part of his family. He wanted to be loved, not merely by his wife and children, but by generations to come. The same applies to Guevara, to Rousseau, and to our other revolutionary leaders.

In each case the rational or ostensible aim of the revolutionary was to "help mankind." Often the exact manner in which this help was to be rendered was at first unclear. Neglect of self can be learned from parents, but only if the child is receptive to such ideas. Guevara was taught by his mother and father to ignore his asthma and engage in vigorous athletic activity. He learned that his body could endure great punishment if he refused to accept his own weakness. But it was Guevara who made the transfer from self-neglect to the care of others. Gandhi learned how to ignore his physical needs from his mother and he was rewarded for his self-sacrifice by his father, but the urge to turn this childhood tendency toward self-sacrifice into some larger mission to save India came from some other source in his adult life. Marx, it would seem, was educated *against* self-neglect. His mother and particularly his father were distressed by his tendency to drive himself, to stay up all night studying, to agonize about his own fate and that of the world in a kind of incurable *weltschmerz* described by his father as "your sickly sensitivity." But in spite of his father's efforts to control his self-neglect—or perhaps because of it, for Marx was extremely oppositional—he continued to forget his basic material needs and those of his family, turning his attention to the larger problems of suffering humanity.

One has to be a terrible egotist to believe one can save humanity. But most of us are cured of this form of egotism early in life. When we no longer have our parents nearby to worry about our self-neglect, we soon learn to care for ourselves, to feed ourselves and our family first and then perhaps to give some minor donation to charity. When this self-neglect is carried throughout the life of the person, despite the many hardships that would tend to extinguish such a response, we must look for some other cause than parental conditioning. Something else must exist within the person, a positive drive beside which self-neglect is a mere by-product, a secondary expression. We might describe this drive as a nurturing impulse, for there is a strong element of caring for and protecting others. But in its final development there is inevitably a mass quality to this impulse. The usual form of nurturing, the usual human contacts, the love of a man and a woman, the attachment to one's children or relatives are, at first, accompanied by, and finally replaced by, the adoption of humanity as a whole. When Gandhi reached this point he wrote to his brother "who had been as a father to me," explaining that while he had given his brother everything he had saved, he must henceforth use his future income for the benefit of the community.

> I could not easily make my brother understand this. In stern language he explained to me my duty towards him. I should not, he said, aspire to be wiser than our father. I must support the family as he did. I pointed out to him that I was doing exactly what our father had done. The meaning of 'family' had but to be slightly widened and the wisdom of my step would become clear. [2]

Is there a general human trait which might help to explain this behavior, or at least one of its elements? Peter Kropotkin believed there was an instinct in both humans and animals that moved some more than others toward this identification with the whole of their species. He examined this trait in his book, *Mutual Aid*. [3] Kropotkin was wary about describing this trait as a "virtue" in the sense of being "higher" than the aggressive impulse to fight others for food and express one's own dominance. However, he pointed out that Charles Darwin, in his *Descent of Man*, regarded it as the basis for man's moral qualities. In his chapter, "On the Development of the Intellectual and Moral Faculties During Primeval and Civilized Times," Darwin emphasized the importance of moral virtues such as courage (risking one's life for others) for the survival of a tribe. [4] In natural selection among animals, it is not the genotype (the internal genetic structure) which is selected for survival, but the phenotype (the outward traits, the real physical and mental characteristics of the individual), so Darwin noted that among human societies it is not the individual whose traits may survive but those of his group or tribe. Thus the social need of humans, their need to be with others of their kind and to find acceptance and approval of others is an important trait for group survival. Individual aggressiveness against one's immediate neighbors—the struggle for existence in the narrow sense—begins to lose its importance beside the tribal and communal traits of courage, faithfulness, and self-sacrifice for the group.

> When two tribes of primeval man, living in the same country, come into competition, if (other circumstances being equal) the one tribe included a great number of courageous, sympathetic and faithful members, who were always ready to warn each other of danger, to aid and defend each other, this tribe would succeed better and conquer the other.[5]

Communal Feeling

I have suggested a direct pleasure in giving up one's immediate physical needs in order to support others. Perhaps the identification of one's self with the group is a part of this total phenomenon. There is, then, on the one hand, a sense of self-abnegation and self-surrender but, on the other hand, a sense of power or an extension of one's ego boundaries. Eric Fromm has suggested some of the negative aspects of the escape from individual responsibility in group identification, but he has pointed out that this behavior fulfills certain psychological needs of the individual, i.e. "secondary bonds to replace the primary bonds which have been lost."[6] We are speaking here of the masochistic feelings associated with powerlessness.

However, there is also a positive feeling of close group association. It is a sense of belonging to a community, similar to the sense of belonging to one's family. This is particularly true at moments of crisis and disaster when people huddle together in bomb shelters or flood relocation centers. There is a sense of community effort for survival. This same feeling can be reawakened in any joint group effort, particularly if there is strong pressure on the group from external sources, such as in a religious minority or a revolutionary movement. The therapeutic communities and encounter groups which have emerged in our modern cities are probably a product of this felt need for community-consciousness which cannot be satisfied in the relationship between the individual and the city or state government.

A leader who takes advantage of these feelings has a powerful ally in his efforts to move large masses of people. Kropotkin was raised in a serf-owner's family, taught to command others and his military experience reinforced this attitude. But he soon discovered in his direct association with the peasants a more powerful source of energy than the command from above.

I began to appreciate the difference between acting on the principle of command and discipline and acting on the principle of common understanding. The former works admirably in a military parade, but it is worth nothing where real life is concerned, and the aim can be achieved only through the severe effort of many converging wills. [7]

Some people are more sensitive to this feeling of group solidarity than others. Kropotkin's deep sense of unity with the peasant and his communal feeling when among them is illustrated in the following account of his experience at a village inn.

Slow, serious conversations with occasional laughter, were going on at the tables, and after the usual introductory questions, I soon found myself engaged in a conversation with a dozen peasants about the crops in our neighborhood, and answering all sorts of inquiries. They wanted to know all about St. Petersburg, and especially about the rumors concerning the coming abolition of serfdom. A feeling of simplicity and of natural relations of equality, as well as of hearty goodwill, which I always felt afterwards when among peasants or in their houses, pervaded me at that inn. Nothing extraordinary happened that night, so that I even ask myself whether the incident is worth mentioning at all; and yet, that warm dark night in the village, that small inn, that talk with the peasants, and the keen interest they took in hundreds of things lying far beyond their habitual surroundings, have made a poor "white inn" more attractive to me ever since than the best restaurant in the world. [8]

So strong is the feeling of equality and communal association in the above paragraph that it is necessary to remind ourselves that these are the words of a Russian prince raised to command. Somehow the training did not take hold with either Peter or Alexander Kropotkin. His closeness to the serfs in his family was possibly a factor in Kropotkin's love of the peasants. In his memoirs he recalled their many kindnesses, including the time they protected him from the wrath of his father by replacing, at considerable expense, some object he had broken while at play with his brother. [9]

While these childhood associations were certainly important influences upon Kropotkin's development, other men could put aside such experiences as the natural deference of servants to one of noble birth. Many a gentleman of the aristocracy was cared for by kind servants and nevertheless learned to establish a distance from them when he came of age. It is not only the behavior of the serfs toward Kropotkin that had such an influence on his behavior. The young Kropotkin had a natural sweetness of disposition that stimulated the warmth and protective feelings in the servants and led to a mutual understanding. He had a strong physical resemblance to his mother who was good to them. They trusted him intuitively; they knew he would tell no one if they concealed his behavior from the master.

Just as we find that some children are aggressive, combative, and domineering from birth, others are naturally gentle and loving. To say that Kropotkin was "conditioned" by the behavior of his servants may be true, in part, but it ignores the important role of heredity. He may have been "conditioned" in part by the servants, but he may also have "conditioned" the servants by his natural sweetness. Out of this mutual conditioning arose a mutual love, later exemplified in theory by Kropotkin's book, *Mutual Aid*, which was the biological antithesis to Darwin's notion of a struggle of one creature against another for survival.

Ego-less Perception

Of course both impulses exist in humans and both are important for human survival. But mutual aid requires an inhibition or holding back of the "natural" impulse of aggression. While this can be partly learned in a logical sense, i.e., a child may be rewarded for sacrifice and praised for his help of others, the sense of communal feeling may also spring forth suddenly in a wave of emotion. We have seen it in Trotsky's speaking experience when he felt incorporated by the crowd. There is, in this experience a loss of the individual ego, a sense that the self has overflowed the boundaries of the body and has permeated all humanity. Sometimes a similar experience can happen when the individual is alone. It can be frightening, particularly in the initial stages, a fear of letting go of one's self and one's very being. But if the person can "let go", it can become very positive.

St. Paul experienced something like this on the road to Damascus when he became a follower of Jesus. Both R. M. Bucke[10] and William James[11] have collected a variety of such experiences. The moment of awakening has often been described as an enlargement of one's perceptual abilities, an expansion of awareness, achieved, it seems, by breaking the ego boundaries. One cannot perceive the world as a single being looking at it with a single pair of eyes. It must be felt, sensed, encompassed. Maslow[12], who has also studied such experiences, stresses the *greater beauty* of the world in this expanded state of perception, which he called "B-Cognition" (Being-Cognition). The greater beauty of the world is probably a by-product derived from seeing things not as objects of need, but as things-in-themselves, deprived of any connection with one's private ego.

Karl Marx, particularly in his early essays, showed evidence of having a similar experience of ego-less perception of the world. Many of his comments anticipate Maslow's later ideas concerning Being-Cognition. Maslow described a way of seeing an object which is free from need-domination, i.e. we see it not in terms of our own need for it, but as a separate entity. We learn to appreciate it for itself: "the object is seen as a whole, as a complete unit, detached from relations, from possible usefulness, from expediency."[13] For Maslow, this was a way of experiencing an object as it is, in full awareness of its beauty. If one is preoccupied with how to use it or sell it, the object itself is not really perceived but becomes a kind of abstract category or commodity.

Marx made a similar point. A starving man cannot appreciate the sensual quality of food. He cannot perceive it apart from its abstract character as food useful for filling his stomach. In like manner the needy man has no appreciation of a beautiful spectacle and the dealer in minerals sees only their commercial value, not their beauty.[14] For Maslow, this capacity for sensual appreciation had its roots in the early development of the individual, the degree to which more primitive needs such as food, sex, and love were satisfied as a child.

Marx probably experienced B-cognition as did Maslow, but his *interpretation* of this experience was different. He looked at the phenomenon in its social context, pointing out that it was private property and not childhood experience which brought about this perceptual dullness. It was individual ownership which stimulated the desire for possession instead of appreciation of an object. This desire for possession clouds the consciousness of the individual and dulls his sensual appreciation.

> Private property has made us so stupid and partial that an object is only *ours* when we have it, when it exists for us as capital or when it is directly eaten, drunk, worn, inhabited, etc., in short, *utilized* in some way. But private property itself only conceives these various forms of possession as *means of life*, and the life for which they serve as means is the *life of private property*— labor and creation of capital.
>
> Thus all the physical and intellectual senses have been replaced by the simple alienation of *all* these senses; the sense of *having*.[15]

Marx considered this interrelationship between perception, social conditions, and consciousness as an essential aspect of the study of psychology. He insisted that no psychology which ignores this relationship can become a real science with a genuine content.[16]

It was from his early studies of this relationship that Marx developed his materialist conception of history, in which he showed the dominant role of the material means of production in a society upon all its "theoretical products and its forms of consciousness, religion, philosophy, morality, etc. . . ."[17] It was, he said, the means of production and the social context of modern production which brought about man's alienation from his own work. Because the capitalist owns the means of production and is in a position to appropriate the products of labor, the worker becomes poorer the more wealth he produces, for the products of his labor can be sold in competition with his future labor. ". . . the object produced by the labour, its product, now stands opposed to it as an *alien being*, as a *power independent* of the producer."[18] The result is the worker's lack of joy in productive activity and his alienation from the sensual experience of work itself.[19]

The Emotional Aspect

Maslow and Marx both emphasize social or environmental causes of this ego-less perception. Bucke was struck by the fact that some individuals are susceptible to it and others are not, regardless of the stimulus that may cause it. In surveying the range of these revelations, the importance of the *person* undergoing the experience cannot be overemphasized. The individual later describes the experience to others and makes his own interpretation of its significance. For the social reformer and revolutionary, the illumination may be as dramatic as for the religious leader, but the former is more inclined to look to his own body for the source of his new-found perceptual ability.

Bertrand Russell, a prominent pacifist and political agitator, was sent to jail several times for his leadership in protest movements. He described his own awakening as an experience that marked a decided change in his *political attitudes.* As a young man his interest was in mathematics. His habit of analysis was his primary mode of thinking. Suddenly, one afternoon, on viewing the wife of his friend in severe pain from an illness, he discovered a deeper, more human sensitivity in himself that he had not previously known. The whole experience was no doubt colored by the fact that Russell was in love with the wife of his friend, but the love he describes in this experience seems to be different from the physical passion between a man and a woman.

> Ever since my marriage, my emotional life had been calm and superficial. I had forgotten all the deeper issues and had been content with flippant cleverness. Suddenly the ground seemed to give way beneath me, and I found myself in quite another region. Within five minutes I went through some such reflections as the following: the loneliness of the human soul is unendurable; nothing can penetrate it except the highest intensity of the sort of love that religious teachers have preached; whatever does not spring from this motive is harmful, or at best useless; it follows that war is wrong, that a public school education is abominable, that the use of force is to be deprecated, and that in human relations one should penetrate to the core of loneliness in each person and speak to that. . . . At the end of those five minutes, I had become a completely different person. For a time a sort of mystic illumination possessed me. I felt that I knew the inmost thoughts of everybody that I met in the street, and though this was, no doubt, a delusion, I did in fact find myself in far closer touch than previously with all my friends, and many of my acquaintances. Having been an imperialist, I became during those five minutes a pro-Boer and a pacifist. Having for years cared only for exactness and analysis, I found myself filled with semi-mystical feelings about beauty, with an intense interest in children, and with a desire almost as profound as that of Buddha to find some philosophy which should make human life endurable. A strange excitement possessed me, containing intense pain but also some element of triumph through the fact that I could dominate pain, and make it, as I thought, a gateway to wisdom. The mystic insight which I then imagined myself to possess has largely faded, and the habit of analysis has reasserted itself. But something of what I thought I saw in that moment has remained always with me. . . .[20]

Russell seemed to break the isolation of his private self in this experience. He felt not only a mystic connection with the wife of his friend but with strangers he met on the street. There was a sense of oneness with others that reached beyond an intellectual understanding of human interrelatedness.

Rousseau had a similar experience in which he believed that the ideas and insights for all of his later books were suddenly revealed to him in one moment of enlightenment.

> All at once my mind was dazzled by a thousand illuminations, a crowd of vivid ideas came upon me, all at the same moment, with a force and confusion

which threw me into an inexpressible turmoil. I felt my head caught up in a giddiness like intoxication. A violent palpitation oppressed me, my chest heaving, no longer able to breathe while walking I dropped under one of the trees on the avenue and passed half an hour there in such agitation that, on arising, I saw that the front of my vest was wet with tears and I was unaware of having shed them. Oh Monsieur, if I could only have written a quarter of what I saw and felt under that tree, with what clarity I would have made men see the contradictions of our social system, with what force I would have exposed all the abuses of our institutions, with what simplicity I would have demonstrated that man is naturally good and that it is only through institutions that he becomes bad. [21]

The stimulus for this experience was an offer of a prize for an essay on the subject: Has the progress of the sciences and the arts done more to corrupt morals or improve them? Rousseau chanced upon the offer while reading the *Mercure de France* on his way to see his friend, Diderot, who had been jailed for writing a political pamphlet. Clearly, Rousseau's personal circumstances, his sense of the injustice of the times, heightened by his friend's imprisonment, influenced the direction and the intensity of his emotional response.

However, like the experience of Russell, his feeling for his friend seemed to generalize to humanity as a whole. He saw and felt the "natural goodness" of humans and he sought to convey this experience in his later work. Through his writings he inspired others with a strong communal feeling, an awareness of equity and the extent to which he saw this equity distorted by the creation of rich and powerful families. It was a perception of reality in striking contrast to the French society of his time and he managed to transmit this view to many who followed him. It was not Rousseau's specific proposals for political change that inspired his followers, but his "spirit of revolt," his altered perception of society.

Rousseau felt this experience not only provided him with an intellectual and emotional revelation but changed his personality as well. In later years he described the experience as follows:

This intoxication had begun in my head, but it has passed to my heart. The noblest pride sprang up there on the ruins of uprooted vanity. I played no part; I became indeed what I appeared; and for the four years at least that this exhilaration lasted in its full strength there was nothing great or beautiful that can enter into the heart of man, between earth and heaven, of which I was not capable. This was the origin of my sudden eloquence, and of the truly celestial fire which burned in me and spread to my early books, a fire which had not emitted the tiniest spark in forty years, because it was not yet kindled. [22]

We see that for both Russell and Rousseau this moment of revelation meant not only an enlightenment, a new way of looking at the world, a deepening of their understanding of their ordinary surroundings and of other people, but a kind of "conversion" or change of personality not unlike religious conversion.

Not all such experiences produce conversions, but they are generally dramatic. They may indeed have a greater significance in the life of the individual than he recognizes at the time, or they may have a different effect on the individual if he is very young or very old at the time he undergoes them. Trotsky was fourteen at the time of his experience. It was associated with an illness, but also with his expulsion from school and the beginning of his antagonism to the state.

> The boy [Trotsky] saw everything in a new light, himself above all. The spring sun stimulated the feeling that there was something immeasurably mightier than the school, the inspector, and the kit hanging aslant on the back—mightier than studying, chess, dinners and even reading and the theater; in short, than all of one's every-day life. And the longing after this something unfathomed, commanding obedience and rising high above the individual, seized upon the boy's entire being down to the marrow of his bones and called forth the sweet pain of exhaustion.
> He came home with a buzzing head, with painful music in his temples. Dropping the kit on the table, he lay down on the bed and, hardly realizing what he was doing, began to weep into the pillow. To find an excuse for his tears, he recalled pitiful scenes from books and from his own life, as if to feed the furnace with fresh fuel, and wept and wept with tears of spring longing.[23]

It is easy to understand how a person who is inclined toward a religious way of life could place a religious interpretation on such an experience, or how the "born again" Christian who has such an experience could feel that he has literally become a new person through the intervention of God. However, it is important to remember that the nature and intensity (as well as the interpretation) of this experience is dependent on the background, the personality, and perhaps even the physiology of the individual. It is clearly possible to perceive it in a non-religious manner. The experience tends to "take over" the individual either with his enthusiastic acquiescence or against his will. It is not the kind of thing that can be planned, directed, or willfully created by the person himself. However, hereditary factors or childhood experiences may well make a person more receptive to such a sudden moment of expanded awareness.

Bucke and Maslow have both suggested that the capacity to have such experiences is a sign that one has attained a higher stage of development, a more exalted personality, but the examination of the individuals who have sudden moments or even long periods of ego-less perception does not seem to confirm this. To accept this would be to affirm that people who have such experiences have tapped into some mystical, eternal truth available only to the great religious leaders and thinkers of the world. I am inclined to accept this ability as merely a different (and not necessarily better) way of perceiving the world. This would suggest that the peak experiences of both Rousseau and Russell as well as Trotsky in his moment of "sweet pain" were states of altered perception and no more.

The capacity to undergo a peak experience is not, then, evidence that we are dealing with an exalted personality. It is not the experience itself, but what the individual does with it that is important. Many left-wing revolutionary leaders seem to make use of this notion of selflessness and non-self-related perception in the development of their ideology. But the feeling of wanting to give up the self and help humanity as a whole is not a pure and isolated experience. It may often become allied with intensely aggressive and destructive tendencies. Selflessness is related not only to the sacrifices of Gandhi, but to the destructiveness of the Bader-Meinhof gang in Germany and the Weathermen in the United States.

Perhaps the chief value of the left-wing revolutionary experience is not the specific ideologies of communism or anarchism as such, but the general spirit of internationalism that has emerged from the movement. It is the recognition of the basic unity of the human race, indeed the unity of all animate and inanimate objects, and the importance of preserving our planet in the face of the growing threat of destruction from thermonuclear war and pollution.

Valuable as have been the contributions of the science of ecology to this general problem, I am not speaking of a logical or scientific approach to the unity of life. Such approaches are important but they do not have the same significance for "knowing" as personal experience. In one sense they are more safe and certain. The experience of letting go of one's ego, while it may involve a pleasant, even thrilling sense of expanded awareness, is not without its dangers. In our normal and usual state of consciousness, a certain fear begins to arise in most of us as we travel along this path. Is it really possible to let in only as much awareness as might be "useful" and stop the process before it goes too far? Or will the door, once set ajar, swing open all the way and refuse to close again? I may feel a sense of brotherhood with the tiger, but the tiger may want to eat me. In like manner, we may feel a sense of common human sympathy with the Russians, but they may want to destroy us.

The fear which practical people of the world exhibit in regard to this type of thinking is not without foundation. To the extent that an expanded awareness is accompanied by a loss of the sense of one's ego, it may involve dangers that we do not yet understand. The human ego appears to be an important mechanism for survival. Like the instinctive startle-reaction of the child to a sensation of falling, the fear of ego loss may be a built-in, instinctive response which evolved in humans because it protected the organism from danger. Certain aspects of the relationship of the human ego to the phenomenon of awareness are imperfectly understood at the present time. The ego appears to serve in both a protective and focusing capacity in the process of understanding. It restricts the individual's perception of the world in terms of those things which threaten or enhance its potency. By placing a limit around a person's own body, the ego restricts the range of sensitivity and pain. By structuring awareness, the sources for pain are reduced and consciousness is focused within a single unified sphere of reference. The ego resists awareness of that which would damage its integrity. National identity operates in a similar manner, as a sort of outer wall of protection for the identity of the individual. The struggle for a larger awareness is essentially a struggle against these barriers.

We have reached a point in the evolution of our species where some of the old protective mechanisms are more of a menace than a source of security. The environment changes and if the species cannot adapt, within limits, it will not survive. The behavior of clutching to one's ego, one's nation, or one's solar system, as a central referent served humans well at a time when they were not sure, from one day to the next, where food would be found. Now, like the heavy armor of the dinosaur, the human ego may prove humanity's ruin if it cannot be discarded or its influence mitigated.

While the experience of a wider awareness may be frightening, risky, and, to some, even fatal, it represents one of the most powerful means for the understanding of the forces around us, both the impersonal forces of nature and the energies of living things. Such awareness has not been a requirement in the past in order to provide food, clothing, and other necessities of life. But with the threat of massive intra-species warfare involving nuclear weapons, we face a problem that our species has never encountered. Like two soldiers who hate each other because they see their world in terms of a struggle for certain necessities, we seem locked into an attitude that will destroy us if we do not find a means of breaking its grip. We are afraid to break that grip because it would mean letting go of an important human instinct for self-protection which, although it places us at odds with all other living things, is nevertheless the built-in basis for our survival.

But man has overcome similar instincts for self-protection which were no longer appropriate for a changing world. He has learned to subdue his most primitive reaction to the sensation of falling. He has, in fact, learned to court it by jumping from a plane in the confidence that his parachute will open, rather than clinging desperately to a craft which will no longer support him. In like manner, he may have to leave this earth for the stars when it can no longer sustain human life, or let go of his narrow concept of self to leap into the vault of a larger consciousness if he is to escape the destructive potential of his own ego.

NOTES

1. Crane, Brinton, *The Anatomy of Revolution* (New York: Vintage, 1958).

2. Mohandas K. Gandhi, *An Autobiography: The Story of My Experiments with Truth* (Boston: Beacon, 1957).

3. Peter Kropotkin, *Mutual Aid* (Boston: Extending Horizons, n.d.).

4. Charles Darwin, *The Origin of Species and the Descent of Man* (New York: Modern Library), 498–99.

5. Ibid., 498.

6. Erich Fromm, *Escape from Freedom* (New York: Hearst, Avon, 1941), 163.

7. Peter Kropotkin, *Memoirs of a Revolutionist* (New York: Dover, 1971), 216–17.

8. Ibid., 107.

9. Ibid., 19.

10. Richard M. Bucke, *Cosmic Consciousness: A Study in the Evolution of the Human Mind* (New York: Dutton, 1969), 125–27.

11. William James, *The Varieties of Religious Experience* (New York: New American Library, 1968), 68–69.

12. Abraham H. Maslow, *Toward a Psychology of Being* (Princeton: Van Nostrand, 1968).

13. Ibid., 74.

14. Karl Marx, *Karl Marx: Early Writings*, edited and translated by T. B. Bottomore, with a new Foreword by Erich Fromm (New York: McGraw-Hill, 1963), 162.

15. Ibid., 159–60.

16 Ibid., 163.

17. Karl Marx and Friedrich Engles, *Collected Works*, vol. 5 (New York: International Publishers, 1975), 53.

18. Marx, *Early Writings*, Bottomore, ed., 121–22.

19. Ibid., 124–25.

20. Bertrand Russell, *The Autobiography of Bertrand Russell*, vol. 2 (New York: Bantam, 1969), 193–94.

21. Jean Jacques Rousseau, *Les Oeuvres Completes de Jean Jacques Rousseau*, vol. 1 (Paris: Gallimard, Bibliotheque de la Pleiade, 1959–64), 1135–36.

22. Jean Jacques Rousseau, *The Confessions of Jean Jacques Rousseau*, translated by J. M. Cohen (London: Penguin, 1954), 388.

23. Leon Trotsky, *My Life: Leon Trotsky*, (New York: Grosset and Dunlap, 1930), 72–73.

Selected Bibliography

I have limited this bibliography to highlight those sources which reveal most about the personality of the political leader. However, occasional use has been made of documents which reveal policy statements or hearings, reflecting some indirect light on the character of the revolutionary as politician. There is great variability in the amount of material available. To some extent this is determined by the importance of the individual and also by his position as leader of a nation. For example, it would not do for Mao Tse-tung to reveal his private masochistic fantasies—even if he had such fantasies. Such a revelation would undermine his image of strength and resolve, an image expected of a national leader. Marx and Gandhi are probably the two most important figures in this study, not only because we have much more information about their childhood and development, but because they represent opposite views in regard to the issue of violence. They are, in essence, the principal theoreticians for the use of violence and nonviolence to achieve revolutionary ends.

In all cases I have made use of the letters, confessions, or autobiographies of revolutionary leaders whenever these original sources were available. In some cases (such as Sun Yat-sen) the life, as told by the individual himself, is not very revealing. In such cases one must rely on friends who have known the leader and sometimes even the account of his enemies. Other individuals (such as Ché Guevara) reveal themselves as much in their political writings and public speeches as in their private letters. In the cases of Mao Tse-tung and V. I. Lenin the public speeches are cautious and orthodox, revealing little of the personality.

General

I have included in this section books on the general subject of revolution as well as those studies covering the relationship between psychological factors and revolutionary behavior. I have also included several studies of individual revolutionaries which appear as part of a larger work. For example, Wolfenstein's study of Gandhi, Lenin, and Trotsky in *The Revolutionary Personality*, is covered in this bibliography rather than in the chapters dealing with the individual revolutionaries.

This study was first initiated with the hypothesis that masochism was a significant motivating factor in revolutionary behavior. In the course of the work I have identified two other needs which I believe play an important role in revolutionary behavior. While they both relate to a lack of self-protective behavior, I believe they can be distinguished as (1) the satisfaction derived from group love or group approval, which Darwin might have described as a communal "instinct," and (2) the pleasure derived from an altered state of consciousness or a loss of the sense of one's ego. This has been variously referred to as "ego-death," "cosmic consciousness," or the "peak experience." I regard all three psychological phenomena as related to a form of self-sacrifice, the key to revolutionary morality. Moral masochism is the abandonment of self-interest in order to do what is right or to "help mankind." The need for group approval, when it involves a complete merging of one's interest with that of the group, represents another form of self-sacrifice. The desire to lose one's ego to achieve a peak experience is a similar, though related phenomenon. Like the other forms of behavior, it is not, in itself, a revolutionary motivation. In fact, it may begin as a simple desire for personal pleasure through a loss of the confined self-image, the desire to break the boundaries of the ego and merge with all life or with the universe.

The sources in this section are from both the Introduction and the concluding chapter, "Beyond Masochism."

Acton, John Emerick and Edward Dalberg. *Essays on Freedom and Power.* Boston: Beacon, 1948. A discussion of the consequences of freedom for social and individual development as well as the influence of power on the personality of the powerful.

Adorno, T. W., Else Frenkel-Brunswik, Daniel J. Levinson, and R. Nevitt Sanford. *The Authoritarian Personality.* New York: John Wiley 1964. A series of studies that seeks to define the psychological characteristics of the authoritarian personality.

Arendt, Hanna. *On Revolution.* New York: Viking, 1975. An essay on the psychological and social factors in revolution.

Aristotle. *Politics.* New York: Oxford University Press, 1962. A general discussion of politics with some reference to the causes of revolution, the emphasis being on poverty and privation.

Baraheni, Reza. *The Crowned Cannibals.* New York: Random House, 1977. An account of some aspects of Iranian psychology and history as well as a description of the author's experience in the prisons of the Shah.

Benda, Julien. *The Betrayal of the Intellectuals.* Boston: Beacon Press, 1955. A classical study of some of the moral factors in the role of the intellectual as critic of the establishment. It is the author's opinion that this role should be one of gadfly in the hide of the state and that the intellectual betrays his calling when he supports the establishment.

Brinton, Crane. *The Anatomy of Revolution.* New York: Vintage, 1958. A development of some of Lyford P. Edward's earlier ideas on the phases in the natural history of revolutions. Brinton is more explicit and attempts to apply Edward's general theory to specific revolutionary movements.

Brown, Roger William. *Social Psychology*. New York: Free Press, 1965. A general review of social psychology which contains a critique of *The Authoritarian Personality*, but also a reaffirmation that there remains a clear relationship between anti-Semitism, ethnocentrism, idealization of parents and self, and a rigid conception of sexual roles.

Bucke, Richard Maurice. *Cosmic Consciousness*. New York: Dutton, 1969. A study of the phenomenon that Maslow was later to call the "peak experience." Bucke takes the position that the capacity to undergo such experiences means the individual has already evolved into a higher moral and intellectual being.

Camus, Albert. *The Rebel*. New York: Vintage, 1958. A study of the psychological, social, and moral aspects of rebellion from an existential viewpont.

———. *The Fall*. New York: Alfred A Knopf, 1959. Camus' self-analysis is essentially an analysis of the sadomasochistic elements in all great reformers.

Christie, Richard and Marie Jahoda. *Studies in the Scope and Method of the Authoritarian Personality*. Glencoe: Free Press, 1954. A compilation and review of some criticisms of *The Authoritarian Personality*.

Darwin, Charles. *The Descent of Man*. Princeton: Princeton University Press, 1931. Darwin's classic study of the evolution of man from the lower animals, and some of the human characteristics that have led to his survival. Of particular importance are his observations on the communal instinct in man.

Edwards, Lyford P. *The Natural History of Revolution*. Chicago: University of Chicago Press, 1973. An attempt to develop a theory of revolution from the early stage of protest through the rule of the moderate revolutionary group, the rise of the radicals, and the final restoration of order.

Erikson, Erik H. *Young Man Luther*. New York: Norton, 1962. A psychological study in which Erikson formulates some of the basic principles of his approach to psychohistory and applies them to the life of Luther.

Fenichel, Otto. *The Psychoanalytic Theory of Neurosis*. New York: Norton, 1945. A comprehensive exposition of psychoanalytic theory by a scholar in the field.

Freud, Sigmund. *The Basic Writings of Sigmund Freud*. Edited by A. A. Brill. New York: Random House, 1938. Contains such early and basic works as *The Psychopathology of Everyday Life* and *The Interpretation of Dreams*. Freud's own exposition of psychoanalytic theory.

———. *Civilization and Its Discontents*. New York: Doubleday, 1950. Freud is critical of religion as a reality outside the psychological development of the individual. Civilization is to blame for much of our misery but also our progress. There is an innate destructive and aggressive instinct in man that is the most powerful opponent to culture.

———. *Collected Papers*. 8 vols. London: Hogarth, 1952. Freud's case studies and speculations on a variety of subjects.

———. *The Future of an Illusion*. Garden City: Doubleday. A psychological study of the development of civilization. Every culture naturally evokes some resistance as men do not willingly work for the welfare of all. Some men will remain asocial because of their natural instinctual vigor. Freud holds some hope for religion as a means for controlling man's instinctual urges.

Fromm, Erich. *Escape From Freedom*. New York: Hearst, 1941. A study of the political implications of sadomasochism, particularly the phenomenon of willing submission to a master or powerful group. Some of this theoretical development was later used in the studies devised for *The Authoritarian Personality*.

Hanfstaengle, Ernst. *Unheard Witness*. New York: Lipincott, 1957. Hanfstaengle's account of the early days of the Nazi movement and his encounters with Hitler in which he played the role of royal clown.

Heiden, Konrad. *Der Fuehaer*. New York: Houghton Mifflin, 1944. A highly critical account of Hitler's period in power, containing many details of his distorted sex life.

Hoffer, Eric. *The True Believer*. New York: New American Library, 1951. A description of the revolutionary as a fanatic. Hoffer describes different types of individuals who lead different stages of revolution—stages, in some respects, comparable to those of Brinton and Edwards.

James, William. *The Varieties of Religious Experience*. New York: New American Library, 1968. An account of religious experiences of both a positive and negative type. Describes some examples of altered states of consciousness in these experiences. Some accounts are not strictly religious, but more like Bucke's "cosmic consciousness."

Krueger, Kurt. *I Was Hitler's Doctor*. Introduction by Otto Strasser. New York: Biltmore, 1941. Numerous personal details, many of them trivial. Perhaps one of the most interesting parts of the book is the revealing introduction by Otto Strasser.

Langer, Walter Charles. *The Mind of Adolph Hitler*. New York: Basic Books, 1972. A psychological study based on interviews and written accounts of Hitler's associates. Psychoanalytic theory forms the basis for the major conclusions.

LaPalombara, Joseph, ed. *Comparative Revolutionary Movements*. Englewood Cliffs: Prentice Hall, 1974. A study of those conditions which coincide with any particular society's capacity for revolution. Not limited to one type of revolution. A discussion of leadership, ideology and social conditions.

Lasswell, Harold D. *Power and Personality*. New York: Viking, 1962. Various types of individuals who strive for power, some principles of leadership and how they relate to the system of government.

_____. *Psychopathology and Politics*. New York: Viking, 1960. A study of the relationship between the psychological problems of the individual and his political behavior.

_____. *World Politics and Personal Insecurity*. Deals with many of the political problems in the world that relate to personal insecurity.

Lasswell, Harold D. and D. Lerner. *World Revolutionary Elites*. Cambridge: MIT Press, 1965. A study of the occupations, geographic distribution, city size, urban or rural background, marital status, education, and other variables in the life of revolutionary leaders.

Lasswell, Harold D. and C. E. Rothwell. *The Comparative Study of Elites*. Stanford: Stanford University Press, 1952.

Lebon, Gustav. *The Psychology of Revolution*. New York: Putnam, 1913.

Lewy, Guenter. *Religion and Revolution*. New York: Oxford University Press, 1974.

Lipset, Seymour Martin. "Some Social Requisites of Democracy." *American Political Science Review*. 53 (March, 1959): 69-105. Lipset found revolutions were negatively associated with the level of educational attainment. This was not supported by Tanter and Midlarsky, but Lipset's study was based on Latin American revolutions that were often palace coups and not the type studied by Tanter and Midlarsky.

Marcuse, Herbert. *Eros and Civilization.* New York: Random House, 1955. An attempt to integrate some of the ideas of Marx and Freud and to go beyond them into some of the requirements for psychological freedom, which the author sees as a prerequisite for any other freedom.

Maslow, Abraham H. *Religious Values and Peak Experiences.* New York: Viking, 1970. An expansion of some of Maslow's earlier work on the peak experience.

_____. *Toward A Psychology of Being.* Princeton: Van Nostrand, 1950. A psychological study of some of the characteristics of an expanded awareness, particularly when this awareness arrives with a sudden rush of feeling and knowing which Maslow calls the "peak experience."

Mazlish, Bruce. *The Revolutionary Ascetic.* New York: McGraw-Hill, 1976. A study of some of the psychological chracteristics of revolutionary leaders with particular emphasis on an evolution of the revolutionary type toward the ascetic character of the successful revolutionary.

Nietzsche, Friedrich. *Beyond Good and Evil.* Chicago: Great Books, 1949. A justification for two separate moralities: the strong (master morality) and the weak (slave morality). Nietzsche favored the former and had contempt for the Judeo-Christian tradition from which the latter developed.

Polanyi, Michael. *Personal Knowledge.* Chicago: University of Chicago Press, 1958. Questions the traditional methodology for establishing scientific proof, and suggests that all real knowledge, in the sense of inner knowing and conviction, arises from a source within the individual.

Putnam, Robert D. *The Comparative Study of Political Elites.* Edgewood Cliffs, Prentice Hall, 1976.

Quandt, William B. *The Comparative Study of Poltical Elites.* Beverly Hills: Sage, 1970.

Reik, Theodor. *Masochism in Modern Man.* New York: Grove, 1941. A psychoanalytic study of moral masochism or what Reik calls "social masochism," and its origins through the use of case histories.

Rejai, Mostafa with Kay Phillips. *Leaders of Revolution.* Beverly Hills: Sage, 1979. A statistical study, using factor analysis, to develop some of the situational chracteristics in the lives of revolutionary leaders.

Russell, Bertrand. *The Autobiography of Bertrand Russell.* 3 vols. New York: Bantam, 1969. Contains Russell's account of his own peak experience in which he changed from a conservative to a liberal and in which he increased his sensitivity to the feelings of others.

Russett, Bruce M., et al. *World Handbook of Political and Social Indicators.* New Haven: Yale University Press, 1964. The authors found a curvalinear relationship between gross national product per capita and domestic violence, suggesting that revolutions seldom occur in very rich or very poor nations, but more often in those which have emerged from poverty.

Sanford, Nevitt. "Authoritarian Personality in Contemporary Perspective." In *Handbook of Political Psychology,* by Jeanne N. Knutson. San Francisco: Jossey-Bass, 1973, 139–70. An update and reaffirmation of some of the findings from *The Authoritarian Personality* and an answer to some of the critics.

Shirer, William L. *The Rise and Fall of the Third Reich.* Greenwich: Fawcett, 1960. A detailed account of Hitler's rise and fall, describing the interaction of many of his chief aids. Records many events leading up to World War II and the meetings of world leaders that followed.

Tanter, Raymond R. and Manus Midlarsky. "A Theory of Revolution." *Journal of Conflict Resolution*. 2:3 (September 1967): 264–80. The authors hypothesized that the duration and violence of a revolution were related to the *change* in GNP: a sharp rise in the years leading to a revolution (producing a rise in expectations) followed by a steep drop in the period immediately preceding a revolution (a disappointment of rising expectations). They studied several types of revolutions and found mixed support for their theory.

Thompson, J. M. *The French Revolution*. New York: Oxford University Press, 1966. An excellent account of the sources of support and resistance to the revolution.

Walzer, Michael. *The Revolution of the Saints*. Cambridge: Harvard University Press, 1965. A study of the interaction between the Puritan religion and the politics of revolt in the English Revolution.

Wilner, Ann Ruth. *Charismatic Political Leadership*. Princeton: Center for International Studies, 1968. Wilner found no really satisfactory means for distinguishing charismatic leadership from charisma in general. The concept itself has also proven elusive.

Wilson, Colin. *The Outsider*. New York: Dell, 1956. Explores alienation of the thinker and the intellectual that may bring about a rebellion (in thought or in action) against conventional beliefs and ways of perceiving the world.

Wolfenstein, E. Victor. *The Revolutionary Personality*. Princeton: Princeton University Press, 1971. A psychological study of Gandhi, Lenin and Trotsky from a psychoanalytic point of view.

T. E. Lawrence

In some respects Lawrence is the most controversial of all the revolutionary leaders in this study. Much has been written to refute what has already been written. The legend created by Lowell Thomas contains many inaccuracies. *Seven Pillars of Wisdom* has been refuted by debunking biographers, serious scholars and Arab leaders who felt Lawrence overstated his own role. He has been variously described as a fraud, an impostor, a great hero and leader of men, a sexual pervert, and a humane honest individual who tried to avoid notoriety. I have included samples of all these views in this selected bibliography. I believe Lawrence had a great respect for the truth and tried to be truthful about himself and the events of his life that he was willing to make public. There is no denying that he was also a very secretive individual and that he concealed many things out of shame. His effort to give an honest account of events was complicated both by his intense desire for fame and his contempt for this quality in himself. This conflict has resulted in, on the one hand, an unconscious overdramatization of everything he did and, on the other hand, an avoidance of publicity, a refusal to talk to the press, a secrecy about his life and his movements and sometimes a revelation of the most embarrassing and degrading experiences. In some respects Lowell Thomas was the ideal biographer for Lawrence. He made a hero of him, despite Lawrence's protests to the contrary. This is exactly what Lawrence wanted—and didn't want at the same time.

Lawrence's full name was Thomas Edward Lawrence, but he was always known, by his own preference, as "T. E."

Addington, Richard R. *Lawrence of Arabia.* London: Collins, 1955. According to the author, Lawrence kept a young Arab boy in his rooms at Oxford and was known by the Arabs as a pederast. He claims Lawrence showed a like affection for other youths. The author doubts most of Lawrence's exploits and even alleges Lawrence planned a meeting with Hitler.

Knightley, Phillip and Simpson Collin. *The Secret Lives of Lawrence of Arabia.* London: Nelson, 1969. The authors claim Lawrence was vastly over-rated and, far from admiring the Arabs, he despised them. They have unearthed the story of the whipping of Lawrence by Tom Bruce (through a pretense that it was ordered by Lawrence's uncle). Bruce was evidently not the only person to beat Lawrence in this manner. The Bey (Hacim Muhittim Bey), who supposedly raped Lawrence, was dead by three years when the authors arrived in Deraa. But they interviewed others and claim the Bey was known as an aggressive heterosexual and his diaries do not mention meeting Lawrence, although Lawrence was known to him.

Lawrence, Arnold Walter, Editor. *Letters to T. E. Lawrence.* London: Johnathan Cape, 1962. Letters to Lawrence from many well-known people.

Lawrence, T. E. *Carchemish.* London: British Museum, 1914. Report on the excavations at Djerabis on behalf of the British Museum.

_____. *Evolution of a Revolt: Early Post-War Writings of T. E. Lawrence.* Edited by Stanley Wientraub and Rodelle Weintraub. University Park: Pennsylvania State University Press, 1968. Letters and manuscripts on the Arab revolt.

_____. *The Home Letters of T. E. Lawrence and His Brothers.* Edited by M. R. Lawrence. Oxford: Basil Blackwell, 1954. Letters from Lawrence and his brothers, primarily to their mother.

_____. *The Letters of T. E. Lawrence.* Edited by D. Garnet. London: Johnathan Cape, 1938. Letters from Lawrence to his many friends.

_____. (As T. E. Shaw) *Letters from T. E. Shaw to Bruce Rogers.* Privately printed by Bruce Rogers at the printing house of William Edwin Rudge, 1933. Letters by Lawrence under the pseudonym of T. E. Shaw, a name he used to avoid publicity during the early period of his post-war military service.

_____. *The Mint.* London: Johnathan Cape, 1973. Lawrence's account of life in the RAF. This is the corrected unexpurgated edition without the name changes that appeared in the earlier version.

_____. *Oriental Assembly.* Edited by Arnold Walter Lawrence. London: Williams and Norgate, 1939. A collection of Lawrence's essays and some notes.

_____. *Secret Dispatches from Arabia.* Edited by Arnold Walter Lawrence. London: Golden Cockrell Press, 1939. Lawrence's contributions to the *Arab Bulletin*: papers of the Arab Bureau 1916-1918.

_____. *Seven Pillars of Wisdom.* Garden City: Doubleday, 1935. An account by the author of his involvement in the Arab revolt, with many personal details and observations that reveal much of his character.

_____. *T. E. Lawrence to His Biographers.* Edited by Robert Graves. London: Cassell, 1963. Letters from Lawrence to Robert Graves and Liddell Hart with commentaries. Graves denies Lawrence's homosexuality, admits his discomfort with women and points out his exaggerated respect for masculinity. He hated being touched by others, seldom ate and then finished in five minutes.

Mack, John E. *A Prince of Our Disorder.* Boston: Little Brown, 1976. A well-researched psychological study, making use of many documentary sources as well as personal interviews with those who knew Lawrence.

Meyers, Jeffrey. *The Wounded Spirit.* London: Martin, Brian and O'Keeffe, 1973. In part, a psychological study of Lawrence's sexual pathology and his self-torture, asceticism and masochism to achieve his goal. The mother often punished Lawrence with a humiliating whipping of his bare body.

Mousa, Sulayman. *T. E. Lawrence: An Arab View.* London: Oxford University Press, 1966. Downplays the role of Lawrence. Upgrades Feisal and other Arab leaders as motivators and planners. Claims *Seven Pillars of Wisdom* is decorated with many events that did not happen at all. Doubts the Deraa incident happened.

Robinson, Edward. *Lawrence the Rebel.* London: Lincoln Preager, 1946. Personal account of some of Lawrence's actions by one who served with him. Claims there was much untruth told about Lawrence's activities at the Peace Conference.

Stewart, Desmond Stirling. *T. E. Lawrence.* London: Hamish Hamilton, 1977. A biography with considerable discussion of his letters and other works.

Thomas, Lowell Jackson. *With Lawrence in Arabia.* London: Anchor, 1962. Highly dramatized and somewhat inaccurate version of Lawrence's Arabian adventures, based on interviews by Lowell Thomas.

Wilson, J. M., ed. *Minorities.* London: Johnathan Cape, 1971. A collection of Lawrence's favorite poems, including a biography with some information not previously available.

Jean Jacques Rousseau

These items were selected from the larger bibliography in *Rousseau and the Spirit of Revolt.* There are only a few additions, works that have been published since this earlier study. I have omitted many of the detailed studies of the facts regarding Rousseau's life, the history of his relatives and his relationship with Mme. de Warens, much of which is interesting, but not directly related to his psychology. On the other hand I have included a number of English translations of Rousseau's work. The letters of David Hume throw a particular light on Rousseau's thinking. They demonstrate the basic factual correctness of much that Rousseau has said, but they show a vastly different perspective. The Memoirs of Mme d'Epinay, as well as the French original under a different title, demonstrate that there *was* a conspiracy, of sorts, to discredit Rousseau. It was simply not as extensive, as involved or as explicit as Rousseau believed it to be. Mrs. McDonald's *New Criticism* throws considerable light on this subject. But, here too, as a Rousseau partisan, she distorts the level of the conspiracy and her work is marred by other efforts to prove Rousseau innocent of many "crimes" to which he admitted in his *Confessions.*

Babbit, Irving. *Rousseau and Romanticism.* New York: Meridian, 1957. A highly critical account of Rousseau's ideas and their consequences for modern politics and modern morality.

Blanchard, William H. *Rousseau and the Spirit of Revolt*. Ann Arbor: University of Michigan Press, 1967. A psychological study based on the works and letters of Rousseau.

Cassirer, Ernst. *The Question of Jean-Jacques Rousseau*. New York: Columbia University Press, 1954. A classical study of the philosophy and morality of Rousseau.

D'Epinay, Louise Florence Petronille Tardieu D'Esclavelles D' *Memoirs and Correspondence of Madame D'Epinay*. Translated with an introduction by E. G. Allingham. London: Routledge, 1930. A diary of Rousseau's benefactress, containing much negative material on Rousseau and some possible forgeries of his letters. The book was first written as a novel and the characters were all given fictitious names. Only later was it altered to represent a factual account of her life.

_____.*Histoire de Madame de Montbrillant*. 3 vols. Paris: Gallimard, 1942. The original fictional work from which the supposedly factual memories were derived. Madam D'Epinay is represented by Madame de Montbrillant.

Green, Frederick Charles. *Jean-Jacques Rousseau: A Critical Study of His Life and Writings*. Cambridge: Cambridge University Press, 1955. A study covering Rousseau's contribution to politics and literature, but which also outlines some of the inconsistencies between his democratic beliefs and his authoritarian policy recommendations.

Grimsley, Ronald. *Jean-Jacques Rousseau: A Study in Self-Awareness*. Cardiff: University of Wales Press, 1961. A study of Rousseau's search for himself, covering many of his later writings after the period of his political work.

Guehenno, Jean. *Jean-Jacques Rousseau*. 2 vols. Translated by John and Doreen Weightman. London: Routledge and Kegan Paul, 1966. A thorough, complete and scholarly biography.

Havens, George W. *Voltair's Marginalia on the Pages of Rousseau: A Comparative Study of Ideas*. Columbus: Ohio State University, 1933. An excellent study of the similarities and differences between Voltaire and Rousseau, who lived through the same period, who were both political liberals, but whose basic attitudes toward man and society were very different.

Heidenhain, Adolf. *Jean-Jacques Rousseau: Personlichkeit, Philosophie, und Psychose*. Munich: Bergmann, 1924. A psychological study, lacking in sophistication and placing a heavy causative emphasis on the relationship between his personal sickness and his ideas.

Hume, David. *The Letters of David Hume*. 2 vols, Edited by J. Y. T. Greig. Oxford: Clarendon Press, 1932. Contains many of Hume's letters to Rousseau as well as his letters to other friends describing Rousseau's perplexing behavior.

MacDonald, Fredrika (Richardson). *Jean-Jacques Rousseau: A New Criticism*. London: Chapman and Hall, 1906. Mrs. MacDonald discovered that Madame D'Epinay had rewritten her fictionalized memoirs directly over the faded, but still visible, ink of her earlier memoirs, giving, in the second account, a much more unfavorable record of her interaction with Rousseau. Some of her letters were also changed and a few of Rousseau's. Mrs. MacDonald has done a fine piece of research, but many of her interpretations are suspect, because of her obvious bias in favor of Rousseau.

McDonald, Joan. *Rousseau and the French Revolution: 1762-1791*. London: Athlone, 1965. A good, short, factual coverage showing the emotional links between Rousseau and the French Revolution as well as the absence of a philosophical or policy connection.

Morley, John. *Rousseau and His Era*. London: Macmillan, 1923. A long factual account of Rousseau's life and times, containing extremely judgmental statements about Rousseau's sex life. Morely finds him, at times, loathsome.

Proal, Louis Joseph Cyrille. *La Psychologie de Jean-Jacques Rousseau*. Paris: Alcan, 1930. An early psychological study in which Rousseau is classified as *un dégéréré supérieur*, a highly emotional individual whose feelings could be triggered by the most trivial incident, a lack of balance between the faculties. Proal does make an attempt to separate Rousseau's genius from his mental illness and does *not* represent his ideas as having been "caused" by his illness.

Rousseau, Jean Jacques. *The Confessions of Jean-Jacques Rousseau*. Translated by J. M. Cohen. London: Penguin, 1954. One of the most revealing autobiographies in literature. Rousseau strives to "tell all" about himself, but there is much self-justification, unjustified suspicion and misinterpretation of his own motives and those of others. However, there is also a basic attempt to get at all te facts, which results in the revelation of details about which we would know nothing except through Rousseau's confession.

———. *Correspondance Gérérale de Jean-Jacques Rousseau*. 20 vols. Edited by Theophile Dufour and P. Plan. Paris: Colin, 1924-34. An older edition of Rousseau's correspondence, not the best, containing at least one letter that has since been shown to be not authentic.

———. *Émile*. New York: Dutton, 1955. Rousseau's work on education, revealing both his tenderness for children and his irrepressible impulse to dominate and control them through clever and, at times, sadistic manipulation.

———. *Émile, ou de l'Éducation*. Paris: Garnier, 1961. A good French edition of one of Rousseau's most important works on education. A novelized account of the education of a young man.

———. *Les Oeuvres Complètes de Jean-Jacques Rousseau*. 3 vols. Paris: Gallimard, 1959-1964. The most complete collection of Rousseau's work, excluding only his letters.

———. *The Political Writings of Jean-Jacques Rousseau*. Edited by C. E. Vaughan. Oxford: Blackwell, 1962. A careful edition of all Rousseau's political manuscripts, based on the original documents, with detailed notes and commentary in English. The political writings are in French and are not translated.

———. *The Social Contract and Discourses*. Translated with an introduction by G. D. H. Cole. New York: Dutton, 1950. A good translation with a historical introduction. Covers many details of the writings and publication of Rousseau's works.

Spurlin, Paul M. *Rousseau in America*. University of Alabama: University of Alabama Press, 1969. A study of Rousseau's influence on the American Revolution.

Starobinski, Jean. *Jean-Jacques Rousseau: La Transparence et L'Obstacle*. Paris: Plon, 1957. An existential psychological study by an eminent Rousseau scholar. A work of profound psychological insight and high literary quality.

———. "The Illness of Rousseau." *Yale French Studies*. 28 (Fall-Winter 1961-1962): 64-74. A detailed study of Rousseau's urethral condition by an M. D. who has read the autopsy report on Rousseau and who is an experienced Rousseau scholar. He concludes there was a psychological component in Rousseau's urinary difficulty.

Talmon, Jacob Lieb. *The Origins of Totalitarian Democracy*. London: Secker and

Warburg, 1952. An attack on Rousseauism as the source of the repressive aspect of modern democratic governments.

Tolstoy, Leo Nikolayevich. "Rousseau." *Annales de la Societe Jean-Jacques Rousseau.* 1 (1905): 7.

Leo Tolstoy

I have not listed Tolstoy's individual works separately. They are all to be found in his *Collected Works*. The most revealing are his autobiographical novels: *Childhood* and *Boyhood*. There are at least three different versions of *Boyhood*. Tolstoy had much more difficulty with this second novel and lost interest in it for long periods of time. His *Confessions*, also found in the *Collected Works*, is particularly useful in what it tells us about his inner thoughts and some of his memories from childhood. Other works of a religious and political nature such as *The Kingdom of God is Within You* and *What Then Must We Do?* suggest the intensity of his guilt and his sense of mission to mankind.

The bibliography also includes works by his children. Unlike the children of Marx, who felt they had to defend their father against the slanders of the world, the children of Tolstoy have been more willing to reveal his dark moods and the way he could spoil their fun with one of his somber looks. Alexandra, in particular, describes his flighty changes in mood and attitude. She was delighted when he admired something she had written, but was always fearful he could take an entirely different attitude toward the same piece if he became unhappy and filled with guilt.

Maude, Aylmer. *The Life of Tolstoy: Later Years.* New York: Dodd Mead, 1911. A revealing account of Tolstoy as field worker and moralist with some record of his political activities.

Noyes, George Rapall. *Tolstoy.* New York: Duffield, 1918. A well-documented biography stressing Tolstoy's Russian heritage, the autobiographical content of his early novels, the influence of Rousseau, his emotional crisis, his religion and his political ideas.

Rolland, Romain. *Tolstoy.* Translated by B. Miall. London: Fisher Unwin, 1911. A well written biography which gives limited attention to his political action and his radicalism.

Simmons, Ernest Joseph. *Leo Tolstoy.* Boston: Little Brown, 1946. A detailed and scholarly biography, making use of Tolstoy's novels as well as his diary and confessions. One of the most complete biographies on Tolstoy.

Steiner, Edward Alfred. *Tolstoy the Man.* New York: Haskell House, 1969. A biography with strong emphasis on his moral and religious development with scant attention to his political activism.

Sukhotin-Tolstoy, Tatiana. *Diaries of Tatiana Sukhotin-Tolstoy.* Translated by A. Brown. New York: Columbia University Press, 1951. A revealing account of Tolstoy's character as seen through the day-to-day reflections of his daughter.

Tolstoy, Aleksandra L'vovna. *Tolstoy: A Life of My Father.* Translated by E. R.

Hapgood. New York: Harper and Row, 1953. A description of Tolstoy's effect on his children, particularly the influence of his severe morality and his tenderness about the suffering of friends.

———. *The Tragedy of Tolstoy*. Translated by E. Varneck. New Haven: Yale University Press, 1933. Stresses the later years, his political actions with much material taken from his diaries.

Tolstoy, Ilia L'vovich. *Reminiscences of Tolstoy*. Translated by George Calderon. New York: Century, 1914. A personal account of Tolstoy's son Ilia, covering his experiences with his father in helping the poor as well as their family life together.

Tolstoy, Leo Nikolayevich. *Collected Works*. 15 vols. Translated by Leo Weiner. Boston: L. C. Page, 1904. Tolstoy's novels and his political writings as well as some of his more personal autobiographical works.

———. *The Complete Works of Count Tolstoy*. 18 vols. Boston: Dana Estes, 1904. A complete collection of Tolstoy's novels, articles on education, confessions, religious and moral works.

———. *Last Diaries*. Translated by Lydia Weston-Kesich. Edited by Leon Stilman. New York: Putnam, 1960. The day-to-day record of Tolstoy's thoughts and actions toward the end of his life.

———. *New Light on Tolstoy*. Edited by Rene Fülöp-Miller. Translated by P. England. London: George Harrap, 1931. Little known letters and esays by Tolstoy.

Tolstoy, Sofia Andreevna (Bers). *The Diary of Tolstoy's Wife, 1860-1891*. Translated by A Werth. New York: Payson and Clarke, 1928. A record of Sonia's conflict with Tolstoy and her growing confusion and depression as their personal difficulties increased.

Troyat, Henri. *Tolstoy*. Translated by N. Amphoux. Garden City; Doubleday, 1967. A well-written biography giving a good description of Tolstoy, the man, and some of his psychological conflicts.

Peter Kropotkin

Kropotkin, unlike Tolstoy and Gandhi, married late in life and little is known of his relationship with his wife. While she shared his poverty after his return to Russia, we have no record of her suffering or any of her complaints. Kropotkin is clearly one of the most reticent of the *early* revolutionaries (who generally tell us more about themselves than those who gain power). Despite the fact that he has written an autobiography that tells us much of his earlier years, including his love for friends and servants, almost nothing is known about his sex life, except that he was repelled by the "oriental pleasures" (presumably the homosexuality) that he found in the school for pages to the Russian court. The biography by Woodcock and Avakumovic is the most complete story of his life and it presents many details about his later years which are missing from his own autobiography. In many respects Kropotkin reveals himself through his works, which offer a testimony to his faith in the communal-cooperative instinct in man and his conviction that it will manifest itself in all men, only if they are no longer pressured from above or confined in prison.

Avrich, Paul Henry, ed. *The Anarchists in the Russian Revolution*. Ithica: Cornell

University Press, 1973. Contains documents supporting the role of anarchists in the Russian Revolution, also describing blunders of the Bolsheviks and their final suppression of the anarchist movement. Some of the works are by Kropotkin, including two of his letters to Lenin.

Durant, Will and Ariel. *Will and Ariel Durant: A Dual Autobiography.* Contains only a brief encounter with Kropotkin, but worthy of note.

Kropotkin, Peter. *The Conquest of Bread.* Edited by Paul Avarich. New York: New York University Press, 1972.

————. *Ethics.* New York: Benjamin Blom, 1960. An incomplete work, representing Kropotkin's effort to develop a natural ethics which did not rely on divine authority.

————. *Fields, Factories and Workshops.* London: Thomas Nelson (no date). A description of the inhuman working conditions in centralized factories and farms. A plea for decentralization, more effective electrification, and a better mixture of brain work and manual work.

————. *The Great French Revolution.* New York: Schocken, 1971. A study of the French Revolution, stressing the anarchist elements as well as the attempt to overthrow the middle-class, which gathered steam as the movement evolved into its more radical phase.

————. *Kropotkin's Revolutionary Pamphlets.* Edited by Roger N. Baldwin. New York: Dover, 1972. An excellent collection of many of Kropotkin's smaller pamphlets, including some of his appeals to young people and an article for the *Encyclopedia Britannica* on anarchism.

————. *Memoirs of a Revolutionist.* New York: Dover, 1971. Kropotkin's autobiography. An interesting personal account, but reserved and even oblique about much of his sexual and sensual life.

————. *Mutual Aid.* Boston: Extending Horizons (no date). Kropotkin's answer to Darwin. Not a refutation of *The Origin of Species*, but an attempt to show that animal development and evolution were influenced by mutual aid as well as mutual aggression. Stresses the role of mutual aid in survival of a species and how it has evolved in man.

Shatz, Marshall S. *The Essential Works of Anarchism.* New York: Bantam, 1971. A compilation of the works of Kropotkin and other anarchists, describing the evolution of anarchist ideas.

Woodcock, Geroge and Ivan Avakumović. *The Anarchist Prince: A Biographical Study of Peter Kropotkin.* New York: Schoken, 1971. A well-written and thorough coverage of the life and work of Kropotkin.

Mohandas Gandhi

There is an abundance of material on Gandhi and many biographies. Most biographers present Gandhi as a saintly figure, ignoring his controlling and dominating side. One exception is the work of N. K. Bose, his secretary who left him because of numerous disagreements, including his feeling that Gandhi should read a bit of Freud to understand his own dynamics in sleeping with young girls. Erikson's psychological study is perhaps the most balanced, showing the moral qualities as well as the tyrant. Tendulkar has provided the most complete factual record of the events of Gandhi's life and Dalal has supplemented this with a chronology, but only for the years after 1915.

It is difficult to maintain one's distance in dealing with Gandhi. One has a tendency to become a worshipper at the shrine or, more rarely, an antagonist. A serious attempt to evaluate the implications of Gandhi's work for modern India has recently been edited by B. C. Das and G. P. Mishra and Judith Brown has given us an acocunt providing important insight into the British view of Gandhi, as he appeared at the time, including the belief that he was a dangerous Bolshevik revolutionary. Gandhi was not only his own man, but a highly idiosyncratic individual, as revealed by his letters and many personal anecdotes from his friends.

Birla, Ghanshyam Dass. *Bapu, A Unique Association.* 4 vols. Bombay: Bharatiya Vidya Bhavan, 1977. A collection of Gandhi's letters to the author and replies. Many letters by others including Gandhi's secretaries, covering his work in politics and government from 1919-1947.

Bose, Nirmal Kumar. *My Days with Gandhi.* Calcutta: Nishana, 1953. Of particular interest is Bose's description of Gandhi sleeping with young women to "test" himself to see if he could discern the slightest awakening of sensuality. He called this an "experiment." Bose was critical of this practice. He felt Gandhi was using the women as objects in his study without their real consent and that he had made some of them hysterical.

Brown, Judith M. *Gandhi's Rise to Power.* Cambridge: Cambridge University Press, 1972. An account that shows how the British came to regard Gandhi as a dangerous revolutionary and how he was rejected by many of the practical politicians in his party.

Chitambar, J. R. *Mahatma Gandhi: His Life, Work and Influence.* Philadelphia: Winston, 1933. The work of an Indian Christian who was basically a supporter of Britain and one who believed the U. K. always intended dominion status for India.

Dalal, Chandulal Bhagubhai. *Gandi 1915-1948: A Detailed Chronology.* New Delhi: Gandhi Peace Foundation, 1971. A valuable chronology covering the years from 1915 to his death.

Das, B. C. and G. P. Mishra, eds. *Gandhi in Today's India.* New Delhi: Ashish, 1979. A discussion of some of the implications of Gandhi's thought for modern India. A series of papers by Indian scholars.

Devanesen, Chandra David Srinjvasagam. *The Making of the Mahatma.* New Delhi: Orient Longmans, 1969. An attempt to trace the development of Gandhi through cultural anthropology. Makes a strong point of his Indian acculturation and his negative reaction to Western culture.

Diwkar, Ranganath Ramachandra. *Glimpses of Gandhiji.* Bombay: Hind Kitabs, 1949. A tribute by a follower, containing many personal observations of Gandhi with workers, politicians in jail, etc.

Erikson, Erik H. *Gandhi's Truth.* New York: Norton, 1969. A psychological study following Erikson's usual approach of focusing on a single incident in order to reveal the dynamics of his subject.

Fischer, Louis. *The Life of Mahatma Gandhi.* New York: Collier, 1973. An excellent and detailed biography of Gandhi.

Gandhi, Mohandas Karamchand. *An Autobiography: The Story of My Experiments with Truth*. Boston: Beacon, 1957. Gandhi's autobiography. A very readable and revealing account of his early life. It ends around 1920, thus omitting many important events of his later years.

———. *Bapu's Letters to Mira*. Ahmedabad: Navajivan, 1959.

———. *Collected Works*. 32 vols. Ministry of Information: Government of India, 1958-1980. A complete collection of Gandhi's work.

———. *The Collected Works of Mahatma Gandhi*. 30 vols. Ahmedabad: Navajivan Trust, 1965. Contains all the early papers, letters to newspapers, drafts of proposals and many other documents not previously published.

———. *Communism and Communists*. Compiled by R. K. Prabhu. Ahmedabad: Navajivan, 1959. A compilation of Gandhi's remarks concerning communism.

———. *The Essential Gandhi, His LIfe, Work and Ideas: An Anthology*. Edited by Louis Fischer. New York: Vintage, 1962. A collection of some of Gandhi's most important work.

———. *Gandhiji's Correspondence with the Government*. 3 vols. Ahmedabad: Navajivan, 1957. Contains most of Gandhi's official correspondence.

———. *Hind Swaraj or Indian Home Rule*. Ahmedabad: Navajivan, 1909. An account of the principles and some of the events of the Indian Home Rule movement.

———. *Satyagraha in South Africa*. Madras: Ganesan, 1928. A more detailed account of Gandhi's period in South Africa than can be found in his *Autobiography*.

———. *Selected Works of Mahatma Gandhi*. 7 vols. Edited by Shriman Narayan. Ahmedabad: Navajivan, 1968. Highlights some of Gandhi's political contacts and his personal conflicts with other leaders.

———. *Self-Restraint Versus Self-Indulgence*. Ahmedabad: Navajivan, 1947. Philosophical discussions of self-control with examples and anecdotes.

———. *Speeches and Writings of Mahatma Gandhi*. Madras: G. A. Natesan, 1933.

Hutchins, Francis G. *India's Revolution: Gandhi and the Quit India Movement*. Cambridge: Harvard University Press, 1973. The book documents some of the connections between Gandhi's statements and the violent acts during the Quit India Movement.

Keer, Dhananjay. *Mahatma Gandhi: Political Saint and Unarmed Prophet*. Bombay: Popular Prekashan, 1973. Presents Gandhi as a great leader, but also reveals his tyrannical character and his absolute control over the lives of others. Describes his conflict with Subhas Bose, the right-wing, violent rebel.

Mehta, Ved. *Mahatma Gandhi and His Apostles*. New York: Viking, 1977. The author traveled throughout several countries collecting oral testimony on Gandhi's life. Covers several incidents told by those close to him.

Pyarelal, Sri. *Mahatma Gandhi*. 3 vols. Ahmedabad: Navajivan, 1965. A lengthy account covering many interesting details not available in other sources. Pyarelal was one of Gandhi's secretaries.

Radhakrishnan, Sarvepalli, ed. *Mahatma Gandhi: Essays and Reflections*. London: Allen and Unwin, 1939. A tribute to Gandhi in essays from his friends, describing his contributions to the freedom and policy of India and his personality.

Ramchandran, C. *A Sheaf of Gandhi Anecdotes*. Bombay: Hind Kitabs, 1945. Stories which highlight Gandhi's idiosyncratic character.

Shulka, Chandrshanker. *Incidents in Gandhi's Life*. Bombay: Vora, 1949. Describes

events in Gandhi's life, many of them in more detail than can be found in the
Autobiography.

Tedulkar, Dinanath Gopal. *Life of Mohands Karamchand Gandhi*. 8 vols. Bombay: The
Times of India Press, 1950–54. A thorough and complete coverage of Gandhi's life,
with frequent references to documentation and quotation from official sources.
Another edition published by the Times of India Press, 1950–54.

Karl Marx

The literature on Marx is extensive. I have limited this bibliography to his actual
works and the literature dealing with his personal life and his political ideas. I
have omitted the many specialized researches which cover specific phases of his
life, using, instead, major biographies or short personal sketches by his friends
or enemies. Seigel's book on *Marx's Fate* is a psychological study, but it is more
than that. It covers much of his reading and thinking as well as his attempt to link
thought with action. While I disagree with many of Seigel's interpretations, I have
found much of value in his work and his sources. While Padover disavows any
interest in psychohistory as such, his fine scholarly biography clearly brings out
many examples of paranoid ideation in Marx, as well as the role of hate in
reshaping the humanism of the communist movement and distinguishing it from
the various forms of socialism which supported a belief in the brotherhood of
man.

Today there are many Marxisms and communisms. For this reason I have
indicated some of those writers who distinguish the original ideas of Marx from
the elaborations of his followers. The works of Tucker, Deutscher, Burns and
Foner are particularly useful in this regard.

Alport, Gordon W. *The Nature of Prejudice*. New York: Doubleday, 1958. Covering all
forms of prejudice as well as self-hatred of the oppressed individual and his ethnic
group.

Annenkov, Paul V. *The Extraordinary Decade*. Translated by Irwin R. Titunik. Ann
Arbor: University of Michigan Press, 1968. Annenkov, a wealthy Russian friend of
Marx, describes a number of their encounters. Perhaps the most dramatic account
of Marx as the representative of communist beliefs, containing the table-thumping
session with Weitling in which Marx denounced Weitling before a small assembly of
fellow-communists.

Anonymous. *Reminiscences of Marx and Engels*. Moscow: Foreign Language Press
(no date or editor). A collection of many personal observations about Marx and
Engels from a variety of people who knew them.

Bottomore, T. B., ed. *Karl Marx*. Oxford: Blackwell, 1979. An excellent compilation of
essays on Marx by A. Schumpeter, Isaiah Berlin, Benedetto Croca, H. B. Acton and
others. Berlin's complete critique of each of Marx's seminal works is superb in its
balance and perceptivenes.

Burns, E. *A Handbook of Marxism*. New York: Random House, 1935. A collection of
extracts from Marx, Engels and their followers designed to give a comprehensive
account of Marxism. The autor has added bibliographical notes and an explanation of
circumstances in which the book was written.

Cantril, Hadley. *The Politics of Despair*. New York: Basic Books, 1958. Presents the thesis that many people, particularly Europeans, vote for communists as a protest against the current system. However, he contends they do not really want communists in power. He backs up his assertions with interviews and voting statistics.

Deutscher, Issaac. *Marxism in Our Time*. Edited by T. Deutscher. Berkeley: Ramparts Press, 1971. A study of the varieties and the distortions of Marxist ideas, written by an ardent Marxist who stresses the continued need for democratic criticism within the Marxist movements of the world.

Dornemann, Luise. *Jenny Marx: der Lebensweg einer Sozialistin*. Berlin: Dietz Verlag, 1970.

Emmett, William Henry. *The Marxian Economic Handbook and Glossary*. London: G. Allen and Unwin, 1925. Containing numerous corrections, explanations and elaborations of the English version of Capital, volume I, the only volume actually written by Marx. Excellent for students of Marx's ideas.

Fackenheim, Emil L. *God's Presence in History*. New York: New York University Press, 1970. Fackenheim, a rabbi, discusses the role of God in history, but also covers the anti-semitism of Marx as well as other aspects of religious belief and its influence on historic events.

Foner, Phillip Sheldon. Editor. *When Karl Marx Died*. New York: International Publishers, 1973. A compilation of speeches and articles at the time of Marx's death, demonstrating his world-renown as well as his notoriety.

Footman, David. *Ferdinand Lassalle: Romantic Revolutionary*. New York: Greenwood, 1947. The story of one of the great revolutionary figures of the Nineteenth Century who, for a time, eclipsed even the influence of Marx in his meteoric rise. However, while he was a student of Hegel and a dramatic speaker, he was not a theoretician in his own right and he applied the principles of Hegel in an uncritical manner.

Kapp, Yvonne. *Eleanor Marx*. 2 vols. New York: Pantheon, 1972-76. A very readable and well-researched account of the life of Marx's youngest child. She was the only one to grow to maturity in London and to develop not only a sense of her Jewish origins but her father's heritage. The book also contains many observations of Marx, himself, and the many visitors encountered by Marx.

Kunzli, Arnold. *Karl Marx: Eine Psychographie*. Vienna: Europa Verlag, 1966. A psychological study with a Jungian orientation, stressing Jewish self-hatred and Marx's choice of a profession as an effort to find a certification of non-Jewishness. Maintains his delay in finishing *Capital* was fear of criticism.

Lafargue, Paul. *Karl Marx: The Man*. New York: New York London News, 1947. A brief article, separately bound, containing a description of Marx by his son-in-law. A vivid description of Marx's personal habits.

Levin, Kurt. "Self-Hatred Among Jews." *Contemporary Jewish Record*. 4 (1941) 219-232. An analysis and description of the phenomenon.

Marx, Karl. *Capital*. 3 vols. New York: International Publishers, 1967. One of the best English translations, unabridged. Includes not only the first volume written by Marx, but the other two edited by Engels from the notes of Marx, with much addition and rephrasing.

_____. *The Civil War in France*. Introduction by Friedrich Engels. New York: International Publishers, 1940. Official addresses and documents of the 1871 war. Address of the General Council of the International Working Men's Association and Marx's own history of the period, including the last battle and slaughter of the Paris commune.

_____. *Grundrisse*. New York: Vintage, 1973. A huge rambling collection of notes and observations which form the basis for the later development of *Capital*. Manuscripts written from October 1857 to March 1858, but not published during Marx's lifetime.

_____. *Karl Marx Dictionary*. New York: Philosophical Library, 1965. Ideas, including actual quotes from the works of Marx, arranged in alphabetical order.

_____. *Karl Marx: Early Writings*. Translated and Edited by T. B. Bottomore. Foreword by Erich Fromm. New York: McGraw-Hill, 1964. Excellent translation of Marx's early *Paris Manuscripts* (as they are called today) as well as his two essays on the Jewish question. Commentary by Erich Fromm, who is insightful, but a bit too biased in Marx's favor.

_____. *The Karl Marx Library*. 16 vols (planned). Some in preparation. Arranged and edited with an introduction and new translations by Saul K. Padover. New York: McGraw-Hill, 1971–. Perhaps the best collection in English of the works of Marx, prior to the *Collected Works* by International Publishers (which is also still in preparation). The volumes cover his many letters and shorter articles as well as his more important works. Arranged by major area of subject matter. Each volume contains an introduction describing the documents.

_____. *Letters to Dr. Kugelmann*. Moscow: Cooperative Publishing Society of Foreign Workers, 1934. Letters of Marx to Louis Kugelmann.

_____. *Manifesto of the Communist Party*. Edited by Friedrich Engels. London: Lawrence and Wishart, 1888. The authorized English version of the *Manifesto*.

_____. *A World Without Jews*. Translated by D. D. Runes. New York: Philosophical Library, 1959. The translator invents his own title to cover Marx's two essays on the Jewish question. The title and the introduction are a one-sided distortion of Marx's ideas, giving the impression they were the basis of all his later thinking, that he was as anti-Semitic as Hitler and Stalin and that his essays are the basis for modern Russian anti-Semitism. Erich Fromm sums up this book very well in his Introduction to Bottomore's *Karl Marx: Early Writings*.

Marx, Karl and Friedrich Engels. *The American Journalism of Marx and Engels*. Edited by H. M. Christman. Introduction by C. Blitzer. New York: New American Library, 1966. A selection of articles from *The New York Daily Tribune*, many of which were written by Engels but signed by Marx. In other cases Engels acted as translator.

_____. *The Civil War in the United States*. New York: International Publishers, 1937. A complete compilation of everything written by Marx and Engels about the American Civil War, including their newspaper articles for the American and German press as well as remarks in their private correspondence.

_____. *Collected Works*. New York: International Publishers, 1975–. When finished it will probably be the best and most complete English translation of the works of Marx and Engels. A cooperative effort among British, Russian, German and American scholars. The only defect is in the commentary which, in obvious deference to the Russian contributors, avoids serious critical appraisal of the works. The same applies to any details supplied regarding Marx's personal life. Events that reflect negatively on him are generally omitted.

_____. 6 vols. *Gesammelte Schriften von Karl Marx und Friedrich Engels*. Berlin: Dietz Verlag, 1920.

_____. *Gesamtausgabe*. Number of volumes not known, incomplete (MEGA). Berlin: Dietz Verlag, 1975–. A new critical edition of the complete works of Marx and

Engels first published in 1927–1935 and edited by D. Ryasanoff and V. Adoratsky in Moscow and Berlin.

———. *Ireland and the Irish Question*. New York: International Publishers, 1972. A collection, from the writings of Marx and Engels, which illustrates the extent to which they investigated the economy, politics, government and working conditions of every potential source of revolution against the capitalist system.

———. *Selected Correspondence, 1846–1895*. Westport: Greenwood, 1975. Contains those parts of letters which relate to the political beliefs and speculations of Marx and Engels. Missing are those many interesting personal interactions (in the same letters) in which Marx speaks of his debts and touches Engels for a loan or which describe the horror of Marx's poverty and his many physical ills.

———. *Selected Works*. Moscow: Progress Publishers, 1970. A selection of the political writings of Marx and Engles, which were particularly influential in developing their communist doctrine.

———. *Werke*. 39 vols. Berlin: Dietz Verlag, 1968. A comprehensive coverage of the work of Marx and Engles, including their letters, but not a complete collection.

McLellan, David. *Karl Marx: His Life and Thought*. New York: Harper and Row, 1973. An excellent factual summary of Marx's life with an extensive evaluation of the interaction between his life and work. Commentaries and observations about his behavior.

Nicolaievsky, Boris and Otto Maenchenhelfen. *Karl Marx: Man and Fighter*. London: Methuen, 1936. A very pro-Marx biography, but rich in factual detail regarding the interaction of Marx and his friends. Extensive quotations from letters and other sources.

Olsen, Richard. *Karl Marx*. Boston: G. K. Hall, 1978. A good short study of Marx's ideas and a brief biography.

Padover, Saul K. *Karl Marx: An Intimate Biography*. New York: McGraw-Hill, 1978. A good book, based on a profound understanding of Marx. While Padover does not approve of psychohistory, he finds it impossible to avoid some psychological observations about Marx, most of which are well-reasoned and well-documented.

Payne, Robert. *Marx*. London: W. H. Allen, 1968. Like his *Unknown Karl Marx*, this is a well-written, scholarly book, but very biased against Marx. Payne sees the demonic side of Marx almost exclusively. He seems to miss Marx's tenderness and his human qualities as well as his genuine effort to save mankind from exploitation.

———. *The Unknown Karl Marx*. New York: New York University Press, 1971. Contains many of the little-known works of Marx, including some of his early poetry, his story of the life of Lord Palmerston, and the letters of Eleanor Marx to Frederick Demuth, after she discovered that Frederick was her father's illegitimate son.

Prawer, S. S. *Karl Marx and World Literature*. Oxford: Clarendon Press, 1976. Corrects a common impression that Marx had a narrow view of literature, for example, the belief that he saw working class oppression as the only fit subject for tragedy. Often critical of Marx, but fair.

Raddatz, Fritz Joachim. *Karl Marx: A Political Biography*. Translated by R. Barry. London: Wiedenfield and Nicolson, 1975. A highly critical, but well-written and well-documented book. Much more intimate than the title suggests. Filled with details of Marx's personal relationships and examples of his extravagance with money.

Ruge, Arnold. *Briefwechsel und Tagebuchblatter*. Berlin: Weidmannsche Buchhandlung, 1886. Ruge's own account of his relationship with Marx as well as his own political development.

Siegel, Jerrold. "Marx's Early Development: Vocation, Rebellion, Realism." *Journal of Interdisciplinary History.* 3 (1972): 475–508. Comparing Marx's early vocational and philosophical changes with those of his father. The interaction between his Jewish origin and his vocational and philosophical development.

_____. *Marx's Fate.* Princeton: Princeton University Press, 1978. A psychological study with an unusual orientation, making an attempt to integrate psychological and intellectual history.

Schwarzschild, Leopold. *Karl Marx: The Red Prussian.* New York: Grosset and Dunlap, 1947. A rather caustic study of Marx's life, emphasizing his egotism, ambition and anti-Semitism, including his infamous remarks about Lassalle: "Baron Issy" and the "Jewish Nigger."

Schwerin-Krosigk, Lutz. *Jenny Marx: Liebe und Leid im Schatten von Karl Marx.* Wuppertal: Stats Verlag, 1976.

Tucker, Robert. *Philosophy and Myth in Karl Marx.* Cambridge: Cambridge University Press, 1961. An excellent study of Marx's ideas. Makes a developmental connection between early Marxism, in the *Paris Manuscripts*, and the "mature" Marxism in his later work.

_____. *The Marxian Revolutionary Idea.* New York: Norton, 1969. Covers Marxism as a theory as well as its impact on modern social thought. Also examines the strategies by which communist movements have come to power and the varieties of communist ideology that have evolved from different world leaders. Studies the process by which deradicalization begins in Marxist movements.

von Bohn-Bawerk, E. *Karl Marx and the Close of His System.* Edited with an Introduction by P. M. Sweezy. New York: A. M. Kelley, 1949. Criticism of Marx by Bohn Bawerk and Rudolf Hilferding with an appendix consisting of an article by L. Von Bortkiewicz on the transformation of values into prices of production in the Marxian system.

Wilson, Edmund. *To the Finland Station.* Garden City: Doubleday, 1953. A story of the rise of socialism in Europe, from Vico to Lenin and Trotsky. Many personal details from the lives of Marx and other revolutionary theoreticians and activists, told by a master story-teller, but based on factual information. No footnotes.

Wolfson, Murray. *Marx: Economist, Philosopher, Jew.* New York: St. Martin's Press, 1982. Relates Marx's rebellion to the rebellion of the assimilated Jew and his search for more universal doctrines. Sees Marx's rebellion against the "commercial" Judaism of his father, but does not draw a clear line from this to his anti-capitalism.

Sun Yat-sen

Very little is known of the childhood of Sun. His own account of his life tells us little of his interaction with his family and his experiences as a child. His story is told in retrospect and, as he looks back, he appears always more radical than he was at the time. He mentions nothing about his ideas for the reform of China, picturing himself as a revolutionary from the beginning. Lyon Sharman has given us the most complete life of Sun and one of the more objective views of his character. However, her view of his authoritarian side is in marked contrast to that of his friend and fellow-physician, James Cantlie.

Anonymous. *Dr. Sun Yat-sen.* Peking: Foreign Language Press, 1957.

Cantlie, James and C. Sheridan Jones. *Sun Yat Sen and the Awakening of China*. New York: Fleming H. Revell, 1912. An excellent account of the personality of Sun, his early life and Cantlie's work with him as a fellow-physician.

Hall, J. W. (Upton Close). *Eminent Asians*. New York: Apppleton, 1930. A good short account of Sun's life and some aspects of his character.

Linbarger, Paul Myron Anthony. *Sun Yat Sen and the Chinese Republic*. New York: Century, 1925. A highly flattering account of Sun's life. Source material is not clearly indicated.

Restarick, Henry B. *Sun Yat Sen: Liberator of China*. New Haven: Yale University Press, 1931. Emphasis is on Sun's political and military activities.

Schiffrin, Harold Z. *Sun Yat-sen and the Origins of the Chinese Revolution*. Berkeley: University of California Press, 1968.

Seton, Grace T. "The Great Leader of China." *American Reveiw of Reviews*. 67; 630 (June 1923): 634. A brief account of the character of Sun Yat-sen.

Sharmon, Lyon. *Sun Yat-sen: His Life and Its Meaning*. Stanford: Stanford University Press, 1968. A good complete biography. Covers the major events of his life.

Sun Yat-sen. *Kidnapped in London*. London: China Society, 1969. An exciting account of Sun's experience in captivity at the Chinese Embassy. This became the basis for many newspaper stories and did much to publicize his role as the liberator of China.

_____. *Memoirs of a Chinese Revolutionary*. New York: AMS Press, 1970. This is Sun's autobiography, but it is lacking in personal detail. He covers much of his arguments with his colleagues and some of his early ideas for necessary changes in China.

_____. *San Min Chu I*. Translated by Frank Price. Chungking: Republic of China: Ministry of Information, 1943. The basic revolutionary philosophy of Sun, compiled from his lectures. It covers his verison of the ideas of Marx, Rousseau, Jefferson and other major thinkers of his time, as well as Sun's own revolutionary philosophy.

Wang Chi Sing. *The Foundations of San Min Chu I in Chinese Culture*. Shanghai: Kuo Hsueh Press, 1927. A description of some of the Chinese sources for Sun's major ideas.

Leon Trotsky

Trotsky gives a fairly detailed description of his early years in *My Life*, but when he begins to tell of his work on *Iskra* and his commitment to communism, the book becomes more dry and factual. There are no details of his courtship or personal relationship with either of his wives. Deutscher has presented the most complete life of Trotsky and gives us some insight into the long period when Stalin was climbing to power and Trotsky, the one person who might have stopped him, waited and did nothing. Segal, in his biography, also reveals some of Trotsky's conflict during this period. Even Trotsky's so-called "diaries" are remarkably sparse in their comments about what he does or thinks about the behavior of others. Instead they tend to be political reflections on world events. Exceptions are those periods of extreme tragedy when something happens to his former wife, his current wife, or one of his children.

Soviet writers, when they speak of Trotsky at all, tend to regard him as some kind of demon without any truly human characteristic. As a result these works have little interest and tell us almost nothing about his character. The hearings of the commission headed by John Dewey have done much to clarify the charges against Trotsky by the Soviet Regime and to give an objective evaluation.

Deutscher, Isaac. *The Prophet Armed: Trotsky 1879–1921*. The first volume in a trilogy. New York: Random House, 1945. The first volume of Deutscher's excellent study, covering the life and works of Trotsky. A sympathetic account, but well-documented.

_____. *The Prophet Unarmed: Trotsky 1921–1929*. New York: Random House, 1959.

_____. *The Prophet Outcast: Trotsky 1929–1940*. New York: Random House, 1963.

Dewey, John, Carleton Beals, Otto Ruhele, Benjamin Stolberg, and Suzanne La Follette. *The Case of Leon Trotsky*. New York: Merit, 1968. A verbatim transcript of a hearing held by the Preliminary Commission of Inquiry into the charges made against Trotsky in the Moscow trials. The Hearing was by a panel in the United States.

Eastman, Max. *Leon Trotsky: The Portrait of a Youth*. New York: Greenberg, 1925. A biography covering Trotsky's early years to the relationship with Lenin. Stresses Lenin's confidence in Trotsky.

Heijenoort, Jean Van. *With Trotsky in Exile*. Cambridge: Harvard University Press, 1978. A record of Trotsky's continuous battle for the ideological purity of the communist movement as well as his personal struggles against persecution by Stalin.

Mosley, N. *The Assassination of Trotsky*. London: Michael Joseph, 1972. Many details of Trotsky's final months and the character of his assassin.

Nevada, Joseph. *Trotsky and the Jews*. Philadelphia: Jewish Publication Society, 1971. Biographical study of the influence of Trotsky's Jewish background. The author questions Max Eastman's assertion that Trotsky was entirely free of a "Jewish complex."

Payne, Robert. *The Life and Death of Trotsky*. New York: McGraw-Hill, 1977. A well-written biography, describing the breakdown of Bolshevik ideals into a party dictatorship. Good character study of Trotsky, good bibliography.

Segal, R. *The Tragedy of Leon Trotsky*. London: Hutchinson, 1979. A vigorous defense of Trotsky and his ideas, giving one the feeling that the revolution might have been saved if he had remained in power. Many details of his exile and death.

Seth, Ronald Sydney. *Lev Davidovich Trotsky: The Eternal Rebel*. London: Dennis Dobson, 1967. A biography which stresses the role of Trotsky as rebel and exile, too confident of his moral rightness to recognize that he could be deposed by force.

Serge, Victor and Natalie Sedova Trotsky. *The Life and Death of Leon Trotsky*. London: Wildwood House, 1975.

Smith, Irving H., ed. *Trotsky*. Englewood Cliffs: Prentice Hall, 1973. A collection of writings by Trotsky and by others who observed him, talked with him and argued for and against his ideas.

Trotsky, Leon Davidovich. *Chapters from My Diary*. Edited by Paul Mattick. Boston: The Revolutionary Age, no date. A personal account of Trotsky's troubles in France and his expulsion in 1916.

_____. *My Life*. New York: Grosset and Dunlap, 1930. An autobiography which begins with much personal detail and feeling, but trails off into a mere recitiation of political events. The first half of the book is lively and fascinating.

———. *Permanent Revolution and Results and Prospects.* New York: Pathfinder, 1978. The best statement of Trotsky's beliefs with particular reference to his differences with Marx, Lenin and Stalin. It reaffirms the international quality of the communist revolutionary movement and it places him closer to Marx than any of his contemporaries.

———. *Trotsky's Diary in Exile.* Cambridge: Harvard University Press, 1958. Mostly political commentaries, but frequently Trotsky allows himself some personal comments regarding his feelings and those of his wife. He is particularly stricken by the attack on his first wife and children.

———. *The Trotsky Papers 1917–1922.* 3 vols. London: Mouton, 1964. Correspondence between Trotsky and Lenin, but including the letters of many other writers.

———. *Writings of Leon Trotsky 1929–1940.* 12 vols. New York: Pathfinder, 1975. Pamphlets, articles and interviews written during his exile, in defense of his brand of communism and in opposition to the acts and charges of Stalin.

Ernesto (Ché) Guevara

We have more information on the personality of Ché Guevara than on most modern revolutionaries, not only because of his diaries and letters, but because the testimony of his friends and at least one former wife reveal much of his character and the source of his revolutionary motivation. Ché was regarded as the ideologist of the Cuban revolution and it is true that Fidel Castro relied on him for much of his early education about communism. But José Martí was an equally important source for the roots of the Cuban Revolution and in this area Ché learned from Fidel.

Ché is, in some respects, a prototype of the early revolutionary whose letters and public speeches were a fruitful source of information about his character. I have emphasized several of these speeches and writings in the bibliography. I have also included one book on Tania because she has become such an important element in the legend of Ché Guevara. She was physically attractive and she died fighting in the Bolivian jungles as part of Ché's guerrilla force. For this reason she has become a heroine to the Left. Daniel James, in his biography of Ché, has cast some doubt on her status, but there is little solid support for his assertion that she deliberately betrayed Ché.

Bly, Robert, ed. *Neruda and Vallejo, Selected Poems.* Boston: Beacon, 1971. The poems of Pablo Neruda (one of Ché's heros) are particularly worthy of note. Highly evocative imagery and strong anti-U.S. attitudes.

Gadea, Hilda. *Ernesto: A Memoir of Ché Guevra.* New York: Doubleday, 1972. A very personal account, containing many details of Hilda's life with Ché, describing some of his difficulties with asthma and its psychological meaning for him.

Goodwin, Richard N. "A Footnote." *The New Yorker.* May 25, 1968: 23. Goodwin's encounter with Ché.

Guevara, Ernesto (de la Serna). *Ché: Selected works of Ernesto Guervara.* Cambridge: MIT Press, 1969. A very good and more readable translation of many of Ché's famous works and speeches, some of which have appeared elsewhere.

_____. *The Diary of Ché Guevara.* Edited by Robert Scheer. Published by arrange-ment with *Ramparts Magazine.* New York: Bantam, 1968. A Diary of Ché's Bolivian adventure. An unrestrained commentary on the positive and negative characteris-tics of himself and his men as well as his terrible struggle with asthma.

_____. *Guerrilla Warfare.* New York: Random House, 1969. Ché's description of the methodology of guerrilla warfare, including his romanticism, his almost religious zeal and his compassion for fallen comrades.

_____. *Reminiscences of the Cuban Revolutionary War.* Translated by Victoria Ortiz. New York: Monthly Review Press, 1968. A detailed battle-by-battle account by one of the chief combatants.

_____. *Venceremos!* Edited by John Gerassi. New York: Macmillan, 1968. An enthusi-astic and vivid account of Ché's life and many of his major works. Many are, unfortunately, poorly translated.

James, Daniel. *Ché Guevara.* New York: Stein and Day, 1970. A well-written, detailed and complete biography. The author reaches rather far for some of his conclusions, but he is free from obvious political bias and does not paint Ché as either a saint or a devil.

Lowy, Michael. *The Marxism of Ché Guevara.* Translated by Brian Pearce. New York: Monthly Review Press, 1973. A study of Ché's ideological contribution to revolution with particular emphasis on his supposedly direct connection between theory and practice. The real Ché was more impulsive and romantic and less deliberate.

Rojas, Marta and Mirta Calderon Rodriguez, eds. *Tania: The Unforgettable Guerrilla.* New York: Random House, 1971. An English translation of the book that has done much to make Tania (Tamara) Bunke Bider a revolutionary legend. She was the last lover of Ché Guevara and died fighting in the Bolivian jungles. A highly romanticized book, full of pictures, letters from Tania, anecdotes about her by friends. There is a slight physical resemblance between Tania and Patricia Hearst, who took her name after she was kidnapped by the Simbionese Liberation Army in San Francisco.

Rojo, Ricardo. *My Friend Ché.* New York: Dial, 1968. Good descriptive detail, based on Rojo's actual experiences with Ché. Many anecdotes known only to the author and Ché.

Fidel Castro

Despite the number of reporters who have interviewed Castro, few have uncovered much information about his personal life or his childhood. From the content of most of these interviews, it would seem that Castro is adept at focusing attention on modern Cuba and the political situation. Herbert Matthews seems to have uncovered more of Castro's personal moral conflicts about leader-ship than most interviewers. While Castro was strongly influenced by the communism of his brother, Raul, and by the ideological writings and discussions with Ché Guevara, it is impossible to understand the political views of Castro without examining the life and writings of José Martí. Martí was not only a Cuban national hero who died in combat while fighting Spanish colonialism, he was educated in Spain, lived in New York for several different periods of his life and traveled extensively throughout Latin America. He was a man steeped in the

Hispanic culture with a broad international view of the future of the Latin American states. He spoke of "Our America," meaning the Hispanic culture in America (North and South) and he detested luxury and capitalism. Today both Castro and the anti-Castro Cubans in Miami invoke his name as the philosophical inspiration of their cause. MIT Press is beginning a series of volumes that will be devoted to the complete works of Fidel Castro. This will become a standard reference work on the origins and development of the Cuban Revolution.

Castro, Fidel. *Revolutionary Struggle: The Selected Works of Fidel Castro 1947–1958.* Edited by Rolando E. Bonachea and Nelson P. Valdes. Cambridge, MIT Press, 1972. This series of volumes is more than an editorial work. It is a complete and well documented account of the details of the Cuban Revolution with much useful information about the life of Castro.

Caususo, Teresa. *Cuba and Castro.* Translated by Elmer Grossberg. New York: Random House, 1961.

Draper, Theodor. *Castroism: Theory and Practice.* New York: Fredrick Praeger, 1965.

———. *Castro's Revolution: Myths and Realities.* New York: Fredrick Praeger, 1962.

Dubois, Jules. *Fidel Castro.* New York: Bobbs-Merrill, 1959.

Lockwood, Lee. *Castro's Cuba, Cuba's Fidel.* New York: Random House, 1969. A series of interviews giving a good flavor of Castro, the man, but mostly about Cuba today. Little historical or biographical information.

Martí, José. *Inside the Monster.* Edited by Philip Foner. New York: Monthly Review Press, 1975. Excellent selection of Martí's writings on the United States including both his admiration of our power and our quest for freedom and his horror of U.S. capitalism. His piece on Coney Island is particularly good.

———. *Our America.* Edited by Philip Foner. New York: Monthly Review Press, 1979. Selection of Martí's writings on Latin America and the struggle for Cuban independence, including some of his letters to other leaders in this movement.

Martin, Lionel. *The Early Fidel.* Secaucus: Lyle Stuart, 1978. Much useful factual information, but the author tries too hard to prove Castro was always an ideological communist through his use of selective quotation.

Matthews, Herbert. *Fidel Castro.* New York: Simon and Schuster, 1969. A good biography based on research and personal interviews.

Schlesinger, Arthur M. *A Thousand Days.* New York: Houghton Mifflin, 1965. Contains an excellent account, from the U.S. veiwpoint, of the Cuban invasion by CIA-backed anti-Castro Cubans.

Urrutia, Manuel. *Fidel Castro and Company, Inc.* New York: Fredrick Praeger, 1964. A negative account of Castro's rise to power after his military victory. The thesis is that Fidel was a closet communist and intended to take power even before he appointed Urrutia President of Cuba. Urrutia was one of Cuba's most courageous jurists, and a strong believer in democracy.

Weyl, Nathaniel. *Red Star Over Cuba.* New York: Devin-Adair, 1961. A highly biased and subjective account of Castro's early life and his rise to power, painting him as a scheming devil.

V. I. Lenin

The pictures of Lenin's childhood are fairly consistent from one writer to the next. There was an attempt by Soviet writers to show that his mother and father were both revolutionaries at heart and entertained political refugees in their home, but there seems to be little substance to these stories. Valentinov has given us perhaps the most complete account of Lenin's early years and these are the years of greatest importance for a psychological study. Lenin stands out as one who developed slowly, but soon learned to dominate others, not through emotion, but through a steady and forceful insistence of his desires. Deutscher, a thorough and careful researcher, began a life of Lenin, but, unfortunately, all that remains is a fragment of his written work which was put together by his wife after his death. Fischer has also written a complete and well-documented life of Lenin. Another interesting book in this section is the comparison of Lenin and Gandhi by Rene Fülöp-Miller. He reveals a similarity in their moral attitudes and the absoluteness of their convictions, which suggests a strong parallel in the psychology of the two men. Lenin, in his letters to Trotsky and Gorky, is the consumate politician, always careful not to take offense, looking for areas of agreement, trying to sooth ruffled feelings. This is in striking contrast to Lenin the bully-boy, which is the usual picture of his childhood character. However, this picture of his self-control and even his conformism, is remarkably similar to accounts of him as a student. Lenin was evidently capable of strict control of his emotions whenever he wanted something.

Conquest, Robert. *V. I. Lenin*. Edited by F. Kermode. New York: Viking Press, 1972. A largely factual account of Lenin's life, but supports the idea that Stalin followed the policies of Lenin. Regards the Russia of Stalin as a natural consequence of the ideas of Lenin.

Deutscher, Isaac. *Lenin's Childhood*. London: Oxford University Press, 1970. Unfortunately a mere fragment of Deutscher's planned work on Lenin. As it stands this is an incomplete account of Lenin's early years. Lenin is seen as a loud robust bully who bossed his younger sister, Olga, and played with her so loudly that the younger children could not do their homework. His fierce courage with other children and with physical obstacles is stressed. In school, however, he was very attentive, quiet and orderly. He envied his older brother, Sasha, and tried to live like him.

Fischer, Louis. *The Life of Lenin*. New York: Harper and Row, 1965. Exellent biography. Typical of Fischer's detailed research and readable style.

Fox, Ralph Winston. *Lenin, A Biography*. London: Victor Gollancz, 1933. A basically positive account of Lenin and his rise to power, picturing him as a man who worked for the good of others.

Fülöp-Miller, Rene. *Lenin and Gandhi*. Translated by F. S. Flint and D. F. Tait. London: Putnam, 1927. Describes both as men who spoke with the disturbing arrogance of a Gospel. Ties them together in their pity for mankind and their deep sense of responsibility for the suffering of others. Both prepared an indictment of European culture.

Gorky, Maxim. *Lenin*. London: Morrison and Gibb, 1967. A short but interesting personal sketch, containing many details from their meetings.

Krupskaya, Nadezhda K. *Reminiscences of Lenin*. New York: International Publishers, 1970. An account by Lenin's wife, but lacking most of the details of their personal life and focusing, instead, on his political accomplishments. A rather dull book.

Landau-Aldanov and Mark Aleksandrovich. *Lenin*. New York: Dutton, 1922. Short on biographical detail. An abundance of opinions, emphatically expressed, against visionaries and utopians of the Lenin school. Opposed to the violence of the revolutionary and convinced that regimes built on violence must perish in violence.

Lenin, Vladimir I. *Collected Works*. 34 vols. London: Lawrence and Wishart, 1977. A recent translation of the early collected works first published by Progress Publishers in Moscow.

Lenin, Vladimir, I. and Gorky A. Maxim. *Lenin and Gorky: Letters, Reminiscences, Articles*. Translated by B. Isaacs. Moscow: Progress Publishers, 1973. Primarily the correspondence between Lenin and Gorky. Shows Lenin's effort to cultivate Gorky's literary talent in the service of the party. His tact, his special privileges for Gorky.

Mirsky, Dimiti Petrovich. *Lenin*. Boston: Little Brown, 1931. An account of Lenin and Leninism, showing the relationship between his ideas and acts. The author deliberately avoids the human touch.

Trotsky, Leon. *Lenin: Notes for a Biographer*. New York: Minton Balch, 1925. The story of Lenin's role in the revolution. Not a complete biography or character study. It is, essentially, an incomplete manuscript which Trotsky published only because he felt he might never be able to finish the work he had in mind.

_____. *The Young Lenin*. Garden City: Doubleday, 1972. A brief account containing a few details of Lenin's early life, including his late development, a point on which biographers all seem to agree.

Valentinov, Nicolai Vladislavovich (N. V. Volski). *The Early Years of Lenin*. Translated by H. W. Theen. Introduction by B. D. Wolfe. Ann Arbor: University of Michigan Press, 1969. A superb, scholarly work, using original sources. Denies the stories of revolutionary sympathies in Lenin's family (mother and father).

Mao Tse-tung

Little is known in the West about the life of Mao, particularly his early years. Mao's own account is rather stylized. It is clear that he allied himself with his mother against a rather stern father. Most sources support this picture. But Wilson also provides some information to suggest that Mao learned to conform and to please his father in order to appease him long enough to enjoy his favorite reading. This would indicate more deliberation and adaptation, a picture similar to Lenin.

Perhaps the most revealing event in Mao's later years was his initiation of the Cultural Revolution. For this reason I have included several documents that focus on this era, as well as Lifton's interpretation of the psychological significance of Mao's policy. When a leader provides us with a great success in policy we may commend his logic. When he produces a monstrous failure, we are more inclined to look to his personality and ask what peculiar personal need caused him to be so wrong about the psychology of his people and the effectiveness of certain methods. The Cultural Revolution is now almost universally regarded as Mao's major failure, even by the Chinese.

Asia Research Center. *The Great Power Struggle in China.* Hong Kong: Yee Tin Tong Press, 1969. A collection of documents, circulars and some Red Guard publications which tell the story of Mao's Cultural Revolution and some attempts to control it.

Karnow, Stanley. *Mao and China.* New York: Viking, 1972. Karnow sees the Cultural Revolution as an effort to change the *personality* of the Chinese people. Mao wanted to cleanse his people of materialism. Outbursts of violence against the technical experts as well as foreign embassies marked this period.

Lifton, Robert Jay. *Revolutionary Immortality: Mao Tse-tung and the Chinese Cultural Revolution..* New York: Random House, 1968. An intriguing attempt to study the psychology of Mao through his policy moves.

Li-Jui. *The Early Revolutionary Activities of Comrade Mao Tse-tung.* Translated by A. W. Sariti. White Plains: M. E. Sharpe, 1977. A biography covering a much neglected period of Mao's student years as well as his role in the agrarian revolution. Previously published in China.

Lindqvist, S. *China in Crisis.* Translated by S. Clayton. New York: Thomas Crowell, 1963. An interesting first-hand account of China during the economic chaos following Mao's first Great Leap Forward. Half-finished factories, abandoned buildings, food shortages and repression characterized this period.

Mao Tse-tung. *Mao.* Edited by Jerome Ch'en. Englewood CLiffs: Prentice Hall, 1969. A brief biography followed by the works of Mao, some not previously published.

––––––. *Mao's China: Party Reform Documents.* Translated by B. Compton. Seattle: University of Washington Press, 1952. Report of the Propaganda Bureau, reform in learning and literature, investigations into village life.

––––––. *Mao Tse-tung: An Anthology of His Writings.* Edited with an introduction by Ann Fremantle. New York: New American Library, 1972. Containing a biography as well as some of Mao's principal works.

––––––. *Quotations from Chairman Mao Tse-tung.* Peking: Foreign Language Press, 1967. The famous "Little Red Book," containing short quotations from Mao's work. Highly concrete and simplistic, such as his well-known remark that "political power grows out of the barrel of a gun."

––––––. *Selected Readings from the Works of Mao Tse-tung.* Peking: Foreign Language Press, 1971. An extensive selection of Mao's work, but no information about his life. This is probably significant in that it was published in China during Mao's lifetime. He felt his work was more important than the events of his life. There are many slogans and commands to action, much concrete thinking.

Meisner, M. *Mao's China.* New York: Free Press, 1977. A history of the rise of Mao with particular emphasis on the defection of the intellectuals. Stresses cultural iconoclasm and nationalism in the intellectual class. Follows revolutionary structure outlined by Brinton and Edwards including Thermadorian reaction.

Payne, Robert. *Mao-Tse-tung, Ruler of Red China.* New York: Schuman, 1950. A biography representing some new interpretations of Mao's development, suggesting he was more influenced by Spencer than by Marx. Some account of his early years as a Buddhist and his physical frailty.

Pye, Lucian W. *The Man in the Leader.* New York: Basic Books, 1976. A psychological study stressing Mao's principle of arousing emotions in others, but keeping his own in check. Description of his "feminine" qualities. Influence of his mother. Some details about his relationship with women.

Snow, Edgar. *Red Star Over China.* New York: Garden City Publishing Company, 1939. The most interesting part of the book is Snow's attempt to extract autobiographical details from Mao. Mao is rather guarded and speaks in generalities, but personal details escape him in spite of himself.

Uhalley, Stephen, Jr. *Mao Tse-tung: A Critical Biography*. New York: New Viewpoints, 1975. Not very critical. The author even glorifies the Cultural Revolution.

Wilson, D. *Mao, The People's Emperor*. London: Hutchinson, 1979. A biography telling some details of Mao's parents, contrasting the personalities of Mao's father and mother. Additional material on Mao's childhood. Good list of sources.

Yeh Ch'ing (Jen Tso-hsuan). *Inside Mao Tse-tung Thought*. Translated by S. Pan, T. H. Tsuan and R. Mortensen. Hicksville: Exposition Press, 1975. A critique of Mao's thought, stressing his links with Sun yat-sen. A biased account, attempting to show Mao's "error," "dangerous ideas," etc. Lacking in real sources of evidence.

Index

Action, political, xvii, xx
  psychological basis of, xv–xvi
  theory vs., 127–131
Administration, post-revolutionary, 137–138,
  190–191, 212
Aggressive revolutionary, 87
Ahimsa (nonviolence), 66, 68–69
Aim, inhibition of, 25–26, 126
Alexander II, 53, 55
Alliance of Socialist Democracy, 56
All India Home Rule League, 76
Altuski, Enrique, 188
Ananiev, Sophie, 57
Anarchism, 54–57
Anarchist movement, 56–59
Anger, Gandhi's struggle against, 69–71
Anna Karenina (Tolstoy), 35
Anti-Semitism of Marx, 97–100, 108–109, 120
Armand, Inessa, 223
Asceticism, 232
  of Lenin, 220–222
  of Mao, 226
  of Rousseau, 22–24
Assassination, desire for, 84
Authoritarianism of Trotsky, 170–171
Authority, moral, 149–150
Awareness, expanded, 242–243

Babbitt, Irving, 15
Babeuf, François Émile, 116
Bakunin, Michael, 53, 56–57, 104, 125, 129
Baraheni, Reza, xxi
Bauer, Bruno, 95, 97
B-Cognition (Being-Cognition), 237, 238
Belief, life-style and, 17–19
Bers, Sonia, 35, 37, 38, 41, 203
Besant, Mrs. Annie, 73, 76
Bider, Haydee Tamara Bunke (Tania), 192, 193
Bolivia, Guevara's struggle in, 192–194
Bolshevik party, 163–164, 167–168

Bonachea, Rolando, 211
Brinton, Crane, xvi, 232
Bronstein, Lev. *See* Trotsky, Leon
Bucke, R. M., 237, 238, 241
Burns, Mary, 104, 125

Cantlie, Dr. James, 138–140
Capitalism, Marx on, 97–100, 108–109
Capital (Marx), 125
Castro, Fidel, 6, 143, 185, 199, 202, 205–216,
  219
  attraction to dirt and disorder, 206–207
  early years, 205–206
  evolution of new system, 214–216
  Guevara in disagreement with, 191
  marriage, 207–208
  Marti's influence on, 208–210
  Moncada attack, 210–211
  refusal of power, 211–213
  Urrutia's presidency, 213–214, 216
  victory and power, 211
Castro y Argiz, Angel, 215
Cause, identification with, 8
Celibacy
  Gandhi and, 63, 72
  Tolstoy and, 40
Chang Ni-isi, 144
Charisma, 214
Chen, General Chiung-ming, 147
Chertkov, V. G., 38, 39, 40, 42
Chiang Kai-shek, 147, 148, 227
Chibas, Eduardo, 209
Chibas, Paul 212
Childhood (Tolstoy), 34
Chinese revolution, 143–148
Christianity, Sun Yat-sen and, 141–143, 145
Civil disobedience, Gandhi's program of,
  76–77
Civil War in France 1870–71 (Marx), 125
Close, Upton, 139

275

Communal feeling, 163, 235–237, 240
Commune of Paris, 116
Communism, 117, 147, 212, 214
    anarchism vs., 56–57
    Marxist, 103–104, 109–111, 115–116
Communist Correspondence Committee, 116
Communist League, 116–117
Confessions (Rousseau), 22, 24–25, 26, 161–162
Confessions (Tolstoy), 33
Consciousness, revolutionary, 110, 149, 223–224
Control, suffering and, 62–64
Conviction without combat, 45–60. *See also* Nonviolence
Crowned Cannibals (Baraheni), xxi
Cruelty, xx–xxi, xxv, 159
    Kropotkin's horror of, 52–53
    Tolstoy's horror of, 32–33
Cuban revolution, 210–213, 215
Cultural Revolution, 137, 227, 228
Culture, master-slave, xviii–xix

Darwin, Charles, 234–235
Deception during revolutionary struggles, 78–79
Degradation, 10, 11
de la Serna, Celia, 181–182
Delay
    dynamics of, 165–166
    intellectualism and, 157–159
    masochism and, 126–127, 131
    rationalization of, xxix
    urge for immortality and, 228
Demuth, Helene (Lenchen), 111–112, 124
Deniken, General Anton Ivanovich, 169
Descent of Man (Darwin), 234
Deutscher, Isaac, 160, 161, 171, 172
Deutsch-französisch Jahrbucher, 96, 97
Development of Capitalism in Russia (Lenin), 159
Diaz Balart, Mirta, 207
Diet, Gandhi and, 71–72
Discipline, Gandhi and, 62
Doctor-revolutionaries, 49
Dominance and submission, xxi–xxii
Dorticos Torrado, Osvaldo, 215
Dress, 6, 17, 182–183, 207. *See also* Life-style
Durant, Will, 59
Dzerzhinsky, Feliz, 173

"Economic and Philosophical Manuscripts" (Marx), 106–107, 109
Economics of Marx, 106–109
Education, 50, 110, 149–150
    of Gandhi, 64–66

Ego-less perception, 237–238, 241–243
Eisenhower, President Dwight D., 216
Eloquence, 161–163
Émile (Rousseau), 5, 26, 31, 32, 200
Emotional aspect of political attitudes, 238–243
Engels, Friedrich, 47, 48, 110, 111, 124, 153
    Communist League and, 116–117
    Marx and, 104–106, 121, 125, 126
    during revolutions of 1848, 119–120
Epinay, Mme. Louise F. P. de la live d', 23–24
Erikson, Erik H., 73
Expanded awareness, 242–243

Family
    break with traditions of, 141–142
    Gandhi and, 69–71, 200–201
    revolutionary leaders' attitudes toward, 199–203
    Tolstoy and, 38–40, 201–202
Fanon, Franz, 49
Fantasies of homosexuality, 9–11
Fasting, Gandhi's use of, 71–72, 73, 80–83
Femininity of submission, xxi
Ferreyra, Maria del Carmen, 182
Flacon, Ferdinand, 119
French Revolution of 1789, xviii
Freud, Sigmund, xviii, xxii–xxiii, 26
Fromm, Eric, 108, 235

Gadea, Hilda, 182, 183–185, 192
Gandhi, Kaba, 62–63
Gandhi, Mohandas K., 6, 13, 21, 37, 47, 48, 61–85, 141, 144, 145, 149, 162, 231, 233, 234
    ahimsa (nonviolence), 66, 68–69
    application to politics, 66–67
    celibacy, 63, 72
    childhood, 61–62
    civil disobedience program, 76–77
    commitment to sacrifice, 67–68
    death of, 83–84
    education and vocation, 64–66
    family and, 69–71, 200–201
    fasting of, 71–72, 73, 80–83
    masculinity and courage, 63, 74
    problem of power and nonviolence, 84–85
    Quit India movement, 77–78
    religion and, 49–50
    revolution, 78–83
    in South Africa, 65–69, 71–72
    struggle against anger, 69–71
    suffering and control, 62–64
    violence and, 73–82
Gandhi, Putlibai, 203
"German Ideology, The" (Marx), 112

Gomez, General Maximo, 208, 209
Goodnow, Professor F. J., 146
Goodwin, Richard N., 185
Gorky, Maxim, 221–222
Granados, Alberto, 185
Group identification, 163, 233–237
Guerrilla warfare, xxxi
Guerrilla Warfare (Guevara), 185
Guevara, Ché, 6, 13, 49, 137, 143, 149,
    181–194, 228, 233
  asthma and oppression of, 181–184, 193
  in Bolivia, 192–194
  characteristics of, 184–186
  dual role of, 186
  family and, 202
  identification with underdog of, 181–183
  internationalism, 186–187
  religion and, 189–190
  revolutionary morality of, 187–189
Guevara de la Serna, Ernesto, 181
Guevara Lynch, Ernesto, 181
Guillaume, James, 55
Guilt, 5, 41, 155

Hanfstaengl, Ernst, xxiii
Hegel, Georg Wilhelm, 94, 95
Heiden, Konrad, xxiii
Herzen, Aleksandr, 35, 53
Hess, Moses, 95, 96, 103, 104, 111, 116
Historical materialism, theory of, 128, 238
History of the Soviet (Trotsky), 165
"History Will Absolve Me" (Castro), 210
Hitler, Adolf, xxiii–xxiv, xxv
Holy Family, The (Engels and Marx), 111
Homosexual fantasies, 9–11
Hume, David, 24, 26
Hutchins, Francis G., 80

Identification
  with cause, 8
  with group, 163, 235–237
  with oppressed, 20–22, 181–183
  See also Mother, identification with
Immorality, revolutionary, 51, 227–229
Indian revolution, 78–83
Inhibition of aim, 25–26, 126
Injustice, sense of, 32–33, 52–53
Intellectualism, 98, 157–159
Internationalism, 242
  of Guevara, 186–187
  of Marx, 98, 127
  of Trotsky, 158, 165–166, 169
International Workingmen's Association, 55

James, Daniel, 181, 182, 185, 192

James, William, 237
Jefferson, Thomas, 149
Jewish question, the, 96–100, 169
Jung, Carl, 89
Jura Federation, 55

Kallenbach, Herman, 71
Kennedy, President John F., 216
Kerensky, Aleksandr, 58, 167
Kierkegaard, Sören, 37
Kolchak, Admiral Aleksandr V., 169
Kropotkin, Alexander, 236
Kropotkin, Prince Peter, 4, 51–59, 234,
    235–237
  Anarchist movement and, 56–59
  childhood, 51–53
  exile, 53–54
  religion and, 49
  as revolutionary, 54–56
Kung, H. H., 145
Kuomintang (National People's Party),
    144–145, 147

Lafargue, Paul, 104
Langer, Walter, xxiii
Lassalle, Ferdinand, 99, 129, 131
Lawrence, T. E., xxi, 5–14, 199, 231, 233
  final act of self-abnegation, 12–13
  leadership of, xvii
  self-sacrifice, suffering, pain, and morality
    of, 11–12
  sexual masochism of, 9–11
  uniqueness of, 7–9
League of the Just, 110
Lenin, Krupskaya, 219, 222
Lenin, V. I., 131, 143, 159, 175, 199, 219–224
  ascetism of, 220–222
  attitude toward family, 202
  invisible personality of, 219
  revolutionary consciousness and, 223–224
  self-denial and self-neglect, 221–223
  Stalin and, 172
  Trotsky and, 161, 163–173
Liberals, 18, 35
Lie, Trygve, 176
Liebkneckt, Wilhelm, 111
Life-style, 6, 38, 41, 103, 107, 223
  ascetic, 22–24
  belief and, 17–19
  as revolt, 16–19
Lifton, Robert, 137
Li Hung-chang, 142
Linebarger, Paul, 139, 140
Linlithgow, Lord (Victor A.J. Hope), 77, 79,
    80, 81, 82
Li Yuan-hung, 147

Lloyd, Sir George, 77
Lockwood, Lee, 215
Long March, The, 227
Lu Hao-tung, 141

Mack, John E., 7, 9, 10, 11
McLellan, David, 88, 132
Makovitski, Dr. Dushan Petrovich, 41–42
Manifesto of the Communist Party (Marx), 118, 119, 121
Mankind as It Is and Ought to Be (Weitling), 110
Mao Tse-tung, 131, 137, 147–148, 149, 150, 199, 225–229
    asceticism of, 226
    childhood, 225–226
    embodiment of others by, 226
    family and, 202
    revolutionary immorality and, 227–229
    revolutionary romanticism of, 226–227
March, Aleida, 182, 188, 192
Martí, José, 208–210
Martin, Lionel, 211
Martov, Julius, 161
Marx, Heinrich, 87–88
    relationship with Karl, 92–93, 94, 99–100, 130–131
Marx, Henrietta, 100
Marx, Jenny, 105–106, 115, 123, 132
    domestic situation, 121–125. *See also* von Westphalen, Jenny
Marx, Karl, xxvii, 47–48, 50, 56–57, 87–133, 137–138, 143, 149, 153, 201, 223, 231, 232, 233, 234
    anti-Semitism of, 97–100, 108–109, 120
    attitude toward family, 200
    attitude toward own work, 120–121
    break with Ruge, 103–104
    on capitalism, 97–110
    childhood and youth, 87–90
    communism of, 103–104, 109–110, 115–116
    Communist league, 116–117
    contradictions in, 133
    economics of, 106–109
    education of 90–91
    ego-less perception of, 237–238
    Engels and, 104–106, 121, 125, 126
    eve of revolution, 115–116
    evolution of theory, 111–112
    final years, 125–126
    identity crisis, 94–95
    influence on Trotsky of, 158–159
    inhibition of aim, 126
    Jenny and, 90–94, 96, 100, 200
    Jewish question, 96–100
    London period, 121–125
    lure of politics, 95–96

    masculinity and, 92–94
    masochism and dynamics of delay, 126–127, 131
    revolutionary agitation, 117–119
    revolutions of 1848, 119–121
    role of suffering, 131–132
    theory vs. action, 127–131
Masculinity, xxi, 63, 74, 92–94
Maslow, Abraham, 94, 188, 237, 238, 241
Masochism, xxvii, 56, 132, 231–243
    characteristics of masochist, xxviii–xxix
    defined, xxii–xxiii
    dynamics of delay and, 126–127, 131
    as productive force, 58
    psychological basis for, 187
    public display and, 162–163, 220–221. *See also* Moral masochism; Sexual masochism; Social masochism
Master-morality, xxv
Master-slave culture, xviii–xix
Materialism, historical, 128, 238
Material needs, neglect of, 233–235. *See also* Self-neglect
Matthews, Herbert, 207, 208, 212, 215
Mazlish, Bruce, 220
Menshevik party, 163–164
Message to the Tricontinental (Guevara), 185, 186, 187
Metternich, Prince Klemenz von, 118
Mirabeau, Marquis de (Victor Riqueti), 26, 27
Moncada attack, 210–211
Money, Marx's inability to manage, 99–100
Moral authority, 149–150
Moral belief, emergence of independent, xvii–xix
Moral indignation, 154
Morality
    of the communist, 117
    master and slave, xx–xxi, xxv
    motivation through, 187–189
    relationship between pain and, xix–xx
Moral masochism, xxii, xxvi–xxvii, 150, 231–232
    of Kropotkin, 58–59
    Marx and, 132
    of Rousseau, 231, 232
    of Sun Yat-sen, 148–150
    Trotsky and, 149, 232. *See also* Social masochism
Mother, identification with
    of Gandhi, 61, 62, 68
    of Kropotkin, 52
    of Mao, 225–226
    of Rousseau, 19–20
    of Tolstoy, 31
Motivation, revolutionary, xxix
    masochism as, 233
Mutual Aid (Kropotkin), 234, 237

Narayan, Jayaprakash, 79
Nashe Slovo (Our Word), 167
Nationalism, 128
Nehru, Jawaharlal, 77–78
Neitzsche, Friedrich, xx–xxi
Neruda, Pablo, 185
Neue Rheinische Zeitung—Politish-Oekonomisch Revue, 121, 138
Nonviolence, xxix, 45–50, 57
  Gandhi's version of, 61, 66, 68–69
  problem of power and, 84–85
Nuturing impulse, 48–50, 234–235

Oppressed, identification with the, 20–22, 181–183

Padover, Saul, 109, 132
Pain, xix–xx, 11–12. *See also* Suffering
Paranoia in Rousseau, 24, 26–27
Partido del Pueblo Cubano (PPC), 209
Parvus (A. L. Helphand), 163, 167
Payne, Robert, 89
Pazos, Felipe, 212
Perception, ego-less, 237–238, 241, 242–243
Perez Serantes, Monsignor Enrique, 210
Permanent Revolution (Trotsky), 137, 164–166
Philosophy of Poverty, The (Proudhon), 129
Political action, xvii, xx
  psychological basis of, xv–xvi
  theory vs. 127–131
Political attitudes, emotional aspect of, 238–243
Politics, 66–67, 95–96, 157
Post-revolutionary administration, 137–138, 190–191
Poverty of Philosophy, The (Marx), 129
Power, xiii–xxiv, 211
  problem of nonviolence and, 84–85
  refusal of, 169–170, 173, 211–213
Prince of Our Disorder, The (Mack), 7
Prosper China Society, 142, 143
Protestor, characteristics of, xv–xvi
Proudhon, Pierre, 35, 104, 129
Provocation, 159–160
Psychodynamics, revolutionary, xxix–xxx
Psychological analysis, limits of, 28–29
Public display, masochism and, 162–163, 220–221
Punishment, desire for, 10. *See also* Masochism; Suffering

Quit India movement, 77–78

Racism, Gandhi's fight against, 65–66

Raubal, Geli, xxiii
Ray, Manuel, 215
Rebel, xxiv–xxvi, 5, 138
Red Guard, 227
Red Star over China (Snow), 225
Reik, Theodor, xxii, xxvi–xxvii, xxviii, 126, 129, 162, 228
Religion, 48–50, 117
  Guevara and, 189–190
  Marx and, 87–88
  Sun Yat-sen and, 141–143, 145
  Tolstoy and, 37–38, 49
Revolt, 16–19
Revolt in the Desert (Lawrence), 12
Revolution, moral aspects of, xvi–xviii
Revolutionary psychodynamics, xxix–xxx
Revolutionary consciousness, 110, 149, 223–224
Revolution Betrayed, The (Trotsky), 174
Revolutions of 1848, 119–121
Rheinische Zeitung, 96, 97, 103, 104
Risk, delight in, 13
Rivera, Diego, 175
Rojo, Ricardo, 182, 188, 189
Romanticism, revolutionary, 186–187, 226–227
Rousseau, Jean Jacques, 5, 15–29, 49, 73, 120, 143, 148, 149, 199–200, 201, 223, 225
  childhood, 19–20
  communal feeling of, 239–240
  eloquence of, 161–162
  fall of, 27–28
  final years, 26–27
  identification with oppressed, 20–22
  influence on Sun Yat-sen of, 146–147
  influence on Tolstoy of, 5, 31, 32, 33–34
  inhibition of aim in, 25–26
  life-style, 6, 16–19, 22–24
  moral masochism of, 231, 232
  need for suffering, 19–20, 43
  role of trust for, 24–25
Rowlatt, Sir Sidney, 76
Ruge, Arnold, 96, 103–104
Ruskin, John, 71
Russell, Bertrand, 222, 239
Russian revolution, 167–168, 169

Sacrifice, xxxii, 88, 117
  family and, 199–203
  Gandhi's commitment to, 67–68. *See also* Self-sacrifice; Suffering
Sadism, xxii
Sadomasochism, xxiii–xxiv, 138, 148
Sadomasochistic personality, xxii, xxv
Saint-Thomas, Prosper, 32–33
San Min Chu I (Three Principles of the People, Sun Yat-sen), 143, 146–148

Sarabhai, Seth Ambalal, 73
Sarria, Lieutenant Pedro, 210
Satyagraha, 64
Schapper, Karl, 110, 116
Schpentzer, Moissey Filippovich, 154
Sedova, Natalia, 171
Self-abnegation, 12–13
Self-aggrandizement, 36–37
Self-denial, 74, 220, 222–223
Selflessness, 237–238, 241–243
Self-neglect, 222–223, 233–235
    by Castro, 206–207
Self-sacrifice, 11–12, 170–171, 233–235
Seven Pillars of Wisdom (Lawrence), 10
Sex, 59, 63–64, 223
Sexual masochism, 9–11, 20, 231
Sharman, Lyon, 141, 148
Shaw, George Bernard, 12
Sheth, Abdulla, 65
Short Account of the Gospels (Tolstoy), 38
Sickness unto Death (Kierkegaard), 37
Siegel, Jerrold, 109
Sierra Maestra Manifesto, 212–213
Simmons, Ernest J., 36
Sincerity, 6
Slave-master culture. *See* Master-slave culture
Slave-morality, xx, xxi, xxv
Snow, Edgar, 199, 225
Social Contract (Rousseau), 146
Socialism, Castro and, 215–216
"Socialism and Man in Cuba" (Guevara), 188,
    189
Social masochism, xxii–xxiii, xxvii, 31, 43, 58,
    126
    immorality and, 228–229. *See also* Moral
    masochism
Social rebel, 5
Sokolovakaya, Aleksandra, 174
Sonderbund, 117–118
Soong, Charlie, 143, 145
Soong, Ching-ling, 145
Soviet Union, Cuba and, 215
Stalin, Joseph, 158, 166, 170, 172
    Trotsky and, 171–174, 175
Stone, I. F., 185
Strasser, Otto, xxiii
Submission, dominance and, xxi–xxii
Success, revolutionary, xxix, 199–203
Suffering, xxvi–xxvii, xxxii
    ability to use, 232–233
    control and, 62–64
    endurance of, 33
    Kropotkin and, 53
    Lawrence and, 11–12
    of Mao, 225–226
    Marx and role of, 131–132
    psychological, 42–43
    Rousseau's need for, 19–20, 43

Tolstoy and, 31–33, 40–42
Trotsky and, 154–157
Suicide, element of in deaths of revolution-
    aries, 13, 177–178, 193–194
Sun Yat-sen, xvii, 49, 137, 139–150, 226
    Christianity and, 141–143, 145
    communism and, 147
    education and, 50
    marriage of, 142–143
    moral masochism and, 148–150
    personality, 139–140
    as revolutionary, 143–146
    San Min Chu I, 146–148
    youthful rebel, 140–143
Sun Yat-sen: His Life and Its Meaning
    (Sharman), 148
Superego, xviii–xix
Survival instincts, 242–243
Swaraj (Indian home rule), 74

Tai Chi-Tao, 139
Taiping Rebellion, 141
Theory, xxx
    action vs., 127–131, 137
Thoreau, Henry David, 6
Tolstoy, Count Leo, 3, 6, 31–43, 50
    celibacy and, 40
    childhood, 31–32
    early years, 33–35
    family and, 38–40, 201–202
    influence on Gandhi, 71
    marriage and development, 35
    period of reflection, 36–37
    religion and, 37–38
    social masochism of, 43
    suffering and, 31–33, 40–42
Trotsky, Leon, 13, 50, 84, 131, 137, 143,
    153–178, 241
    assassination of, 175, 176–177
    attitude toward enemy, 175–177
    attitude toward family, 202
    authoritarianism of, 170–171
    background, 153
    childhood, 153–154
    eloquence of, 161–163
    intellectualism and dynamics of delay,
    157–159
    internationalism of, 158, 165–166, 169
    Lenin and, 161, 163–173, 220
    moral masochism of, 159, 232
    Permanent Revolution, 164–166
    in prison, 159–160
    provocation of, 159–160
    rebel within party, 166–167
    refusal of power by, 169–170, 173
    Stalin and, 171–174
    suffering and, 154–157

Trotsky, Leon *(continued)*
  suicide motive, 177–178
Trust, role of, 24–25
Typology, revolutionary, xxx–xxxii
Tyranny, morality of, xx–xxi, xxiv–xxvi, 138

Ulyanov, Vladimir Ilyich. *See* Lenin, V. I.
United League (Tung Meng Hui), 144
United States, Cuba and, 215–216
Unto This Last (Ruskin), 71
Urrutia Lleo, Manuel, 213–215, 216

Valdes, Nelson, 211
Victory
  Castro's power and, 211
  resignation in, xxix
Village Soothsayer, The (Rousseau), 18
Violence
  Gandhi and, 73, 82
  innocence of provoked, 80
  as nonviolent, 74–76
  provocation of, through nonviolence, 66

Voltaire (François Marie Arouet), 17, 22
von Westphalen, Baron Johann Ludwig, 88
von Westphalen, Caroline, 111
von Westphalen, Jenny, 90–94, 96, 100, 200.
  See also Marx, Jenny

War and Peace (Tolstoy), 35
War and the International (Trotsky), 167
Wavell, Lord A. P., 83
Weitling, Wilhelm, 117, 119, 129, 138
Weyl, Nathaniel, 206
What I Believe (Tolstoy), 39
What Is To Be Done? (Lenin), 223
Wife, revolutionary, 199–203
Wolfenstein, 61, 155, 219, 220
World War I, 72, 74–76

Yuan Shih-kai, 145, 146

Zimmerwald Manifesto, 167

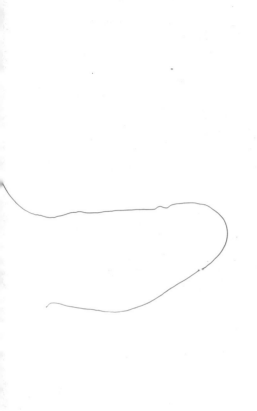